LUIGI RUSSOLO, FUTURIST

The publisher gratefully acknowledges the generous support
of the Ahmanson Foundation Humanities Endowment Fund
of the University of California Press Foundation.

LUIGI RUSSOLO, FUTURIST

NOISE, VISUAL ARTS, AND THE OCCULT

Luciano Chessa

UNIVERSITY OF CALIFORNIA PRESS

Berkeley   Los Angeles   London

University of California Press, one of the most distinguished
university presses in the United States, enriches lives around the
world by advancing scholarship in the humanities, social sciences,
and natural sciences. Its activities are supported by the UC Press
Foundation and by philanthropic contributions from individuals
and institutions. For more information, visit www.ucpress.edu.

University of California Press
Berkeley and Los Angeles, California

University of California Press, Ltd.
London, England

© 2012 by The Regents of the University of California

Library of Congress Cataloging-in-Publication Data

Chessa, Luciano, 1971–
   Luigi Russolo, futurist : noise, visual arts, and the occult /
Luciano Chessa.
    p. cm.
   Includes bibliographical references.
   ISBN 978-0-520-27063-3 (cloth : alk. paper)
   ISBN 978-0-520-27064-0 (pbk. : alk. paper)
   ISBN 978-0-520-95156-3 (ebook)
   1. Russolo, Luigi—Criticism and interpretation.
2. Futurism (Music).   I. Title.
   ML410.R966C44   2012
   700.92—dc23   2011046516

21 20 19 18 17 16 15 14 13 12
10 9 8 7 6 5 4 3 2 1

To Troy

CONTENTS

List of Illustrations	ix
Acknowledgments	xi
Introduction	1

PART ONE. Luigi Russolo from the Formative Years to 1913

1.	Futurism as a Metaphysical Science	13
2.	Occult Futurism	43
3.	Spotlight on Russolo	71
4.	Painting Noise: *La musica*	98
5.	Russolo and Synesthesia	110
6.	Russolo's Metaphysics	122

PART TWO. The Art of Noises and the Occult

7.	Intonarumori Unveiled	137
8.	The *Spirali di Rumori*	151
9.	The *Arte dei "Romori"*	169
10.	Controversial Leonardo	197
11.	Third Level	209

Conclusion: Materialist Futurism?	225
Notes	231

ILLUSTRATIONS

1. Luigi Russolo, *Autoritratto con teschi* (1908) / *6*
2. Fillìa, title page of *Arte fascista*, December 1927 / *9*
3. Umberto Boccioni, *Città che sale* (1910–11) / *29*
4. Giacomo Balla, *Trasformazione forme spiriti* (1918) / *33*
5. Giacomo Balla, *Mercurio passa davanti al Sole, visto da un cannocchiale* (1914) / *40*
6. Luigi Russolo, *La musica* (1911–12) / *77*
7. Luigi Russolo, *Autoritratto* (1940) / *80*
8. Luigi Russolo, *Maschere* (1907–08) / *82*
9. Luigi Russolo, *Autoritratto (con doppio eterico)* (1910) / *86*
10. Luigi Russolo, *Autoritratto (con l'ombra)* (1920) / *87*
11. *Luigi Russolo seduto in mezzo ai suoi rumorarmoni* (1924–28) / *88*
12. Luigi Russolo, *Ricordi di una notte* (1912) / *91*
13. Luigi Russolo, *Linee-forza della folgore* (1912), central panel / *93*
14. Annie Besant and Charles W. Leadbeater, illustrations 22 and 23 from *Thought-forms* (1901) / *94*
15. Luigi Russolo, *Solidità nella nebbia* (1912) / *95*
16. Luigi Russolo, *Compenetrazione di case + luce + cielo* (1912) / *96*
17. Umberto Boccioni, caricature of the futurist *serata* in Treviso on June 2, 1911 / *99*

18. Annie Besant and Charles W. Leadbeater, plate W, "Wagner: Overture to Meistersingers [sic]," from *Thought-forms* (1901) / *105*
19. The Three-Level Process / *139*
20. Luigi Russolo, musical example from *Risveglio di una città* (1913) / *152–53*
21. Paolo Buzzi, *Pioggia nel pineto antidannunziana* (1916) / *165*
22. Luigi Russolo, *Impressione di bombardamento shrapnels e granate* (1926) / *166*
23. Leonardo da Vinci, Codex Arundel 263, fol. 175r / *175*
24. Luigi Russolo, drawing for the patent *Intonatore dei rumori* (1914) / *178*
25. Luigi Russolo, drawing for the patent *Descrizione della prima aggiunta al brevetto depositato l'8/10/1921* / *179*
26. Luigi Russolo, drawing for the patent *Apparecchio acustico producente sotto l'azione di un rumore qualsiasi dei suoni la cui tonalità e il timbro sono definiti* (1921) / *180*
27. Luigi Russolo, drawing for the patent *Instrument de musique* (1931) / *183*
28. Leonardo da Vinci, sketch of the viola organista, Madrid MS II, fol. 76r / *187*
29. Adolfo De Carolis, header for *Il Leonardo* (1903) / *203*

ACKNOWLEDGMENTS

Like every work that aspires to be scientific, this book is not the result of a solitary effort; rather, it is the product of a multifaceted dialogue. My thanks therefore go first to Mary Francis for having encouraged me from the inception of this dialogue, for her constant and enthusiastic support, and for guiding me through the treacherous traps that accompany all publications.

Other key participants in the dialogue were Barbara Moroncini, who gave this work its first edit; Julie Brand, who provided a thorough final edit; and Rose Vekony, the project editor. Their help was crucial in making this book speak to you as it does.

The dialogue started while I was in graduate school at the University of California in Davis, and this book follows on the completion in 2004 of my PhD dissertation, "Luigi Russolo and The Occult." I should like to thank my dissertation committee, David Nutter, Douglas Kahn, D. Kern Holoman, Pablo Ortiz, and Margherita Heyer-Caput, for their trust, generous exchange of ideas, and advice. I wrote the dissertation in Italian. It was translated by Tamsin Nutter, and her translation was revised by Beth Levy, Marit MacArthur, and Ramón Sender Barayón: I thank them all for their time and help.

Justin Urcis, Mark Gallay, Nathan Kroms Davis, and Beverly Wilcox read this manuscript and gave me their feedback. Ellen Fullman, Gregory Moore, and Theresa Wong discussed specific sections of it with me. I am grateful to them all.

Thanks go to my family—my father and mother, and my sister and brother and their families—without whom I would not have been able to accomplish this. Thanks also to Troy Boyd for his unwavering support throughout the entire process and beyond. This book is dedicated to him.

A version of chapter 9 appeared twice as an article: "L'arte dei romori: Leonardine Devotion in Luigi Russolo's Oeuvre," *Leonardo* 41, no. 1 (February 2008); and "L'arte dei romori: Del culto leonardesco nell'opera di Luigi Russolo," in *Musica e arti figurative: Rinascimento e novecento*, ed. Gerhard Wolf and Mario Ruffini (Venice: Marsilio, 2008). Both articles were based on chapter 11 of my dissertation, and it is on this version that I have based the material presented here.

I was able to improve the section on the mechanisms of the intonarumori with the help of a commission I received from RoseLee Goldberg of the New York–based Biennale of the Arts *Performa* to direct the first reconstruction project of Russolo's earliest intonarumori orchestra. Together with Esa Nickle, I curated a concert program that featured music specifically commissioned for this orchestra, which the *New York Times* hailed as one of the best events in the arts in 2009, and which subsequently toured internationally.

My thanks go also to Mary Ellen Poole and John Spitzer at the San Francisco Conservatory of Music and to Tom Welsh from the Cleveland Museum of Art for their indirect and direct support. Finally, thanks to Margaret Fisher who upon reading my "Luigi Russolo and the Occult" first convinced me to revise and submit the work for publication.

Introduction

To enrich means to add, not to substitute or to abolish.

—Luigi Russolo, *The Enharmonic Bow*

On a summer evening the Russolos were entertaining a guest, when Russolo, pleading fatigue and sleepiness, went to bed. The lady and the guest continued chatting for a little longer, until she, the good nights said, retired. While ascending the internal staircase, her gaze was attracted upward: something that had never happened to her. It was then that she saw a kind of white ghost appearing at the banister of the landing, and quickly recognized its familiar face: it was Russolo, leaning on the banister, all illuminated by the full moon.

His wife gazed at him amazed and asked what he was doing and why he was standing there so calmly, and wrapped up in his white nightshirt. He did not respond, nor did he move. Alarmed by his silence, Madame Russolo descended the few steps to call on the guest so that she could be reassured that this was not an illusion. But at their return the white vision had disappeared. She felt humiliated and almost offended by the teasing of her guest, who treated her as a visionary. They quickly entered Russolo's room and found him deeply asleep, calm, breathing very regularly. In silence, they left. Later, rethinking the incident, the wife was not able to convince herself that it had been a hallucination.

The morning after the event Madame Russolo recounted the scene to her husband, who, with evident satisfaction, asked: "Ah! Do you really say? You saw me, actually me in that state? But then I have finally succeeded! I have obtained the doubling of my body. That which you saw, you really saw it: it was my etheric body, perhaps coming to see you go up to your room, while my physical body lay inert in bed. Good! Good! I am more than happy about this. But I pray you: don't tell this story to anyone now; the reasons for silence are obvious and you understand them by yourself."

The preceding paragraphs are a verbatim translation of an anecdote that Maria Zanovello, the widow of the futurist Luigi Russolo, recounted in the third person in the biography of her husband that she published after his death.[1] Her experience can confidently be dated in the late 1930s, years the Russolos spent in Cerro di Laveno, a small and idyllic northern Italian town on the shores of Lago Maggiore. Surprising as it may seem, this anecdote was not the result of Russolo's wife's fevered imagination; rather, it can be directly linked to Russolo's writing (and practices) at the time, as the following passage from his 1938 book *Al di là della materia* exemplifies:

> By continuing the process of magnetizing a subject, once the phase of exteriorization of sensibility has begun, the layers of sensibility around the subject becomes larger and larger in concentric layers that gradually condense in two masses: one on the left, colored in orange, and one on the right, colored in blue. These two masses soon connect, as they are attracted one by the other—the right one, usually passing from behind the subject, reunites with the left one. These two masses, now joined, take a shape vaguely resembling a human body a little bigger than the subject's body, and that stays, at least at first, on its left. This form is connected to the body of the subject via a special tube or vapor-like cord about a finger in thickness, departing from the stomach region (solar plexus) and joining this vaporous mass at the same point. This is a true ghost or, as occultists call it, an etheric double.
>
> To follow the phases of this phenomenon, it is necessary that clairvoyants be present, or that a subject in somnambulic state sees and describes the unfolding of the phenomenon. Other experimental tests have been run to ascertain the presence of this double. A screen of calcium sulfide becomes brilliant and luminous if this double, which one can also cause to move to a nearby room, passes over or near the screen. It is possible to cause this double to execute actions like moving light objects: it is, in short, something resembling the apparitions of ectoplasm that occur and have been photographed in séances such as those done by Crookes.[2]

At this time in his life Russolo had set aside musical research and was almost exclusively writing about spirituality and the occult, as well as practicing meditation and yoga. Most scholars familiar with Russolo's late writings consider them to indicate a departure in his thinking; some have been quick to follow Adorno and label them regressive, arguing that by abandoning the technologically inspired modernity of futurism for esoteric gymnastics, Russolo had de facto "abdicated"—as one Hegelian critic put it—from following the "spirit of the avant-garde."[3]

This view makes sense: nothing would seem to be conceptually further from futurism than outlandish stories such as the one that opens this chapter. Yet this reading is troubling. If spirituality constituted a late but entirely new course for Russolo, what happened to change his trajectory so radically? To my great surprise I discovered in the course of my research that throughout his active years not much changed in the way that Russolo viewed the world.

Luigi Russolo (1885–1947)—painter, composer, builder of musical instruments, and a member of the Italian futurist movement from its inception—represents a crucial moment in the evolution of twentieth-century musical aesthetics. He is generally considered the father of the first systematic poetics of noise and by some even the creator of the synthesizer, and his influence on the likes of Edgar Varèse, Pierre Schaeffer, and John Cage is well documented.[4]

Notwithstanding the increasing interest surrounding his activity, very few studies have been dedicated to Russolo. Apart from the above-mentioned—rather hagiographic—biography published by his wife, Maria Zanovello, in 1958, there are only a few scholarly studies, principal among them an edition of Russolo's musical writings with an introduction by Gian Franco Maffina that appeared in 1978; both Zanovello and Maffina contain useful bibliographic and documentary information but both are slight from a hermeneutical point of view. Besides these two sources there are four pamphlets on Russolo and the visual arts by Maffina (1977), Ethel Piselli (1990), Diego Collovini (1997), and Franco Tagliapietra (2000), respectively.

Of these writers all but Zanovello are art historians; they have focused on Russolo's connections to the visual arts, and their discussions of sound are limited. This is also true of the most recent publication on Russolo, *Luigi Russolo: Vita e opere di un futurista*, the catalog of a retrospective of Russolo's painting and printmaking hosted by the Museo di arte moderna e contemporanea di Trento e Rovereto (MART) in 2006. This catalog presents an updated chronology of Russolo's artworks by Franco Tagliapietra, but it, too, includes hardly any discussion of Russolo's musical contributions.

This state of the affairs is all the more curious given Russolo's current reputation among musically literate audiences and the importance that Russolo gave to sound investigations. Yet little is available on Russolo's musical activities apart from introductions to various editions of Russolo's 1916 key book, *L'arte dei rumori*; among these are one in French by Giovanni Lista (1975), which was translated into Italian and revised in 2009, and one in English by Barclay Brown (1986), as well as a handful of articles, master's theses and book chapters, which are for the most part concerned with repeating much of the information found in Lista, Maffina, and Brown rather than engaging in reexaminations of primary sources.

None of these writings is more than one hundred pages in length, and most of them focus on Russolo's futurist period. Even so, likely because of a common view that futurism was a movement devoid of spiritual concerns, these contributions pay little or no attention to Russolo's occult interests. My research began when I came to realize that these interests are crucial for a full understanding of his futurist aesthetics.[5] In 2004 my "Luigi Russolo and the Occult," which focused on the importance of Russolo's interests in spirituality—the present book constitutes an expansion of that earlier work—inaugurated a shift in Russolo scholarship.[6] The present book intends to continue this shift.

The premise of my work is that the theosophical phase of his late period—what is often considered his regressive change of direction—was linked to his longtime interest in the occult arts. This interest is already evident in his formative years and, more important, it profoundly influenced what was possibly Russolo's most significant futurist achievement: the concept of an art of noises.

My focus is on Russolo's first phase of futurist musical activity: from 1913, the year of his Manifesto on the Art of Noises, to 1921. The year 1913, when he formulated the art of noises and began the construction of instruments to realize it, the *intonarumori* (noise intoners), constituted the beginning of Russolo's public involvement with music, whereas 1921 was the year of the intonarumori's last patent, the year of Russolo's last intonarumori concert, and the year in which he decided to direct his energies toward the construction of another instrument, the *rumorarmonio* (noise harmonium).[7] Given the fundamental continuity of Russolo's intellectual activities, my study is not entirely confined to this chronological period but also takes into account both earlier and subsequent manifestations of his interests in the occult arts. Diachronical referencing to Russolo's occult beliefs was not only essential for my research but should also provide a useful tool for future research on other periods of Russolo's life.

Until the publication of my "Luigi Russolo and the Occult," Russolo scholars accepted several unfounded claims made by earlier writers. In her biography Maria Zanovello wrote: "In Paris Russolo met an Italian scholar of occult arts and every artistic activity was thereafter absorbed by a science that was for him *still something new*."⁸ Maffina, repeating that claim, again stressed the novelty: "As he had done with painting, now he immediately abandoned his musical activities, throwing himself body and soul into a *new and fascinating experience*." A bit later Maffina adds, "With the rise of the new passion, the psychological change is evident in him. This asceticism seems even more absurd if we think that this is the same Russolo who took an active role in futurist activities, activities that are very distant from those of the *new experience*."⁹

Both Zanovello and Maffina underline how "new" this interest in the occult was, which Russolo, according to them, developed *ex novo* at the beginning of the 1930s. The most recent scholarship echoes this opinion. In MART's catalog, for example, Lombardi writes of the 1929 performances with the noise harmonium: "These last activities [i.e., the 1929 noise-harmonium performances] preceded Russolo's change of direction toward spiritualism and a metaphysical path, which he made without ever returning to the *strong material physicality* of the noise of his *ululatori, ronzatori, scoppiatori, crepitatori*"; in this same catalog Franco Tagliapietra writes: "Russolo's work toward the end of his Parisian years is little known: he *developed rather different interests* from painting and music, and soon after he moved away from Paris."¹⁰

Of course these frequentations were nothing new: the merest glance at Russolo's *Autoritratto con teschi* of 1908 (fig. 1), his first documented oil painting, shows how untenable this interpretation is and that in fact his interest in the occult arts was already evident in his earliest works.¹¹

Maffina in 1978 wrote of the "complex personality of Russolo and his various interests in painting, music and the occult arts, among which it seems impossible to find any links."¹² If Maffina was unable to find a link among Russolo's eclectic interests, it can only have been because he never seriously considered the spiritual and occult aspect of Russolo's research. Yet they constitute the *constant* in his evolution.

In analyzing Russolo's writings and works what strikes us above all is the peculiar continuity and coherence of his concepts, and how they migrate from painting to music to philosophy.¹³ Since the occult is an inquiry that often embraces synesthesia, a critical acceptance of Russolo's continual interest in the occult reconciles the seeming conflicts among the various activities—and their related expressive sensory fields—that he undertook.¹⁴ Moreover, his theosophical explorations reconcile his apparently irreconcilable interests in science/technology and spirituality/occult. These interests characterized not

FIGURE 1. Luigi Russolo, *Autoritratto con teschi* (1908). Milan, Museo del Novecento e Case Museo. Copyright Comune di Milano; all rights reserved.

only Russolo's research but also the research carried out by other futurists; both sets of interests find common ground in theosophical thought.

To grasp the continuity of Russolo's spiritual studies and the coherence of his thought one must patiently compare Russolo's early writings with those of his mature period; analyze the cultural context in which he operated, influenced as he was throughout his futurist years by French symbolism; and read the stormy reviews of the *intonarumori* concerts, or the war testimony describing Russolo at the front. Only then does it become obvious that Russolo's interests did not change direction, and that he never truly reoriented his aesthetics.

If it is true that Russolo's last phase was a coherent development of, rather than a radical deviation from, his early principles, this premise offers the key to better understanding Russolo's futurist years and seeing their importance from a new critical perspective.

The two principal contributions of my book are a reconsideration of Russolo's musical career in the light of his occultist interests and an alternative reading of the art of noises, which he and his contemporaries understood to be an ambitious, if occult, experiment. Russolo's passion for the occult arts was decisive both for his theoretical elaborations and, even more important, in his practical realization of this theory in the whole intonarumori ordeal, which, when analyzed through the prism of the occult, presents a new and previously hidden interpretive angle.

Whereas Barclay Brown considered the intonarumori to be the forerunner of the synthesizer and therefore concentrated exclusively upon the instrument's engineering aspects, I focus on what for Russolo was the intonarumori's occult meaning.[15] I base this avenue of investigation also on Russolo's persistent admiration for the alchemical implications and metaphysical aims of the work of Leonardo da Vinci, especially da Vinci's mechanical instruments, which—I argue—were the most important model for Russolo's intonarumori.

How is it that the connections between Russolo's art of noises and the occult have until now been underestimated, given that he himself believed firmly and coherently in their correlation all of his life? The answer to this question may provide some epistemological insight into the field of musicology in the twentieth century.

One reason why this type of investigation has never been undertaken is certainly methodological. Until recently, musicological research dealing with the twentieth century has labored under an abundance of musical sources, which fostered preoccupations with score analysis. But in a case such as Russolo's, where the sources are almost entirely lacking (none of the intonarumori escaped the bombs of World War II, and a fragment of seven bars is all that remains of Russolo's scores), the scientific process of reconstructing history must rely on a very different type of primary evidence—paintings, novels, poetry, letters.

In studying Russolo it is necessary to use an approach similar to that of the medievalist whose eye has been trained by the scarcity of sources. No one would find it strange if, to gain insight into the modalities of listening to music in thirteenth-century France, it were suggested to read, say, the elusive

Roman de la rose; similarly, in the case of Russolo, we should not ignore any element useful for integrating and reconstructing the mosaic of his musical career, regardless of how elusive or poetical it may be.

A second reason for the lack of critical attention to Russolo's occult work is ideological. Interest in the occult has been ignored by scholars whose modernist approach to musicology accepts and rewards only contributions that can be considered progressive according to a narrow, selective, and fundamentally ideological idea of progress in art. Most likely this judgment is also based on a fear of the supposed connection between irrational occult theories and fascism.[16]

Russolo's documented involvement with fascism has until now been erased from Russolo scholarship; his participation in the Duce-endorsed futurist exhibit at Turin's Quadriennale in May 1927 has been thoroughly suppressed, as has his involvement with the exhibit at Milan's Pesaro Gallery in October 1929. His fascist connection is further covered up with the designation "antifascist," which Giovanni Lista first applied to him in 1975. Lista supported this designation with a number of disputable post–World War II testimonies, and he claimed that in 1927 Russolo voluntarily went into exile in Paris to protest fascism (fig. 2).[17]

What led Russolo to Paris were professional opportunities, not politics. In fact, his permanent return to Italy in 1933, as well as some of his subsequent writings, signal first acceptance of and then allegiance to the fascist regime. Yet the fable of his antifascism runs through all Russolo scholarship—it is still maintained in Tagliapietra (2007) and Lista (2009)—with no convincing evidence to support it.

This book focuses on the 1913 formulation of the art of noises. Since *fascism* at that time was not even a word in the dictionary, this book cannot be the place for a detailed discussion of the connection between Russolo and fascism. The occult was part of Russolo's set of interests from early on, and fascism—if only for chronological reasons—could not have been; therefore, though it cannot be argued that the two were not connected, the connection only becomes relevant and critically useful in analyzing futurist works produced after the foundation of fascism.[18]

What modernist ideology tried to dismiss or cover up we can now see with more clarity, thanks both to the evolution of hermeneutical strategies and to a more advantageous historical perspective. Since Russolo's occult

FIGURE 2. Fillìa, title page of *Arte fascista*, Edizione Sindacati Artistici Torino, December 1927. Courtesy of Beinecke Rare Book and Manuscript Library, Yale University.

interests were not a sign of late blooming but had been present from early on (and since not all such interests end up in fascism), they cannot be read or dismissed as aesthetically and philosophically regressive.[19] Through careful analysis of Russolo's occult interests I was able to perceive the continuity of his research activities, and that in turn gave me access to the occult intention of the art of noises.

Unveiling associations with the occult within Russolo's futurist poetics reinforces the connections between his most important aesthetical ideas and their migration in the spiritually charged works of Varèse, Schaeffer, and Cage. But my work aspires above all to change the perception of Russolo's musical activities, from that of a rational scientist devoted to positivist thought to that of a multifaceted personality in whom the drive to keep up with the latest scientific trends coexisted with a deeply felt spiritual interest and the aversion to positivism and materialism that he shared with the futurist movement.

With my research, a new portrait of Russolo emerges—a more unified and, I hope, richer one. In this portrait the occultist is as evident, and is accorded as much attention, as the scientist. My portrait should give a new interpretive perspective to studies of Luigi Russolo without conflicting with the common perception of him as a talented inventor. As he himself wrote, "to enrich means to add, not to substitute or abolish."[20]

PART ONE

Luigi Russolo from the Formative Years to 1913

CHAPTER 1

Futurism as a Metaphysical Science

It is surprising how little the common perception of futurism has changed since 1967, when Maurizio Calvesi complained about the "reductive general idea of Italian futurism as a simple exaltation of the machine and superficial reproduction of movement."[1] Although the futurists did not always agree among themselves on a definition of the movement, they certainly would not have shared a view that reduces futurism to merely materialistic terms.[2] If a similarly reductive attitude can already be found in Varèse as early as 1917, the reduction of futurism to a materialistic movement within post–World War II art criticism was likely determined, as noted in the introduction, by a need to downplay the uneasy relationship between futurism and fascism.[3]

Yet futurism was a movement animated by contradictory ideas, constantly oscillating between science and art, the rational and the irrational, future and past, mechanical and spiritual. Indeed, it may well have been these very tensions and frictions that gave futurism its dynamic force.

Defining the futurist movement and analyzing its aesthetics is not an easy task. To the casual observer the futurists seem to present a united front, unified by the charismatic personality of Marinetti, but analysis shows them to have been highly diverse intellectual personalities, each with slightly different opinions and conceptions of life and art and sometimes in open and violent opposition to one another. They may have found themselves (for reasons of convenience, if nothing else, and perhaps sometimes opportunism) under one ideological roof, but individually they maintained autonomous physiognomies and attitudes and peculiarities of their own. It seems, then, impossible to hope to find coherence inside the different poetic positions of the futurists, let alone to formulate an organic presentation with which they would have been satisfied.

Marinetti's work and personality succeeded in maintaining a certain order, at least in the beginning. It is well documented that Marinetti initially subsidized all the initiatives of the movement (including publications and exhibitions), and, like a good impresario, he reserved the right to supervise the work of the other artists of the group, to the point that all the first futurist manifestos unquestionably ran the gauntlet of Marinetti's censorship; this explains their similar tone.[4] But in the privacy of living-room discussions or personal correspondence—or anywhere outside Marinetti's public control—the futurists' aesthetic visions diverged synchronically and diachronically; they were in continual growth and in a restless state of becoming, changing along with the shifting alliances within the movement.

Critically the most lucid figure among them was probably Umberto Boccioni. Perhaps owing to a predisposition of spirit, and despite the brevity of his career, which almost did not leave him time to conclude a cycle of thought, Boccioni was one of the very few futurists to produce a volume that presented his poetics systematically.[5]

The other exception was Luigi Russolo. Although he was not as socially exuberant as Boccioni was, his thought was characterized by a surprising coherence of themes—many so extraordinarily close to those of his friend Boccioni as to suggest a sort of intersecting pollination between the two. Russolo was to repeat these early themes, unchanged in their substance, for the rest of his life; being spiritual in character, they corresponded well with futurism's occult side.

To summarize all the instances that show connections between futurism and esoteric preoccupations at various levels—ranging from spirituality to interest in and practice of the occult arts, and also including black and red magic and spiritualism—would be an ambitious undertaking. Here I shall simply create a backdrop against which to project the fruit of research on Russolo's interest in the occult and my reinterpretation of his sound-related activities in the context of this interest.

I am not the first to mention the influence of the occult arts on the futurist movement. Sporadic references to this influence can be found in volumes, catalogs, and essays on futurism and the visual arts edited by Calvesi and Maurizio Fagiolo dell'Arco. Until a few years ago the only contributing monographs available were a brief article by Germano Celant titled "Futurismo esoterico," published in *Il Verri* in 1970, and Calvesi's very brief article "L'écriture médiumnique comme source de l'automatisme futuriste et surréaliste," published in *Europe* in 1975, in which Calvesi shows connections between mediumistic phenomena and the poetics of the automatic writing adopted first by Marinetti and then by the Surrealists. To these should certainly be added Calvesi's above-mentioned 1967 classic *Il futurismo: La fusione della vita nell'arte*, in which occult and spiritualist themes, however eccentric, occasionally color the overall discussion.

Renewed interest in the topic began first with the extensive catalog of a 1995 Frankfurt exhibition titled *Okkultismus und Avantgarde*, which devoted much space to the futurists; this was followed by Flavia Matitti's writing on Balla and theosophy, as well as by the handsome volume by Simona Cigliana (*Futurismo esoterico*), which takes its title from Celant's essay and is the most complete contribution to the topic to date. In contrast to the earlier sources cited, some of which are limited to a list of facts, Cigliana's book offers a convincing in-depth analysis of the futurists' occult frequentations, albeit primarily limited to the field of literature.

The futurists' interest in the occult can be attributed to their full immersion in the culture of their period, principally inspired by French symbolism, which was in turn a reaction to Comte's mid-nineteenth-century positivism and absolute materialism. In Italy, critiques of positivism and materialism also attacked idealism, and not just in rational and dialectic Hegelian formulations but also in idealism's mainstream Italian dissemination through the writings of the philosopher Benedetto Croce.

It has been maintained that interest in the occult arts and metapsychics can be attributed to the futurists' attraction to the then current understanding of science. There were those who, considering the future of scientific research, maintained that science should include among its fields of inquiry the study of paranormal phenomena and confer legitimacy upon it, since this was the natural direction toward which science was already tending. This view may be true, but it offers only a partial picture of futurism, and it bears the further defect of again putting science and technology at the center of the futurist poetic meditation, as if they were the end of this meditation instead of, as we will see, the means.

Already at this stage, however, it is clear that these occult interests were poles apart from an aesthetic conception preoccupied exclusively with the "simple exaltation of the machine and exterior reproduction of movement." The futurists' interest in science was not always exclusive or absolute, and it was not always blind idolatry. Calvesi addresses this point when he writes, "Boccioni did not want a scientific aesthetics, that is, definable into scientific rules, but only an aesthetics that took the acquisitions of science into account: which is very different."[6] For Marinetti the situation was entirely similar: "Art assimilates science intuitively, analogically, by parallelism and also by benefiting from science's technical discoveries, but never by a substitution of methodologies."[7] For the futurists, science was above all a means; it was not the end of their aesthetic vision.

The present and following chapters consider the movement's interest in the occult—alongside its interest in science and technology and its greatly underexplored interest in altered states of consciousness—as a means to achieve out-of-body experiences. Such experiences, in turn, would permit the futurists to observe reality from a hyperreal point of view, as well as to re-create reality through a new, spiritual mode of artistic creation. Subsequent chapters add Russolo's musical activity to those expressions of futurism that are indebted to the occult tradition.

SCIENCE AND THE OCCULT AT THE TURN OF THE TWENTIETH CENTURY

Interest in the occult would seem to contradict the attention the futurists gave to the latest discoveries of the science and technology of the period.[8] But from the middle of the nineteenth century on, interest in the occult was increasingly shared by scientists and occultists alike, generating such terms as "scientific occultism," which further muddied the waters.[9] Increasingly spreading an image of the universe as an organism animated by mysterious and supernatural forces, new scientific discoveries made between the second half of the nineteenth century and the first years of the twentieth showed that idealism, positivism, and materialism gave too restricted a vision of natural phenomena and the cosmos.[10]

A more dynamic conception of experimental science led various intellectuals of the time to consider occult manifestations as phenomena not yet known because of imperfect human senses and the limitations of human research tools; sooner or later, however, the scientific community was expected to be in a position to measure, understand, and explain. Heisenberg's uncertainty principle would eventually limit, if not altogether undermine, this hope for accurate measurements.

Exhortations to avoid reducing existence (and so the world) exclusively to what human senses can perceive came from all sides, as exemplified by the famous astronomer Camille Flammarion's comment that X-rays were a further proof that "sensation and reality are two very different things."[11]

Among the many attempts to systematize ways of understanding, ranging from alchemy to metapsychics to spiritualism, and drawn from sources as diverse as the *Corpus Hermeticum*, medieval mysticism, the neoplatonism of the Renaissance, freemasonry, and Eastern philosophies, was the philosophy of the Rose+Croix, which is worth citing for its direct influence on artistic disciplines.[12] But even more relevant was the influence of theosophy.

Blavatsky's theosophy, with its comparativist and encyclopedic popularizing approach, which embraced Eastern philosophical thought as well as having numerous points of contact with scientific research, found fertile ground in the cultural context of the epoch. In fact, it became fashionable in those end-of-the-century artistic circles that still believed in romantic philosophical ideas or had aligned with the new symbolist trend. Theosophy famously called for systematic research of parascientific phenomena that would apply the same criteria used by scientific method to investigate other natural phenomena. Such spiritual research was never intended for utilitarian purposes but only for the spiritual advancement of humanity.

In Italy theosophy paid particular attention to the study of the human psyche. In fact, perhaps because of the charismatic presence of the celebrated Turinese psychiatrist and anthropologist Cesare Lombroso, psychiatry and neurology were in Italy the first disciplines to take an interest in various forms of the occult. Among these forms were parapsychology and parascience (telepathy, clairvoyance, possession, psychokinesis, ideoplastic), as well as correlated mediumistic phenomena.[13] The need to push beyond the appearance of things to understand the world and the belief that mediums and artists were gifted with more highly developed spiritual faculties—both principles that betrayed connections with romantic aesthetics—were propositions that futurists maintained on several occasions.

In this "sounding out" of reality the new frontiers of science were certainly helpful. Among the scientific discoveries of the age, that of Röntgen's X-rays in 1895 was one of the most suggestive, because its application implied a complete revolution of the perceptive act itself. Unlike the theories on the fourth dimension or the study of non-Euclidean geometries that affected the *representation* of the perceptive act, X-rays revolutionized the very act of seeing. This discovery was fundamentally important in the development of theories of the pictorial avant-garde in the first years of the century—and not only for the futurists.[14]

X-rays bore a metaphoric weight: they encouraged one to view things profoundly rather than occupy oneself with the surface perceptible via the five senses. And an even closer relationship with mediumistic phenomena circulates in the scientific literature of the time: Lombroso, Flammarion, Ochorowicz, and Zoellner all drew a direct connection between Röntgen's research on the vibration of ether waves and the phenomena of ectoplastic condensation.[15] It is not surprising, then, to learn that X-rays thoroughly fascinated Boccioni, Balla, and Russolo, and that they offered a concrete way of achieving (through the extension of human senses of perception) the futurist interpenetration of planes they promoted in the manifestos of futurist painting.

The futurists' fascination with this new technology is first documented in a passage in the technical manifesto of futurist painting of April 11, 1910: "Who can still believe in the opacity of bodies, while our acuity and multiplied sensitivity makes us intuit the obscure manifestations of mediumistic phenomena? Why must one continue to create without taking account of our visual power that can give results analogous to those of X-rays?"[16]

The futurists were convinced that X-rays and X-ray-like clairvoyance could help to register otherwise invisible aspects of reality, such as the residual traces of the movement of bodies or the luminous emanations produced by the brain and projected in the surrounding aura—emanations that theosophists called "thought-forms." This protocol of perception based on light and movement permitted one to grasp the spiritual level of reality. The technical manifesto claimed that "by the persistence of the image in the retina, objects in motion multiply, deform, following one another, as vibrations, in the space that they pass through [i.e., of their trajectory] [. . .]. To paint a figure one does not need to make the figure: one needs to render its atmosphere. [. . .] Motion and light destroy the materiality of bodies."[17]

These convictions would be summarized at the end of the manifesto in the concept of *complementarismo congenito* (congenital complementarism), a notion that the art historian Marianne Martin, in her *Futurist Art and Theory*, considered "an occult spiritual experience bringing the artist in closer touch with the universal forces."[18] The term *complementarismo congenito* readily promotes a union of opposites that rings distinctively alchemical, and thus occult.

SPACE AND TIME TAMED: MARINETTI'S ECTOPLASM

An examination of the critical texts of Calvesi, Fagiolo dell'Arco, and Celant reveals that all of the most representative futurist artists were to varying degrees concerned with the occult.[19] This is certainly true of Marinetti. By celebrating action and movement—a celebration clearly intoxicated with Nietzscheanism—his aesthetics celebrated the energy manifested in every vibration of the cosmos, that is, energy itself.

Far from being a proposition of materialistic thrust, Marinetti's obsessive celebration of movement and vibration reflects an occult, symbolist-derived substratum.[20] Central to this view is the idea that matter is constituted by condensation of waves vibrating at different intensities; as such, through movement, matter either vanishes or better reveals its implicit spirituality. Basing his ideas on Nietzsche's theory of action, his personal reading of Bergson's vitalism, and Einstein's theory of relativity (which Marinetti probably encountered by way of the popularizing work of Minkowsky), the founder of futurism derived a conception of the world in which, if only because we lack absolute parameters to show stasis, all is perpetual movement.[21]

According to Marinetti, "absolute space and time do not preexist, nor do any absolutely immovable points nor any objects in absolute movement, because there is no absolute term of reference: object and subject are, always, correlatively but discontinuously mobile."[22] According to Calvesi, futurists did not regard "spirit and matter (and therefore [. . .] intuition and intellect)" as separate; they saw them as a unity, under the "same principle of energy."[23] As is also true of Boccioni, Marinetti overcame Bergson's dualism of matter versus movement. Matter never exists as absolute inertia: "Matter and movement, rather than contradictory ends, became ends that could be brought back to one single principle."[24]

Behind this theory of energy we find not only the influence of Nietzsche's interpretations and Einstein's suggestions but also one of the core propositions of alchemy that futurists may have derived from pre-Socratic philosophies: the belief in a universe that may be synthesizable into a single generating principle, a *primal matter*, existing in various levels of density and from which all things derive.²⁵ This primal matter, a wave vibrating at different frequency, was often referred to as the ether.

The interest in waves and vibrations, and in their relationship to occult themes, is a constant in Marinetti's prose. In his *Manifesto della declamazione dinamica e sinottica* he writes that the futurist poet/performer will have the task of "metallizing, liquefying, vegetalizing, petrifying, and electrifying the voice, fusing it with the vibrations of matter, themselves expressed by Words-in-Freedom,"²⁶ whereas in *La grande Milano tradizionale e futurista* Marinetti recognized in Russolo's enterprise the capacity to "organize spiritually and fantastically our acoustic vibrations."²⁷

A similar transformative approach is found in the manifesto *La radia*, published with Pino Masnata in 1933. Among other things, the radio set (Marinetti and Masnata have recourse to the feminine gender for the word, *radia*) is here considered to be:

4. Reception amplification and transformation of vibrations emitted by living beings by living or dead spirits noisy dramas of states of mind without words.
5. Reception amplification and transformation of vibrations emitted by matter Just as today we listen to the song of the woods and of the sea tomorrow we will be seduced by the vibrations of a diamond or of a flower.²⁸

It is, furthermore:

6. Pure organism of radiophonic sensations
7. An art without time or space without yesterday or tomorrow [...] The reception and amplification, through thermionic valves, of light and of the voices of the past will destroy time [...]
9. Human art, universal and cosmic, that is like a voice with a true psychology—spirituality of the noises, of the voices and of the silence.²⁹

In these passages points of contact with panpsychism are evident. The idea that everything is vibration is an eminently occultist one, as it implies that all phenomena occurring in the world are in some way secretly linked. Once the corpuscular theory of light, inspired by Democritus and upheld by Newton, was put aside in favor of the theory of waves traveling through ether, which lasted until Einstein, it was as if the scientific community implicitly validated the long esoteric tradition that had always included a belief in the correlation between light and sound. The discovery of electromagnetic waves, X-rays, and, shortly after, radioactivity, confirmed this occultist proposition.³⁰ In fact, the theory of waves propagating themselves in the ether reinforced and essentially confirmed an alchemical/synesthetic conception of art, because both sound and light are, according to this vision of physics, waves that only differ in frequency or wavelength—a difference of degree, not of kind.

Futurism was always characterized by a strong synesthetic component, and synesthesia has traditionally been an indicator of the occult (by way of the vibrational tradition).[31] This connection was a remnant of the connection between futurism and French symbolism in the latter's most occultist (and psychedelic) moments—one may think of the Baudelaire of *Correspondances* or the Rimbaud of *Voyelles*—but also of the Italian version of that same symbolism, alcoholic and brilliant, which we call Milanese scapigliatura, an antibourgeois art movement surely characterized, just as futurism is, by an overlap of scientific and occult interests.[32]

The debate about synesthesia was widespread at the opening of the twentieth century.[33] Marinetti's interest in the relationship between the *arti sorelle* (sister arts) and the different senses was ever present, even when not taking center stage as it does in his manifesto "Tactilism" (1921, revised in 1924).

Tactilism, Marinetti claimed, could be considered the result of the mortification of the other four senses, producing an empowered sense of touch; this would occur following a deviation of the sun from its proper orbit that would cause its unusual distancing from the earth.[34] But, Marinetti maintained, the phenomenon was instead created by "an act of futurist caprice/faith/will." In fact, in an extreme situation such as a planetary catastrophe, the five senses would be reduced to only one. Marinetti wrote, "Everybody can feel that sight, smell, hearing, touch and taste are modifications of a single, highly perceptive sense: the sense of touch, which splits into different ways and organizes into different points."[35]

In this manifesto, *tactilism* is a provisional term for a new art form that merges all of the five traditional senses as well as a series of new senses that Marinetti lists. He chooses to give "the name of Tactilism to all the senses that are not specified," since he believes that the perceptive senses are in fact "more or less arbitrary localizations of that confused total of intertwined senses that constitute the typical forces of the human machine"; these forces could in his opinion "be better observed on the epidermal frontiers of our body." Notwithstanding this, the attention here is obviously on the sense of touch; as Marinetti describes it, to arrive at a tactile art, other stimuli (including the visual) must be sacrificed or neutralized.[36]

Marinetti therefore contemplates a synesthetic emotion—which by definition links different senses by means of association—that is evoked and activated by use of specially made implements that he calls tactile tables (*tavole tattili*). In tactile art it is exclusively through touch that the perceiver reconstructs, by association, stimuli that, while similar, belong to other expressive fields such as music or painting; this kind of reconstruction is encouraged in the tactile tables. Marinetti chose not to integrate the expressive protocol of the tactile tables with expressive modalities derived from other art forms (like painting or sculpture)—a choice made not to prevent a dialogue between the arts but to protect the newborn art form tactilism and permit it, at least in the beginnings of its journey, to develop autonomously.

Marinetti believed that the sense of touch, when empowered, permits seeing beyond the physical—permits seeing even inside objects, as if by a sort of tactile X-ray vision: "A visual sense is born, at the fingertips. *Interscopia* is developed, and some individuals are able to see inside their own bodies. Others can dimly discern the insides of nearby bodies." The connection with Boccioni's interpenetration of planes, and of its occult and scientific matrices (or implications), could not be clearer.

At its core, Marinetti's tactilism aimed at the perfecting of "spiritual communications between human beings, through the epidermis." Often read as merely an erotic proclamation, this statement was, rather, the testimony of Marinetti's spiritual and occult attitude, perhaps even traceable to the conversations with his father, who was an enthusiastic reader of Eastern philosophy.[37] With Tactilism, Marinetti proposed to "penetrate better and outside of scientific methods the true essence of matter" and to promote the type of spiritual experience that could reach the point of "negating the distinction between spirit and matter," an affirmation that in substance overcomes, as stated above, Bergson's dualism of movement versus matter. Marinetti believed that comprehension of the essence of matter could be obtained by eliminating the mediation of the brain (i.e., of human reason), which is guilty of polluting the virgin, immediate perfection of the tactile experience. As he wrote: "Perhaps there is more thought in the fingertips than in the brain that has the pride of observing the phenomenon [the act of touching]."

According to Marinetti, the new art had more relations with spiritualism and could better demonstrate the validity of theories of reincarnation than other arts: "The futurist Balla declares that by means of Tactilism everyone can enjoy again with freshness and absolute surprise the sensations of his past life, that he could not enjoy again with equal surprise by means of music nor by means of painting."[38]

Only a few years after this manifesto, the *Manifesto della fotografia futurista*, a collaboration between Marinetti and Tato published on April 11, 1930, proposed updating Anton Giulio Bragaglia's *fotodinamica* (photodynamics) by taking advantage of the new technological possibilities. The aesthetic coordinates of this book however are not that distant from Bragaglia's, who was from the beginning of his career interested in phenomena of mediumistic materialization.

The goals of futurist photography in 1930 included, among other things:

4. The spectralizing of some parts of the human or animal body isolated or joined nonlogically; [...]
11. The transparent and semitransparent superimposition of concrete persons and objects and of their semiabstract phantasms with simultaneity of memory/dream; [...]
14. The composition of absolutely extraterrestrial landscapes, astral or mediumistic by means of thicknesses, elasticity, turbid depths, clear transparencies, algebraic or geometric values, and with nothing human, vegetable, or geologic;[39]

But in *L'uomo moltiplicato e il regno della macchina*, part of *Guerra sola igiene del mondo* of 1915 (and originally in *Le futurisme* of 1911, perhaps even drafted as early as 1910), Marinetti aspired to a structural modification of man that in future would, thanks to the materialization of wings produced with the force of thought, allow man to fly.[40]

In *L'uomo moltiplicato*, Marinetti wrote: "The day it is possible for man to exteriorize his will such that it extends outside of him like an immense invisible arm—on that day Dream and Desire, which today are vain words, will rule sovereign over tamed Space and Time."[41] Having lost the reader in this forest of his postsymbolist prose, Marinetti then showed us the way. He believed that this prophecy, which he himself recognized as paradoxical, could be more easily understood by "studying the phenomena of exteriorized will that constantly manifest themselves in séances."

This *uomo moltiplicato*, a metallic alter ego that would duplicate man without duplicating his defects, would even have the gift of clairvoyance and, in addition to being a "non-human and mechanical type, constructed for an omnipresent velocity, it will be naturally cruel, omniscient and combative." The figure of the multiplied man shows interesting similarities with the metallic animal of the subsequent manifesto, "Ricostruzione futurista dell'universo" by Balla and Depero, the aggressiveness of which would unquestionably have been inebriated with the spirit of World War I interventionism.

For Marinetti, the man of the future was not so much the product of Darwinian evolution as, rather, the transformist hypothesis of Lamarck (whom, indeed he cited in his essay): not an evolution of man but his alchemical transformation into a more perfect being *created* by the futurists, a "non-human type in whom moral pain, kindness, affection and love, i.e., the only corrosive poisons of inexhaustible vital energy, will be abolished"—in short, a man aiming for a suspended, ataractic, beyond-good-and-evil spiritual state.

These scientific-alchemical themes never disappeared from Marinetti's repertoire. In his 1933 manifesto *La radia*, he again announced the "overcoming of death" through futurism "with a metallizing of the human body and the appropriating of the vital spirit as machine force."[42] In this proclamation, Marinetti reelaborated his 1915 position, according to which the futurists had the power to reawaken mummies with the charismatic electricity of their hand movements. In a passage of "Guerra sola igiene del mondo," Marinetti recounts some of the brawls after the futurist evenings of the first years: "Everywhere, we saw growing in a few hours the courage and the number of men that are truly young, and [we saw] the galvanized mummies that our gesture had extracted from the ancient sarcophagi, becoming bizarrely agitated."[43] By now it should be clear that Marinetti's will futuristically to abolish death is a trope, a trope that will recur frequently in Marinetti's writings (e.g., the closing of the manifesto "La matematica futurista immaginativa qualitativa"). [44]

PAINTING THE INVISIBLE: BOCCIONI'S SIXTH SENSE

Contro ogni materialismo.
—Umberto Boccioni, "Note per il libro"[45]

At the intersection of romantic impetuousness and Bergsonian critique of materialism, the personality of Umberto Boccioni stands out dramatically. Departing from a type of formation close to Marinetti's, yet influenced by Marinetti's theories, Boccioni too demonstrated a strong interest in the occult. Drawn to symbolism, Nietzsche, and Bergson, familiar with the ideas of Einstein, admirer of Wagner, and more generally attracted to the titanic and romantic aesthetic, Boccioni had the vocation and the presumption of the demiurge, the creator of worlds, the materializer.

Boccioni, like Marinetti, overcame the Bergsonian dualism of matter and movement by wedding himself to Einstein's vision (and perhaps to that of Steiner, if one substitutes the term *energy* for *spirit*).[46] Everything moves, everything vibrates (all bodies are "persistent symbols of the universal vibration," can be read in the technical manifesto of futurist painting), all creation is energy, existing in the form of waves that organize the primal matter, the ether, into different levels of density or, as Boccioni puts it, of *intensity*. There is no separation between one body and another: in Boccioni's thought, continuity is preferred. In fact, in his article "Fondamento plastico della scultura e pittura futuriste," which appeared in the periodical *Lacerba* on March 15, 1913, Boccioni writes that "*distances* between one object and another are made up not of empty spaces but of the continuities of matter of different intensity," immediately adding that in the paintings of the futurists one does not have "the *object* and the *emptiness*, but only a greater or lesser intensity and solidity of spaces."[47]

And he adds, further advocating for continuity,

> They accuse us of doing "cinematography," which is an accusation that really makes us laugh, so much it is vulgarly moronic. We do not subdivide visual images: we search for a shape, or, better, a single form [*forma unica*] that would substitute the new concept of continuity to the old concept of (sub)division.
>
> Every subdivision of motion is completely arbitrary, as it is completely arbitrary every subdivision of matter.[48]

In confirmation of this proposition, Boccioni presents two quotes form Bergson.

This passage can be better understood after reading the futurist Ardengo Soffici's restatement of this principle of continuity, since he returns the concept to what would have been its original theosophical coordinates. In his article "Raggio," published in *Lacerba* on July 1, 1914, and republished not by chance a few months later in the Roman theosophical periodical *Ultra* with the eloquent title "La teosofia nel futurismo," Soffici wrote that bodies are not separated from one another but that "the entire universe therefore is a single whole without interruption of continuity," and that, moreover, "the world is not a molecular aggregate, but a flux of energy with varied rhythms, from granite to thought."[49]

Soffici goes on to maintain that "a privileged organism, a center of extrapowerful vital force, can in a certain moment and under certain circumstances attract and concentrate within itself its distant parts, the peripheral waves of its energies, making them concrete," and that "an artist can live and make concrete in a work the life of another being, of things, of places that he has not visited. A prophet [can] see and reveal future events—future for sensibilities less acute than his own." In a crescendo of self-centered hubris, Soffici maintains that his consciousness is "a globe of light that shoots its rays all around in accordance with its force," and he concludes, "I am the point of confluence of history and of the world. I am one with eternity and with the infinite."[50]

Soffici's claim that the psychic energy of the artist could not simply *reproduce* but must *re-create* reality was shared by all futurists. I shall investigate how determinative this proposition is in analyzing the work of Russolo. This idea led to the futurists' interest in the creation of ectoplasmic forms by sensitive subjects in a mediumistic trance. In "Fondamento plastico della scultura e pittura futuriste," Boccioni wrote:

> When, through the works, one understands the truth of futurist sculpture, one will see the form of atmosphere where before one saw emptiness and then with the impressionists a fog. This fog was already a first step toward atmospheric plasticity, toward our *physical transcendentalism* which is then another step toward the perception of analogous phenomena until now occult to our obtuse sensitivity, such as the perceptions of the luminous emanations of our body of which I spoke in my first lecture in Rome and which the photographic plate already reproduces.[51]

A year later, at the close of his volume *Pittura, scultura futuriste*, Boccioni wrote: "For us the biological mystery of mediumistic materialization is a certainty, a clarity in the intuition of psychic transcendentalism and of plastic states of mind."[52] In his preparatory notes for the book, which were published posthumously, Boccioni formulated yet another eloquent phrase: "Our painting is esoteric."[53]

In the passage from "Fondamento plastico della scultura e pittura futuriste" quoted above, Maurizio Fagiolo dell'Arco read an allusion to the photographs of ectoplasms produced at the beginning of the century by the notorious Neapolitan medium Eusapia Palladino.[54] Both Marinetti and Boccioni were fascinated by Palladino's séances.[55] These séances had became still better known after the director of the *Corriere della sera* tried to discredit them.[56]

Palladino based her credibility on the fact that she had agreed to repeat her mediumistic séances in the presence of neurologists and psychologists, and she was defended fiercely by the anthropologist Lombroso. Celant records that Lombroso, along with a Turinese group of faithful followers, was in those years investigating the study of phenomena of psychic condensation and materialization. Lombroso's theories would have been fairly widespread in the artistic circles of the time. Kandinsky, for example, was well informed about the studies on spiritualism that Lombroso conducted in Palladino's mediumistic séances,[57] and the young Balla in his early years in Turin took Lombroso's classes.[58]

Materialization phenomena were also the point of departure for the work of Anton Giulio Bragaglia, the author of that "futurist photodynamism" that incited Boccioni's wrath. In two articles from 1913 titled "I fantasmi dei vivi e dei morti" and "La fotografia dell'invisibile," Bragaglia published photos of fake ectoplasms; in doing so he was following a well-established international trend.[59] But the year before, influenced by mediumistic photos and those theories of chronophotography of Muybridge or Maray on which Giacomo Balla based his 1912 paintings of the frame-based breakdown of movement (*scomposizione del movimento*), Bragaglia had already produced the first works of photodynamism.[60] In these works he retraced blurs and trajectories of bodies in movement, aiming to reveal that spiritual essence that is lost as a result of the limitations of the human eye: "In motion, things, dematerializing, become idealized," he declared in his *Fotodinamismo futurista*.[61] Calvesi, considering this phrase to be a departure from Bergsonian ideas, linked it to one of the key phrases of the technical manifesto of futurist painting of 1910: "Movement and light destroy the materiality of bodies." Bragaglia's interest in the supernatural did not exhaust itself in this first phase, as testified by his 1932 photograph *Alchimia musicale*.

But the passage from *Lacerba* of March 15, 1913, in which Boccioni talked about "perceptions of the luminous emanations of our body," seems actually to refer to the particular metapsychics phenomena that Annie Besant and Charles Webster Leadbeater called "thought-forms." Their book *Thought-forms* of 1901 was read assiduously in the early twentieth century by artists who were interested in abstract painting. In fact, it exerted great influence over the work of Kandinsky, Kupka, Malevich, and Mondrian.

The book's central proposition is that all thoughts and emotions create corresponding forms and colors in the aura that surrounds the physical body of every human being. These forms and colors are directly determined by the vibrations of the aura, which only clairvoyants can perceive. According to Besant and Leadbeater, the aura of an individual is composed of the union of different "bodies," among which are the astral body, generated by the passions, and the mental body, generated by the thoughts. The vibrations of the astral and mental bodies have the power to produce special psychic forms, both concrete and abstract, which they called thought-forms. Thought-forms can move freely, and they can distance themselves from the body if the energy of the mind that produced them is sufficient. Their color is based on the quality of the thought, their form on its nature, and their sharpness on its clarity.[62]

Besant's and Leadbeater's book contain a famous series of color plates painted by various artists on indications furnished by the authors after experiencing trances. Their indications were intended to document scientifically, down to the smallest detail, the thought-forms produced by subjects while feeling emotions ranging from devotion to fear and rage that were collected on specific occasions, at specific times of the day. The largely abstract plates attracted the interest of artists of the time, as did the illustrations of Leadbeater's *Man Visible and Invisible* of 1902. *Thought-forms* was quickly translated into a number of languages; in Italy it was first disseminated in the 1905 French translation, in which version it was read by Luigi Pirandello and influenced his poetics from the writing of *Il fu Mattia Pascal* onward.[63]

It is useful, however, to remember that Boccioni first expressed interest in the occult in that Roman lecture of 1911 that he referred to in his *Lacerba* article of March 15, 1913, a lecture in which his spirituality is clearly revealed. The text of the lecture, which remained unpublished for a long time, represents one of the high points of Boccioni's poetics. Conscious of its relevance, he referred to it often in his subsequent works. His familiarity with the books of Leadbeater and Besant, particularly *Thought-forms*, emerges from the very opening lines of the lecture, where, in prophesizing the art of the future, Boccioni affirms:

> There will come a time when a painting will no longer be enough. Its immobility will be an archaism when compared with the vertiginous movement of human life. The eye of man will perceive colors *like feelings in themselves*. Multiplied colors will have no need of forms to be understood, and pictorial works will be whirling musical compositions of enormous colored gases, which on the scene of a free horizon, will move and electrify the complex soul of a crowd that we cannot yet imagine.[64]

The reference to the use of colors as "feelings in themselves," the use of "colored gases" that can electrify the soul, and the synesthetic link between colors and musical composition are all concepts from *Thought-forms*. In that same year,

FIGURE 3. Umberto Boccioni, *Città che sale* (1910–11). New York, Museum of Modern Art.

1911, Luigi Russolo exhibited perhaps his most ambitious canvas, on which he had worked for many years.[65] Titled *La musica*, it represents a whirling azure wave that unfolds in the air while the protagonist of the painting, a pianist, executes equally whirling musical figurations on a keyboard. Russolo's painting probably inspired Boccioni's visionary remarks above; and it certainly inspired some elements of *Città che sale*, Boccioni's masterpiece of 1910–1911 (fig. 3).[66]

The synesthetic hypothesis returned in the closing words of Boccioni's 1911 lecture, where Boccioni clarified that by painting the sensation, the futurists stop "the idea before it can be localized in any one sense and be determined either as music, poetry, painting, architecture, that way capturing without any mediation the primal universal sensation."[67] Moreover, because futurists live in the absolute, Boccioni maintained that it was necessary for those wishing to understand their works to be not only extremely intelligent but also ready "to enter into contact with pure intuition," which is possible only "after a long and religious preparation."[68]

Thanks to this spiritual preparation, we are endowed with a new sensitivity that, through new perceptive and psychic means, guides us in the search for the absolute. Boccioni writes:

> We painters [. . .] feel that this sensitivity is a psychic divining force that gives the senses the power to perceive that which never until now was perceived.[69] We think that if everything tends toward *Unity,* that which man until today has sought to perceive in unity is still a miserable blind infantile decomposition of things.[70]

Boccioni believed that the artist must aspire to re-create this unity from the "chaos that envelops things." Sensation is the synthesis, the essence of things, their transfiguration. It is the "subjective impression of Nature."

Moving from the more spiritual aspects of the artistic currents that had gone before (divisionism, impressionism, symbolism), Boccioni arrived at a definition of futurism as the culmination and overcoming of these previous artistic currents. Divisionism represents for Boccioni the achievement of a "symphonic and polychromatic unity of the painting that will become more and more a universal synthesis." With the impressionists, figures and objects, although still in a fairly embryonic way, "are already the nucleus of an atmospheric vibration." But the impressionists exchanged "appearance for reality." It was their limit, and as a result they were trapped in a superficial representation of nature.

Boccioni considered the painting style of the Italian symbolist Gaetano Previati—in which he noted contacts with the "Rosa Croce"—to be the direct predecessor of futurist painting. In Previati, "forms begin to speak like music, bodies aspire to make themselves atmosphere, spirit, and the subject is ready to transform itself into a *state of mind."*

Boccioni perceived futurism as a new kind of impressionism: "Our impressionism is absolutely spiritual since more than the optical and analytical impression, it wishes to give the psychic and synthetic impression of reality." The spiritual role of futurist painting and the psychic force that it develops exhibits far loftier ambitions than French impressionism. In Boccioni's words, it "hypnotizes, grasps, envelops and drags the soul to the infinite." Boccioni had already defined this psychic synthesis as "simultaneity of state of mind." It was a mnemonic-optical representation of what is remembered and what is seen; in substance, it was a *spiritualization* of the perceptive experience. As if it were an X-ray view, this psychic synthesis offered possibilities of "penetrating the opacity of bodies."

The influence of X-rays and the mythology that the futurists developed around them returns with Boccioni's mention of X-rays in a catalog note for the painting *La risata* (also painted in the year 1911), which was prepared for the program of the 1912 London exhibition: "The scene is round the table of a restaurant where all are gay. The personages are studied from all sides and both the objects in front and those at the back are to be seen, all those being present in the painter's memory, so that the principle of the Roentgen rays is applied to the picture."[71]

This quote shows similarities with his affirmations in the Roman lecture. For Boccioni the model of the modern artist was the "clairvoyant painter," capable of "painting not only the visible but that which until now was held to be invisible."[72] He believed that the modern painter "can only paint the invisible, clothing it with lights and shadows that emanate from his own soul." Thanks to the progress—spiritual and technological—of the modern age, the five senses can again be transcended: "It is our futurist hypersensitivity that guides us and makes us already possess that sixth sense that science strains in vain to catalog and define."[73]

This perceptive sensitivity permitted the futurist artist to understand the spiritual essence of the movement of bodies. Everything is perennially in motion, all is composed of the same waves that have various grades of density and that vibrate at different intensities. "Bodies are but condensed atmosphere," Boccioni wrote, and minerals, plants, and animals are composed of "identical nature." This new sensitivity is a true and real "psychic divining force" that allows one to grasp that substantial "Unity" of everything that Boccioni considered—as he phrases it in his lecture notes in a crossed-out line—the symbol of the "universal vibration." [74] Futurist painting aspired to reproduce a more profound reality as it is perceived by the subject and as it produced states of mind in the subject: "If bodies provoke states of mind through vibrations of forms, it is those that we will draw."

The following excerpt from the closing paragraph of the Roman lecture is both the most visionary passage of that document and the one where Boccioni's familiarity with Leadbeater is most evident:

> There is a space of vibrations between the physical body and the invisible that determines the nature of its action and that will dictate the artistic sensation. In short, if around us spirits wander and are observed and studied; if from our bodies emanate fluids of power, of antipathy, of love; if deaths are foreseen at a distance of hundreds of kilometers; if premonitions give us sudden joy or annihilate us with sadness; if all this impalpable, this invisible, this inaudible becomes more and more the object of investigation and observation: all of this happens because in us some marvelous sense is awakening thanks to the light of our con-

sciousness. *Sensation is the material garment of the spirit* and now it appears to our clairvoyant eyes. And with this the artist feels himself in everything. By creating he does not look, does not observe, does not measure; he feels and the sensations that envelop him dictates him the lines and colors that will arouse the emotions that caused him to act.

THE CRAFT OF LIGHT: BALLA'S OCCULT SIGNATURE

In Balla one finds again the confluence of two streams common among many of his futurist comrades: the scientific/positivist and the spiritualist.[75] The merging of these two tendencies into a sort of metaphysical rationality would constitute, toward the end of the nineteenth century, one of the aims of theosophy. As Linda Henderson maintains, the preferred meeting place between science and spirituality is the theory of vibrations.[76] In the light of this convergence of ends, it is no surprise that Balla, literally obsessed with vibrations, was involved with theosophy for many years, and that an understanding of his relations with it are crucial to reconstructing his artistic journey.

During his formative years in Turin, Balla studied with Cesare Lombroso (whose contacts with spiritualism have been mentioned by Germano Celant, among others).[77] But the encounter first with freemasonry and occultism, and later with theosophy, occurred only in 1895, once Balla had moved to Rome. In the first years of the century, Balla furthered his interest in psychiatry by reading Hoepli's popular compendia and manuals.[78] His interest in X-rays may have been piqued by his acquaintance with Professor Ghilarducci, an expert on radiology, psychology, and electrotherapy, whose portrait Balla painted in 1903.[79] This is indicated in an undated entry in his notebooks: "Roentgen rays and their applications."[80] I believe he made this entry to remind himself to look into Ignazio Schincaglia's popular 1911 book *Radiografia e radioscopia: Storia dei raggi Roentgen e loro applicazioni piu importanti*.

The supernatural element is already present in some of Balla's first Roman works, both in the impressive dimensions of *Ritratto della madre* from 1901 and in the metaphysical angle and hyperrealism of the formidable *Fallimento* of 1902.[81] As early as 1904 he maintained a friendship with Ernesto Nathan, an occultist and freemason (he was grand master of the Grande Oriente d'Italia in 1899 and again in 1917), who in 1907 became the first anticlerical mayor to take office in the Campidoglio. Nathan acquired nine canvases from Balla and commissioned a portrait in 1910, and Balla even taught painting

FIGURE 4. Giacomo Balla, *Trasformazione forme spiriti* (1918). Rome, Galleria Nazionale d'Arte Moderna. © 2010 Artists Rights Society (ARS), New York / SIAE, Rome.

to Nathan's daughter, Annie.[82] Notwithstanding his contact with Nathan, Balla apparently never affiliated himself with a lodge.[83]

Information about Balla's first contact with theosophy comes from Balla's daughter Elica: "In 1916 Balla is also interested in psychic phenomena and attends the meetings of a society of theosophists presided over by General Ballatore; they hold, in said society, séances. [...] Inspired by this interest, [...] he outlines some sketches on this subject and then a larger painting, aptly titled *Trasformazione forme spiriti*" (fig. 4).[84]

Flavia Matitti has reconstructed the history of the circle around Generale Ballatore, the "Gruppo Teosofico Roma," and Balla's relationship with that circle. Gruppo Roma was founded in 1897 and recognized as a theosophical association in 1907. In the same year, the first issues of the periodical *Ultra* came out; in it Ballatore published articles on hyperspace and the fourth dimension; later he wrote on radioactivity. *Ultra* was the official organ of Gruppo Roma until 1930. In October 1914, Ardengo Soffici published his article "La Teosofia nel futurismo" in Ultra.[85]

Gruppo Roma's activities included the production of their periodical, regular meetings, and the organization of lectures by illustrious speakers; among these Matitti mentions Annie Besant in 1907, and above all Rudolf Steiner, who in 1909 held a series of Roman lectures on different themes (Christ and theosophy, theosophy and Rose+Croix, occultism in Goethe's *Faust*) and drew so much attention that he was invited again the following year.[86]

A careful analysis of Balla's canvases from those years offers evidence that Balla had contact with Gruppo Roma before 1916, perhaps even as early as 1914. In Balla's signatures on the paintings from *Iniezione di futurismo* (1913–14) onward, the two "L" and the "A" of Balla's name intertwine to form a swastika in which the hooks are oriented toward the right. The swastika becomes more evident in the signatures of Balla's "patriotic" and interventionist paintings from 1915, among them *Canto patriottico in piazza di Siena*, *Forme grido "Viva l'Italia,"* and *Bandiere all'Altare della patria*, and it is definitely noticeable in *Trasformazione forme spiriti*.

The swastika has a millennial history; the symbol reappears in a range of latitudes, principally in relation to the cult of light and sun. Especially the right-facing version (in which the hooks are flexed in a clockwise direction) is considered auspicious because it describes the apparent motion of the sun from east to west, thus representing light, life, energy, and the masculine principle.[87]

Because of the presumed Indo-Iranian (i.e., Aryan) origins of the Germanic peoples, Germany's National Socialist German Workers' Party appropriated the swastika in their emblems as a symbol of the purity of "Aryan" blood. But the swastika had been utilized in other historical and geographical contexts well before the Nazis, with quite different meanings. In Madame Blavatsky's posthumous theosophical glossary, the term *svastika* is defined as follows:

> **Svastika** (Sk.). In popular notions, it is the Jaina cross, or the "four-footed" cross (*croix cramponnée*). In Masonic teachings, "the most ancient Order of the Brotherhood of the Mystic Cross" is said to have been founded by Fohi, 1,027 B.C., and introduced into China fifty-two years later, consisting of the three degrees. In esoteric philosophy, it the most mystic and ancient diagram. It is "the originator of the fire by friction, and of the 'Forty-nine Fires.'" Its symbol was stamped on Buddha's heart, and therefore called the "Heart's Seal." It is laid on the breasts of departed Initiates after their death; and it is mentioned with the greatest respect in the *Râmâyana*. Engraved on every rock, temple and prehistoric building of India, and wherever Buddhists have left their landmarks; it is also found in China, Tibet and Siam, and among the ancient Germanic nations as Thor's

Hammer. [. . .] Finally, and in Occultism [sic], it is as sacred to us as the Pythagorean *Tetraktys*, of which it is indeed the double symbol.[88]

According to Blavatsky the swastika was known in India (and other regions of the world that had contact with Buddhism), among proto-Germanic populations, and in China; above all it is a key symbol for freemasonry and theosophy, so important for Madame Blavatsky that she adopted it as one of the symbols of the mystic brooch she designed for herself.

The swastika was an important symbol within Gruppo Roma. For the 1922 design of "Spiritualist Movement," a column header in *Ultra*, Nicola D'Urso adopted a right-facing swastika inscribed in a winged disc and surrounded by stars and concentric orbits.[89] Since at the turn of the century the swastika was regarded in Masonic and theosophical circles as a symbol of light, it is not surprising that Balla, too, would have been fascinated by it. The hidden swastika I detected in Balla's signature on a 1914 work may well indicate that his theosophical influences date back to that year or earlier.

Balla's belief in the mysticism of light, initially inspired by symbolism and divisionism (from Segantini to Pellizza and Previati), followed his early interest in the representation of light in the dark.[90] This interest became stronger over the years, to the point of becoming the most important element of the scene depicted in *Elisa sulla porta* of 1904, in which Balla's wife, Elisa, who was expecting their first daughter—Balla would name her, appropriately enough, Luce—provided the background to a manifestation of light as magical and luminous phenomenon behind a door.[91]

The culmination of Balla's early research into light, and his first futurist work, is however *Lampada ad Arco*, dated 1909 on the canvas, though very probably painted in 1910.[92] This painting, which was certainly influenced by Marinetti's manifesto "Uccidiamo il chiaro di luna," represents the symbolic victory of electric light over the moon and starry sky.[93] In the technical manifesto of futurist painting of 1910, the signatories (Balla among them) proclaimed themselves "Lords of Light" who drink "at the living fountains of the Sun." This openly pagan adoration of the sun includes, among other elements, echoes of the poet Giosuè Carducci and the Milanese Satanism of the scapigliato Emilio Praga.[94]

But this is not the whole story. Besides being a symbolic work, *Lampada ad Arco* is also a scientific work, in which Balla analyzed and pictorially rendered the division of the spectrum; divisionists had largely concentrated on that issue. On the occasion of the canvas's acquisition by the Museum of Modern Art of New York in 1954, Balla wrote: "The canvas of the 'lamp' was painted by me during the divisionist period (1900–1910); in fact the dazzle of the light was obtained by means of the combination of pure colors. This canvas, besides being original as a work of art, is also scientific because I tried to represent the light by separating the colors that composed it. [...] Rendering light has always been my favorite study."[95]

In its ambitious, successful joining of science with spirituality, *Lampada ad Arco* represents an appropriate homage to the genius of Edison, who was a member of the Theosophical Society;[96] as such, the painting may even be considered an homage to theosophy itself. *Lampada ad Arco* was not Balla's last work to betray theosophical leanings. The above-mentioned cycle of 1916–18 titled *Trasformazione forme spiriti*, for example, or *Forme e pensiero—visione spiritica*, exhibited by Bragaglia in 1918, show an evident relationship not only with theosophy, but even more particularly—down to their titles—with Besant and Leadbeater's *Thought-forms*.[97]

Calvesi has written of Balla's self-portrait *Auto-stato d'animo* of 1920, "The attempt seems evident [on Balla's part] to 'dematerialize' his own image by rendering it like an ectoplasm, an ideation very near to that of Bragaglia's Autophotodynamism of 1911; in this portrait, the intent is not so much to suggest a sensation of movement as to spiritualize his own face through the unfocusedness of the repeating and moving of his features."[98]

Balla's interest in spiritualism also surfaces in brief autobiographical descriptions. Describing himself, Balla wrote: "He is a little temperament (he would say) who prefers to hang out with the voices of the infinite than with our own."[99] In a brief autobiographical note from 1920, he affirmed: "In 1500 they called me Leonardo or ... Titian after 4 centuries of artistic decadence, I reappeared in 1900 to shout to my plagiarizers that it is time to end it because times have changed. They called me crazy: poor blockheads !!!!!!!!! I have already created a new sensitivity in art that is expression of future ages that will be colorradioiridesplendorideal luminosissssssssssimiiiiii."[100]

Matitti considered this biographical note to be "in jest."[101] But if the style is in jest, the substance is less so, insomuch as Balla offers a precise and aware self-portrait of himself. The "colorradioiridesplendorideal luminosisssssssssimiiiiii," a portmanteau word that comprises the terms *colori, radio, iride, splendori, ideali*, and *luminosissimi* (colors, radio, rainbow, splendors, ideals, and most luminous), summarize extraordinarily well the coordinates between which

Balla's research moved; "luminosissimi" returns us to the word *luce*, "light," which is so central to his work, and "colori-radio-iride" to the notion of light as radiant wave *and* of the colors of the rainbow as a range, a spectrum of different frequencies of this same wave. Thus in but a few words Balla covered the critical and intellectual distance that separates the mysticism of colors, alchemy, and science.

Another point of contact with the theosophical mysticism of colors emerges with clarity in the series of *Compenetrazioni iridescenti* of 1912–14, real meditations in which the penetrating dynamic-spiritual form of the triangle and the colors of the rainbow, matched together with calculation and elegance, become a symbol of the reunion of two opposing principles, the "compenetration of the self with the universe"—the title Balla later gave to one of the coeval preparatory studies for his now lost *Spessori d'atmosfera*, on which he worked in 1913.[102]

Whereas the idea of rejoining opposites can be connected with the central thesis of Nietzsche's Zarathustra, the animistic ideas of pantheism and panpsychism, which return in Bragaglia and Balilla Pratella, are always present in Balla.[103] Calvesi finds these concepts in *Trasformazione forme spiriti*, a work that he in fact considers a perfect example of the "compenetration between spirit and matter, between creatures and creation."[104]

As Calvesi emphasized, "compenetration [. . .] returns to that idea, fundamental in the theosophical and hermetic sphere, of integration or mercurial *coniuctio*."[105] In the alchemical process the *coniuctio* takes place with the union of opposites, and its catalyst is the principle of light, symbolized by mercury (which is simultaneously a god, a planet, and an element). For alchemy—the hermetic science par excellence—as for theosophy, compenetration is possible since everything in the universe is intimately connected.[106]

This interconnection, then, reveals the occult roots of synesthesia as they are found in the symbolists, the scapigliati, and the futurists. According to these roots, sound, color, and scent are connected because they are different manifestations of one energy. The same holds for alchemy, which appears to be one of the most paradigmatic forces driving Balla's poetics. In alchemy, material objects are essentially variations of weight, form, and color of one single principle, to which they can all be reconducted; this leads naturally to one of the central aspects of this science: through the operation of transformation we can in fact pass from one substance to another. For example, to pass from iron to gold, the secondary properties, which are the distinctive characteristics of the first material (iron), are subtracted to reobtain the primal matter, and, in turn, properties of the second (gold) are introduced into the primal matter in the form of a seed.[107]

The function of compenetration, or *coniuctio*, of opposing elements is to reconstruct the primal matter, the principle common to every existing thing, and thus re-create the totality present in God's work (i.e., creation) through a process of artificious conjoining. The rainbow, as a symbol, is the natural equivalent of this process. Here the colors of the spectrum lie side by side, their conflicts smoothed out by way of attraction, to join together in a comprehensive universality of ranges in solemn harmony: white light as the primal energy that unites opposite, complementary colors.

Since everything derives from a single element, and everything constitutes but a variation of it, it is possible, with detailed observation and analysis of nature and through comprehension of its structure, to deduce the universal principles of these variations (the abstract equivalents that inform creation). It is then possible to reproduce in vitro (with artifice) a sample of the harmony of nature that has the same properties as the natural, divinely created phenomenon and in this way give new form, according to the deduced principles, to the primal matter. The deduction is possible through a hermetical theory of correspondences, according to which the microcosm corresponds structurally to the macrocosm, and so for every object on earth there exists an abstract, celestial ideal. The general laws of the entire universe are thus faithfully reproduced or mirrored in the earthly detail. This theory, central in Plato and famously found in the opening of Hermes Trismegistus's Emerald Tablet—"That which is above is like that which is below and that which is below is like that which is above, to achieve the wonders of the one thing."—returns constantly in all occult thought and is also present in Swedenborg, Steiner, and the Hinduist-inspired nineteenth-century organicism of Goethe. By means of contemplation, one may read in the particular the very metaphor of the totality; one may grasp this idea of totality because in the particular is reflected the structure of the cosmos and its harmony of proportions. This theory of correspondences explains the scientific, analytic-deductive, and alchemical point of view of Balla's research, characterized by meticulous study of details and their re-creation; it also explains his admiration for Leonardo da Vinci.[108]

Balla's ambition to re-create reality through thorough observation and then (re)production of that reality via a detail, or sample, is already perceptible in the hyperrealism of his 1902 *Fallimento*; to create this painting Balla stood tirelessly for hours before a closed door on Via Veneto. In 1950 Balla wrote on the back of the painting:

THIS PAINTING PAINTED BY ME FROM MEMORY IS OF A REALITY THAT NO ONE HAS EQUALLED! LEARN TO LOOK AT IT, TO KNOW IT PURIFIES THE EYES AND THE HEART
BALLA 1950; THOUGHTLESS CHILDREN SCRIBBLE ON THE DOOR OF A FAILED STORE A.D. 1902[109]

A similar attitude can be seen in Balla's *Lampada ad Arco*, which its author also considered, not by chance, "scientific." Fagiolo dell'Arco noted that in this painting Balla "humbly analyzes the most intimate substance of light, wants to find the structure inherent in the object, not the modifications brought by the subject; neglecting the effects he wants to arrive at the cause."[110] An example of Balla's attention to detail is in the recursive structure of the *Compenetrazioni iridescenti*, in which the basic, modular element—the primal matter—is the triangle, which symbolizes movement and light.[111] This attention is also present in the rhythms of the circular figures of *Spessori di atmosfera*, which are scaled down "to human dimensions by way of lines-of-force that connect them to the earth."[112] This painting is now unfortunately lost, but preparatory studies and photographs reveal Balla's use of relations between alchemy and astrology that will culminate in his allegorical canvas *Mercurio passa davanti al Sole, visto da un cannocchiale* of 1914 (fig. 5).

Preceded by a series of preparatory studies and existing in various versions—in which the experience of *Compenetrazioni iridescenti* and *Spessori di atmosfera* is clearly visible—*Mercurio passa davanti al Sole* aims to re-create the experience of seeing the partial solar eclipse caused by Mercury on November 7, 1914, by reproducing the sublime and grandiose harmony of such natural phenomena through forms that are ideal, platonic, abstract. Balla was interested in astronomy and especially familiar with the research of the astronomer and theosophist Flammarion.[113] Thus he observed the 1914 eclipse through a telescope, capturing on canvas the circular forms of Mercury, depicted in a spiral trajectory representing the different phases of the planet's motion, as they overlap with bold vigor against the mass of the sun, the solar rays, and the refractions of the focal lens itself. Mercury, placing itself in between the earth and the sun, acts as a catalyst in the union of the opposed entities of Sun and Earth; Balla was able to downscale this cosmic union to a microcosmic, human level because, thanks to the technology of the telescope, it had become fully perceptible to human eyes.

FIGURE 5. Giacomo Balla, *Mercurio passa davanti al Sole, visto da un cannocchiale* (1914). Gianni Mattioli Collection (on long-term loan at the Peggy Guggenheim Collection, Venice). © 2010 Artists Rights Society (ARS), New York / SIAE, Rome

This scientific-alchemical attitude can be found also in the 1915 manifesto *Ricostruzione futurista dell'universo*, signed by Balla and Depero but enriched with interpolations by Marinetti. In this manifesto we see the artist playing God. Though the attempt is overambitious, it is far from Boccioni's titanic "frescoes." Balla created the detail; he did not expect to create the entire universe in one single shot but, rather, patiently to populate it through example and its multiplications.

Consistent with all the aesthetic coordinates Balla had elaborated until then, the manifesto proposed to discover the pure and ideal forms that shape nature to produce a true tridimensional abstract art in which the synesthetic interaction—of painting, sculpture, the art of noises, and even odors—is once again decisive:

Pictorial futurism evolved, in six years, as the overcoming and solidification of Impressionism, plastic dynamism and molding of an atmosphere, interpenetration of planes and states of mind. The lyric valuation of the universe, by means of Words in Freedom [*Parole in libertà*] of Marinetti and the art of noises of Russolo, fuses itself with the plastic dynamism to give a dynamic, simultaneous, plastic, noisy expression of the universal vibration.

[...] We will give skeleton and flesh to the invisible, the impalpable, the imponderable, the imperceptible. We will find the abstract equivalents of all the forms and of all the elements of the universe, then we will combine them together, according to the caprices of our inspiration, to form plastic complexes that we will put in motion.[114]

A few paragraphs later, Marinetti intervened in the manifesto in the form of a citation, in which he gave his blessing to Balla's and Depero's plastic complexes: "Therefore art becomes Presence, new Object, new reality created with the abstract elements of the universe. The hands of the artist who worships the past (*passatista*) suffered for the lost Object; our hands were impatient to create a new Object. That is why the new Object (plastic complex) appears miraculously between your hands."[115]

As in the case of the *Compenetrazioni iridescenti* of the preceding year, behind this theory of creation, which moves from an ideal level and lands at a analogous concrete materialization, there is the influence of the theory of correspondences: to every object that our mind can imagine, a material object can correspond, according to the assumption that what exists in the macrocosm must have a correspondent in the microcosm, and vice versa.

Side by side with the alchemic/philosophic aspect in the manifesto stands a more playful magic, an ideal meeting point between Marinetti's *Manifesto del teatro di varietà* (1913), Palazzeschi's manifesto *Il controdolore* (1913), and what would be Depero's marionette. The manifesto's section "Miracle and Magic" has more to do with the tricks of the illusionist than with the scientific seriousness of the alchemist and betrays Depero's imprint. Balla the "magician" entertains with tricks of conjuring, appearing, and disappearing among unexpected firecracker explosions, as if in a performance dedicated to children.[116] In the rhetorical elaboration of the futurist toy and its pyrotechnic marvels, however, their contradictory nature is revealed; these are creations in which the game overlaps frighteningly with militaristic propaganda, and fantasy with the reality of war.

In closing the manifesto, just before their customary patriotically based claim for the "Italian genius," Balla and Depero adopted a messianic tone and affirmed that "we have descended into the profound essence of the universe, and we master the elements." With such elemental control, and by way of the fusion of art and science, they declared that they could repopulate the earth with the multiplication of new samples of reality, true futurist *homunculi* that are either the innocuous *fiori magici trasformabili motorumoristi* (transformable magical motor-noisy flowers) or the dangerous metallic animals that, mass produced in millions of units, would have the task of re-creating in the field of art the hoped-for political conflagration of the Great War, which had just broken out and for which the futurists forcefully promoted intervention.

The idea of materialization, and above all the desire to give "skeleton and flesh to the invisible, the impalpable, the imponderable, the imperceptible" to obtain "a dynamic, simultaneous, plastic, noisy expression of the universal vibration," denotes the influence on this manifesto of *Thought-forms*, which is already an influence present in *Compenetrazioni iridescenti*, and also in *Trasformazione forme spiriti* and *Forme e pensiero—visione spiritica*.

One last proof of Balla's interest in the theosophical mysticism of colors and their associations with states of mind, as documented in *Thought-forms*, appears in a note never actually transcribed but reproduced in a manuscript by Maurizio Fagiolo dell'Arco. The note is dated 1914–15, the period in which Balla and Depero were producing the plastic complexes now lost but documented in photographs in the manifesto, and also a period in which Balla was still working on the series of *Compenetrazioni*. In this note, *passatisti* and *futuristi* colors are contrasted in the form of scenic action: the *passatista* yellow is depressing, whereas the *futurista* yellow is joyous; the *passatista* blue is monotonous, whereas the *futurista* blue is spiritual; the *passatista* red is mistrustful, whereas the *futurista* red is violent; and the *passatista* white is filthy, whereas the *futurista* white is clairvoyant.[117]

CHAPTER 2

Occult Futurism

PROVINCIAL HIPSTERS:
THE COUNTS GINANNI CORRADINI

Celant maintains that both Balla and Bragaglia were pointed to the reading of occult texts by the brothers Arnaldo and Bruno Ginanni Corradini, counts of Ravenna. Given the brothers' precocious interest in the occult sciences, their influence on the futurist movement in occult matters during the early years may have been decisive.[1] Describing them as "the most esoteric futurists," Celant cites a claim by Ginna that illustrates their formative readings: "We provided ourselves with spiritualist and occult books, my brother and I, through the publishers Dourville and Chacormac. We read the occultists Elifas Levi, Papus, theosophists like Blavatsky and Steiner, Besant, secretary of the Theosophical Society, Leadbeater, Edoard Shure [sic]."[2]

Ginna's note is not dated, but it is reasonable to think that the brothers' readings began around 1910. Their first pamphlet, Metodo of 1910, which both of them signed with the pseudonym A.B.C., clearly established the coordinates of their theoretical position and aesthetics. The signature refers to their initials (Arnaldo Bruno Corradini), but of course it also references the first three letters of the alphabet and the "abecedario," the alphabet book. This is appropriate, given that the brief treatise had an educational purpose. The physical, intellectual, and spiritual education of the individual promised in its pages is obtained through gymnastics (or exercises), diet, the study of Eastern disciplines, meditation, and yoga.[3] In time, Russolo, too, would pursue these interests.

43

Metodo is accompanied by exercises—physical, mental, breathing, and autosuggestion—and it is pervaded by theosophical concepts. The following passage, for example, lays out the theosophical doctrine of vibrations:

> In Nature is present a force that is in everything. This force is in perpetual vibration; this vibration or undulation of the atoms that constitute matter manifests itself to us in different forms, as for example, in light, heat, electricity, attraction, repulsion, harmony, dissonance, magnetism, thought, etc. If our thinking, our acting, is not in harmony with the laws by which everyone without exception must abide, it is clear that we will suffer from its evil effects.[4]

The treatise, written more than twenty-five years before Luigi Russolo's *Al di là della materia* (1938), mentions suggestive therapy, yoga, hypnotism, and magnetism and cites the experiments of Mesmer, Puységur, and Baraduc. *Metodo* had considerable success and acquired numerous admirers and followers for the Corradinis.[5]

That same year the two Ravennese counts also published the pamphlet *Arte dell'avvenire*, in which they attempted the difficult marriage between art and science. The aesthetic vision that emerges from its pages substantially preserves a romantic system of thought, as revealed by the Wagnerian cast of its very title, and by the series of artists cited (Gluck, Mozart, Beethoven, Weber, Berlioz, Wagner, Verdi, Meyerbeer, etc.).[6] But in their aesthetic vision, the model composer was not so much Wagner, a genius "hampered by the nightmare of the word," who gave too much importance to the literary text in a musical composition, but Hector Berlioz. He, having learned better than Wagner, and much earlier, the lesson of Beethoven's late symphonies, knew how to create true "dramas without words," though according to the brothers these were unfortunately misunderstood. "Few realized that the way indicated and in part traveled by Berlioz was the true, the only one," they solemnly conclude.[7]

Occasional deviations from this romantic system occur wherever traces of occultist readings surface: "It is necessary that we give our passion to the dead things of nature so they acquire in our eyes the vitality of the artwork."[8] The idea of the artist as someone who could animate "the dead things of nature" certainly has a mesmeric side; this is followed by an exposition of the theory of correspondences, here understood as a protocol that regulates the relations between physical world and spiritual world:

The artist is he who takes from nature its [. . .] fundamental elements and, conscious of the correspondences between them and his sentiments, composes them variously to represent the passions and games of force among them. Thus is defined the work of art: passions in such reciprocal relations as to form a system— a system *identical* to those that revolve in the Heavens or to those between the molecules of matter: neither more nor less.[9]

A direct consequence of the systematic identity of art and the heavens is synesthesia. As the brothers explained, "Among all the arts there exists parallelism and a correspondence of absolute forms." This idea had already been proclaimed in the Giuseppe Mazzini epigraph used in the first edition of the text: "The Arts need someone who can tie them together again. This person will come."[10]

The synesthetic ideal is further amplified in the closing sentences of the pamphlet's revised and augmented edition, published one year later: "This treatise includes the already evolved arts; there remain the arts that are linked to the other senses. On the art of flavors I lack experience; of the music of odors I could produce a very complete treatise if an exact and complete nomenclature existed in this field."[11]

Further evidence of theosophical thought can be found in *Musica cromatica* of 1912, which, though only Bruno Corradini is listed as author, was clearly the theoretical work of both brothers. In this pamphlet, which reelaborates essential points of *Arte dell'avvenire*, they aimed to illustrate the result of their studies on the physics of light and sound that is intended to produce "chromatic" (as in color-based) music.

In an early phase, color-based music was generated by a color-based keyboard, whose twenty-eight keys controlled an equal number of colored lightbulbs that lit up to produce "color" chords; a prototype of this keyboard was completed in 1909.[12] Color-based keyboards were a commonplace in occult and synesthetic circles, presumably dating back at least to Newton's color music disc, but the Corradinis' experimental keyboard brings to mind one of the most famous of their time: the luminous keyboard called for in the score of Scriabin's *Prometheus* of 1908–10, a work in which theosophical influence is well documented.[13]

The Corradinis' aim, unlike Scriabin's, was not so much to associate sound and color as to spiritualize the visual arts by adopting the formal and expressive articulation of a piece of music "translated" into combinations of colors. But their experiment was not satisfactory. The brothers therefore next attempted to realize the music of colors without the aid of a keyboard, by first theorizing and then producing what may very well be the first example in history of abstract cine-painting, which they called *cinepittura*. In this phase of their work, they painted directly on film, determining the color of each individual frame. Here the color chords were produced through an optical trick that depended on the persistence of images in the retina; by projecting differently colored frames in rapid succession, one could obtain the effect of overlapping colors.[14] The synesthetic ideal was fundamental to the entire treatise, as was the theosophical influence; the brothers even discussed Claude Bragdon's theosophical text *The Beautiful Necessity—Seven Essays on Theosophy and Architecture*.[15]

In *Pittura dell'avvenire* of 1915, Arnaldo Ginna investigated further theosophically derived ideas. This essay opens with the idea that "Minerals live, hurt, sicken, and die like plants and animals. Every discovery, however apparently unrelated to others, forms with them the line of conjunction between the essential points-laws; the universal line-law already dreamed of by alchemists of the Middle Ages and by poets of all ages."[16]

Ginna is well informed about tension between the sciences and the occult. In *Pittura dell'avvenire*, he considers the occult disciplines of alchemy, spiritualism, mediumism, telepathy, water divination, astrology, magic, and magnetism to be "sciences of tomorrow"; he complains that though these subjects are studied at the *École de psychologie* of Paris, and though scientific proof of the magnetic fluid (a property which could explain all of these manifestations) exists, the processes by which these sciences operate are still largely unknown.[17]

Ginna then describes his pictorial process in the light of these future sciences:

> Human thought and sentiment are vibrations that are certainly not delimited by our physical body, but it is both evident and *experimentally proved* that they are a force similar to electricity or to the Hertzian wave that propagates itself indefinitely in the ether. The living forms created by this vibratory force are the essence of our tremors of hate, love, lust, mysticism, fear, courage, self-abnegation, sacrifice, etc. I paint therefore not the attitudes of a human, contorted in pain but the vibration of his pained soul or PAIN ITSELF.[18]

The direct influence of theosophy is confirmed by Ginna's citing from *Thought-forms* and *Man visible and invisible*. He calls for the artists of the future to follow the example of such "ultrasensitive mystics" as Leadbeater who, "with a very different purpose from that of creating a painting, drew forms that express a state of mind."[19] Such individuals, able to grasp and reproduce the forms and colors of the etheric vibrations generated by bodies in different emotional states, were for Ginna "mediums that claimed to be guided by an entity outside of their own will and personality. And they were mystics that claimed to be inspired by a Divinity. But in any case they were always hypersensitive men, armed with a power of sight and thought beyond the ordinary."[20]

Ginna emphasized the fact that one cannot "avoid observing the similarity of representational approach between the states of mind of a highly sensitive mystic such as Leadbeater and those of a most modern painter."[21] And in fact it is in the act of comparing mediumistic and artistic activity that the roots of Ginna's abstract painting can be located; he himself defined his work as "Occult Painting."[22]

Nevertheless, in Ginna's occult painting the equivalence of painter and medium is controlled. He described his artistic process as follows:

> The state in which I put myself, for the most part voluntarily, is not mediumistic or somnambulistic, because I do not fall into a trance. The definition of this exact state, although difficult to explain, is *conscious subconsciousness*. This approach to painting, invisible to others, is formed of mostly very bright colors in very fast vibration in the air . . . (or in the ether). This painting is the expression of a sentiment of mine or of others; or it may be provoked by a piece of music or by noise. [. . .] With all this I CANNOT SAY if they are astral or mental vibrations; AND I DO NOT KNOW if these *forms*, living a life a thousand times more intense than our own, are created by my psyche or if they themselves come to me when I open the window of my soul. We are not advanced enough in experimental and scientific method to be able to verify these phenomena.[23]

The affinity this passage bears with certain writings by Kandinsky could be considered embarrassing, but Ginna claimed poetic autonomy and maintained that inspired artists are able to attain abstraction by similar paths, even without knowing about each other's work.[24] In the final note of his essay, however, Ginna also claimed originality that sets him apart from the crowd of "abstract painters of the state of mind"; this was perhaps an indirect attack on one of Boccioni's signature terms, his "states of mind" painting.[25] Ginna in fact maintained that he had already formulated his aesthetic in 1910, while he was in exile in the Ravennese countryside, thereby claiming authorship of the first "*non-representative*, unreal, *occult* paintings constructed with abstract forms."[26]

The question of precedence aside, many of the aesthetical positions in Ginna's *Pittura dell'avvenire* can already be found in Boccioni's work. The conception of the artist as a medium (Boccioni would say *clairvoyant*) and the aim of painting "not the attitudes of a human, contorted in pain, but the vibration of his pained soul or PAIN ITSELF," are positions that Boccioni had established in his 1911 Roman lecture.[27] It is possible that Ginna (a documented occultist at least from the *Metodo* of 1910 onward) might have influenced Boccioni (and with him Marinetti, Russolo, Pratella, Balla, and other futurists), but it seems more feasible that their respective research would have proceeded on parallel courses. Certainly it is conceivable that all drew from the same parascientific, alchemical, and theosophical sources, which in turn all derived from French symbolism.

Still, even in Ginna's late work *L'uomo futuro*, published in 1933 and pervaded by fascist rhetoric, the influence of the occult is far from extinguished. Throughout that pamphlet, including in the introduction by Marinetti, Ginna is the "precise alchemist of infinite scientific and mediumistic researches."[28] In fact, once more reconciling fascism and futurism, Ginna theorized in this book a future man resembling a "'Homunculus' arisen from the greatest revolution recorded in history [i.e., the fascist revolution]."[29]

This future man, generated by an alchemical process but with an obvious relationship to Nietzsche's superman, was an allegory for Mussolini's process of biologically forging "il nuovo italiano," the new Italian race. For Ginna the future man would be "naturally inclined toward the future, and always futurfascistically *[futurfascisticamente]* at the orders of the Duce."[30] Among the opinions printed at the end of the book and signed by eminent personalities who supported Ginna's ideas—Benito Mussolini is the first in the series—one proclaiming "The Futurists are the mystics of action" is mysteriously signed "The Theosophists."[31]

Of the two brothers, the elder, Arnaldo, is difficult to pin down, not only because he signed his works with eight different pseudonyms, including the name of his brother.[32] He defined himself as "ungraspable" because of his "encyclopedic" approach to life and art.[33] And it is true that he occupied himself with many disciplines in many different scientific and artistic fields, including literature, cinema, painting, photography, "cine-painting," and the technology of sound; the list is long.

Of his activity as a painter, which shows links to postsymbolist and occult aesthetic, his *Nevrastenia* of 1908 deserves mention; Mario Verdone has called it the first example of abstract painting, for it precedes by two years Kandinsky's first abstract work.[34] Furthermore, Ginna was the one responsible for the sections of *Arte dell'avvenire* that deal with the visual arts. In a late writing titled *A proposito dell'arte dell'avvenire*, he stressed the primacy of his 1908 abstract painting activity and backdated to that same year the ideas expressed in the pamphlet *Arte dell'avvenire*, claiming that they were his.[35]

According to Ginna's testimony, Ginanni Corradini's early relations with the futurist movement and Marinetti were maintained through Paolo Buzzi, at the time when Buzzi worked for Marinetti's periodical *Poesia*.[36] This was probably in 1910, the year in which the Corradinis also began their association with Balilla Pratella. Ginna recorded that Marinetti exposed Boccioni, Carrà, and Russolo to the Corradinis' ideas early on, and he remembered that in 1910 Marinetti sent the first edition of *Arte dell'avvenire* fresh off the press as recommended reading to the futurist group in Milan.

Boccioni thereupon became interested in the theories laid out in that pamphlet and in the Corradinis' researches on "chromatic music": one cannot help but suppose that both *Arte dell'avvenire* and, even more so, *Metodo*, which was unquestionably the better known of the two pamphlets, were topics of discussion within the group of futurist painters.

The theories presented in the Corradinis' essays, together with their practical application in painting, were only sporadically appreciated by the futurists. Eventually Boccioni criticized their efforts as a too "literary" kind of pictorial art. Lista claims that the disagreement between Ginna and Boccioni hinged on the way in which dynamism came to be understood: whereas Ginna (in line with Balla and later Evola) understood it as a formal speculation aiming toward the abstraction of forms, Boccioni understood it as a vitalist and figurative perception of modernity.[37] The polemic they engaged in was overcome with the exhibition in 1914 at the Galleria Sprovieri in Rome; on that occasion Boccioni cordially invited Ginna to show his works with the rest of the futurist group.

Though the group of futurist painters would have been familiar with the researches of the Corradinis at least from 1910 on, Ginna in his memoirs claims that the actual meeting *de visu* with Marinetti, Boccioni, Carrà, and Russolo did not occur at the Casa Rossa before 1912, the year of Ginna's *Musica cromatica*. While the Milanese futurists may have encountered theosophy at the same time as the Corradinis did, the influence of the Corradinis on the Milanese group is noteworthy. The Corradinis' writings surely anticipated by decades, and perhaps even influenced, some aspects of Russolo's late research. In fact, they dealt, as Russolo later did, with meditation, yoga, magnetism, and the experiments of Mesmer.

In any case, the Corradinis' visit to the Casa Rossa conferred an official tone to the brothers' adhesion to the futurist movement, an adhesion that, although meeting some resistance from Boccioni, was being discussed by Marinetti and Pratella at least by the beginning of 1911. It was the composer Pratella, in fact, who pleaded the brothers' cause when they wished to join the futurist group, as confirmed by an exchange of letters among Ginna, Corra, and Pratella, and between Pratella and Marinetti, from the end of 1910 to the early months of 1911.[38]

PRATELLA, KANDINSKY, AND THE EXTRA-HUMAN

The Corradinis' first direct contact with Pratella, who was also from Romagna, came at the end of 1910, and their friendship with him lasted for the rest of their lives. Traces of their influence can be observed in Pratella's writings, but it is undeniable that they too benefited from the exchange. In the conclusions of his 1910 "Manifesto dei musicisti futuristi," published on January 11, 1911, Pratella invited young composers to

> FEEL AND SING WITH A SOUL TURNED TO THE FUTURE, DRAWING INSPIRATION AND AESTHETICS FROM NATURE, THROUGH ALL ITS PRESENT HUMAN AND EXTRAHUMAN PHENOMENA; TO EXALT THE MAN AS A SYMBOL RENEWING HIMSELF PERPETUALLY IN THE VARIOUS ASPECTS OF MODERN LIFE AND IN HIS INFINITE INTIMATE RELATIONS WITH NATURE[39]

According to the musicologist Luigi Rognoni, this paragraph betrays familiarity with Kandinsky's "Spirituality of Art."[40] Pratella may well have been introduced to Kandinsky by the Ginanni Corradinis.

Alternatively, the link between Pratella (or Marinetti, who most likely edited the above passage) and the ideas of Kandinsky may have resulted from Pratella's familiarity with Schoenberg's work. Pratella was certainly well informed about the latest trends in contemporary music, since Marinetti kept him up to date. Pratella's rather provincial anxiety about keeping up with the latest musical trends can be deduced from a letter that Marinetti wrote to Pratella on April 12, 1912, to accompany a package of newly published scores that Pratella was requested to study. Marinetti wrote: "I send you everything there is of the most advanced as far as music in Paris."⁴¹ And this was not a single instance. Daniele Lombardi claims to have observed numerous first editions in Pratella's library of scores by Scriabin, Debussy, Ravel, and others, signed as gifts by the xenophilic young Marinetti, who evidently force-fed Pratella with musical novelties as they became available in Paris.⁴²

Pratella's musical knowledge was, however, limited mostly to what was musically fashionable in Paris, at the time an important center of European cultural life and the place where, as Marinetti tells him in his April 1912 letter, Pratella would have to achieve artistic victory if he wanted "to appear to the eyes of all Europe as an absolute innovator." If Pratella's musical knowledge was indeed limited to Parisian fashions, then he may well have had a merely superficial acquaintance with Schoenberg's theories and music, as Rodney Patyon has pointed out.⁴³ This superficial knowledge may explain Pratella's harsh—and groundless—critique of Schoenberg in his essay "Musica futurista e futurismo" of May 4, 1914.⁴⁴

Yet it is also possible that Pratella (and Marinetti) were drawing not directly on Kandinsky but on the Ginanni Corradinis, who, though unacquainted with Kandinsky's ideas, were influenced by similar theosophical sources and may thus have arrived at related aesthetic positions. Pratella knew the Corradinis' work well, as is clear from his epistolary exchanges with them. In a letter to Pratella of April 8, 1911, Ginna outlined his synesthetic credo by citing a phrase of Tiberghein: "The sensory organism that comprises hearing, sight, smell, taste, and touch is like a keyboard that resounds to impressions of the physical world and perceives what happens outside."

Other writings of Pratella reflect that pantheistic approach found in the January 11 manifesto quoted above, and one that is in line with that found in some of the Corradinis' statements.⁴⁵ In his "La musica futurista: Manifesto tecnico" of March 29, 1911, Pratella declares:

> Sky, water, forests, rivers, mountains, tangles of ships, and swarming cities are transformed by the souls of musicians into marvelous and powerful voices, which sing humanly the passions and the will of mankind, [which sing] for its human joy and griefs, and which unveil, through art, the common and indissoluble bond that bounds it to all of nature. Musical forms are only appearances and fragments of a single and entire whole.⁴⁶

On February 28, 1915, at the height of the polemical debate between Papini, Soffici, and Palazzeschi, on the one side, and Marinetti on the other—

the quarrel between the "futurists" and the "Marinettists" that was to end in a historic break—Pratella published a letter in *Lacerba* addressed to Palazzeschi, Soffici, and Papini, in which he proclaimed his principles:

> You three [...] will never be able to comprehend what Futurism is: because though you may have the virtue of laughing scornfully, you do not have that of loving. We futurists have them both. Be as shocked as you like, call me an idiot, a cretin—I am used to the harmless stoning of loud idiots—that will not prevent me from affirming before all of you and others my *religious faith, pantheistic and futurist,* in *life*.[47]

Traces of the theories expounded in the Corradinis' *Arte dell'avvenire* (and *Musica cromatica*) can be seen in what is considered to be Pratella's most ambitious work from the years of his adherence to futurism: the opera *L'aviatore Dro*, written between 1913 and 1914.[48] The libretto, described by Pratella as "a modern and humanized variation of the myth—Daedalus, Icarus, Phaeton," already makes clear that this opera is a metaphor for Dro's progressive purification of body and spirit.[49] The spiritual ascension occurs in three stages: that of potential aviator, earthly aviator, and, finally, celestial aviator, at which point, in Pratella's words, "the hero Dro, liberating himself from matter and now finally purified, begins his real and eternal flight of the spirit."[50]

As in work of Marinetti and Boccioni, the machine is only a *means* to elevate the spirit—or, in the Blavatskian terminology of the manifesto *La radia*, to "immensify" the spirit. Payton has correctly explained that "Dro's machine and his technical achievement in mastering it are only means to his spiritual enlightenment. Indeed, on the purely mechanical and technical level, Dro fails, and the aircraft falls."[51] The opera's unstated reference to Marinetti's 1910 novel *Mafarka il futurista*, in which the protagonist, gifted with wings, aspires to fly toward the sun to dethrone it, would have been obvious to Pratella's intended audience.

L'aviatore Dro is a work of total theater that uses lights, colors, sounds, noises, and scents according to synesthetic principles that betray theosophical origins. In the opera's first act, the sequence noted as "Dreams" is composed of eight distinct sections in which the music is paired with scents and different-colored light that are meant to flood the scene, as indicated in the score:

> At the first diffusion of aromatic vapors, a very thin veil will fall upon the stage, behind which all subsequent action will develop.[52] The sequence is divided in

these eight sections: "Dark-blue light.—Sleep-nightmare. [...] Light-blue light.—serene. [...] White Light.—Flowing sweetness. [...] Yellow gold light.—Sun—Blazing joy. [...] Orange light—Sensuality. [...] Rosy light—Desire—Impatience. [...] Bright red light—Spasm—Charm. [...] Dark red light—Pleasure, blood, fire.

These sections were to be followed by one with "very intense lunar light; the shadow of the internal half."

In this work, Pratella merges his knowledge of the Corradinis' *Arte dell'avvenire* and *Musica cromatica* with what he learned from studying Scriabin's *Prometheus*, which Marinetti had urged on him; indeed, the use of stage scents in Pratella's opera also points to his having known of Scriabin's unfinished *Mysterium*.[53]

Prometheus was so famous in Paris that it is unthinkable that Marinetti did not at least know of it; it would not be implausible that it was among the Scriabin scores Marinetti sent to Pratella. In his article *Musica futurista e futurismo* of May 4, 1914, Pratella not only demonstrated familiarity with *Prometheus* but recognized its importance—though he also strongly criticized some of its elements.[54] Here Pratella characterizes the luminous keyboard in *Prometheus* that pairs sound and colored lights, which is one of the score's best-known—and overtly theosophical—features, as a courageous invention.

Pratella was aware of the relations between mediumistic activities and composing techniques; this is clear from his description of Satie's music in the essay *Musica futurista e futurismo*. Pratella first mentions that Satie was part of the circle around "Sar Peladan," whom Pratella defined as orientalist, spiritualist, half mystic, and half presumed magician. He goes on to discuss Satie's use of agogic performance indications, observing that Satie at times substitutes for the usual indications (adagio, allegro, etc.) instructions of a mystical or mediumistic character such as "ignore your own presence"; Pratella may have lent this issue particular attention because Marinetti, in one of his letters, had rebuked him for not being sufficiently "futurist" in his own use of performance indications.[55]

Pratella's synesthetic interest is also evident in his *Giallo pallido*, one of the most inspired works in his oeuvre. This single movement for string quartet, written in 1920 as an intermezzo for Luciano Folgore's drama *Rose di carta*, was published in 1924 by Bongiovanni as opus 39.

The "pallid yellow" of the title might be more easily linked with D'Annunzio's decadentism, or even some of the crepuscolari poets' languor—aesthetics that were fully in agreement with the theories of Achille Ricciardi—than with the ultra-brilliant colors theorized and employed by futurist painters a few years earlier.[56] However, the color choice is in fact the result of Pratella's and Folgore's alignment with the artistic group Novecento and its motto "return to order." Although futurism's synesthetic interest survives even in this later Pratella work, the brilliant proclamation of color certainly disappears, just as the "polenta yellows, the saffron yellows, the brassy yellows," obviously not found in Achille Funi's canvases, had disappeared from Carrà's canvases of the 1920s. *Giallo pallido*'s distance from the early phase of futurism is embodied in the aesthetics found in Folgore's drama: whereas Carrá in his manifesto of 1913, *Pittura dei suoni, rumori e odori*, railed against "the banal sense [...] of flowers too pallid and withered," *Giallo pallido* is the story of three women of withered beauty, symbolized by the paper roses in pallid colors.

FLORENTINE SPIRITUALITY: THE CEREBRALIST GROUP

In 1912 a relationship began between the Corradinis and what was to become the Florentine wing of the futurist movement. This wing was the group around Emilio Settimelli and Remo Chiti, which published the periodical *La difesa dell'arte* and, starting in 1912, *Il centauro*, and which separated from the group around Papini, Prezzolini, and Soffici, who in 1912 were publishing the futurist-inspired journal *Lacerba*. At the end of the *Lacerba* adventure, following the break between Marinetti and Papini, Ginna and Corra put Marinetti in contact with Settimelli and Chiti. Thereafter, and for years to come, Corra's and Settimelli's periodical *L'Italia futurista* replaced *Lacerba* as the official organ of the Florentine wing of the futurist movement. The group around *L'Italia futurista*, sometimes called the "cerebralist group," in addition to Corra and Settimelli included Ginna, Chiti, Irma Valeria, Maria Ginanni, Rosa Rosà, Russolo, and many others: this group focused in particular on the study of the occult sciences.[57]

Early evidence of their interest is the manifesto "Pesi, misure e prezzi del genio artistico" of 1914, in which Corra and Settimelli proposed radically to reform art criticism. In addition to addressing art terminology, they aimed to demystify artistic production and to value and evaluate on the basis of calculating the psychic energy used in the process of artistic production. The 1914 manifesto was conceptualized in the same year in which Corra published the first "synthetic" futurist novel, *Sam Dunn è morto*. This work, which constituted a pivotal stage in Corra's career and anticipated the stylized writing of Massimo Bontempelli, was first published by Marinetti for the Edizioni di Poesia in 1914; then, most likely for its occult overtones, it was republished in serial form in 1916 in *L'Italia futurista*. The protagonist of the novel, Sam Dunn, is a man gifted with extraordinary psychic powers with which, through patient mental work, he proposes to act as a go-between and "channel into our reality energies belonging to a world of more complex phenomena."

Sam Dunn releases a flux of occult energies that initiate what Corra calls a "psychic revolution": he primes a chain reaction of bizarre events centered around the city of Paris. But when opposing energies resist this revolution, Sam Dunn, despite having the strength to fight them, chooses to sacrifice himself; he is barbarously slaughtered, his head repeatedly struck by his maid's voluminous butt. On the mysterious location that Corra called the Norwegian *Keidelstruk*, his sacrifice produces a mountain of phosphorescent waters in the form of buttocks, from which once a year, on the sixth of June, a series of greenish elliptical stones erupts, which bear Sam Dunn's initials incised on one side.

Like Corra's other writings from these years, this brief, bizarre novel is an allegory of the futurist revolution that Corra's group was calling for, a revolution in which the unforeseeable, irrational, occult, spiritual, and fantastic would shake to its foundations bourgeois science and society. In the last chapter of the novel, Corra prophesied: "It is unavoidable that our entire lifestyle will soon be crumbled, fluidified, and lyricized by an invasion of fantastic energies. The fantastic revolution of Sam Dunn was only a sign. *We live above a powder magazine of fantasy that will not be long in exploding.*"[58]

An accurate picture of the Florentine *L'Italia futurista* group is presented in the manifesto "La scienza futurista," published in the June 15, 1916, issue and signed "Bruno Corra—A. Ginanni—Remo Chiti—Settimelli—Mario Carli—Nerino Nannetti." Here the attack on bourgeois science is more explicit than the call for renewal of art criticism of the preceding "Pesi, misure e prezzi del genio artistico" and extended to the field of scientific and philosophical discoveries. The new futurist science being promoted here is an aggressive thirsting for the unknown, which hurls itself against both acquired certainties and the yawning pedantry of an official science that is suspicious of the occult forces that animate the universe. The eighth point of the manifesto reads: "We attract the attention of all the audacious minds toward that less probed zone of our reality that comprises the phenomena of mediumism, psychism, water-divining, divination, telepathy."[59]

Particularly from 1917 onward, when Ginna took over from Corra as codirector of *L'Italia futurista*, the journal's occultist focus intensified. In the issues edited by Ginna and Settimelli, a motto from the Corradini brothers, presumably chosen by Ginna, was placed under the title to confirm the journal's occult and synesthetic gospel: "Words, the sounds, colors, forms, lines are means of expression. The essence of the arts is one."[60]

In the May 6, 1917, issue, Ginna published a short article titled "Il coraggio nelle ricerche di occultismo," in which he aimed to explode the myth that "occultist research" must stay secret. He wrote the article with the goal of popularizing science, in pure Blavatskian style. In this contribution, although a few years and some brawls have passed, the legacy of the Florentine group that produced the earlier periodical *Leonardo* is summed up by the paraphrase of *Leonardo*'s Leonardine motto "He does not turn who is fixed on a star" (*Non si volge chi a stella è fisso*): "To those who counsel me prudence I respond that he who set out on a road by night fixing upon his own guiding star, sees nothing but the splendor of that star and will never be able to see anything else."[61] At the end of the article, Ginna promises to dedicate space in *L'Italia futurista* to articles concerning "occult science and art"; his own *Pittura dell'avvenire* was thereafter published in its entirety (in installments), and a brief but highly significant contribution by Irma Valeria titled "Occultismo e arte nuova" (Occultism and New Art) appeared in the June 10, 1917, issue.

Valeria's article opens with the lapidary affirmation that "in short, we are all occultists." This alone reveals the cultural climate in which the entire group operated. Valeria was convinced that the supremely subtle sensations felt by a modern artist in the process of creation are comprehensible only to particularly *sensitive* individuals. Excited by the hyperreal noise of the lighting of a wax match during a noisy dance party, a noise amplified by her auditory hypersensitivity, Valeria dispenses pearls of occult wisdom in a brief article that unfolds in a literary register encompassing the most sensual and the messianic.

Valeria believed that the artists of the new generation have the duty to penetrate and fuse the "perfectly neat, rigid and glaze-like polished surface" of reality with "the luminous rays of the spirit" so as to "reconnect the mysteries of the universe with those of art [in] a single harmonic and majestic music." Adopting the animistic theses of panpsychism, she also asserts that "the newest art" seeks to penetrate "the soul of the objects [...] and to make them live not through the observer's personal sensations but through sensations that belong to [the life of] the objects themselves." This statement is a reference to the theatrical syntheses of Marinetti, but also to the *drammi d'oggetti* (object-based dramas) in Ginna's, Settimelli's, and Corra's lost film *Vita futurista*.[62]

In line with the Florentine group's agenda, Valeria toward the end of her article attacks materialist and positivist science, declaring that it is incapable, because of its skepticism, of understanding "an art made of inner, musical, subtle, complex, and mysterious tremors," which can only be understood by the occultist. Microcosm and macrocosm are mutually identified in an effort to understand the hidden soul of the universe: "The occult atom of our being and that of the world unify: they mingle because they are nothing but the same thing." Her exalted writing style reaches its apex in the closing sentence: "I firmly believe that the new art will attain this simple and immense result like the fall of a luminous drop of ruby in the crystal vase of an ecstatic and timorous night."

Another important exponent of *L'Italia futurista*'s Florentine group was Maria Ginanni.[63] Her interest in the occult sciences can be documented from her first years in Rome, when she attended the lectures at the Roman Theosophical Society and read assiduously both theosophical and other French occultist texts. Following her move to Florence, she came into contact with the group around *L'Italia futurista*. In 1917 she published *Montagne trasparenti* in Edizioni dell'Italia Futurista, a series of publications of which she later became the editor in chief. Passages such as the following are in line with the cultural beliefs of the group:

> I rose up thinly in the air to the maximum limit of the atmosphere, whose last stratum tangentially caressed my head. I could have leaned out into the emptiness. [...] I preferred to peep out into the Universe with the most ironic fragility: holding out my little index finger immersing it and stirring it around in the ether, with a grimace on the nose of all the Secrets.[64]

The kind of interest aroused by *Montagne trasparenti* can be seen in the *L'Italia futurista* issue of April 1, 1917, which includes a page of opinions about Ginanni's book:

> "[Maria Ginanni is a] poet ascended on the trapezes of the sky, engaged in genius matches with the beyond. [...] Nothing is more cerebrally enharmonic and more

cordially melodic at the same time, as if the genius of the most modern Italian musicians were soaking in a bath of prose." —Paolo Buzzi (Gli Avvenimenti)

"Your transparencies see the infinite!" —Giacomo Balla

"[...] for two hours *I lived*, saturating myself with her vibrations [...]" —Mario Carli

"Maria Ginanni gathers all the infinite sensations. [...] futurism! Maria Ginanni more than a futurist; she is a profound clairvoyant..." —Robertson (Gazzetta di Torino)

"Everything is transparent for Maria Ginanni because her brain is a veritable mine of radium." —F. T. Marinetti

Ginanni's writing style did not change with her second effort. The following passage, from an extract of her novel *Luci trasversali* published in the *L'Italia futurista* issue of April 8, 1917, includes all the key words of esoteric literature: "The night is the ethereal soul of space, it is *the soul of the light*, hidden and elusive like our soul. Spiritual constellations of ether break and escape...."

FUTURIST OUTSIDERS

Occult sentiments can be identified in the work of several other futurist painters, even those who were futurists for only a limited time or not centrally connected to futurist activities. Romolo Romani was the only painter from the prefuturist Milanese "Poesia" group to join the futurist movement, and he was also the first futurist to retract his allegiance and break ranks with the futurist group; although he decided to defect only one month after signing the painters' first manifesto, his influence on the futurist group in its initial phase was decisive. Most of his output, cut short in 1916 by his early death from an incurable disease, has a spiritual character, aiming to capture what occult reality can reveal only to the perceptive effort of the patient eye of the initiated.

Silvia Evangelisti has written on the connections between Romani and the Milanese occultism of both the *Società per lo studio dei fenomeni psichici* and the *Salone delle conferenze Spiritualiste*, the circle around Marzorati; at the same time she has emphasized the influence of Lombroso's Turinese group and its interest in the examples of Palladino's materialized will, both ideoplastic and ectoplastic.[65] Among Romani's earliest works, the series titled *Sensazioni* (1903–04) and *Simboli* (1906) have been considered "remarkable examples of representation of the more spiritual states of consciousness."[66]

Other works, too, testify to Romani's interest in these theme: *L'incubo* (1904–05), an intriguing altered projection of reality; *Ritratto di Dina Galli* (1906), in which the corporeal figure is portrayed by means of a ghostly luminous emanation, diaphanous and fluctuating, while behind it can be seen a menacing demonic mask; *Riflessi sonori* (1907–08), which unveils Romani's synesthetic interest; *Prismi* (1908), a study on the diffraction of luminous waves, which Balla must certainly have known; and finally a series of works including *La goccia che cade sull'acqua* and *La goccia* (both 1911), a study of the vibration generated by a drop falling on water and the concentric waves that thereupon emanate at regular intervals from the center. These works suggest a familiarity with the experiments of Chladni, and perhaps even with *Thought-forms*, where Chladni's experiments are reproduced.

The propagation of vibrations, together with its implicit synesthetic value, would interest Russolo as well: in fact, concentric circles representing waves are found in Russolo's *La musica*, also painted in 1911.[67] Marianne Martin has detected several tropes, both pictorial and literary, that Romani shared with other futurists, including Munch's sense of anguish, and Poe's taste for the macabre, adding that Romani's paintings show elements of Redon's psychoanalytic symbolism mixed with Piranesi's perverse perspectives.[68]

A trace of occult frequentations is surely also present in Carrà's work, though more in his theoretical writings than in his paintings. Perhaps no more than a second-hand reflection of the activities of other futurists, this trace is still worth investigating. Carrà's most important theoretical contribution about the futurist years, the manifesto "La pittura dei suoni, rumori e odori," published on August 11, 1913, is essentially an exposition of synesthetic theories and the energy-based theory of vibrations, both of which have a likely theosophical provenance. The manifesto affirms that "sounds, noises, and odors are nothing but diverse forms and intensities of vibration" and that "a succession of sounds, noises, and odors imprints in the mind an arabesque of forms and colors. It is therefore necessary to measure these intensities and intuit this arabesque."[69] Carrà continued with the following passage:

THE PAINTING OF SOUNDS, NOISES AND ODORS REQUIRES:

[...]

17. The continuity and simultaneity of the plastic transcendences of the animal kingdom, the vegetable kingdom, the mechanical kingdom.[70]

18. Plastic abstract installations, that is, installations resulting not simply from the sense of sight but from sensations born of sounds, noises, and odors and produced by *all the unknown forces that envelop us.*[71]

Point 17 shows links to pantheism, whereas point 18 unquestionably reveals associations with Leadbeater, an association that is also evident in the *Thoughforms* reference contained in the phrase "arabesque of forms and colors," quoted above. These references to the occult are not isolated cases in Carrà's writings. *Guerrapittura*, a volume he published in 1915, contains a section of Words-in-Freedom by the eloquent title "Mediumistic Digressions," in which the fragmentation of the text and the associations that spring from it are related to the revelations of a medium in a state of trance.[72]

A differently colored spiritual attitude and investigation pervade the work of Gino Severini. The beginning of his "Analogie plastiche del dinamismo," a manifesto drawn up in 1913 but unpublished for many years, provides a good example of his views. In it he claims emphatically that

> we want to enclose the universe in the work of art. Objects no longer exist. It is necessary to forget exterior reality and the knowledge that we have of it [...] because by now exterior reality and knowledge [...] no longer have any influence on our plastic expression, and, if we consider the action of memory upon our sensitivity, only the memory of the emotion persists, and not that of the cause which produced it.

Severini continued:: "The abstract forms and colors that we draw belong to the Universe outside of time and space."[73]

These propositions show an aesthetic vision linked to scientific theories about the fourth dimension, which Severini cites in his next work, *La peinture d'avant-garde*, published on January 1, 1917.[74] Theories about the fourth dimension, as well as the study of non-Euclidean geometries, offered avant-garde artists the possibility of (re)formulating alternative systems of representing the world. Invitations to observe the world in depth and overcome the illusoriness of exterior reality, which accompanied such reformulation, were leitmotifs in all futurist poetics; they betray familiarity with that critique of materialism that was likewise omnipresent in futurist discourse.

Severini's spirituality soon thereafter became redirected toward Christian mystical religiosity. Calvesi later recalled the painter's friendship with Jacques Maritain, to whom he was devoted.[75] Severini's leaning toward spirituality was, however, already present in his *Maternità* of 1916, a madonna with child in Godardesque clothes, and in his "futurist frescoes [...] in Swiss churches," which Marinetti and Fillìa mentioned in their "Manifesto dell'arte sacra futurista" of 1932.[76] Notwithstanding—and perhaps to honor a fashion of the time that spared neither D'Annunzio nor Russolo—Severini's wife, Jeanne, claimed that she and her husband, though devoted Christians, participated in numerous séances.[77]

Spiritually remote from Severini—though sharing with him Balla's training—was Baron Julius Evola, who, more than any of the other artists closely associated with futurism, cultivated the study of occult sciences and eventually even made the writing of esoteric texts his profession. "Practically a student" of Balla's, whose studio he visited regularly, along with Prampolini, Depero, and the Corradinis, as of the tender age of seventeen (in 1915), he continued painting with great dedication until 1921.[78] A contributor from 1922 to 1927 to *Ultra*, the periodical of Gruppo Teosofico Roma, Evola was also the aristocratic author of various volumes (some published by Bocca, others by Laterza) on subjects ranging from race theory to occultism, mysticism, alchemy, and political and moral philosophy. He had complex relationships with Fascism and Nazism, being opposed to both regimes but at the same time became an important theoretician for the right wing during and following World War II, which earned him a considerable cult following. Early on he was close to the Roman futurist circle, but later he became one of the few Italian dadaists.

Following the example of Balla, who in 1915, the year he met Evola, began calling himself "futurist abstract painter" (*astrattista futurista*), and Ginna, who had by then been producing abstract paintings for several years, Evola favored abstraction from the start.[79] In this early phase, which the artist himself defined as one of "sensory idealism," and which lasted from 1915 to 1918, abstract painting was Evola's escape from reality, which permitted his intuiting the transcendent.

In Evola's second phase (he called it "mystic abstraction"), which lasted from 1918 to 1921, he brought into focus, always using abstract pictorial formulation, astral and cosmological signs, and, especially, alchemical symbols. In this phase he adhered to dadaism, of which he was possibly the most important Italian exponent. Evola had made contact with the dadaist group as early as 1918, maintaining in those years a fruitful correspondence with Tzara, Arp, and Schad. The esoteric overtones, sometimes collected through altered states of consciousness, are accentuated and harmonize surprisingly with the automatisms (and the depersonalization) of dadaist poetics.

Toward the end of this phase, Evola turned increasingly to philosophy, politics, meditation, occultism, and the study of race, and these were to occupy him for the rest of his life.[80]

PRAMPOLINI'S SPIRITUALIZING MACHINES

The polymateric compositions of Enrico Prampolini offer yet another interesting point of contact between Futurism and the occult. The first polymateric experiments in futurism were conducted by Boccioni between 1911 and 1912, in a series of sculptures now lost. His subsequent theoretical formulation can be found in his manifesto of futurist sculpture of April 11, 1912. Prampolini may have derived not only the polymateric idea but also the spiritual aim itself (of Bergsonian inspiration) from Boccioni; regardless, Prampolini in time became the principal theoretician of futurist polymateric art.

Prampolini was influenced by Boccioni, but even more so by his mentor, Giacomo Balla, who discovered him and in whose spiritual orbit he spent his formative years, until a quarrel over polymateric theorization eroded their friendship. Calvesi describes a series of letters from May 1915—a couple of months after the publication of Balla's and Depero's manifesto "La ricostruzione futurista dell'universo" (March 11, 1915)—in which Prampolini accused his mentor of plagiarism and maintained that he had been the first, in an article published in March 1915, to lay down the theoretical foundations of noisy sculptures, or toys, which he too had called "plastic complexes."[81]

Prampolini believed that one could, by using different materials, compose a painting as a heterogeneous universe. This was a way of injecting reality into a work of art so as to achieve an "absolute realism."[82] By absolute realism Prampolini did not mean the positivist realism of the late nineteenth century but rather Boccioni's occult realism of the simultaneity of states of consciousness.[83]

Prampolini followed this direction with great orthodoxy. As late as 1938 he still maintained that "the polymateric compositions' power to impress and represent is the power to spiritualize matter."[84] Soffici had written something similar in his "Primi principi di una estetica futurista," datable somewhere between 1914 and 1917: "*The matter used by the artist stays entirely and always inert, dead, inexpressive if it is not led by the genius to* SPIRITUALIZE ITSELF; *to become what is pure element of symbolic lyrical representation. That is equivalent to disappearing as matter.*" In this statement, italicized for emphasis, Soffici confirmed the "necessity of spiritualization of expressive means."[85]

In his article "La cromofonia—Il colore dei suoni," published in *Gazzetta Ferrarese* on August 26, 1913, Prampolini dealt with the well-known theory according to which a sound source can generate a light vibration, explaining how this vibration can influence the "atmospheric aura that surrounds a body."[86] Certainly relating to this article is the subsequent synesthetical manifesto by S. A. Luciani, Anton Giulio Bragaglia, and Franco Casavola titled "Le sintesi visive della musica," first published in the Prampolini-edited periodical *Noi*, and later republished with the more convincingly synesthetical title "Le atmosfere cromatiche della musica."[87]

In the manifesto "L'arte meccanica," written in 1922 by Prampolini, Pannaggi, and Paladini and appearing in *Noi* in May 1923, which hews closely to Marinetti's 1916 manifesto "La nuova religione-morale della velocità," the machine is not a simple material object but rather a sacred and spiritual element, the "most exuberant symbol of the mysterious human creative force."[88] The *Noi* manifesto, which invites the machine to "tear itself from its practical function, rise up to the spiritual and disinterested life of art, and become a lofty and fecund inspiration," further exhorts the reader to distinguish between "exteriority and spirit of the machine" and attack artists who in their work have until then contemplated only the exterior aspects of the machine, or have added to their compositions purely decorative mechanical elements without expressive and spiritual ambition. The manifesto confirms the futurists' intention to render the spirit and not the exterior form of the machine, turning the machine into the authentic place of the sacred, a vengeful divinity toward whom to direct their pagan prayers. The manifesto closes on this note: "The Machine is the new divinity; in our futurist time, that is, time devoted to the great Religion of the New, the Machine illuminates, dominates, distributes its gifts and punishes."

One year later, in an article titled "Orientamento spirituale contro ogni reazione," published in July 1923, Prampolini invited artists to turn toward the spiritual world as a wellspring of inspiration, now that they had "exhausted the plastic and pictorial possibilities of the physical world."[89] He added:

> The evolution of the plastic arts demands [. . .] a *spiritual orientation*, and if yesterday we explored and discovered the new values of human sensitivity by eternalizing them in new plastic symbols, today we must turn ourselves to the *spirit* [of these values], understand their intimate spiritual meaning, their internal and occult physiognomy, gather from them the misunderstood echo of a thousand different voices and find in these voices the unique faculty of expression of the art of tomorrow.

In other works as well Prampolini lauded the machine as the spiritual reality from which to draw inspiration. In an article written for the *Little Review* in 1926 and titled "The Aesthetic of the Machine and Mechanical Introspection in Art," Prampolini amplified the ideas of the writings cited above.

In Prampolini's animistic conception, the machine exists on a level that is metaphysical, ideal, spiritual, and mythic. The machine became the new source of artistic inspiration because nothing else can offer symbols with such archetypal force and inspiring function as those that the religious symbols of the Assumption, the Deposition, and the Crucifixion had for the artists of the past. Criticizing a materialistic portrayal of machinery, Prampolini in 1926 still reaffirmed this position: "The plastic exaltation of the Machine and of mechanical elements must not be conceived of in its exterior reality, that is, in the formal representation of the elements that compose it, but rather in the plastic-mechanical analogy that the Machine itself suggests to us in relation to the various spiritual realities." And again: "The machine marks the rhythm of the human psychology and beats the time for our spiritual exaltations."[90] As in Pratella's *Dro*, the machine is for Prampolini the principal means to attain spiritual elevation.

PAOLO BUZZI FLYING HIGH

The works of Paolo Buzzi, though marked by stylistic inconsistencies and crossover among literary genres, were classified by Glauco Viazzi into four creative periods encompassing: the adoption of a late-classicist learned style; the conquest of the symbolist expressive world; futurist experimentation; and the return to free-verse prosody.[91] All of these categories, undoubtedly attributable to a restless personality and constantly oscillating between symbolism and futurism, and between tradition and novelty, can be found within a single work. Buzzi's spiritualist-esoteric interest, sometimes extending into the realms of the occult sciences or alchemy, seems the only common denominator in his oeuvre and provides continuity to his work.

From 1902 onward, well before the *Poesia* adventure began, Buzzi was Marinetti's friend and comrade-in-arms. Some literary topoi flow freely between Marinetti's and Buzzi's writings, revealing the nature of their exchange. Compare, for example, a passage about the "sunset-conductor" in Marinetti's *Battaglia di Tripoli* (1912) with the "very strange concert of noises" in the chapter "La diana enarmonica" in Buzzi's *L'ellisse e la spirale* of 1915, and

"La diana enarmonica" with the vegetable orchestra in Marinetti's *Indomabili* of 1922.

The case of the "diana enarmonica" demonstrates Buzzi's intent to describe and re-create musical suggestions through the medium of the word, and it points to the omnipresent synesthetic aspect of his work, which is evident in the numerous references to the sonorous world but also in the associations of images and sounds in his poetry.[92]

I shall begin this synesthetic survey with the long poem *A Claude Debussy* from 1908, written on the occasion of the first performance of *Pelléas et Mélisande* at La Scala in Milan. Already its first lines reveal the neoplatonic theme of the illusoriness of the world—only a shadow of the ideal, which Buzzi harmonizes with a transposition in the occultist key (for Viazzi "rosacrociana") of Democritean atomism. The poem closes with a further triangulation between the music of Debussy and the hypermusical poetry of Mallarmé that inspired it (*L'après-midi d'une faune*). The erotic languor of Mallarmé and Debussy—the symbolist and Wagnerian dialectic of *Eros* and *Thanatos*—comes to be framed in fitting metaphysical, spiritualist terms.

In *Canto di Mannheim* of 1913, Buzzi invokes as inspirational muse "the musics of the future song or orchestra" that produce the "shiver that assassinates the souls and the spheres," and, borrowing lines from his own *Inno alla Poesia nuova*, he sings (with a motif derived from Russolo—the first manifesto on the art of noises that was published in March of that year) of the "Machine" as the new "Lyre"—a lyre that could accompany the bard of the new poetry, but also the lyre as "vortex of different gigantic invisible wheels," the only one that can produce the music of the present day.[93] The harmony of the spheres, (re)produced by the chaotic noise of mechanical parts, will resound with spiritual implications in Russolo's intonarumori.[94]

These themes return in *Concerto di Cetre* of 1952, in which Buzzi evokes the vortices of dream to attempt to send the listener's soul flying through the ether with the velocity of electric discharge, to attain what he called the "Planet of Music," the celestial sphere where the concert of an orchestra of angels takes place. Buzzi finds the Paradise alluded to in the poem in the canvases of a recently deceased friend, in the

> waves [of the paradisiacal echoes] and the admirable swimming ghosts,
> like in the plastic trigonometries
> by Rùssolo [sic],
> iridescent on the large canvas-space.[95]

The reference to Russolo's *La musica*, a painting often cited by Buzzi and one of his favorite paintings, is almost obligatory. In the next chapters I will discuss the complex relationship between Buzzi and Luigi Russolo, who were close friends and became even closer during the last years of Russolo's life; their common interest in spirituality and the occult brought them together.[96]

In Buzzi, occultist themes like those just described mingle with others, equally occultist, of alchemical thrust. In *Luna di Cannocchiale* of 1933, the quintessential alchemical experiment—the union of sulfur and salt—becomes the center of the poem, a metaphor for the creation of art (poetry, in this case) as the production of an organism by means of the synthesis of opposites.

On the synesthetic side, "Aereopoesia per Aereopittura" (in *Poema di radioonde*, 1933–1938) describes the intoxication of flying, celebrating noted heroes of the air (Lindberg, Balbo, Agello, Stoppani) and exhorting painters to become flying aces. Evoking the elegant trajectories of forms and colors observable from an airplane taking off, the poem connected with the young genre of aeropainting (the "Manifesto della aeropittura" was published in 1929) and served as a commentary on the works of such aeropainters as Benedetta, Dottori, and Tato, to whom the poem indirectly alludes.

An inattentive reader could mistake the poem "Aereopoesia per Aereopittura" to be merely the result of Buzzi's having aligned himself with the *diktat* of Marinetti's "Manifesto dell'aeropoesia" of 1931. In truth, the "Manifesto della aeropittura" provided a questionable chronology in dating the "lyrical exaltation of flight by means of free verse" to Marinetti's *Le monoplane du Pape* (The pope's airplane) and claiming that that work was from 1908, even though *Le monoplane du Pape* was first published in 1912 by Sansot in Paris and the Italian translation, published by the Edizioni Futuriste di "Poesia," did not appear until 1914.[97]

Aereopoesia per Aereopittura was thus more of a revindication, since in Buzzi this aerial, "lyrical exaltation" is documentable at least from *Aeroplani (Canti alati)*, a volume of poems in free verses written between 1906 and 1909, and published in 1909 by the Edizioni di "Poesia" with a "Futurist Proclamation" by Marinetti. (Marinetti eventually fully exploited aerial aesthetics, as in the opening of his *Manifesto tecnico della letteratura futurista* of May 11, 1912.)

Already in *Volo*, Buzzi's Words-in-Freedom, published in the *Lacerba* issue of January 1, 1914, perceptions that originated in visual, auditory, tactile, and even gustatory fields were vigorously forced to overlap and, well over fifteen years before the manifesto of aereopoetry, associated with aviatory inebriation. Further, the will to reproduce the suggestion of flight, and the accompanying sense of the sublime, gave Buzzi the opportunity to free himself from the constrictions even of free verse and unhinge syntax, thus giving life to one of the most visionary poems in his entire body of work and an authentic tour de force whose ultimate aim is to capture the pilot's emotion and allow the reader share it by reproducing the pilot's bravery with poetic audacity.

The consumption of absinthe gives the starting signal for spirals of free associations, with synesthetic, protopsychedelic images that produce verbal expression that resembles the tone of a mediumistic trance as well as that of hallucinatory delirium. The technological, mystical-spiritualist, and psychedelic universes could not be more thoroughly entangled than in this poem. Analyzing the work consequently helped me to frame futurist aesthetics from a new point of view, for which reason I shall now take this narrative on a short yet pertinent detour.

FUTURIST ALTERED STATES OF MIND

Just as it was the main goal of futurism to understand the essence of reality, so the futurists believed that this comprehension could be obtained by way of extracorporeal experience aimed at reaching an altered state of consciousness, and that there were three avenues to achieve such an altered state: through experimentation with the instruments of technology, metapsychics, or chemistry. These three avenues harmonized with one another, and probably the futurists' experience of altered states of consciousness went hand in hand with their interest in the occult sciences and the study of the latest scientific and technological discoveries. All three avenues (including technology) were no more than *means* for achieving extracorporeal experiences; the ultimate goals were to understand reality at a deep level, understand Creation, and try to imitate its process.

An investigation of the futurists' use of drugs (not only alcohol, with which, according to Boris de Schloezer, Scriabin experimented to attain spiritual peaks otherwise inaccessible, but also, and especially, the absinthe dear to many French intellectuals, the hashish associated with Baudelaire, and such drugs as opium, laudanum, and morphine), goes beyond the scope of this work.[98] I will simply mention that absinthe was cited not only by Buzzi, in *Volo*, but also in 1919 by Armando Mazza, in *Tormenti*, and that it was the subject of a painting by Carrà titled *La femme et l'absinthe* of 1911. Similarly, hashish inspired Cangiullo's poem *Narcosi d'haschisch* of 1919, and until 1921 Evola made use of narcotic substances (on which he was dependent for a time), allegedly as a support to meditation.

Russolo was not immune to the attraction of drugs, as documented by an early etching titled *Morfina*. In a document from 1909, in which Russolo promised to send three prints to the tenth *Internationale Kunstausstellung* (1909) in Munich, he indicates that this work was then lost.[99] In the MART catalog, Tagliapietra has suggested that the sleeping figure portrayed in *Morfina* is the same as that portrayed in an etching and aquatint on the back of the plate of Russolo's 1910 etching *Mamma che cuce*.

This is an interesting hypothesis, but I would rather propose that *Morfina* was Russolo's explicit title for an earlier etching of 1906–07, which, by the time it was reproduced in MART, was circulating with the alternative titles *Testa e fiore* and *Donna fiore*. Because of the exceptionally realistic portrayal of two opium poppy flowers in two different stages of blooming —this in my opinion makes a compelling iconographical case—and even more so because of the sweetly seductive gaze of the young woman depicted, I am convinced that this 1906 etching was Russolo's prosopopeia of morphine.

Opium was present in a phase that may be considered the "prehistory" of the futurist movement. In February 1905 a cartoon appeared in the Florentine periodical *Leonardo*, showing a man listening to a gramophone and smoking a pipe, which Martin has identified as an opium pipe. In August 1906 Prezzolini published, also in *Leonardo*, the story of a young man possessed by a mysterious voice inviting him to take part in a quest for spiritual purification and personal and communitarian elevation. Prezzolini later recognized in this story the inspiration for the decision to found the new periodical *La Voce*.

The second wave of futurism in Florence, the cerebralist group, was interested in the study of science and occult sciences but equally dedicated to the use of narcotic substances, which helps to demonstrate that these three passions went hand in hand."[100] It is not by chance that the interest felt by this group of intellectuals in the work of Marinetti and the Milanese group around *Poesia* actually occurred primarily through the poetic (and narcotic) work of Paolo Buzzi.[101] Settimelli, in *Sinfonia* of 1912, and Corra, in the *Talis-*

mano Giallo of 1913, both mention morphine addiction, and the protagonist in Corra's *Sam Dunn è morto* reaches the most elevated state of meditation after having "gulped down three liters of whisky, five bottles of champagne, and twenty-seven shots of espresso, together with fifteen doses of opium and hashish: all that while smoking a hundred cigarettes and inhaling frequently from a small bottle of ether."[102]

BOCCIONI VS. BALLA

The list of futurists interested in the occult sciences is long, and there are others I could include in this context.[103] I hope that those I have discussed here suffice to bring into focus the preoccupations of a spiritual, ontological order within the futurist thinking. The idea that futurist art does not intend to represent the exterior and sensory reality of the world—which the futurists believed had characterized the aesthetic of the impressionist painters—recurs in many of their theoretical writings.[104] Futurism, the futurists claimed, instead sought to re-create in art the true essence of reality, as spiritualized by the subject observing it.

If impressionism allowed itself to be enchanted by the illusoriness and sensuality of the surface, and cubism, prisoner of a coldly static aesthetic (and therefore from a Bergsonian point of view, evoking death images), was a "frozen fabrication of images," then futurism, in exalting (psychic) energy, placed itself in opposition to both those currents as a movement of spiritual vitality and depth.[105] The eye of the futurist artist adopted various cognitive strategies with the goal of sounding out the diverse densities of matter; perceiving and reproducing the aura that emanates from bodies (and, influencing it, thereby influencing mood); penetrating bodies themselves to reach the ideal and perceiving in the world cues of the beyond.

In the futurist context, the ambition of re-creating reality through the work of art carries with it magical implications. Most of the divergences within the futurists' theorizations (principally pictorial) can be reduced to the contrast between Boccioni's subjective synthesis and Balla's objective analysis of, a contrast that Calvesi proposed and discussed at length in his writings, and one which we can adopt as a useful critical paradigm throughout this book.[106] Whereas Balla reconstructed and reproduced the harmony of natural phenomena by extracting from them the ideal, platonic, abstract forms, Boccioni aspired to re-create the dynamic chaos of nature by using techniques of interpenetration of planes and simultaneity to produce grandiosely conceived figurative works.[107]

These two approaches to producing art are polar—and complementary—opposites. Moreover, when applied to Russolo's poetics, this binary critical paradigm will reveal an artist who, while showing some common elements with Balla's objective analysis, was more closely connected with the subjective synthesis of Boccioni.

CHAPTER 3

Spotlight on Russolo

A NEW READING

At its core, the art of noises was for Luigi Russolo a process of conjuring the spirits, a process he divided into two parallel moments: one in which noise became spiritualized, the other in which spirits materialized. Russolo first painted this process in 1911, and he began to put it into practice a year later.

Some scholars have mentioned the relationship between Russolo and the occult arts in his early years as a painter (either when analyzing key artworks, or in passing), and the occult is certainly part of all discussions of his late creative phase—for several years after 1930, the occult arts were his only interest. But the role the occult arts played between 1913 and 1930, during the years he focused on music as theoretician, composer, builder of musical instruments, conductor, and improviser, has so far been ignored.

Given Russolo's occult interests during both the early and late periods, this critical vacuum seems curious. It becomes even more curious if one looks at the cultural environment in which he took part during his formative and futurist years and the early post–World War I period. Surrounded by companions with similar occult interests, it seems strange that Russolo would not have participated (or would have stopped participating) in the debate that preoccupied those he associated with daily.

It seems highly improbable that the Russolo who was a close friend of Romolo Romani, who assiduously frequented the society of Filippo Tommaso Marinetti, Paolo Buzzi, and Carlo Carrà, who was probably familiar with the early writings of Arnaldo Ginna and Bruno Corra, and who was fraternally attached to Umberto Boccioni, would have developed a musical aesthetics completely shielded from the occult interests of his futurist friends.[1] And, in fact, the opposite was true: on many occasions Russolo promoted the occult arts within the futurist movement.

Occultist theories circulated in the environment that Russolo frequented in his futurist and musical years, which constitutes some proof of his interest in the subject. I am convinced, however, that, proof of the connection must be found in his works. My aim, therefore, is to uncover points of contact between Russolo and the occult not merely in texts written by other futurists but also in Russolo's own musical research and writings; this connection, once uncovered, could be a key to reinterpreting both Russolo's work as a builder of musical instrument and his futurist aesthetics.

Many of the usual sources for this kind of investigation—printed scores, manuscripts, drafts, and musical instruments—are no longer extant. Other materials therefore become all the more precious, including iconological sources (paintings, photographs, films), letters, newspaper articles and reviews, contemporary literary sources that cite Russolo (factual, fictionalized, and poetic), and written evidence from friends and relatives.

Russolo's activity during his association with futurism has been studied principally within musicology, a discipline that, when dealing with the twentieth century, is often spoiled by a great exuberance for sources. That may be why, in the case of Russolo, since the preferred primary sources are largely missing, musicologists have not yet reconstructed a complete picture of his activities. It seems as if Russolo scholars have been reluctant to adopt critical instruments used to comprehend and reconstruct musical repertoires more distant in time, as in the field of medieval studies. In Russolo research, information often comes from a detail of a painting, or a novel or poem; such information should be regarded with caution, but it should be considered.

If one investigates Russolo's artistic work from this angle, the occultist aspect can be observed in all of his works, beginning with his early artworks and continuing through his futurist phase and, as has been recognized, from the 1930s onward. Russolo was interested in the occult all of his life: this interest gives continuity, unity, and coherence to his figure. Thus, the occult is a fine thread unifying all of his works, starting in the years when he espoused symbolist aesthetics and quite likely continuing throughout his futurist years and beyond.

Throughout this book I have resisted the temptation to apply Russolo's later formulations to interpretation of his early works, yet I have been surprised by the consistency of his ideas. Naturally, Russolo's thought processes evolved, but differences in his beliefs are those not of kind but only of degree.

Both Zanovello and Maffina have mentioned Russolo's period of intense theosophical and occultist studies, starting in the 1930s (these studies included the practice of magnetism, yoga, techniques of doubling the body, and materialization), as an unexpected, and unpredictable, change of interest. Like Giovanni Lista, they were surprised at an aesthetic maneuver they considered incomprehensible and possibly even regressive.[2] The notion of sudden regression is still found in all of the general biographical references on Russolo.[3] They neglect the occultist sources that would have been available to Russolo long before 1931—the periodical *Ultra* from 1907 on, and the work of the young Romani, Ginna (by 1910), and Boccioni (by 1911).[4]

Notable is Celant's seminal article "Futurismo esoterico," in which the author maintains that "there is no trace of Carrà's and Russolo's attention to the esoteric," save for Russolo's interest in "the penetration of the ultrasensitive realm in *La musica*."[5] But Carrà, himself interested in the occult, had quite a different opinion of Russolo's "attention to the esoteric." In his review of Russolo's late treatise *Al di là della materia*, published in the *Ambrosiano* issue of July 28, 1938, he wrote that "the book appears open to every kind of reading. Nor could it be otherwise for those who, like we, have *known for many years* of Luigi Russolo's fervid passion for all that which is a spiritual problem."[6]

The critical silence on Russolo's interest in occult practices, which the artist deliberately cultivated throughout his "progressive"—futurist—phase, came about because scholars deemed these preoccupations aesthetically regressive. They were thought to constitute Russolo's abdication from the avant-garde, and modernist critics therefore condemned them as a volte-face.[7] A similar fate befell the other exponents of the futurist group, whose occult interests were until recently neglected by many critics.[8]

A TINKERING LINEAGE: THE RUSSOLOS' CUTLERY NOISES

Luigi Russolo's father, Domenico (1847–1907), must have been a singular character. As we learn from Maria Zanovello, Domenico's eccentric personality probably left a mark on the equally eccentric soul of his son. To his profession of watch- and clockmaker, inherited from his father, Domenico Russolo early on added the study of music, and he instilled this passion in his children as well.

Zanovello introduces information about Domenico's earliest musical training by means of the following anecdote. Following a series of lessons from an elderly Portogruaran musician, Domenico decided to study the pianoforte. He received as a gift an old piano, which he placed by his father's watch shop, facing the town's main square. Only the frame of the piano was intact, so that "the old keyboard produced such sounds that his friends kept teasing him, asking, 'Menegheto, are you moving the cutlery drawer?'"[9]

Zanovello can have learned these things only from her husband, who probably enjoyed telling the story. But this fleeting reference to his father's "art of noises" should not be overlooked by the attentive historian, especially as cutlery noises would appear in Russolo's music. In his preface to Zanovello's biography, Russolo's friend Paolo Buzzi recalled the famous concert of 1914 at the Teatro dal Verme, at which Russolo's three *spirali di rumori* were performed for the Milanese public. About the second piece in the concert's program, *Si pranza sulla terrazza del Kursaal*, Buzzi remarked on the "effects of a terrace of a large restaurant with echoes of a small orchestra interspersed with the sound of waiters' footsteps and noises of plates and of cutlery."[10]

Domenico Russolo studied music intensely and soon became the town organist, responsible for regularly tuning and playing the handsome mechanical action organ of the cathedral of Portogruaro. To investigate, if briefly, the instrument's type and resources will prove useful. The cathedral of Portogruaro now unfortunately hosts a dubious electronic pipe organ, that was forced into the somber sixteenth-century organ loft designed by Pomponio Amalteo, a pupil of Pordenone. The electronic organ replaces a previous organ constructed by Beniamino Zanin in 1911, which the Zanins expanded in 1942 by reusing material from an earlier organ of the Venetian school. The instrument that Domenico Russolo played and tuned was almost certainly a nineteenth-century Venetian organ. The sonoral characteristics that the young Russolo heard would have been those typical of Venetian organs constructed by the Callido or Nacchini families of organ builders.

Although not endowed with the rich timbral resources that the organ builders of other northern Italian areas could provide (for example, the birdsong [*Rosignuoli*] or bell-like [*Campanelli*] organ stops of the Bernasconi or

Tamburini organs), this type of organ could display sophisticated acoustic and mechanical tricks. These included such effects as the characteristically Venetian regal stops called *Tromboncini* and *Violoncello* (similar to the sound of the *Regale*) and, above all, the *Rollo* (drum-roll), a sort of rumble produced by two very deep pipes, tuned almost to the unison and controlled by a pedal that, by means of the two frequencies sounding simultaneously, produces very fast beats and gives a surprisingly accurate illusion of the roll of timpani.[11]

Domenico Russolo eventually became director of the Philharmonic School of Portogruaro and entered on a fertile compositional period. The Russolos then moved to the near town of Latisana, where Domenico took the job of maintaining the town clocks. In Latisana, Domenico assumed direction of the Philharmonic School and the Schola Cantorum, opened a photographic laboratory, and occupied himself with the tuning of organs and pianos.

All of Domenico Russolo's professions—watch- and clockmaker, organist, piano and organ tuner, and later photographer—required considerable mechanical competence, and they were undoubtedly an important influence on his son, Luigi. A passion for levers, cogwheels, and sophisticated clockwork mechanisms, together with acquaintance with the mechanical principles of keyboard instruments such as the organ (justly considered the most complex machine of antiquity), were fertile seeds in Luigi's development.

Luigi Russolo's interest in organ building can be seen in the earliest models of his rumorarmonio (noise harmonium), the instrument that Russolo built in the 1920s, which reproduces and controls the same timbres as the intonarumori through an organlike keyboard mechanism.[12] Russolo's passion for organs in 1928 led him to propose a modification of organ pipes (and wind instruments) with which he sought to reduce the instruments' production costs.[13]

Domenico Russolo taught his children music and succeeded in preparing Russolo's two brothers, Giovanni (born in 1874) and Antonio (1877–1943), for the entrance exam to the Conservatory of Milan. They passed the exam brilliantly, and whereas one graduated with degrees in violin, organ, and viola, the other took degrees in piano and organ. Luigi took a different path. He started studying piano but passed quickly on to the violin, and then as quickly abandoned that instrument when he became interested in painting.

While studying music, Russolo completed his secondary education at the Seminary of Portogruaro, an institution that gave him a solid, if orthodoxly

Catholic, spiritual education. As his writings reveal, his interest in all that is spirit and its emanation was never to diminish: those years of seminary training may explain the Christian mysticism of Russolo's later years, a leaning that in fact prefigures his later interest in Steiner's anthroposophy, found in *Al di là della materia*. Indeed, Zanovello, referring to the last spiritual period of Russolo's intellectual activity, considers the Seminary of Portogruaro to have been "the origin of the religious-Christian substratum of this artist's soul."[14]

But Russolo did not choose ordination. In 1901, his seminary training completed, he rejoined his family, who had moved to Milan so that his brothers could attend the conservatory, and, once there, found himself increasingly drawn toward visual arts.

DETECTING THREADS

Mention of the relationship between Russolo and the occult prior to 1930 can be found in books of art criticism, but only when authors attempt to contextualize some of his early works as a painter and printmaker. With the single exception of Gasparotto's contributions in the MART catalog, these references appear only sporadically and often in the context of a general discussion. Ester Coen, for instance, comparing Russolo to Boccioni, emphasizes the preferential use of color to suggest an atmosphere of "impalpable, magical manifestations."[15] Calvesi compares Russolo to Balla and mentions fleetingly, without developing the claim or giving it precise chronological coordinates, the interests common to both men toward "theosophy, anarchy, freemasonry, and humanitarian socialism," to which Calvesi also adds sympathy for those theories of Nietzsche and patriotism that ended up being common to the entire futurist group.[16]

Lista has advanced the hypothesis that Russolo began to take an interest in occultism in 1910–11, but pointed to his intellectual independence from Boccioni. He wrote: "It is possible that his research into metapsychics and Eastern doctrines dates back to these years [1910–11], although it would be difficult to maintain whether these studies were an autonomous interest of his own or a common direction of research for the futurist group, still little studied [. . .]. The second hypothesis seems the more probable."[17]

Jean-Marc Vivenza confirmed the hypothesis of an early occultist interest when he commented on Russolo's large canvas of 1911–12, *La musica* (fig. 6),

FIGURE 6. Luigi Russolo, *La musica* (1911–12). Estorick Collection, London, UK / The Bridgeman Art Library.

which he felt "reveals a strong interest in metapsychics and especially in occultism, an interest that would become, some years later, his only intellectual preoccupation."[18] Like Lista, Vivenza does not develop the point, nor does he analyze the painting.

Germano Celant also related *La musica* to Russolo's interest in occultism, but he is among those who consider this interest to have been a pallid reflection of Boccioni's theories, absorbed almost by osmosis through "having lived in the same Milanese environment."[19] Celant believed that *La musica* attests to Russolo's interest in "the penetration of the ultrasensitive realm;" in this painting "musical ultrasensitivity is recalled, on the canvas, by the 'traces' of the pianist's face, residual images spread and dispersed in an undulatory and sinuous turbine of blue, red, and yellow bands; *La musica* reproduces, in a metaphysical light that can be found also in the *Vinti*, traces produced by the pianist (the residual images converge toward the focal center constituted by the subject) in a particular state of mind."

According to the art historian Marianne Martin, the many-armed pianist in this painting represents Siva Nataraja, the "creator and lord of the cosmic dance in the Hindu pantheon": an element that could further prove Russolo's early interest in Eastern philosophies, which were a main source of theosophy.[20] Martin is the only scholar to recognize the conceptual originality of Russolo's painting and its independence from the cubist influence so clearly seen in the other painters of the first futurist nucleus (above all, Boccioni and Carrà, but also Severini). Martin sketches Russolo as a "sensitive and mystical temperament," and she hints at his interest in synesthesia, attributing it to his symbolist background but never linking his synesthetic interest to that in the occult arts.[21]

Martin noted, moreover, that it may have been Russolo's two explicitly synesthetic paintings (*Profumo* of 1910 and *La musica* of 1911) that inspired Boccioni in his Roman lecture of May 1911 to theorize "paintings [as] whirling musical compositions of enormous colored gases": something that should have signaled the future development of painting in the direction of dematerialization (or, even better, of spiritualization).[22] If this were true, *Profumo* and *La musica* would constitute a further step toward the dematerialization—moving from sense to sense, and vibration to vibration—that Russolo's research aspired to enact. In interrupting his pictorial activity to take up musical research, then interrupting his musical research to concentrate on metaphysics, and finally returning, with eyes profoundly changed, to painting, Russolo was motivated throughout by his occult interests.

In an article by Mario Verdone, published in the catalog of the exhibition *Okkultismus und Avantgarde*, Russolo's name is mentioned first in an incomplete list of futurists interested in the occult arts (the list further included Benedetta, Giuseppe Steiner, Thayaht, etc.).[23] Russolo's name does not, however, reappear in the article. In the same catalog, an essay by Lista titled *Futurismus und Okkultismus* refers to Russolo on two occasions, recording that some of his first engravings (*Trionfo della morte* and *Tentazione*) adopt themes of mystical, visionary, and demonic symbolism. Lista also affirmed that the powerful and shocking *Autoritratto con teschi* (1908) could have been inspired by practices of clairvoyance using a black mirror. As the subject of this painting is similar to that of the late painting *Lo specchio della verità* of

1944, this idea advances, albeit briefly, the hypothesis of a continuity between the occultist themes of Russolo's first and last periods.[24]

Ilaria Schiaffini resolved the question of who influenced whom in her discussion of Russolo's and Boccioni's mutual interest in "occult sciences and paranormal phenomena which, although not actually documented before WWI [sic], have a primary inspirational role in Russolo's painting."[25]

SPIRITUAL 1940S

Occultist themes pervade Russolo's last paintings. To analyze the late works—from 1940 until the year of his death—would strain the limits of this work. A brief overview of these works would be useful however, not only because this is a vast body of work with considerable artistic merit but because these paintings occupied Russolo during the time he systematically committed into writing his metapsychic investigations. Thus they provide a fitting visual complement for the investigations that are the primary subject of this book.

No formalized studies of Russolo's late paintings existed before the publication of the MART catalog; in fact, Russolo's activities of the 1930s and 1940s have never been seriously studied in their entirety.[26] The late paintings have suffered from the negative judgment of modernist-inspired criticism (that of Maffina, among others), which considered Russolo's return to the figurative to be unpardonable. This superficial point of view ignores the fact that Russolo—like Boccioni—had never completely abandoned the figure, not even during the years of his most radical pictorial experimentation. Russolo never, in fact, produced an abstract painting.

The many remarkable works from his later years—*Autoritratto* (1940; fig. 7), *Eremo sotto la luna* (1942), *Il fico* (1944), *Trio* (1946)—are marked by allegory and absolute clearness of tone; the atmospheres evoked are pervaded by a moving spirituality. Purity of line, stasis, silence, and an intense sense of calm are some of the elements that distinguish these works. They point to a religious aspect implicit in reality and nature, and they reveal the superior metaphysics that manifests itself once the appearance of things is overcome and the supreme harmony reverberating through and in them is heard.

Russolo defined this style of painting as classical modern.[27] These late canvases, in their timeless classicism, are certainly distant from futurism, but Russolo actually planned them as a further evolution of futurism—a further synthesis, and a natural continuation of investigations never abandoned.[28]

FIGURE 7. Luigi Russolo, *Autoritratto* (1940). Portogruaro, Collezione del Comune di Portogruaro.

Rather than the "return to order" generally promoted by the "Novecento" group—a group Russolo vehemently criticized—his late paintings show the influence of Achille Funi's magical realism; more than a *naïf* element in general, here surfaces the spirit of *le Douanier*.[29] But over every influence there predominate the lessons of the great Italian painting tradition, from Giotto to Masaccio, Titian to Leonardo da Vinci, Giovanni Bellini to Michelangelo.

OCCULT BEFORE THE NOISE

It is not difficult to demonstrate the influence of the occult arts in Russolo's visual work: most of his canvases are laden with symbols of death, skeletons, skulls, globes of fire; supernatural, hallucinatory, ethereal, and residual images; and synesthetic representations—in short, all the *caravanserai* of icons typically associated with the occult.

Certainly the study of symbolism and decadentism helps explain the presence of these subjects in Russolo's paintings. The most immediately evident sources of literary influence are Baudelaire, Mallarmé, Rimbaud, Laforgue, Huysmans, and Péladan; also evident is the influence of Poe, whom Russolo and Marinetti knew well, as well as that of Bergson and, even more so, Nietzsche, whose ideas the futurists probably became acquainted with through Gabriele D'Annunzio's disseminatory work.[30]

In fact, the young Russolo must have been first led to the study of the occult arts by symbolism, a movement that matured in France from 1880 on, when materialism and positivism were no longer fashionable. During this time, theosophy—and the publication of works by Papus, Éliphas Lévi, and Éduard Schuré—reconnected with the esoteric tradition, returned to concepts of platonic philosophy and Swedenborgian mysticism, revived the cabalistic tradition, and promoted a rebirth of spirituality in the arts.[31]

The influence of the Belgian painter James Ensor and his allegorical works was more important in Russolo's early works than Lista and Maffina have acknowledged. Ensorian elements can be perceived in a number of Russolo's early works, in particular in the subject matter of *Carezza-Morte* (1909), which is strongly allegorical and Düreresque, as well as in *Autoritratto con teschi* and *Maschere* (fig. 8), both from 1908, and the subsequent *La musica* (1911). Russolo adopted some of Ensor's preferred themes—masks or skeletons dancing in grotesque formation, *memento mori* orchestrating a satire of society (as can also be found in Aroldo Bonzagni and the early, Jarry-influenced Marinetti)—but in his works he gave these themes a spiritual, rather than political, spin.[32]

If Martin is right, Marinetti may have been the first of the futurists to become familiar with Ensor. According to Martin, Marinetti visited the Ensor exhibit promoted by *La Plume* in 1898, and he was credited with introducing Ensor to Russolo and the other futurists.[33]

Russolo shared Ensor's rejection of impressionist painting for its sensual superficiality, and both men began their artistic careers as printmaker. Half of Ensor's work is printmaking; as the artist explained in his famous letter to Albert Croquez: "Pictorial materials still worry me. [...] I dread the fragility of painting, exposed to the crimes of the restorer, to insufficiency, to the slander of reproductions. I want to survive, to speak to the people of tomorrow for a long time yet. I think of solid copper plates, of unalterable inks, of easy reproductions, of faithful printing, and I am adopting etching as a means of expression."[34]

Other important models for Russolo, Boccioni, and Balla were the sym-

FIGURE 8. Luigi Russolo, *Maschere* (1907–08). Milan, Civica Raccolta delle Stampe "Achille Bertarelli" Castello Sforzesco.

bolist painter and printmaker Odilon Redon and, among the Italians, the symbolist painter Gaetano Previati, who in 1892 exhibited in Paris with the *Rose+Croix* group of painters (Boccioni mentioned this event in his 1911 Roman lecture). The allegorical world of Previati, infused with mysticism and symbolic proclamations of the victory of light, soon found a place of honor in futurist poetics. This is clear from the technical manifesto of futurist painting, cosigned by Russolo, which closed with words that strike a disturbingly Luciferesque tone: "We proclaim ourselves Lords of Light."[35]

Russolo was also influenced by Romolo Romani who was himself influenced by Ensor and Redon. Romani is known to have been always extremely sensitive to occult themes. Many of Romani's paintings are based on observation of the spiritual levels of reality; this is in line with one of futurism's defining goals, to plumb the depths, without stopping at the superficial and sensory level. This irrational, antipositivist component unites futurism and occult study and practice. Romani's painting was also solidly grounded in synesthetic interests and on the relationship between music and painting, which would also concern Russolo. In his autobiography, Carrà declared that Romani "following the guide of the aesthetic principle, valid in the musical world, wanted to require from painting an effect similar to that of music."[36]

Apart from these influences, Russolo seems also to have been inspired by his direct interest in symbolism (which he shared with Kandinsky) and, possibly, the theories of the Munich circle *Der Blaue Reiter*, as well as of those of Schoenberg.[37] Sixten Ringbom, in his seminal book *The Sounding Cosmos*, has shown clearly the direct relationship between the ideas of Kandinsky in *The Spiritual in Art* and theosophy. I am convinced that Russolo, like Kandinsky and Ginna, drew directly from theosophy: by 1908 he must already have been exposed to the occult and theosophy, and he may even have read Besant's and Leadbeater's *Thought-forms*.[38] As Martin has noted, it is plausible that Russolo influenced Boccioni in spiritual matters, rather than vice versa.[39]

Death themes with a strongly symbolist flavor pervade some of Russolo's early etchings and aquatints of 1908–09, including *Carezza-Morte*, *Medio Evo*, and *Il Trionfo della Morte*; the last-named even borrows its title from a novel by D'Annunzio, the acknowledged source of Italian symbolism. Even more clearly occultist, in my opinion, is the climate of the etching and aquatint *Maschere*, also of 1908. If Ensor and Munch influenced Russolo in the choice of subject, the work's grotesque character and the peculiar deformations of the figure reveal Romani's prominent influence.[40]

Russolo's *Maschere* bears no relationship to the Nietzschean mask—this hypothesis was advanced by Ethel Piselli—or to the mask as a Baudelairean image.[41] Instead, I believe that Russolo must have found inspiration in Romani's analysis and reproductions of diverse expressions of the human face, which Romani transformed into comic or tragic masks (*Il riso* and *Il crapulone* of 1903–04, *Il risentimento* and *Il dubbio* of 1905, *Il ricco* of 1905–06, and *Il guerriero* and *Lo scettico* of 1905–07).[42] Evangelisti has correctly related this series of masklike portraits, executed from 1904 on, to the ideoplastic experiments (*mediumistic* images materialized and transmitted at a distance) of Eusapia Palladino.[43]

Far from being an ingenuous early exercise in composition, *Maschere* is a precocious representation of forms of fluctuating thought (thought-forms) produced by the mental energy of a subject in a trance who has been able to overcome the barrier of the aura: a process thoroughly illustrated in *Thought-forms*. *Maschere* is a representation of different states of mind that only a sensitive subject (a *clairvoyant* painter, Boccioni would say) has the power to see and eventually himself produce.[44] In other words, *Maschere* is a representation of a plastic materialization.

It may be impossible to prove definitively that Russolo was familiar with Besant's and Leadbeater's book already in 1908, but certainly the concept of thought-form was known at the turn of the twentieth century, particularly in the circles Russolo traveled in. Russolo's awareness of these theories convincingly explains why *Maschere* shows resemblances not just with his 1910 etching and aquatint *Città addormentata* (see the masks visible in the upper margin) but also with the masks in the more overtly occultist *La musica*, a painting essentially inconceivable without assuming Russolo's familiarity with *Thought-forms*.[45] Much like *Maschere*, *La musica* presents a series of flying masks with different expressions that can easily be read as a visualization or materialization of the different states of mind induced in an interpreter-medium by spirits he himself has evoked.

The striking *Autoritratto con teschi* can be analyzed using this same critical frame. Despite being Russolo's first canvas, it already offers a complete synthesis of the artist's intellectual world. Painted in the same year of *Maschere*, this self-portrait seems to have been particularly dear to Russolo's heart: he mentioned it more than twenty years later in a letter to his wife of December 5, 1929.[46] Buzzi wrote about this painting with a display of futurist code words: "There Russolo, *almost mediumistically* approaching the self-portrait, where the shadow of the intellectual goatee has the power of an essential poem, overflows with his enharmonic genius onto the walls of a kaleidoscopic constellation of masks that have all the supreme vehemence of a great Verdi chorus." [47]

Giovanni Lista related the *Autoritratto con teschi* to a specific practice of the occultists: divination through a black mirror. By observing a black mirror for ten consecutive minutes, Lista claimed, one can enter into a trance in which hallucinatory or prophetic images emerge into view.[48] It is impossible to claim that the clearly hallucinatory vision represented in Russolo's painting derived from his direct experience with the black mirror. But Lista believed that it did, seeing confirmation in the fact that Russolo returned to the subject of this painting in his *Lo specchio della verità* of 1944.

Russolo's self-portrait of the artist crowned by skulls, a most evident symbol of death, was probably inspired by the Northern-European tradition of *memento mori*. This reading is confirmed by Zanovello's claim that the painting represents nothing less than "a preoccupation with death."[49]

Russolo's careful reproduction of skulls from different angles may be one of the first instances in his work of the influence of Leonardo da Vinci.[50] But in the self-portrait, the focal point around which the whole painting revolves is not the crown of craniums but rather the gaze of the artist. This painting inaugurates a long series of self-portraits in Russolo's oeuvre in which the gaze will be the focus. The 1910 etching *Autoritratto* plays mysteriously with light and shadow on a face distinguished by deep-set eyes; the *Autoritratto (con doppio eterico)* of 1910–11 (fig. 9), which features Mephistophelean eyes, shows a Russolo with his etheric double in a pose that surprisingly matches Stravinsky's description of Russolo: a figure "with wild hair and beard." [51] A 1911 study for an *Autoritratto* in watercolor and tempera reproduces a sharpened face, highly stylized, with enigmatic eyes and almost extraterrestrial features.[52] If this sketch is authentic, it might be a preparatory study for the so-called *Autoritratto "verde"* of 1913, which shows a face whose features are almost entirely obscured and a spiral line that repeats and amplifies its form, like an aura, or a double. In both of these works, the mannequinlike interrogative aspect of the face is almost metaphysical, and it resembles the work of De Chirico, a painter hardly associated with futurism.[53]

Russolo's series of self-portraits continued with *Io Dinamico* of 1912–13, which was lost after the futurist exhibit at the San Francisco Universal Exposition of 1915, and in which the angular features of the face commence a whirling rhythm of turbulent, spiraling, rotating lines amplifying the figure in a double. This work was followed by the greater realism of the 1920 *Autoritratto*, where Russolo shows his double as a diabolic shadow on the wall (fig. 10), and the *Autoritratto* in black and red chalk of 1925, in which the refined features are negotiated between the two contrasting colors (red and black) without, however, any diminution of the magnetism of the eyes.[54]

There is, in addition to the series of self-portraits a sequence of photographic portraits of Russolo: *Il fumatore*, an ectoplasmic example of the photodynamic trajectory, taken by Arturo Bragaglia in 1913; a second portrait by Bragaglia reproduced in Maffina, in which an older Russolo looks into the

FIGURE 9. Luigi Russolo, *Autoritratto (con doppio eterico)* (1910). Location unknown.

lens with a penetrating eye; a conceptual double portrait of Russolo taken in the mid-1920s and featuring him in front of his *La musica* and between two keyboards of two models of his noise harmonium (fig. 11); and the portrait featured on the dust jacket flap of the second edition of *Al di là della materia* in 1966, in which Russolo wears what looks like a priest's robe. Crowning Russolo's many portraits and self-portraits, however, is the superb and hypnotizing *Autoritratto* in oils of 1940.

Maurizio Calvesi once said of *Auto-stato d'animo*, a self-portrait by Giacomo Balla of 1920, that it was an attempt on the part of the artist to "*dematerialize* his own image, rendering it like an ectoplasm [. . .] to spiritualize his own gaze."[55] It seems that Russolo's principal objective in many of his self-portraits was precisely that: the spiritualization of his features. It is interesting to note how constantly, throughout his life, he pursued this objective in the representation of his own figure.

Immediately evident in many of the portraits is the aura, which Russolo represented in various ways around the face. Buzzi, in a description of Rus-

FIGURE 10. Luigi Russolo, *Autoritratto (con l'ombra)* (1920). Florence, Galleria degli Uffizi.

solo from January 1918, wrote: "Whence he passed [...] there was a burst of sparks that resembled an *aura*. Moreover, his brain added there *the halos* of scintillations of his genius."[56]

The gaze is crucial. In all of the above-mentioned representations, and, for that matter, in most of the surviving photographs of Russolo, the eyes are always fixed, profound, magnetic, enchanting. This visual rhetoric evokes in the observer that reverential fear arising in encounters with a spiritual master; this is certainly the function of the serious, even severe, gazes found in portraits of Madame Blavatsky and Rudolf Steiner, both of whom aspired to build a cult of personality. The iconographic nature of Russolo's portraits solidifies the continuity of his interests.

Most of Russolo's works reveal his occultist sensitivity and prove that his interest in theosophy and spiritualism must have preceded his taking part in séances in Paris in the mid-1920s.[57] Already in 1911, *Uomo che muore* repro-

FIGURE 11. *Luigi Russolo seduto in mezzo ai suoi rumorarmoni* (1924–28; photographer unknown). Rovereto, The Museum of Modern and Contemporary Art of Trento and Rovereto Archivio del '900, Fondo Fortunato Depero.

duced spirit in the act of abandoning a dying body.[58] The original of this work disappeared, but Russolo was so attached to the subject that he repainted it completely in 1941 with the title *L'uomo morente*. The subject of *Uomo che muore* was one of the topoi of occultist iconography, as shown, for example, in an illustration taken from *The Projection of the Astral Body* by Muldoon and Carrington.[59]

The doubling of the etheric body by the material body, a recurring theosophical theme, interested Russolo for most of his life.[60] The *Autoritratto (con doppio eterico*) is overwhelming proof of this and aptly subtitled.[61] Zanovello explains that in the portrait "the author, with an almost diabolical effect, appears near his 'etheric double,' who commiserates with him."[62]

The other, above-mentioned *Autoritratto*, which Lista has claimed was painted in 1930, was a kind of "remake" of his *Autoritratto (con doppio eterico)*. This painting, for years known only in the reproduction in Apollonio, and now in MART (where we learn that it is now owned by the Galleria degli Uffizi in Florence), effectively shows the face of its author accompanied by a mysterious shadow projected on the wall, which sharpens the contours of Russolo's profile.[63] This is the self-portrait "with the shadow" that Russolo mentioned in a letter to his wife of December 5, 1929.[64] I have argued that it must have been painted before 1922, in the period preceding Russolo's departure for Thiene, and this is confirmed by the reproduction in the MART catalog, where, unlike in Apollonio, the signature and the year 1920 are clearly visible.[65]

The fact that in 1910 Russolo worked on a painting titled *Autoritratto (con doppio eterico)* demonstrates that at that time he was already well informed about the key notions of occultist thought popularized by theosophy. The various bodies (material, mental, astral) and the etheric double are frequent topics in theosophical literature. Leadbeater mentions the etheric double in both *Thought-forms* and *Man Visible and Invisible*, as well as in his 1913 book *The Hidden Side of Things*, a collection of articles that had appeared in various theosophical magazines (principally *The Theosophist*) over the preceding twelve years.[66]

The subject of the doubling of the material body was eventually treated in *Alla ricerca del vero*, the first of the three parts of *Al di là della materia*, Russolo's most ambitious work in his later period; the first edition was printed by Bocca in 1938.[67] In the paragraph titled "The doubling of the body or etheric double," Russolo explains how the densification of two masses (presumably mental body and astral body) into a single form vaguely resembling the human body—here still defined as "etheric double"—is the result of magnetizing a subject once the subject has passed the phase he calls "exteriorization of the sensitivity."[68] The etheric double is thought to be linked to the human body that produces it through a sort of umbilical cord attached to the solar plexus.

In this paragraph, as we have seen, Russolo mentions experiments conducted to verify the existence of the double: "A screen of calcium sulfide becomes brilliant and luminous if this double, which one can also move to a nearby room, passes over or near to the screen." He adds, "It is possible to cause this [etheric] double to execute actions, like moving light objects: it is in short something resembling the manifestations of ectoplasm that occur and have been photographed in séances by William Crookes."[69]

In the same paragraph Russolo again takes up the subject of *Uomo che muore*, this time in the form of a rhetorical question: "And isn't it true and established that this astral body with its etheric double, when death occurs, is seen by clairvoyants or magnetized subjects under magnetic sleep, to leave the physical body, its separation determining, in such physical body, death?"[70] The theme of the etheric double recurs in Zanovello's description of the event in Cerro di Laveno with which this book opened.[71]

The etheric double is not the only evidence of occultist themes in Russolo's painting. Another doubling is represented in *Nietzsche e la pazzia* (the etching and aquatint of 1909; the canvas of the same name, from 1910, is lost). In an article cited by Zanovello, Amedeo Mazzotti explains that the woman's image, which appears next to the philosopher's head, is "that which Plato would have called his *daimonos*, his genius, which talks to him, drives him, incites him."[72] Martin has read the feminine figure as the philosopher's alter ego, a muse, or the prosopopeia of madness.[73] Madness is not simply a tragic reference to Nietzsche's biography but a celebration of Nietzsche's philosophy of the irrational, which, for Gasparotto, was one of Russolo's avenues to overcome the reductive positivistic view of the world.[74] The uncanny, Freudian trope of the double seems just as evident in this allegorical representation.

According to Lista, *Ricordi di una notte* of 1911 deals with an experience of *hypermnesia*: it is in all probability a pictorial transcription of mental images produced by a subject (presumably the artist himself) during a metapsychic session (fig. 12).[75] The artist's sensitivity, empowered by the state of trance, permits him to reconstruct in this painting a nocturnal experience as a hallucinatory simultaneity of the images that surface in his memory.[76] The result is a re-creation, for Russolo perhaps the most faithful and spiritual, of reality and of life. According to the occult aesthetic the futurists espoused, reality could be observed, produced, and endowed with its own spiritual life only through a medium able to help spirits reincarnate. To the eyes of the "clairvoyant painter *(pittore veggente),*" as Boccioni called it, reality reveals itself for what it truly is: as chaotic as the universe, a monstrous cacophony of many events and sensations all occurring simultaneously.[77]

In this canvas Martin has noted the influence of Bergson's theories of *psy-*

FIGURE 12. Luigi Russolo, *Ricordi di una notte* (1912). Location unknown.

chic time, which in these years also influenced Marinetti and Boccioni. In particular, Russolo applied Bergson's theory of the interior duration as a "qualitative multiplicity [...] an organic evolution [...whose] moments [...] are not external to one another," and for that reason they interpenetrate and overlap.[78] This theory here results in a highly chaotic quality, which finds order only in the mind of the subject perceiving—and perhaps, as implied by Boccioni's concept of *complementarismo congenito*, generating—such complementary chaos. Yet this theory not only provides a spiritual key to understanding the futurist poetics of optical-mnemonic synthesis—or the "synthesis of what one remembers and what one sees"—but is also fundamental to understanding the occult direction of Russolo's research and how it led naturally to the art of noises.[79]

In the presentation catalog of works exhibited at London's Sackville Gallery in March 1912, Russolo described his *Una-tre teste* (1912) as a study of the transparency that light confers on bodies.[80] That work is now lost, but judging by the photographic reproduction, it seems to lack the technical, compositional, and conceptual sophistication of other coeval works by Russolo. It is therefore difficult to say whether or not the three heads here represented are the result of the optical, frame-based breakdown of the movement of a single head, shown in three different positions in three different moments in time, a technique also found in the hands of the pianist in *La musica* and in the horse's legs in *Ricordi di una notte*, both from the previous year.

Russolo's application of the techniques of optical synthesis are primitive variations of those that became central in Balla's works of 1912 (*Le mani del violinista*, *Dinamismo di un cane al guinzaglio*, and *Ragazza che corre sul balcone*), which Boccioni criticized for their frame-based, discontinuous portraying of movement, as well as for being the center (and essence) of these paintings.[81] Russolo's optical synthesis is technically more primitive than Balla's, but he employed the technique sparsely, never exclusively, and in a conceptually more refined way that resembles Boccioni's use of it (consider the blurs of the men in *Città che sale*).[82]

This similarity with Boccioni is also revealed in another aspect of Russolo's *Una-tre teste*: the painting can be read as an optical-mnemonic simultaneity (i.e., as a synthesis of what one sees and what one remembers), but the three heads, diaphanously illuminated by light, which in all probability comes from a window, can also be read in another way: as a physical body accompanied by its mental and astral bodies, the two elements that according to theosophical teachings constitute the aura.

Russolo's reading of *Thought-forms* and Leadbeater's essay on sonic forms probably influenced one of his most icastic canvases, *Linee-forza della folgore* (1912; fig. 13), which, according to Zanovello and Martin, the artist broke into pieces in 1943 while experiencing a *raptus*.[83] Russolo treated the same lightning theme in a more traditional manner in the series *Lampi* (1910), only to repeat it two years later in a far more personal and not the least impressionistic form.

This masterly stylization of the rapid course of a bolt of lightning across an urban sky, and the spectacle of elemental, electrical, luminous, and sonic power thus evoked—reflecting Nikola Tesla, Henry Adams, and Benjamin Franklin—suggests an animistic and pantheistic devotion to the forces of

FIGURE 13. Luigi Russolo, *Linee-forza della folgore* (1912), central panel. Portogruaro, Collezione del Comune di Portogruaro.

nature.[84] At the center of the painting, the complex of forces becomes concentrated in the lightning, creating an electrical unity of remarkable formal and visual power.[85] The undulating bands represent the shock wave—the sound wave—that according to scientists is as dangerous to contact as the lightning itself.

Russolo portrayed the sonic forms of this shock wave with great care, as can be seen in the newly rediscovered central panel of the painting as well as in some of the other remaining fragments. The figures, like triangular yellow-green rays on a dark blue-black background can in my opinion be derived from the thought-forms depicted in plates 22 and 23 of *Thought-forms* (fig. 14). In that book, the two stiletto-like figures on the illustration's black background are explained as follows: "The keen-pointed stiletto-like dart [#23] was a thought of steady anger [. . .] murder, sustained through years, and directed against a person who had inflicted a deep injury on the one who sent

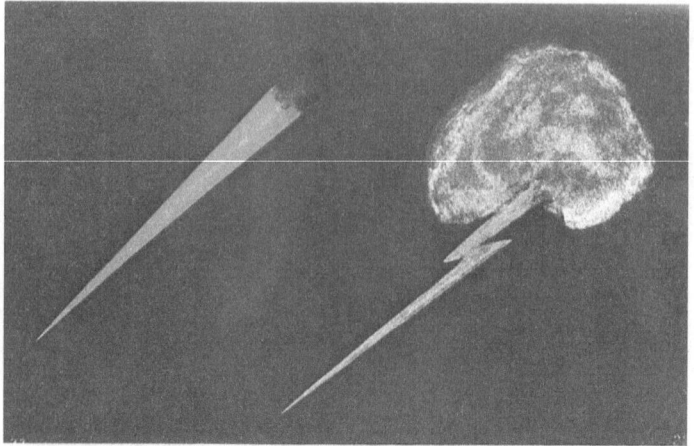

FIGURE 14. Annie Besant and Charles W. Leadbeater, illustrations 22 and 23 from *Thought-forms* (1901). Reproduced by permission of The Theosophical Publishing House, Adyar, Chennai 600 020. India. © The Theosophical Publishing House. www.ts-adyar.org & www.adyarbooks.com.

it forth. It will be noted that both of them [#22 and #23] take the flash-like form of a lightning bolt."[86]

The triangular image of the shock wave in *Linee-forza della folgore* is extraordinarily close to the description of the sonic forms of a tempest found in the chapter on sound-forms in Leadbeater's *The Hidden Side of Things*: "The majestic roll of a thunderstorm creates usually a vast flowing band of colour, while the deafening crash often calls into temporary existence an arrangement of irregular radiations [. . .] or sometimes a huge irregular sphere with spikes projecting from it in all directions."[87] These irradiating spikes resemble projectiles of sound, which can wound the astral bodies of surrounding persons like swords.[88] In this excerpt the image of the lightning and the metaphor of the sword are intertwined.

In *Solidità della nebbia* of the same year, Russolo once again confronted the problem of representing waves, though the type of wave remains unclear (fig. 15). Evangelisti has read the painting as a representation of sonic waves radiating outward and propagating themselves in an atmosphere of different levels of density like that offered by fog banks; these waves are thus related to the wave forms of Romani's *La campana* of 1912.[89] Lista thought that the painting represents the "materializing of waves of an energy field" and refers therefore to the waves of an electromagnetic field.[90]

FIGURE 15. Luigi Russolo, *Solidità nella nebbia* (1912). Gianni Mattioli Collection (on long-term loan at the Peggy Guggenheim Collection, Venice). © 2010 Artists Rights Society (ARS), New York / SIAE, Rome.

In my opinion, however, the painting has to do with light rather than sound waves. The concentric bands of color of *Solidità della nebbia* represent the banks of fog influencing the light and the visible surrounding bodies, almost giving them different degrees of density. In this way, the images are spiritualized, like incorporeal phantasms or spirits; with these images Russolo again "destroys the materiality of bodies."[91] Here I agree with Martin, who maintains that the canvas shows the "gradual approach and ultimate union of two independent, slowly expanding, curving rhythms—those of the

FIGURE 16. Luigi Russolo, *Compenetrazione di case + luce + cielo* (1912). Basel, Kunstmuseum.

street light above and the pavement below," effectively transforming the fog into "a potent conductor of universal dynamism."[92]

In *Compenetrazion di case + luce + cielo* (1912), a work of surprising economy of pictorial gestures, Martin notes a similar attempt to represent the spiritual union between earth and sky, a union that evokes images of an unknown world that is pure and ethereal (fig. 16).[93] The buildings are the bridge between the earth and the sky, and in fact *Le case continuano in cielo* was the alternative title under which the painting exhibited. The buildings symbolize the work of man upon nature, of technological artifice. As it was for such futurist heroes as Mafarka and Dro, the futurist credo of technology is here the principal means of spiritual elevation—true catalyst of the union of earth and sky. Both *Solidità della nebbia* and *Compenetrazione di case + luce + cielo* anticipate by a couple of years the principles that became fundamental to various works by Balla (for example, *Mercurio passa davanti al sole, visto da un cannocchiale*, 1914), which, in representing the union of two opposites, bright and dark, light and shadow, can be read as an allegory of the alchemical process.

As discussed in the previous chapter, Russolo's paintings also manifest the relationship between synesthesia and the occult. At least two works by Russolo, *Profumo* and *La musica*, clearly reveal his interest in synesthesia and therefore highlight the correspondences between luminous and sonic vibrations. In this field, Russolo was probably influenced by French symbolism, Italian scapigliatura, and theosophical texts.

Profumo exists in two versions, both from 1910, and both in some way linkable to Boccioni's *Studio di testa femminile* of the previous year. The mezzotint is probably the first version, since it retains a distinctly art nouveau flavor that can be seen both in the slightly curved upper side of the frame (this appears not only in Boccioni's *Studio di testa femminile* but also in Romani's *Ritratto di Dina Galli*) and in the way Russolo represents the ramifications of scent in the lower right corner.[94]

The diffusion of light came to symbolize in Russolo's painting the spreading of a scent, suggesting that luminous waves and scents of perfume were in some way secretly and elegantly linked. (Boccioni's work completely lacks the synesthetic reference present in these two works of Russolo.) *Profumo*, as Carlo Cohen wrote in the Florentine *Nazione* on May 25, 1911, "indeed gives a sense of voluptuousness and of the indulging."[95] The title's suggestion of olfactory perceptions can be related to Russolo's reading of one of the most important reference texts for D'Annunzio's decadentism, Huysmans's *A Rebours*, where, in chapter 10, the protagonist, Des Esseintes, experiments with exotic perfumes and rare essences, intoxicating himself to the point of physical collapse.

The analysis of Russolo's second important synesthetic painting, *La musica*, demands a separate chapter, as the cornerstone of my investigation of the relationship between Russolo's visual and aural occult explorations.

CHAPTER 4

Painting Noise: *La musica*

LA MUSIQUE

La musique souvent me prend comme une mer!
Vers ma pâle étoile,
Sous un plafond de brume ou dans un vaste éther,
Je mets à la voile;

La poitrine en avant et les poumons gonflés
Comme de la toile
J'escalade le dos des flots amoncelés
Que la nuit me voile;

Je sens vibrer en moi toutes les passions
D'un vaisseau qui souffre;
Le bon vent, la tempête et ses convulsions

Sur l'immense gouffre
Me bercent. D'autres fois, calme plat, grand miroir
De mon désespoir!
—Charles Baudelaire, from *Les fleurs du mal*

THE PROCESS

Russolo's interest in synesthesia and the occult is most in evident in what is undoubtedly his best-known work, the large oil painting *La musica*. This painting is centrally important to my investigation, as it sets out the poetics of music that Russolo was working out in the years immediately preceding his manifesto on the art of noises.

Buzzi has confirmed the importance of this work in Russolo's artistic and intellectual development, claiming that the painting was Russolo's "work in

FIGURE 17. Umberto Boccioni, caricature of the futurist *serata* at the Politeama Garibaldi in Treviso on June 2, 1911, reproduced in *Uno, due, tre*, Milan, 17 June 1911.

progress since the years of his earliest youth."[1] The different versions of the painting are evidence of a complex gestation period.

A first version in ink on paper (1911) shows many of the elements of the final version of the painting yet also significant differences. This version of *La musica* has neither hands nor masks, and its crudity suggests that it may be a forgery.[2] If proved authentic, it would most likely have preceded the first oil-on-canvas version of the same subject, which was shown in Milan at the *Prima Esposizione d'Arte Libera* on April 30, 1911, with its first title, *Dinamismo musicale*. Early in 1912 Russolo painted the subject again, this time changing the title to *La musica* and creating the version known today.[3]

Dinamismo musicale is fully documented in Boccioni's caricature of the futurist *serata* held at the Politeama Garibaldi in Treviso on June 2, 1911, and reproduced in the Milanese *Uno, due, tre* on June 17, 1911. This *vignetta* shows three futurist paintings: Russolo's *Dinamismo musicale*, an early version of Boccioni's *La risata* (before it was repainted after having been disfigured by an anonymous viewer), and Carrà's *Nuotatrici*. Although Boccioni's vignette offers only a caricature of Russolo's painting, it is nonetheless possible to distinguish in it Russolo's central figure of the many-armed pianist (fig. 17). In place of the masks that appear in the final version of *La musica*, here the pianist's head is surrounded by a multitude of insects, which are meant to represent materializations of a spiritual energy that, in the form of a wave, is gushing vigorously from the pianist's open head.[4]

WHAT EXPERIENCE?

In a letter to Pratella of January 20, 1913, Marinetti introduced Russolo as a "formidable pianist" and proposed that he be asked to perform a piece of Pratella's synesthetically titled *Poema dei colori* at a futurist soiree being planned at the Teatro Costanzi.[5] Marinetti's hyperboles asides, Russolo was likely a competent keyboard player; possibly Russolo painted himself as the pianist in *La musica*.[6] However, since the central character in that painting lacks the distinctive features that characterize Russolo's many self-portraits (particularly the spirited eyes and pointy Mephistophelian goatee), this remains debatable.

The final version of *La musica* shows a pianist performing in a state of rapturous enthusiasm, as it can be understood in its etymological connotation of *possession*. The features of the pianist's face, moved by excitement, can barely be distinguished. The hands are represented in a mad, virtuosic dash along an infinite keyboard.

Like other canvases by Russolo, the painting has an almost hypnotic character, evoked in this case by the series of concentric circles that gradually shade from palest to darkest blue and radiate from a point behind the pianist, who remains the painting's center of gravity.[7] Beyond the concentric circles, two other elements frame the figure and underline its central position. A wave of blue rises from the instrument to spread into the air; and, like the skulls of the *Autoritratto con teschi*, a great number of red-, yellow-, and green-colored masks converge at great speed around the pianist, leaving luminous blurs of color behind them.

In portraying the movement of the hands, arms, and face, and above all the blurs produced by the apparent motion of the masks, Russolo used the technique of optical frame-based breakdown of movement, similar to that which Balla adopted in his paintings of the following year, and which can also be found, though produced with different means, in the photodynamic compositions of Anton Giulio Bragaglia. With Boccioni's *Città che sale* (1910–11), Carrà's *Le nuotatrici* (1910–12), and *Funerali dell'anarchico Galli* (1911), Russolo's *La musica* is one of the first futurist paintings in which the illusion of matter in movement is shown through blurs of residual images.[8]

For these reasons, I believe that *La musica* was intended not merely as a self-portrait but as a documentation of a direct experience. But what experience?

A SUMMARY OF CRITICAL JUDGMENT

Interpretations of *La musica* tend to follow similar paths. Zanovello cited the first public reviews of the painting, which indicate that the work generated substantial interest in the artistic community. Filippo Quaglia wrote in the *Avanti!* issue of June 11, 1911: "With the painting *La musica*, Russolo achieved clamorous success; he knew how to represent the keys, the sounds, the chords, the melodic line that writhes over and through all the keys. But these words of mine cannot give an idea of the painting; it is necessary to see it to take possession of the vision of art."[9]

Other evidence from the time comes from Attilio Teglio in *Il Giornale* (Bergamo) of July 4, 1911:

> A spectral musician, to whom the artist gave the semblance of Beethoven, is seated at the piano; his hands multiply and draw music from the keyboard, guided by inspiration. In the air winds a long flexible blue ribbon: it is the wave of melody that develops and widens on high its spirals to the infinite. A nimbus of concentric circles denotes the vibrations of the sonic wave. The notes, the sounds, the chords are rendered by masks with long colored blurs and each has a special face of its own. They sing in loud and soft voices, laugh and smile, weep and moan, sometimes shout, each bringing its contribution to that complex of feelings from which will result *a symphonic whole*. This canvas rich with bright, efficacious, suggestive colors, is accessible to anyone occupied with music even if he is not *initiated* in futurism.[10]

The following review was essentially a paraphrase of Russolo's critical note on the painting, which similarly analyzed the work within a time and space grid:

> With this painting the author wanted to make a kind of pictorial translation of the melodic, polyphonic, coloristic impressions that constitute the complex of musical emotion. On a blue sky progressively shaded several times, so as to render the spatial widening of the sonic wave, a *ghostly* musician, agitated by the frenzy of inspiration, draws from a vast keyboard a *witches' swarm* of sounds, rhythms, and chords: the development of the melodic line through time is translated pictorially in that

deep blue band that winds and spreads through space, dominating and enveloping the whole painting.

Like unexpected meteors that mark the blur of their route in the blue space, numerous serene, cheerful, or grotesque masks group, intertwine, and overlap to form harmonic or complementary chords of bright colorations, thus translating the indefinite feelings belonging to music into defined human expressions.

These masks variously grouped form around them chords of pictorial colorations, reflections and resonances of chords, and timbres and musical colorations.[11]

One reaction came from no less a personage than Giacomo Puccini, who admired the painting in 1919 at the ex–Caffè Cova exhibit and expressed admiration for Russolo's mastery in "translating in so efficacious a way sounds and timbres into lines and colors."[12]

DECONSTRUCTING *LA MUSICA*

Sensation is the material garment of the spirit and now it appears to our clairvoyant eyes. And with this the artist feels himself in everything. Creating he does not look, does not observe, does not measure; he feels, and the sensations that envelop him dictate to him the lines and colors that will arouse the emotions that caused him to act.
—Umberto Boccioni, *La pittura futurista: Conferenza tenuta a Roma nel 1911*

The critics cited above considered Russolo's large oil painting to be a successful attempt at portraying music with visual means. Yet the constituent elements of the painting can be interpreted at a deep level: the concentric circles symbolize the expansion of the sonic wave in space; the deep blue band shows the development of the melodic line in time; and the masks represent the various states of mind that music can engender. However, this level of analysis is unsatisfactory. Something in the painting—perhaps the type of images reproduced in it, perhaps their restless motion, perhaps the general atmosphere evoked by the painting, both monstrous and enchanting—indicates that this interpretation is too reductive.

On the basis of critical and interpretive readings, I believe that the painting relates to theosophy—not simply in general, synesthetic terms but *specifically* to theosophical principles in the volume *Thought-forms* that I have already observed reflected in other works of Russolo, beginning with the etching and aquatint *Maschere* of 1908.

Calvesi has noted that the visual representation of sound waves in *La musica*, which can already be distinguished in the sketch of the painting, recalls expressive techniques adopted by Munch in *The Scream* (1885) and by

Jan Sluijters in *Bal tabarin* (1907).[13] The concentric circles reminded Calvesi of Romani's work, and he commented on the mysticism of the wheel as a planet-star-sun, all symbols of pantheistic, universal energy.[14] Of great interest, if perhaps a little rash, is Martin's idea that the many-armed pianist represents "Siva Nataraja, the creator and lord of the cosmic dance in the Hindu pantheon."[15]

Long before Calvesi, Carrà maintained that Russolo in *La musica* evoked "the mediumistic masks of the spirits of the great composers." This interpretation was later echoed by Lista, who wrote that the masks represent "the spirits of the great composers of the past that are embodied through their 'mediumistic masks.'"[16]

Russolo's interpretation of his painting shows similarities with the theories that Ginna and Corra were working out in those years under the openly acknowledged influence of theosophy. Further research is needed to map and date the relationships Russolo had with the Corradinis, but for the purpose of the present analysis it is useful to compare Russolo's interpretation with the ideas that the two brothers presented in their *Arte dell'avvenire* of 1910.

Ginna and Corra's goal in this pamphlet was to create a dialogue between painting and music, and even to adopt a musical lexicon to describe elements of their pictorial language (chord, motif). Russolo's *La musica* seems to want to actualize these goals. That Ginna's and Corra's position is indebted to the theories of Besant and Leadbeater is evident from their expressed desire to translate a "system of passions [. . .] into a system of images" and in their aspiration to base their aesthetic on synesthetic laws that would allow them to "re-tie" the arts, as called for in Mazzini's epigraph to the first edition of their pamphlet.[17]

Russolo's fascination with and adoption of these systems is clear. However, if Buzzi is correct in claiming that *La musica* had a long gestation, then Ginna's and Corra's influence on this work suddenly seems less likely. Granted, the principles of *Arte dell'avvenire* had been put into practice for the first time in Ginna's *Accordo cromatico* of 1909, which suggests that the counts Ginanni Corradini had initiated their esoteric readings by that year. But if Ginna and Corra, living in the isolation of the countryside of Ravenna, could furnish themselves "with spiritualist and occultist books" (see chapter 2), it is even more likely that Russolo, living in one of the most culturally dynamic cities in Italy, had access to those same esoteric texts, and probably as early as 1908. That would explain the provenance of the materializations in *Maschere*.[18]

I am convinced, therefore, that the brothers Corradini and Russolo proceeded on parallel courses in their studies and could not have influenced one another until after 1910, the year when Marinetti transmitted the ideas of the Corradinis to Boccioni, Carrà, and Russolo (and vice versa). Moreover, that same year Ginna sent the first edition of *Arte dell'avvenire* to the Milanese futurists.[19] By that time, however, Russolo was already involved with works like the *Autoritratto (con doppio eterico)*.

Regardless of primacy, *La musica* recalls theosophical doctrines with such clarity as to make it unthinkable that Russolo could have painted the work without knowing about theosophy. The ideas of Besant and Leadbeater emerge forcefully from the canvas. Indeed, the painting is structured according to criteria presented in *Thought-forms*, in particular the section of the book that describes the forms produced by music.[20]

Besant and Leadbeater claimed that every time a composer writes music, his states of mind produce luminous projections in the aura around him; they named these projections thought-forms. In the activity of interpretation, the player also expresses his own states of mind, which produce other thought-forms. Moreover, the music produces sound-forms, also referred to as "forms built by music" that, while similar to them, are not technically thought-forms and therefore not projected onto the aura as thought-forms are; instead they are projected onto the sky above the performance venue.[21] Thought-forms are, finally, produced by the audience as a spontaneous reaction to both the music and the forms. To complicate matters yet further, the thought-forms of the musician and audience and the sound-forms produced by the music itself can occur simultaneously, even if the thought-forms do not have the power to interfere with the much more voluminous sound-forms.

Besant and Leadbeater also claimed that, just as thought-forms correspond to thoughts, all features of each sound-form correspond to the musical element that generated that form. For every musical characteristic (harmony, melody, rhythmical articulation, form, timbre, etc.) there exist a corresponding form and color that render that characteristic with extraordinary precision.

The dimensions of the sound-form produced and its permanence in the air vary according to the music, dynamics, timbre, quality of musical execution, and other parameters. The greater the "spiritual" weight of the sound-form, the sharper, brighter, and more voluminous the images. Moreover, the sound-forms radiate vibrations in every direction for the entire duration of their existence (often more than two hours). The contact between these vibrations and the aura of the particular individual they reach will condition that indi-

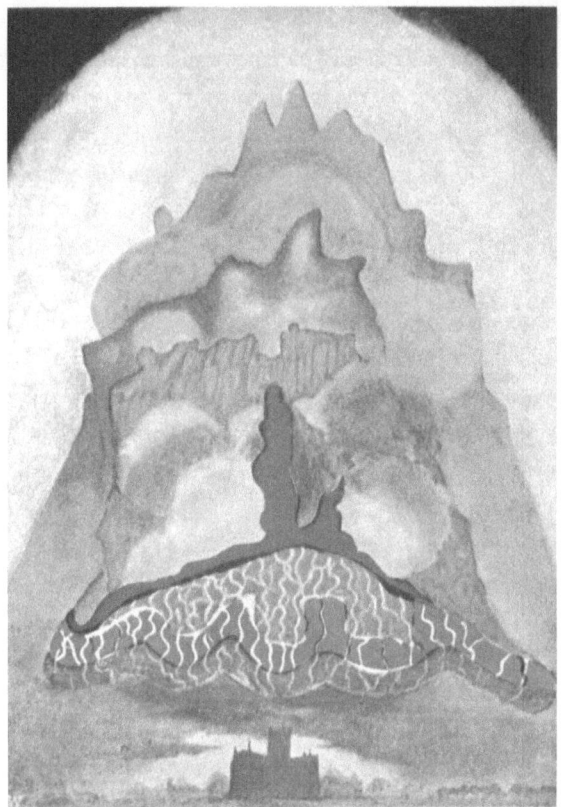

FIGURE 18. Annie Besant and Charles W. Leadbeater, plate W, "Wagner: Overture to *Meistersingers* [sic]" from *Thought-forms* (1901). Reproduced by permission of The Theosophical Publishing House, Adyar, Chennai 600 020. India. © The Theosophical Publishing House. www.ts-adyar.org & www.adyarbooks.com.

vidual's mood. In this way, the musician can influence hundreds of listeners without having a relationship with them on the physical plane.

Thought-forms presents earlier artworks that are conceptually similar to *La musica* in three important plates titled *Mendelssohn, Gounod*, and *Wagner* (fig. 18). In these artworks, the music of the three composers, executed in the same church on the same organ, generates three different sound-forms that project themselves onto the sky above.[22] The plates show three detailed examples of sound-forms that can be observed by clairvoyant subjects "who have eyes to see."[23]

Leadbeater expanded the sound-forms section of *Thought-forms* in an essay dedicated entirely to the subject, which became a chapter in his 1913 volume *The Hidden Side of Things*. Even more than on the book *Thought-forms*, Russolo drew heavily on the expanded essay, not only for a series of key concepts but also for a rhetorical structure that he subsequently applied to the formulation of his art of noises. Leadbetter's essay opens with a "scientifically" argued explanation of sound-forms as forms obtained by the higher harmonics of sound-producing light waves: "There are many people who realise that sound always generates colour—that every note which is played or sung has overtones which produce the effect of the light when seen by an eye even slightly clairvoyant."[24]

La musica represents, to quote Leadbeater, "the hidden side of the performance of a piece of music."[25] If one were to consider the opinions of Carrà (and Lista), according to whom Russolo's masks are mediumistic—and therefore ideoplastic—materializations, and overlap those opinions with the theosophical references on which the painting is evidently based, a more complex reading of *La musica* emerges.

On a first hermeneutic level, the painting represents the act of producing music, complete with the implicit motoric skills and physical effort of execution. According to current interpretations, the concentric circles symbolize the spread of the sonic wave, the blue band the development of the melodic line, and the masks the various states of mind that the music evokes. There is more here, though, than meets the eye: the painting also illustrates a process in which the performer is the medium between spirits and the mechanical means that produced the physical sound—the keyboard. In this process, the spirits that fluctuate on the astral plane dictate the production and improvisation of music to the mechanical means of music production by way of the performer, who is in a state of trance. Through the medium, the psychic energies of the conjured spirits ideoplastically mold thought-forms in the shape of masks and faces, re-creating various and also complementary states of mind: a complete range of emotions, and a universe of spiritualistic expressions, to represent which Russolo in *La musica* references Romani's aesthetics.[26]

La musica celebrates the performance of music as a form of channeling in which the synchronic, discordant choral sum of complementary spiritualistic thought-forms is fused in musical, enharmonic unity by the performer-medium, who reconciles the opposites by means of their common origin (that is, by their congenital complementarism), as the thought-forms are all evoked or generated by the mind of the performer.²⁷ Thus music as acoustic phenomenon, as wave, once finally spiritualized, is represented by the sound-form of the sinuous blue band.²⁸

Masks

The 1911 ink-on-paper version of *La musica* does not contain the masks of the 1912 final version apart from their blurs; the first oil version, at least as far as one can tell from Boccioni's vignette, shows hints of materializations but not the blurs. In the 1912 final version, masks converge and condense at great speed, producing luminous blurs of residual images. The masks are not sound-forms but thought-forms generated by the spirits through the pianist, who is both interpreter and medium. The masks, which show different and even conflicting expressions, must be understood as thought-forms that visualize or materialize the various states of mind induced in a performer-medium by the spirits that he has evoked. The masks are therefore the ideoplastic, ectoplasmic product of the action of the spirits conjured up by the medium, perhaps even the spirits of the great composers of the past embodied through their "mediumistic masks."²⁹ They are, in effect, ideoplastic materializations, or, better yet, representations thereof.

The above process is also theosophical. In *Thought-forms*, Leadbeater explained that the spirits that reside in the astral plane have the energy to change the course of thought-forms that already exist, and to make them move.³⁰ Through the possessed medium, conjured spirits can not only create colors and abstract images but also materialize, animate, and control these images.

Concentric Circles

In this interpretation, the concentric circles of light of decreasing luminosity, which depict the sonic wave's outward radiations, also represent the aura (aureole) surrounding the performer-medium, and they become stronger the closer that aura is to his body. The aura, easily distinguishable from the bands of the sonic wave, was already present in the 1911 ink-on-paper version of *La musica*. Such a portrayal of magic by means of concentric circles and irradiations thereafter became a leitmotif in Russolo, as can be seen in *Notturno + scintille di rivolta* (1910–11), *Linee-forza della folgore* and *Compenetrazione di case + luce + cielo* (1912), and *Solidità della nebbia* (1912–13).

In his unpublished manuscript "Avviamento alla magia (Giuliano Kremerz [sic])," Russolo described the process of irradiation as a "crown of light

[...] to the summit of the head [...] that increasingly irradiates in circles [...] as sound waves [... through] chains of figures."[31] The spiritualization of the figure, notable in Russolo's other paintings as well and often represented by a visible aura surrounding the bodies, is noteworthy. According to theosophical texts, the aura is composed of "spiritual bodies," and among the aura's various functions is that of acting as a screen on which thought-forms, produced by the various states of mind, can be projected. This also seems to be the function of the concentric circles in *La musica*.

The energies of the spirits that induce a state of trance in the performer-medium through him produce states of mind expressed in corresponding colors and forms: masks as thought-forms.[32] Interestingly, the masks have the same dimensions as the face of the interpreter-medium. He no longer has a single expression; now his expressions are as numerous as those generated by the spirits guiding him.

WHICH MUSIC?

The "flexible blue ribbon," the undulating band, is the only image in the painting that can be considered a sound-form; it follows the principles illustrated in the sound plates included in *Thought-forms*.[33] Thus *La musica* perfectly exemplifies futurism's interest in synesthesia as it connects with the theory of correspondence between different senses derived from the study of vibrations—vibrations either of waves in the ether, of sound waves, or of different types of electromagnetic waves (radio, light, X-ray). In this sense Russolo's work can be placed alongside the investigation of waves that Romani pursued in his *La campana* and *La goccia che cade nell'acqua*.

Russolo studied the theory of waves attentively, perhaps more so than the other futurists, and he was with all certainty convinced of the spiritual correspondence between sound and electromagnetic waves. This explains the evolution of Russolo's research, from the study of light and of X-rays, which he conducted in his laboratory on via Stoppani, to his studies on acoustics. The theory of waves links Russolo's interests in light, astronomy, occult arts, and acoustics.

Russolo also devoted time to studying acoustics in depth and focused on how this science connects with the visual arts. Buzzi has maintained that Russolo's work was always "nourished from essential Pythagorean sources."[34] In *L'arte dei rumori*, Russolo does in fact cite Pythagoras and Zarlino, the experiments of Helmholtz, and Chladni's often quoted research on *Klang-*

figuren, the geometrical figures produced on sand by means of bowing on the metal plates that support the sand.[35] According to Lista, Russolo may have derived the idea of studying noises from Helmholtz, whom he cited in his 1913 manifesto, and whose ideas he probably read in popularizing publications.[36] Chladni's experiment is cited in *Thought-forms* and mentioned in the first paragraph of the chapter on sound in Leadbeater's *The Hidden Side of Things*.[37] Russolo, who most likely knew Leonardo da Vinci's writings on acoustics, would probably also have known the precedent for Chladni's experiment: a study by Leonardo on the regular figures produced in dust by the shockwave generated by a hammer striking a dust-covered table.[38]

In *La musica*, sound is visually represented by a blue wave that expands in almost spiral-like fashion. Both the spiral and the undulating line were received positively by the futurists, because, as Carrà indicated in his manifesto "La pittura dei suoni, rumori e odori," these shapes suggest dynamism. Russolo christened all the works he composed in 1913–14 for concerts of intonarumori *spirali di rumori* (spirals of noises).[39] In combining the visual (spiral) and the auditory (noises), this expression, which is, as we shall soon see, spiritually charged, evokes a synesthetic aspect that points directly to *La musica*. Buzzi was referring to the synesthesia in *La musica* when he wrote of the "thin, electric Russolo living in our plane, who painted blue concentric atmospheres of music using elusive flashes of the paintbrush."[40] The flexible, spiral-like continuity of the undulating band reproduces the essence of futurist *enarmonia:* a slide among the infinite frequencies contained between two different pitches. Wrapping the concept in spiritual robes, Russolo defined it in *The Art of Noises* as "dynamic continuity" *(continuità dinamica)*.[41]

If the undulating band is a transcription of a sound-form, a question remains: what kind of music is Russolo portraying? Presumably the discordant choral sum of the various spiritualistic states of mind produces a variety of complementary expressions in the masks. The music in *La musica* is therefore first a deafening *rumorista* chaos, and second a spiral of noises *(spirale di rumori)* that synthesizes this chaos into the sinuous blue band of the enharmonic (i.e., microtonal) continuity. It is thus already an *art of noises*, a subjective *synthesis* of all the complementary acoustic vibrations of the universe superimposed according to the futurist aesthetic of simultaneity and dynamism. Russolo's ambition here was not simply to imitate or represent nature but to *create*, that is provide the spiritual conditions and the spiritual fuel for the creation of a new reality through Artifice. Russolo's musical research had begun.

CHAPTER 5

Russolo and Synesthesia

La nostra sensibilità moltiplicata, dopo essersi conquistata degli occhi futuristi avrà finalmente delle orecchie futuriste.
—Luigi Russolo, "L'arte dei rumori: Manifesto futurista" (1913)

An in-depth analysis of *La musica* is essential to understanding Russolo's research in the transition years immediately preceding his manifesto of March 11, 1913, "L'arte dei rumori: Manifesto futurista," and fully to contextualize the art of noises that the manifesto inaugurated. Read in this context, the painting can be seen to set out a clear and well-conceived poetics of music, and to exhibit the profound spiritual notions that in the brief span of a year had brought Russolo to sound.

The continuity of Russolo's theoretical journey cannot be sufficiently emphasized: his embarking upon full-time musical investigations should not be read as a sudden change in direction. In fact, the music that Russolo imagined and produced in 1913 was not radically different from the music he had painted in the preceding years.

But how did his transition to sound take place? To formulate a convincing hypothesis on the nature of Russolo's activity circa 1912–13, it is useful to sketch his research profile, substantiating it with all the available evidence.

INGENIOUS INGENUOUSNESS

The mantra of Russolo's ingenious ingenuousness, so frequently repeated in the available biographical sketches written about him, implies that his intellectual journey suffered from a lack of technique and, consequently, a lack of continuity, organicness, and deliberation. It suggests that, as engraver and painter, as well as in the field of music, Russolo was a dilettante.

Unlike Balla or Carrà, he was self-taught. And although, as Maffina has emphasized, Russolo's early works were prints (principally etchings), which require considerable technical ability, many have said that Russolo was technically the least accomplished of the five signatories of the technical manifesto of futurist painting.[1]

The cliché of Russolo's ingenuousness is rooted in a legitimate critical opinion, according to which his technical weakness (amply compensated for, it is occasionally recognized, by his theoretical strength) both explains his lack of critical success and, at the same time, constituted one of the primary reasons for his aesthetic originality. As Martin has written, "Russolo's technical innocence may have given him the freedom of a most original interpretation of the revolutionary precepts of the technical manifesto, influencing his colleagues and setting a precedent for the surrealists."[2]

However, this putative ingenuousness is thought to have allowed him to abandon painting, change direction, and undertake full-time musical activity. How could this have happened by chance? Maffina, in describing the sequence of Russolo's diverse interests in painting, music, and the occult arts, judged that among them "no link can be found."[3] This critical model may be partly defensible, but the portrait of Russolo as an ingenuous dilettante, leaping randomly from one discipline to another, fails to convince because it ignores the coherence of his intellectual development.

Russolo never earned a conservatory diploma. It must have annoyed the official musician of the futurist movement, Balilla Pratella, when Russolo invaded his own field, notwithstanding that Pratella, in his first manifesto, had railed against the institutional obsolescence of the *regii conservatori di musica*. Pratella never made his uneasiness explicit, and relations between Pratella and Russolo always appeared to be harmonious. But to avert problems Marinetti decided to carve a separate space for Russolo's art of noises— which in any case had no connections with Pratella's futurist music— within the futurist movement.

Russolo was obviously wary of the fiery Pratella, for at the end of his manifesto he wrote what sounds like a disclaimer: "I am not a musician by profession, and therefore I have neither acoustical predilections, nor works to defend. [. . .] Thus, more temerarious than a professional musician could be, not worried about my *apparent* incompetence, and convinced that audacity has all rights and all possibilities, I was able to intuit the great renewal of music through the Art of Noises."[4]

Critics often cite this passage to confirm the idea of Russolo's ingenuousness. But I would suggest that he is actually boldly claiming a space for himself: he raises the issue of incompetence, but note his use of the adjective *apparent*. Russolo had long been interested in music, and through his synesthetic investigations he had probably already devoted intense hours of study to the theory of vibrations, acoustic science, and the theosophical theories about the forms produced by music, all of which is evidenced by *La musica*.

Russolo was a futurist who could easily be seen as an outsider within the movement. His eclectic development, and his omnivorous curiosity, kept him from crystallizing his interests into a single means of expression, and this in turn allowed him to explore outside of the conventions of any one discipline. He enjoyed being able to cross, almost unobserved, the fences separating the arts, and he thus succeeded better than the other futurists in applying those ideals of synesthesia that the movement in theory continually promoted.

Russolo was aware of his particular circumstances, and he knew how to exploit them to promote his artistic growth. Because he was considered the perfect example of the dilettante he never was, his work did not receive the attention it merited during his lifetime. Russolo's study of the occult arts resulted in a multiplicity of interests, yet that multiplicity was never the byproduct of charlatanism nor the consequence of ingenuousness.

RUSSOLO'S SYNESTHETIC IDEA

Russolo's investigations were driven by the synesthetic ideas of the symbolists and scapigliati: thus they were framed by occultist theories. The perception of all the arts as secretly linked by the theory of vibrations allowed Russolo to move freely between them, without threatening the cardinal ideas of his poetics and consequently having to renounce them.

Paolo Buzzi acutely defined the different phases that constitute Russolo's course of inquiry within a sort of "vibrational poetics." On the subject of the theoretical and philosophical phase of Russolo's late years, Buzzi wrote: "Indeed, Russolo, while engaged in painting and subsequently music, was already directed toward poetry. And poetry was everything during the last years of his life. A poetry, I would say, that was nourished by the Pythagorean and Aristotelian essentials; the two Hellenic thinkers were in fact well aware of the phenomenon of sound vibrations."[5]

Russolo's intellectual life, in the course of which he moved easily among different sensory fields, was a realization of the synesthetic credo expressed by the theory of vibrations, which he must have learned from theosophical texts. Having demonstrated his interest in synesthesia in a number of his pictorial works, he undertook his musical investigation as if it were a further stage of spiritual growth—a continuation of his visual research in another field—and he applied to music the same aesthetic principles, derived predominantly from the readings of occultist texts that had earlier driven his visual activity.

The combination of interests that constituted Russolo's metaphysical views returns at every creative moment of his life, as well as occasionally surfacing in his writings. Russolo, in harmony with the principles of theosophy, derived his metaphysical ideas from the research methods of experimental science, and he adopted laboratory tests and proofs in his research.[6]

I have addressed the apparent contradiction between science and the occult in preceding chapters. Like other intellectuals (many of Symbolist background) who at the beginning of the twentieth century felt that their culture needed radical renewal, Russolo expressed himself extremely polemically, attacking positivism and materialism in all of their forms. These two philosophies were, he felt, responsible for every sort of societal evil—making society increasingly bourgeois, "museumified," and mummified—and he saw in theosophical teaching the antidote to these evils.

Russolo dedicated himself with passion and the rigor of a scientist to the investigations in the physics of light, sound, waves, acoustics, magnetism, spiritualism, and metaphysics. His investigations, which he often referred to in his personal documents and which were frequently mentioned in the accounts of others, were in full agreement with theosophical orthodoxy, according to which the only possible model of science is of a science in contact with the spiritual world. Whether this means that Russolo was attracted by metaphysical rationality, or scientific irrationality, is merely a semantic exercise. The fact remains that he never wanted to compromise his work with anything he thought was shallow or materialistic.

Russolo often engaged in a polemic against materialism, and the spirituality of his approach to research was so crucial to his entire career as to confer upon it a strong poetic unity. In fact, Russolo aspired to an art that would re-create the spiritual side of the world instead of merely imitating it impressionistically. He was after an art that would reflect reality by re-creating its spirit, its essence; an art that would dare to dig into the heart of things and reach their deepest spiritual level.

ANECDOTES

A number of primary sources document superficial, perhaps lesser, aspects of Russolo's personality. Though these aspects may be considered marginal, they are important for me, and not only because of the scarcity of sources. These marginal aspects are valuable for sketching a character endowed with a strong spiritual conception and so immersed in occult and synesthetic practices that typical occultist external traits come to the surface.

Russolo took an eclectic and encyclopedic-comparativist approach to research, which was pedantic and almost obsessive in its intellectual breadth. In a propagandistic article published in installments in the *Gazzetta dello sport* and dealing with the deeds of the futurists at the front during World War I, Marinetti reported that, while such futurist soldiers as Boccioni, Piatti, and himself were busy preparing dinners, lighting fires, or taking turns drawing water, Russolo was "studying the noises of the war and drawing from them improvements for his intonarumori."[7]

In his book *Le serate futuriste*, the futurist poet Francesco Cangiullo portrayed Russolo as a pedant, absorbed in his studies to the point of refusing romantic opportunities: "Russolo had no romantic yearnings: he is a hero, and he pays no attention except exclusively to the intonarumori."[8]

Russolo's pedantic temperament did not change over the years; in *Al di là della materia*, he boasted of having seen all the Titians in the collections of all the most important European galleries.[9] Zanovello's biography offers a further example of his tendency toward pursuing subjects obsessively. After an evening with friends who at dinner talked about dairy, a subject of which Russolo knew nothing, he went out the next morning and bought two Hoepli manuals on cheese making.[10] The "encyclopedicity" of this approach is no different from that practiced by other occultist figures within futurism (Ginna is the best example), but it also mirrors the encyclopedicity of theosophical texts.

Zanovello introduces a second, anecdotal manifestation of Russolo's occult persuasions by relating that he was on several occasions described as a "magician." In one of these instances, she writes, "Russolo's studio came to be defined by Marinetti and his companions as *the house of the Magician*; and that was no hyperbole."[11] Elsewhere Marinetti described Russolo as a "skeletal sorcerer."[12]

A third manifestation of Russolo's occultist tendencies is his peculiar interest in improvising music, which for Russolo, at least according to how he chose to represent it in *La musica*, was mediumistic music. By all accounts,

Russolo was an inspired improviser. On one occasion he reported to his wife that the audience had responded enthusiastically to his successful improvisation on the noise harmonium in a concert in Paris at the École des Autes Études Sociales of the Sorbonne on June 30, 1927.[13]

RUSSOLO THE *INATTUALE*

In a volume published posthumously under the title *La grande Milano tradizionale e futurista*, Marinetti dedicated a brief passage to describing the construction of Russolo's intonarumori. Maffina considered this piece of evidence to be of little interest, criticizing its "generality of references" and noting that its lyricism was "of little use in documentarily rendering the terms of discussion of real events." Yet once the reader knows how to separate style—certainly not devoid of emphases—from content, the following passage is revealing:[14]

> I mean by poetry also the temerarious leap of the investigating spirit and it is poetic my friendship with Luigi Russolo, with his thin *inattuale* face and his ingenuous kindness outside time space
>
> Ecstatic and vibrating afternoons in his laboratory where I assist in the construction of the intonarumori and the noise harmonium
>
> Certainly attentive to our dormer window of mechanical chemistry is the sun, setting while the tormented scientist Russolo bends his head over the immeasurable vacuum tube in the night and here are stars forerunners of electric discharges
>
> In the flooding fluorescence we free ourselves again and outside of ourselves we can contemplate exposed plates and calculate the irradiations
>
> In descending—to help the sun—the twisting slimy dark stairs, Russolo shouts with his red goatee
>
> —Glory to your name Roentgen and glory to the futurist rumorismo[15]

This passage is rich in elements that deserve comment. First, the term *inattuale* is the Italian word traditionally used to translate Nietzsche's *unzeitgemäße*; indeed, it was possibly coined specifically to translate that German word.[16] The term, which can be roughly rendered in English as *asynchronous*, refers to the subversive position that Nietzsche believed a modern intellectual, a superman, should always occupy within the society of his time, so as to constantly to push the envelope. This asynchronicity is a position of outsiderness that the intellectual carries as a cross, but also as a badge of honor. The *inattualità* of Russolo, an intellectual and a scientist "outside time space," rendered him in Marinetti's eyes the perfect prototype of the futurist artist. Marinetti surely saw Nietzsche's *inattualità* as the measure of genius.

The man who is not "in phase" with the rest of society (because he has arrived either too soon or too late in the course of history) is destined as a consequence of his temporal impertinence to break with society itself. But the *inattuale* intellectual and artist must take up this challenge; he must accept this perpetually subversive function if he wants to force the clock hands of history and awaken the slumbering bourgeoisie from its sleep of mediocrity.

In this Nietzschean view, the function of art is to elevate man to a level of eternity (and therefore of atemporality), suggest an alternative route to historicism's absurd pretenses of rationality and truth, and to encourage him to promote his radical views with thoughtless lightheartedness.

For the Hegelian idea of history as a sequence of events developing rationally in a temporal vector (which implies inexorable progress from one epoch to the next), Nietzsche substituted a model of history made up of cycles (including that of eternal return); the *inattuale* man (or artist) is not necessarily the standard-bearer of the "new." He is the intellectual who imposes positions—either after or ahead of his time—that oppose the dominant morality and the too often invoked historical necessity. Working against the tide, he cares nothing for fashions, conventions, and other social practices of his time.

In his passage about Russolo's intonarumori, Marinetti seems to understand and appreciate Russolo's contradictory position: he sees him as an outsider who has committed himself body and soul to the new, but who at the same time and with pedantic passion studies acoustic sciences of the past and the occult tradition—a Janus-like figure among the futurists, one face looking to the future, the other to the past.

Marinetti's reference to Nietzsche and his *Unzeitgemäße Betrachtungen* (usually translated into English as *Untimely Meditations* but meaning, literally, asynchronous observations) is inscribed within an aesthetic of the irrational that futurism had made its own; behind this exaltation of the irrational can be read interest in the occult and a critical position against materialism.[17] Along with active nihilism, the critique of rationalism and idealism offers yet another tool to understanding the futurists' attraction to Nietzschean thought (or interpretations thereof), which is evident not only in their themes but also in the style they adopted—consider, for example, the messianic-allegorical-Zarathustrian tone of such early Marinetti manifestos as "Uccidiamo il chiaro di luna."

In *Unzeitgemäße Betrachtungen*, Nietzsche renewed his attack on Hegel and the philosophy of the Hegelian right. By critiquing the philosophy of David Strauss in the first of the "Asynchronous Observations," Nietzsche is in fact criticizing Prussian military supremacy over France, which Strauss justified as historical, real, and therefore rational. In the second Observation, titled "On the Utility and Liability of History for Life," Nietzsche declared that Hegel's philosophy is responsible for the hyperrationalization of philosophical thought, and in particular for promoting the idea of history as a rational and linear development.

Nietzsche attacked the cult of the past to expose the bourgeoisification of contemporary German culture, which he considers was unaware of the paralysis generated by this cult. Nietzsche is really railing not against the past but against what the futurists will subsequently define as "past-idolatry"—blind faith in the linear development of history as intrinsically rational: the only possible historiographical model. In deluding himself that he is a child of the past and the logical consequence of history, modern man deprives himself of the ability to choose and dare. Thus man relieves himself from responsibility and convinces himself that history justifies and legitimizes his actions. Nietzsche's concern and criticism are at the foundation of Marinetti's early manifestos, written more than thirty years later. By calling Russolo *inattuale*, Marinetti is acknowledging his sources.

X-RAYS AND THE OSCILLOSCOPE

The continuation of Marinetti's text yields further meaning:

> Ecstatic and vibrating afternoons in his laboratory where I assist in the construction of the intonarumori and of the noise harmonium
>
> Certainly attentive to our dormer window of mechanical chemistry is the sun, setting while the tormented scientist Russolo bends his head over the immeasurable vacuum tube in the night and here are stars forerunners of electric discharges
>
> In the flooding fluorescence we free ourselves again and outside of ourselves we can contemplate exposed plates and calculate the irradiations
>
> In descending—to help the sun—the twisting slimy dark stairs Russolo shouts with his red goatee
>
> —Glory to your name Roentgen and glory to the futurist rumorismo

Notwithstanding Marinetti's writing technique—or perhaps, on the contrary, because of its rhetorical tone, resembling that of a sacred book—careful perusal of this text allows the reader to deduce the nature of Russolo's investigations. I believe this passage to be a snapshot of Russolo's experiments of 1912–13, a time when he was engaged in the study of acoustics that eventually led to the construction of the intonarumori.[18]

If we abstract the keywords from their rhetorical context—a hermeneutic operation that is rash but not arbitrary—this is the result:

> vacuum tube / electric discharges / flooding fluorescence / exposed plates / irradiations / Roentgen

The elements thereby laid bare, and above all the reference to Röntgen, lead to the plausible interpretation that the Russolo experiments described by Marinetti involved X-rays.

What is needed to construct the X-ray machine that Röntgen had started developing in 1895 is: a power supply (note the textual reference to *electric discharges*), a Cathode Ray Tube or CRT *(vacuum tube),* and *plates* to be *exposed* to the X-rays *(irradiations);* these rays, if not contained by a thick lead plate, tend naturally to escape in all directions *(flooding fluorescence).*

A range of evidence confirms that Russolo was an ingenious mechanic and that he would have been able to construct such a machine. Russolo built musical instruments, and later in life, at his house at Cerro di Laveno, he succeeded in assembling a telescope using "two lenses, a cardboard tube specially prepared and hardened, and a couple of wood beams that formed the tripod."[19]

Russolo was also a passionate reader of popularized science. From a letter he wrote to his wife upon arriving in Tarragona, Spain, on February 24, 1932, we know that during his Paris years he subscribed to a magazine for astronomy enthusiasts called *Caelum,* which published articles of popular astronomy and amateur microscopic science.[20] Zanovello confirms that Russolo read various Hoepli manuals, publications that deal with such disparate topics as dairy art and spiritualism.[21]

Giacomo Balla cited Hoepli manuals in his notebooks, in the same place where he annotates "Roentgen rays and their applications *(Raggi Roentgen e loro applicazioni)."*[22] And sure enough, several among these popular scientific manuals were dedicated to X-rays and their applications.

Although academic treatments of this subject were previously available, Hoepli was the first Italian publisher to publish manuals on the X-rays.[23] One of the first titles was *Elettricità medica: Elettroterapia, raggi Rontgen [sic], radioterapia, fototerapia, ozono, elettrodiagnostica,* by Adolfo Dario Bocciardo, published in Milan by Ulrico Hoepli in 1904 as part of the popular series Manuali Hoepli. This was followed by Gian Alberto Blanc's *Radioattività del dott. G. A. Blanc con una prefazione del prof. A. Sella ed un'appendice di G. D'Ormea sulle azioni fisiche dei raggi Becquerel*, also published as a Manuale Hoepli in 1907, but this time as part of the "scientific series."

Two other books, also published in Milan and readily available to Russolo, may likewise have been a source: a hands-on approach to X-rays titled *Le correnti variabili e loro applicazioni: Auto-induzione, rocchetto di ruhmkorff, Raggi catodici, Raggi X, radiografia, telegrafia senza fili* by Carlo Laguna, published by the Società Editoriale Milanese in 1909 in the series La biblioteca pratica (The practical library), and Ignazio Schincaglia's *Radiografia e radioscopia: Storia dei raggi Rontgen [sic] e loro applicazioni piu importanti*, published by Vallardi in 1911; the last-named title may have served as a source for Balla.

There were additional sources of information on X-rays; according to Linda Henderson, more than fifty books and pamphlets and over a thousand articles were published on X-rays in 1896 alone, and many of these were published with a large, popular audience in mind.[24] These various publications made the details of Röntgen's experiment, along with full instructional drawings for building the machine, available to amateurs all over Europe. Because X-rays could be produced relatively simply—with only CTR and a power supply—the experiment rapidly went all around the world.

A close cousin to the X-ray machine, a device that utilized CRT technology to analyze the shape of sound waves, was the CRT oscilloscope. First invented by Karl Ferdinand Braun in 1897, when he was experimenting with the 1875 Crookes' tubes (ancestor to both the X-ray machine and the CTR oscilloscope), this device quite quickly became an indispensable tool for acousticians.

Russolo's references to the frequencies and shapes of different sound waves, suggests a familiarity with the CRT oscilloscope beyond that of second-hand information. In chapter 3 of *The Art of Noises*, "Principi fisici e possibilità pratiche," a comparison of the shape of various sound waves (that of a pitch pipe, a violin, and a metal plate) becomes the central argument for one of Russolo's most fundamental claims: that, from a physical standpoint, there is no difference between sound and noise.[25]

Since there is no specific point where sound and noise join, there can be no point where the former stops and the latter begins; rather, the shape (or frequency) of the sound wave merely becomes progressively more irregular. Because Russolo understood sound to be a continuum, he shared the notion that the difference between what is called sound and what is called noise is cultural.

As the basic components of the X-ray machine and the CRT oscilloscope are the same, and given the close ties between Russolo's visual and aural investigations, it is plausible that he may have built first Röntgen's X-ray machine and then Braun's oscilloscope. Scientific inquiry would not have been Russolo's only motivation. Marinetti's text appears to confirm that Russolo was theoretically and practically equipped to build the two machines, but Marinetti's writing style also implies that Russolo was artistically and spiritually motivated to do so.

FUTURIST GOOD VIBRATIONS: X-RAYS, LIGHT, SOUND, AND THE OCCULT

Between 1912 and 1913, Russolo decided to experiment with X-rays in his laboratory in via Stoppani, at first likely animated by his intention to apply the result of his X-ray study to painting. In those same years X-rays and their properties excited avant-garde artists (above all, Duchamp) and, as is evident from their technical manifesto of futurist painting of 1910, futurist painters as well.[26]

X-rays, which penetrate to the hearts of objects, revealed the same profound reality that futurists aimed to paint.[27] Although Russolo arrived at his X-ray investigations directly from his experience on such works as *La musica*, he was from the beginning guided by a general interest in the synesthetical interconnection among the perceptive senses that is implied by the theory of vibrations. These studies occupied Russolo on the many afternoons that Marinetti called "ecstatic and vibrating."

Confirmation of the link between his pictorial investigations and the X-ray experiments that led Russolo to explore sonic waves with the CRT oscilloscope is found in the following passage from the technical manifesto on futurist painting: "Who can still believe in the opacity of bodies, while our acuity and *multiplied sensitivity* makes us intuit the obscure manifestations of mediumistic phenomena? Why must one continue to create without taking account of our visual power that can give results analogous to those of X-rays?"[28] A similar declaration of intent appeared in Russolo's manifesto on the art of noises from 1913: "Our *multiplied sensitivity*, having conquered futurist eyes, will finally be endowed with futurist ears."[29] Russolo transferred the *multiplied sensitivity* that first allowed for the perception of the imperceptible ghostly vibrations—and had previously granted the spiritual amplification of the sense of sight—to the equally spiritual empowering of the sense of hearing, something that the CRT oscilloscope made visible and thus tangible.

Following the thread of the theosophical doctrine of vibrations, we can observe that Russolo's engagement with acoustics and vibrations of sound waves deepened once he encountered Röntgen's theories on the vibration of waves in the ether. By juxtaposing the name of Röntgen with the art of noises, Marinetti's last sentence, shouted by a possessed Russolo—"Glory to your name *Roentgen* and glory to the futurist *rumorismo*"—factually sanctioned the synesthetic interconnection of light waves, X-rays, and sound waves. These, according to what Russolo knew about physics, were manifestations of the same phenomenon, differentiated only by frequency and wavelength.

The study of X-rays was a natural point for science and occultism to converge.[30] Russolo's study, then, fit perfectly within the theosophical doctrine of vibrations. X-rays, as both a scientific and cultural phenomenon, pointed to the imperfection of human senses in the act of perceiving the world; thus X-rays served to confute the philosophical positions of materialism. Moreover, they served indirectly to validate the photography of ghosts and phenomena such as exteriorization of sensitivity and materialization of ectoplasms. A photographic plate could register ghostly manifestations and spiritual emanations from the human body because those were also composed of vibrations of different wavelengths, vibrations that leave incontrovertible traces.

These phenomena prompted scholars such as Crookes, Flammarion, Lombroso, and Zollner to adopt Röntgen's experiments for the analysis of mediumistic condensation.[31] In particular, as Celant wrote in his "Futurismo esoterico," X-rays served to "demonstrate how the action of the thought is often accompanied by certain molecular movements that act upon internal and external molecules," which in turn justified "the formation and visualization of ectoplasms."[32]

Russolo's interest in X-rays during the time he was working on the intonarumori was not the result of mere scientific curiosity but had, rather, deeper and occult motivations. The whole of his intonarumori adventure—from the time he first conceived it—must therefore be fully and radically reinterpreted in the light of his occult motivations.

CHAPTER 6

Russolo's Metaphysics

Futurism is concerned with the essence of reality, because all that exists is *essentially* composed of vibrations of different intensities in the ether. Like Boccioni and Carrà, Russolo was convinced that an artist's true objective was to penetrate bodies and discover this essence. Futurists believed that investigation, analysis, and comprehension of the real ought to be guided by an epistemology founded on a solid metaphysical basis that would allow them to look into the depths.

To those who have recontextualized it in these terms, art can no longer be mere imitation of the surface of the real but instead becomes (re)creation *ex novo* of the spirit of reality, achieved by infusing matter with the spirituality of the artist—or, better yet, with the creative, spiritualistic forces the artist can evoke. In Russolo's own words, the spirit of the artist has "the insatiable desire to raise matter up to its own level, to see it spiritualized in the work of art."[1]

Within that proposition lay the crux of the futurists' polemic against the impressionists, for it defined the fundamental difference between impressionist art and their own. Although they believed that impressionist painting deserved praise for having anticipated avenues of investigation (such as the treatment of light) that were later pursued by divisionists and thereupon by some of their own, impressionism, in their opinion, was based on the reproduction of sensory illusoriness and concerned with superficial levels of reality. Therefore it lacked spirituality.[2]

Similarly, Russolo never understood his the art of noises as a simple imitation of superficial sensation. In his 1913 manifesto of the art of noises, Russolo, to avoid misunderstanding, emphasized this point in boldface type: "Although the characteristic of noise is that of reminding us brutally of life, the **Art of Noises should not limit itself to an imitative reproduction.**"[3] In point 6 of his manifesto, Russolo writes that that art of noises cannot limit itself to a "succession of noises imitative of life" but must be based upon "a fantastic association of the different timbres."[4]

Russolo's deviation from impressionist imitation is captured by a French press release of September 1913: "Les quatre *réseaux des bruits* ne sont pas de simples reproductions impressionists de la vie qui nous entoure mais d'émouvantes syntheses bruitistes. Par une savante variation de tons, les bruites perdent en effet leur caractère épisodique accidentel et imitatif, pour devenir des elements abstraits d'art."[5]

Later, in his *L'arte dei rumori* of 1916, Russolo repeated this concept, asserting that his art of noises does not have "a simple-minded imitative [or] impressionistic aim, reminiscent [merely] of the noises of life."[6] Russolo confirmed the concept many years later, when he was defending his aesthetics from the charge of being no more than superficial reproduction of reality: "Mais le nome même, la superficialité de la critique et l'ignorance du public aidant, a crée un malentendu qui a fait croire que dans mes bruiteurs il y avaint une intention imitative et espressionniste des bruits de la nature et de la vie. Mon but a été différent. Dans une livre qui j'ai publié en 1916 j'ai dit très clairement que les timbre nouveaux des mes instruments sont seulement une matière abstraite devant servir au musicien."[7]

Pratella seemed to understand quite well the spiritual implications of Russolo's work and their distance from impressionism. He wrote: "As one very well sees, the intonarumori produce practically every sense of objective reality; they move from an objective reality, immediately distancing themselves from it, and come to constitute a new abstract reality—an expressive, abstract element of a state of mind."[8]

Futurists criticized impressionism for favoring the empirical at the expense of the spiritual, and this rejection overlapped with their rejection of materialism. Russolo, like other futurists, was violently opposed to materialism as a philosophical hypothesis and modus vivendi, so much so that this critical position gradually became the center of his interests. His substantial book *Al di là della materia: Alla ricerca del vero, Alla ricerca del bello, Alla ricerca del bene* (Beyond matter: In search of Truth, in search of Beauty, in search of Good) of 1938, legible even in its title as a treatise on spiritual education, includes a severe critique of materialism as the negative tendency, caused by a lack of spirituality, that dominates society.

Since the true scope of every action is the comprehension of the higher essential unity that resides beyond the material world, material and spiritual levels (the spiritual here intended being the state in which the essential unity of the world is manifest) exist on two parallel planes; their relations are strictly regulated by the theory of correspondences, which dictates their hierarchies and provides the initiated with the keys to the higher level. Russolo incorporated the theory of correspondences—one of the most important beliefs in the occultist tradition—in his personal blend of platonic inspiration filtered through neoplatonism, Ficinian hermeticism, and the thinking of Swedenborg, Bergson, and Steiner.

In this blend of beliefs, man becomes, by means of his incessant spiritual search, the arbiter of the relationship between the material and the spiritual. Carrà formulated this point of view—yet another manifestation of the individualistic aspect of the early (Marinettian) futurist movement and one of futurism's most embarrassing debts to the aesthetics of romanticism—as the concept of "individuation," where the plastic world is "rendered through the individuality of the artist." Carrà believed that individuation was "the only creative force of aesthetic truths"[9] and that, by harnessing the force of intuition (a term dear to Bergson), the futurist artist could "identify himself with the center of things."[10]

Man's central position (in the equation that opposes the material and the spiritual) was at the foundation of Steiner's anthroposophy. The futurist artist is an initiate or, as Boccioni wrote, a clairvoyant: he has the key to that spiritual level where things appear as they really are, in their essential unity. The artist, who is able to see the multiplicity of reality can reproduce (re-create) in his work the spiritual essence implicit in all things.

Besant's and Leadbeater's theory of thought-forms was central to Russolo's formulation of his aesthetics; thoughts produce forms and project or irradiate them into the surrounding aura, thereby enveloping the body. The forms are visible to subjects in a particular state of trance, and they can be indirectly perceived by all whose auras are sufficiently near to the aura of the emitting individual.

As Leadbeater and Besant claim in *Thought-forms*—and Leadbetter further expands in his *The Hidden Side of Things*—sounds and noises, too, create forms visible to sensitive individuals.[11] From this perspective music can be considered a sort of "spiritual painting." The point is important, not only because it provides a way to understand Russolo's eclecticism and his easy, synesthetic transition from painting to music but also because the theory of sound (and noise) forms leads naturally to a reinterpretation of the art of noises as a spiritual operation. Such reinterpretation unveils the occult function of the intonarumori—machines that intone noises and above all permit enharmonic fluctuations, thus enabling the spiritualization and sanctification of brute matter (noise) that is being carried out by the energy of the artist-initiate.

SPIRITUALIZING MATTER

The futurist believed that the mind of the artist-initiate cannot create out of nothing; rather, in line with the alchemical doctrine, the mind must work through a process of transformation. Infusing his own spirit into bare matter, the artist transforms it via the (mechanical) instruments that allow him to give it life: the artist thus creates the only real art, that of a higher spiritual reality. Whether it be a series of noises or a colored canvas mounted on wooden boards, the end of the creative process brings not merely an inanimate material object, a faded copy of the world, but a sort of re-creation, through an artificious mechanism, of life in vitro.

The poetics of the futurists, Russolo included, do not aim for "creation" in a metaphorical sense—that is, creation of material and inanimate art objects, simple metaphors of creation, by means of a process of conceptualization whereby something is realized through effort and passion—but rather real, true, spiritual creation, creation of life. Once the image is created, the possessed artist can make it materialize (as if it were a phenomenon of condensation), and into it, as suggested by the theory of thought-forms, he can instill spirit.[12]

When the creation of the work of art becomes the creation of spiritual reality, such poetics come frighteningly near to black magic. The consequent sin of hubris—from having appropriated the faculty of creating life, which is the prerogative of the divine alone—is inevitable. The heretical belief that the artist was privileged to have been conceded the power to create and instill life (admittedly through artifice, the science of art), circulated widely within the futurist movement. Most futurists, let us not forget, were violently anticlerical and engaged in extreme polemics against Catholicism.

The influence of the occult arts imbued Russolo's poetics with meaning that went beyond a mere postromantic theory of the creative process. Traces of this poetics can be perceived in other futurist writings. One example among many is Balla's and Depero's 1915 manifesto "La ricostruzione futurista dell'universo," which succinctly summarized the futurist position on the creation of works of art.

Although alchemical and theosophical notions led Balla and Depero to a poetics of creation that use a deductive process of objective analysis (it is thus antithetical to the poetics of Boccioni and Russolo), they cited Boccioni's conquests of plastic dynamism and Russolo's art of noises as fundamental guiding experiences. Theorizing a work of art that reconstructs life through artifice and science, they wrote in this 1915 manifesto:

> The lyric valuation of the universe, by means of the Words in Freedom of Marinetti and the Art of Noises of Russolo, fuses itself with plastic dynamism to give a dynamic, simultaneous, plastic, noisy expression of the universal vibration.
> [...] We will give skeleton and flesh to the invisible, the impalpable, the imponderable, the imperceptible. We will find the abstract equivalents of all the forms and of all the elements of the universe, then we will combine them together, according to the caprices of our inspiration, to form plastic complexes that we will put in motion.[13]

Throughout his life, Russolo in his writings espoused the concept of art as the result of a process (carried out by an inspired artist) of transformation of vile matter (be it color or sound) into spiritual reality and life. In an essay published in *Lacerba* on November 1, 1913, and republished in *The Art of Noises* in 1916, Russolo claims: "We finally have the *noise-sound* material capable of assuming without any exception all the forms that the futurist artist may wish and know how to give them."[14]

The theme of the artist-demiurge molding matter is expanded in the final chapter of *The Art of Noises*. The passage below is the most complete (and the most misunderstood) statement of Russolo's poetics. In a messianic tone, Russolo exhorted his readers:

> Make first the senses vibrate, and you will also make vibrate the brain! Make the senses vibrate with the unexpected, the mysterious, the unknown, and you will truly move the soul, intensely and profoundly!
> Here lies the fated and absolute necessity of drawing the timbres of sounds directly from the timbres of the noises of life. Here—sole salvation in the deep misery of orchestral timbres—lays the unbounded richness of the timbres of noises.
> But it is necessary that these noise timbres become *abstract matter* for works of

art to be shaped from them. *As they come to us from [everyday] life*, in fact, noises immediately remind us of life itself, making us think of the [triviality of the] objects that produce the noises that we are hearing. This reminder of life has the character of an impressionistic and fragmentary episode of life itself. And as I conceive it, the *Art of Noises* would certainly not limit itself to an impressionistic and fragmentary reproduction of the noises of life.

The ear cannot relate to the confused and fragmentary noises of everyday life. It is necessary that the ear will perceive these noises as dominated, enslaved, mastered completely, conquered, and constrained to become elements of art. (This is the continual battle of the artist against matter.)

Noise must become a prime element to mold into the work of art. That is, it has to lose its character of accidentality and become an element sufficiently abstract to achieve the necessary transformation of any natural prime element of art into every abstract element of art.

And so, although the resemblance of timbre with natural noises may be attained by my noise instruments even to the point of deceiving the ear, the noise, as soon as it is heard to change in pitch, loses its episodic, solely imitative character. Noise therefore loses entirely its character of *result* and *effect*, which is bound to the causes that produced it (motive energy, percussion, friction through speed, bumping, etc.), causes resulting from and inherent in the purpose of the machine or object that produces the noise.

And since we dominate the noise—which we freed, as described from the necessities that produce it—by deliberately transforming its pitch, intensity, and rhythm, we hear it suddenly become autonomous and malleable matter, ready to be molded by the will of the artist, who transforms it into an element of emotion and, finally, a work of art.[15]

This passage, where Russolo synthesized his creative ambitions, is important, for it contributes to the process of revealing the occult function of the intonarumori.

The concept that requires noises to become "abstract matter" is related to Marinetti's treatment of onomatopoeia in his "Lo splendore geometrico e meccanico e la sensibilità numerica" (The geometric and mechanical splendor and the numerical sensitivity) of 1914, which Russolo cites in the chapter "The Noises of Language" in *The Art of Noises*. In point 8c of his manifesto, for example, Marinetti writes about what he called "abstract onomatopoeia, the noisy and unconscious expression of the most complex and mysterious motions of our sensitivity. (Example: in my poem DUNE, the abstract onomatopoeia *ran ran ran* corresponds to no noise of nature or machine but expresses a state of mind)."[16]

A tendency toward abstraction, and the consequent negation of materiality, can easily lead to occult persuasions. Marinetti's treatment of abstraction, which Russolo eventually incorporated into his sound aesthetics, reflects, as did the aesthetics of Kandinsky and Ginna, occult interests. The connection between Marinetti and Ginna is not incidental: the principle of the onomatopoeic psychic chord that Marinetti espoused in point 8d of his manifesto echoes themes in Ginna's 1909 painting *Accordo cromatico* and the theories of the image chord set out in Ginna's and Corra's *Arte dell'avvenire*. Marinetti knew both sources.

Similar themes are developed and coherently reinforced in Russolo's late writings. In *Al di là della materia* Russolo declared that the artist must point "beyond technique toward the higher spiritual necessities."[17] He goes on to address sound and noise, which, though both are abstract elements and thus perceived as spiritual, can also be seen as matter awaiting to be spiritualized by the artist:

> Music apparently has no need of a universal ideality, nor of any kind of spiritual ideality, because thanks to its fundamentally abstract language, neither narrative nor speculative, it escapes the contingencies of the collective idealities of each work. But sound, let us not forget, is the matter of this abstract language, as the word is for poetry and color is for painting. Let us not confuse the abstraction of this matter with the spirituality to which all matter from which the arts are molded must take us. Music must make the same effort as the plastic arts: music must spiritualize its matter, as the plastic arts must spiritualize theirs. And whereas the plastic arts, when they do not succeed in this, remain either solely descriptive or banally and impressionistically documentary and fragmentary, music, when it does not succeed in this, remains abstractly amorphous. Music must move away from an abstract indefinite, which is the characteristic of its language, and of the matter that it uses, to arrive at a spiritual infinite.

Russolo's approach, as he formulated it here, had not changed much since the time he conceived the art of noises. In the eulogy he held in 1944, on the occasion of Marinetti's funeral, Russolo returned to the theme of the artist-demiurge struggling to spiritualize the materiality of sound, word, and color. Recalling Marinetti's role as guide to the futurist movement, Russolo declared: "I must now say what a marvelous, untiring guiding spirit you were for all of us when discouraged by that greater, deeper, and more difficult struggle: the struggle the artist experiences for the realization of the work of art, that is, the intimate struggle to subjugate matter (be it word, sound, color, clay, or marble) and thereby express the creations of the spirit."[18]

Russolo repeatedly stressed art's need for a spiritual life of its own, as conferred upon it by the artist in the act of wresting it away from materiality. In his *Conferenza sull'architettura*, which he presented at the Galleria Borromini di Como in 1944, he wrote that "the harmony of forms finds correspondence in our spirit, which is equivalent with saying that harmony spiritualizes it. In this process of spiritualization of forms, [our spirit] is the genesis of works of art, it is the reason for their indestructible vitality."[19] In the catalog of his one-man show for the same venue in 1945, Russolo wrote that technique is the "indispensable means for bending matter to the expressions of the spirit."[20]

Russolo returned to the concept yet again in his last writing, *L'eterno e il transitorio nell'arte* of 1947, the text for a lecture written a few weeks before his death:

> When the work of art has overcome the phenomenology of the moment represented by taste, expression, the whole of things or of beings, or the actions of those beings, it is no longer a moment, contingency, event determined by chance, or transitory or variable effectuality; when all this has become essence, understood as the eternity of being absorbed or transformed into eternity and a condition that has overcome space and overcome time, then the work of art has truly overcome the human, its transitoriness, and the ephemeral that is the human characteristic, linked and deeply embedded in the necessities of life itself; it has overcome living and life to the state of "being" as power, cause, origin-demiurge—a being that for itself has no cause or necessity; then the work of art has arrived at the eternal and delivers us, raises us up, sends us into ecstasy. Then the work of art truly *is*.
>
> Then the work of art is pure spirit and lives outside even of its own material body, eternally young even though its body, which is matter, is aged, blackened, cracked as is happening to Leonardo's *Last Supper*, which became in its pictorial materiality a nebulous and evanescent breath without having lost anything of its supreme spiritual life.[21]

SPIRITS

To spiritualize matter, the artist-initiate can invoke the spirits fluctuating in the astral plane he has reached; he can then communicate with them and obtain (as if under their dictation, in a state of trance) the energy for the spiritualizing process.

Russolo believed that these spirits may have been those of the dead awaiting reincarnation. On October 26 and 27 of 1912, Rudolf Steiner gave two lectures in Milan, parts 1 and 2 of "Investigations into Life between Death and Rebirth."[22] Russolo may well have attended these lectures. Steiner illustrated the various phases of the soul's journey after the death of the body in preparation for its reincarnation. In the first phase, the period immediately after the separation from the dying body (a subject Russolo had portrayed earlier in his *Uomo che muore*), the spirits of the dead fluctuate in areas not far from the places they inhabited in life. At this moment it is important that they maintain communication with loved ones who still live. This is the only phase in which the living can enter into contact with the souls of the dead. In theosophical thought, the protocol for such communication is strictly and scientifically regulated.[23] In part 2 of his lecture, Steiner declared:

> Only when those who remain on earth seek us with their souls can a link with them be created. [...] A person who has died before us and whom we completely forget, finds it difficult to reach us here in earthly life. The love, the constant sympathy we feel for the dead, creates a path on which a connection with earthly life is established. During the early stages after death those who have passed on can live with us only out of this connection. It is surprising to what extent the cult of the commemoration of the dead is confirmed in its deeper significance by occultism. Those who have passed on can reach us most easily if they can find thoughts and feelings directed towards them from the earth.[24]

Immediately after death, the souls live "in an objective world that can be compared to that of the initiate," because after death they can no longer perceive things through the senses but only "by the way of visions."[25] Initiates who are on this same plane can communicate with them and in turn be influenced by them. Subsequently, during the various phases of getting away from and reapproaching the sensory world that guide them to rebirth, souls increasingly distance themselves from the earth (in terms of both physical and spiritual distance) until communication becomes impossible. In theosophical thought, communication between spirits occurs by way of waves that travel through the ether, like a radio wave, and the signal weakens as the distance between emitter and receiver increases.

Steiner's position changed over time— he eventually came to condemn mediums, states of trance, and spiritualism—but the positions Steiner disseminated in Milan in 1912 were crucial to the evolution of Russolo's ideas.[26] In fact, less than three months after Steiner's lectures, on February 21, 1913, Russolo published the first manifesto on the art of noises.

Communication with spirits was also one of the preoccupations of Emanuel Swedenborg, whose name Buzzi associated with that of Russolo. As is evident in at least two passages written almost thirty years apart, Russolo believed in the possibility of communicating with the dead.

On August 22, 1916, five days after the death of Boccioni, Russolo wrote a letter from the front to the art critic Margherita Sarfatti in which he confessed being prostrated at the sudden and tragic death of his friend. Russolo railed against "this complicated, beastly, boring life which has taken from me even meditation, and which has taken from me also the time again to take with Him [Boccioni] our strolls in the divinely terrible paths of art! Yes, because I still speak with Him: his spirit, his genius is not dead. He is still alive, he is still with us!"[27] The lapidary claim that "I speak with him" (*io parlo con lui*) at the center of the letter is more profound than it might seem at first glance, given the vehemence of the rhythmic prose Russolo adopted. Yet his claim cannot be taken merely as a literary device.

Almost thirty years later, the opening of Russolo's 1944 eulogy at Marinetti's funeral resounds like a pagan prayer turned toward the dead, filled with the formulaic rhetoric one would expect from a medium at the beginning of a séance to conjure up a spirit: "I speak to you, O Marinetti, I speak to you still because if we are here reunited around the coffin that holds your mortal remains, very surely your thought is in the air here around us. Your spirit, that inexhaustible living fount of *energies*, of courage, of force that you infused upon all of us, your young friends of those days, and which you have continued to spread to the youths that followed and the youths of today."[28]

Here again Russolo is speaking to a recently deceased friend's spirit, which, he is convinced, is floating in the surrounding air; according to what Steiner had declared in his 1912 Milan lectures, this is possible only because the friends gathered around the corpse have all directed their thoughts toward the spirit of the deceased.

PREACHING TO THE MASSES

The art of noises was an experiment born in Russolo's laboratory on via Stoppani out of the creative excitement of, in Marinetti's words, "ecstatic and vibrating afternoons" devoted to occult preoccupations. In *La grande Milano*, where Marinetti recalled the 1914 *Primo gran concerto futurista per intonarumori* at Teatro Dal Verme in Milan, he considered Russolo's intonarumori to be capable "of organizing *spiritually* and imaginatively *our* acoustic *vibrations*."[29] Various testimonies from the time indicate that Russolo considered the art of noises with a kind of reverence half way (as was the theosophical custom) between the reverence reserved for a precise scientific experiment and that generated by an occult, spiritual ritual.

Russolo, too, referred to his studies in terms that were at once scientific and devotional. He recorded the work of those "ecstatic and vibrating afternoons" in via Stoppani with exaltation: "The joy of each successful accomplishment alternated with the anxiety of ever new experiments, and with the delusions of assumptions that proved false, or difficulties not overcome. But we had the *certain, absolute, and unshakeable faith* that made us patiently persist, courageously beginning our studies and labors anew each time that it was necessary."[30] He would return to the reference to "faith."

After Russolo introduced the prototype of the intonarumori to a completely unprepared audience at the Teatro Storchi of Modena on June 2, 1913, the next day's Gazzetta dell'Emilia quoted him verbatim. About the *scoppiatore* (combuster), he had said: "My futurist comrades have encouraged me with *enthusiasm* and with *faith* for the practical result already obtained, and they will encourage me even more for the result that soon we will obtain."[31]

The article went on to describe the presentation of the intonarumori, which apparently followed a protocol such as that of a solemn religious service.[32] According to Russolo's script, the climax of the evening program, the entrance onstage of the intonarumori, was supposed to be heralded by a detailed lecture given by Russolo. However, the public found his lecture pedantic and boring, and he was interrupted frequently by jeers and shouting. The public shouted, "Out with the instrument, we want to see the instrument!" But, like an inspired prophet, and sustained by his "unshakeable faith," Russolo continued to preach to the hostile crowd; he prepared them for the revelation with a laconic, sibylline prediction: "It will come." The instrument finally materialized, an occult epiphany:

> Russolo concluded his oration and together with his collaborator Piatti exited to prepare the unveiling of the *mysterious* contraption that would give the Modenese public a *divine* [...] impression of the new futurist orchestra.
>
> After a time, Russolo and Piatti returned. With *ceremony, almost as if they had in their hands something sacred, mystical, superhuman, or supernatural,* they carried a large object. [...]
>
> Russolo and Piatti tested the instrument twice.
>
> In a *hieratic* pose, moving and agitating God knows which handle, they produce a noise, first weak and muffled, then stronger, higher, more clamorous.

In describing the end of the evening, the article makes one more reference to faith: "Marinetti, Russolo, Pratella, and Piatti saluted their *comrades in faith* and retired to their rooms."

Though likely ironic, the terms used in the article to describe the event are still pregnant with references to a religious, possibly pagan, service, and at the same time the writer chose to depict a rigorous alchemical-scientific experiment—Mondrian later called Russolo a "biologist." The experiment is described as having been carried out by an officiant-magician-scientist and his *faithful* altar-boy-apprentice-assistant with self-satisfied, pompous hieraticity, all participants observing a rigorous etiquette in the presence of a congregation of both *faithful* and skeptical members. The combination of science and metaphysics is typical of theosophical undertakings.

THE INTONARUMORI ON TRIAL

The first public concert of the intonarumori took place on April 21, 1914, at the Teatro Dal Verme. Among the press coverage, one negative review by the Catholic deputy and music critic for *L'Italia*, Agostino Cameroni, so incensed Russolo that he slapped the critic in public.[33] When Cameroni thereupon brought a charge of assault against the artist, Russolo believed that his artistic reputation was at stake and that he would have to defend both himself and his work.

The account of the trial as reported in the newspaper *L'Italia* on October 10, 1914, shows that even Russolo's detractors took a scientific-metaphysical view of him. Describing the appearance in the witness box of the impulsive, hot-blooded futurist, the press described him as "pallid, slight, something like the figures painted in Pisa's Monumental Cemetery."[34]

According to that newspaper article, Russolo in his deposition, proclaimed the "worth of his intonarumori, which he described as the fruit of studies and untiring work, and based on scientific and mathematical laws." Cameroni had questioned the "artistic quality" of the intonarumori, claiming that the art of noises was a regression of music to the "imitation of natural noises." This was one of the main objections of Russolo's detractors and a frontal attack on the spirituality of his operation. Cameroni's position touched a raw nerve in Russolo, to whom the intonarumori were not merely machines designed to produce superficial imitations of noises but means for forcing and forging noise into a spiritual form. His intonarumori produced noise (the raw material) but also intoned it enharmonically, thereby spiritualizing it.

Among the witnesses of both the prosecution and the defense, some perceived the intonarumori in spiritual terms. Not surprisingly, Marinetti, the principal witness for the defense, warned in his deposition that "to understand the intonarumori one needs . . . *religion.*" More surprising, however, was the testimony of the *commendator* Amann, a witness for the prosecution, who maintained that "the intonarumori could and can produce enthusiasm only among the initiates." Precisely because it came from an unbiased place, Amann's choice or words is revelatory. In its etymological derivation, *enthusiasm* indicates possession, the possession of the body of an *initiate* by a divine entity during a ritual ceremony.

In the trial, Marinetti and Amann represented two ideologically opposed positions, yet their perception of the intonarumori was fundamentally similar. Russolo's occult persuasions had penetrated the enemy's encampment to become the platform for the discussion.

PART TWO

The Art of Noises and the Occult

CHAPTER 7

Intonarumori Unveiled

THREE LEVELS

Russolo considered the intonarumori to be more than simply musical instruments. But what then does that make the special compositions Russolo wrote for the intonarumori, which he first called *reti di rumori* (networks of noises) and then *spirali di rumori* (spirals of noises)? And what is the real significance of *Risveglio di una città* (Awakening of a city), the most famous of these spirali?[1]

Like most futurists, Russolo was moved by a cosmogonic ambition. Françoise Escal is the only musicologist to have touched upon this aspect of Russolo's activities. In a brief 1975 article, Escal claims that in the development of the art of noises Russolo's aural frame of reference first shifted from Nature to the Real; Escal understood the Real to be the meeting place of noises from nature and those produced, directly or indirectly as a result of human industry, by machines. When Russolo first turned his attention to the noises of the Real (Nature plus Man), he did not limit himself to merely imitating or representing reality. Escal explained that

> in effect, art is not the re-production, re-presentation, of life, and the art of noises especially is not an inventory, a collection of noises of the exterior world, of the real. [...]
> To an aesthetics of representation, Russolo opposes an aesthetics of creation. Futurist music "will obtain the most complex and new sonic emotions not through a succession of noises imitative of life, but rather through a fantastic combination of these varied tones": in between the noises and the art of noises there is the mediation of the artist as full, inspired subject.[2]

Unfortunately, Escal, instead of elaborating on his own brilliant intuition, reverted to framing Russolo's aesthetics of creation as a mere regurgitation of romanticism, concluding that "Russolo remains a prisoner of the traditional (i.e., romantic) conception of the author as a superior being elected to deliver his message to ordinary mortals."[3]

In 1975 the critical climate was not sufficiently mature, and the debate on exchanges among the disciplines of the artistic avant-garde, science, and occultism had yet to begin. Whereas Lista (who in that same year edited a second French edition of *The Art of Noises*) considered the messianic side of Russolo's thought, which is concerned with the spiritual, metaphysical, and irrational, to be regressive and reactionary, Escal on the other hand dismissed Russolo's thought as conservative. Escal believed that Russolo's occult was a cumbersome and obsolete debt from nineteenth-century romanticism; he interpreted Russolo's approach to be a way of playing with the worn-out metaphor of artistic creation rather than actually engaging in the act of Creation, and therefore considered it unworthy of further investigation.

Within the occultist ferment at the turn of the century among theosophy, science, and spiritism, and as used in séances and materializations, the term *creation* assumed greater significance than it had ever held for the romantic generation. The creation of life as intended by the occultists lay within the field of black magic, since the ability to give life, like that of taking it away, is a divine prerogative and therefore outside the human sphere. Alchemy is the most important of the occult disciplines dealing with creation, and creation was one of its most ambitious goals. Creation never occurred out of nothingness; it was always an artificious operation of transformation, obtained through an infusion of energy.[4]

For Russolo, the intonarumori was an alchemical experiment in the creation of life, which futurists believed was the only process capable of producing an art that could truly be called "spiritual." In Russolo's experiment, raw matter (in the form of pure noise) is transformed by means of a mechanical instrument (the intonarumori) functioning as an alchemical crucible or *vas*, through a cunning process with a mechanical side (enharmonic transformation) and a spiritual one (infusion of energy).[5] At another level, the noises produced by an orchestra of intonarumori (a chaotic, complementary multiplicity that can be read within the alchemical opposites of salt and sulfur, i.e., masculine and feminine) are transfigured through the catalyst (in alchemy

LEVEL I	LEVEL II
Incited by the spirits, the **artist/clairvoyant** spiritualizes noise through mechanical means —the **intonarumori**—which render it continuous and enharmonic	Through a dynamic process of **synthesis** of multiplicity into unity, of chaos into cosmos, the orchestra of intonarumori as a whole creates the **Art of Noises**
↓	↓
thought-forms	*sound-forms*

LEVEL III
The infusion of **life energy** from the
Art of Noises acts as a spiritual soundtrack, so that

thought-forms + matter
result in

**materialization
incarnation, awakening**

FIGURE 19. The Three-Level Process.

the catalyst would be mercury) of futurist simultaneity and dynamism into a synthesis fusing these opposites into unity.

This process is articulated at three levels. In the first level, noise becomes spiritual as a result of the intonarumori being tuned and endowed with enharmonic (i.e., microtonal) possibilities. In the second level, an orchestra of intonarumori produces a spiral of noises that re-creates the world first as a simultaneous chaos and then as a unity. In the third level, the artist-creator-medium who spearheaded the process can communicate with the spirits, who, against the soundtrack of spiritual music, are now able to materialize (fig. 19).

Thus the artist-creator, in the act of producing noise, conjures up the spirits of the dead so that they excite his states of mind to project themselves as thought-forms onto the "bodies" constituting his own aura.[6] The states of mind produced in the artist-creator by the spirits that he himself has conjured up influence him in the process of creation, so that the possessed artist works as if taking dictation. This is precisely the process that Russolo stages in *La musica*; through the intonarumori he transformed raw matter (noise), creating from it what the futurists considered the only true art: new spiritual life.

Creation must occur through a transfer of vital energy.[7] The energy necessary for transformation is achieved with the help of the psychic powers of the spirits conjured by the artist-creator. In his essay "Raggio," Ardengo Soffici offered a synthesis of this process: "A privileged organism, a center of extra powerful vital force, can in a certain moment and under certain circumstances attract and concentrate within itself its distant parts, the peripheral waves of its energies, making them concrete."[8]

The intonarumori is not an instrument that produces noises by imitation: the noise that the intonarumori produces at the beginning of the transformation process is only raw matter awaiting elevation by the artist-creator, who has to struggle against its materiality. Boccioni, recounting the function of the intonarumori to Giovanni Papini, wrote, "Intonarumori (the word itself tells you) does not mean noise pure and simple, i.e., raw reality, but intoned noise, therefore lyrical elaboration of new noise realities, which are acoustically the essence of modern life."[9]

While crusading against materialism, and in line with his interventionist political position before World War I, Russolo described his struggle in militaristic terms, maintaining that noises must be "dominated, enslaved, mastered completely, conquered, and constrained to become elements of art. (This is the continual battle of the artist against matter)."[10]

Russolo understood the intonarumori to be a means with multiple functions; these instruments can thus be illustrated by the three-level outline. At the first level, the intonarumori is a means to produce noise, making it available as primal matter to be transformed; but it can also enable the channeling of the spiritual energy gathered by the artist-creator, infusing its energy into the noise matter and transforming it by elevating it into something spiritual: into art that has the gift of being alive. Marinetti had this function in mind when he claimed the intonarumori's ability to "organize spiritually and fantastically our acoustic vibrations (*organizzare spiritualmente e immaginosamente le nostre* vibrazioni acustiche)."[11]

At a second level, an entire orchestra of intonarumori, conducted by the inspired artist taking spiritual dictation, holds the cosmogonic ambition of re-creating the world (by substitution, not imitation) through the spiritualization and synthesis of the manifold and complementary into essential unity.

At a third level, the intonarumori is a "portal to the beyond": during the process of creation, as the artist-creator is delivered to a more elevated plane of consciousness, he can communicate with the spirits of the dead that he has conjured up, spirits that fluctuate in that same plane awaiting for reincarnation.[12]

Throughout this three-level process, the spirits produce thought-forms—

and, above all, sound-forms—through the mediation of the artist-initiate. These forms in their turn emit vibrations that influence the aura of every individual present in their field of action; under certain circumstances these forms can also materialize into bodies.[13]

FIRST LEVEL: THE SINGLE INTONARUMORI

How does spiritualization of noise matter take place? Russolo effectively described this process of transformation in *The Art of Noises*:

> Noise must become a prime element to mold into the work of art. That is, it has to lose its character of accidentality and become an element sufficiently abstract to achieve the necessary transformation of any natural prime element into every abstract element of art.
>
> And so, although the resemblance of timbre with natural noises may be attained by my noise instruments even to the point of deceiving the ear, as soon as it is heard to change in pitch, the noise loses its episodic, solely imitative character. Noise therefore loses entirely its character of *result* and of *effect*, which is bound to the causes that produced it (motive energy, percussion, friction through speed, bumping, etc.), causes resulting from, and inherent in, the purpose of the machine or object that produces the noise.
>
> And since we dominate the noise—which we freed as described from the necessities that produced it—by deliberately transforming its pitch, intensity, and rhythm, we hear it suddenly become autonomous and malleable matter, ready to be molded by the will of the artist.[14]

Reading the passage metaphorically places Russolo within romantic aesthetics. But the occult meaning of his words is paradoxically revealed when they are read in their literal sense. The intonarumori is an artificious mechanism, or rather, is a medium for spiritualizing matter and, from it, re-creating life. Russolo believed that this spiritualization was possible because when the intonarumori transformed the noise it had produced by rendering it free to exist in what he called enharmonic space. In this way noise loses its materiality: it transforms itself, becomes abstract, and spiritualizes itself.

ENHARMONY

In changing pitch, the intonarumori was not limited to the tempered chromatic scale. Since it is necessary, when creating a spiritual reality, to re-create the same properties encountered in nature and life, and to enslave those properties, the intonation of the noise must use the infinite spectrum of pitches available through the "enharmony" we experience in the everyday world. In Russolo's words: "The infinite ways in which noise is produced in nature, in life, and above all in machines, offer a large field for the study of these different ways of producing noise vibrations; these ways had to be translated so as to make possible variation of tones, semitones, and all the enharmonic passages that other musical instruments do not have but that are so often found in noises of nature and life."[15]

The term *enharmony* is key to the art of noises, but the reader should be aware that, as used by the futurists, it deviates from the common meaning. As used by them (including Russolo), enharmony designates a microtonal musical system that adopts as its compositional material not only every pitch present in the chromatic scale but also all the microtones generated by dividing the octave (and therefore the tone) into infinite parts.

Pratella was the first futurist to use the word with this precise meaning in his "La musica futurista: Manifesto tecnico" of March 29, 1911.

> We futurists proclaim that the search for and the realization of the *enharmonic mode* is a progress and represent the victory of the future over the chromatic atonal mode. Whereas chromaticism only takes advantage of the sounds contained in a scale divided by minor and major [sic] semitones, enharmony, by contemplating also the slightest subdivisions of the tone, not only offers our *renewed sensitivity* the greatest number of determinable and combinable sounds but also provides us with new and more varied relations of chords and timbres.
>
> But above all *enharmony* grants us the natural and instinctive intonation and modulation of the enharmonic intervals, presently unproducible given the affectedness of our tempered system-based scale, which we wish to overcome. We futurists have long loved these enharmonic intervals that we find only in the off-key notes of the orchestra, when the instruments play in different tunings, and in the spontaneous songs of the people, when they are intoned without preoccupations of art.[16]

The term *enharmony* derives from ancient Greek musical theory. In its original meaning, the term *enharmonic* designated one of the three systems of Greek music—the other two being the diatonic and the chromatic. The enharmonic system was based on a scale obtained from the union of two descending enharmonic tetrachords. Because an enharmonic tetrachord contains a central interval smaller than a semitone, Pratella extended the meaning of enharmonic to designate a musical system in which all of the infinite microtonal pitches could be used.[17]

Russolo took up the term in its Pratellian meaning in *The Art of Noises*. In the chapter "La conquista dell'enarmonismo" ("The Conquest of Enharmony"), he elaborated upon Pratella's conception, even citing part of his "Manifesto tecnico della musica futurista."[18] Russolo began by attacking the tempered system, the adoption of which, he argued, had not only caused the richer, Greek meaning of the term *enharmonic* to disappear but also reduced the term exclusively to define the relationship of the homophony between two notes that carry different names (e.g., C-sharp and D-flat). The greatest fault he found in this system was not a matter of terminology, however: "Dividing the octave into only twelve *equal* fractions and adopting this temperate scale in all of the instruments, has lead to a considerable limitation of the number of available sounds and made strangely artificial the few that are available. [. . .] *Temperament*, with its homophony, has in a sense *torn* the notes *apart* from each other, taking away the most subtle bond that joins them together, i.e., the fractions of a tone smaller than the present—artificial and monotonous—semitone."[19]

Russolo contrasts the equal-temperament system with the enharmonic one he realized in the intonarumori, by means of which he was able finally to "overcome the stupid barriers of the semitone" and which allowed sustained notes to change pitch "*by enharmonic gradations*" instead of by leap.[20] The noises emitted by the intonarumori in fact move from one pitch to the next in glissandi, like sirens, showcasing both their conferred enharmonic properties and the theory upon which these properties are based.[21]

ENHARMONY'S SPIRITUAL PROPERTIES

Natura non facit saltus.
—Linnaeus, *Philosophia botanica*

To explain how noise can become spiritual, that is, explain the connection between enharmony and spirituality, I must introduce the philosophical (and theosophical) notion of continuity. The futurists believed that the term *continuity* designated the continuity of ether, the matter that composes both bodies and the spaces between bodies, and vibrates in waves of varying intensity. This conception, which theosophy endorsed and popularized, was strongly rooted in early twentieth-century spirituality. As Linda Henderson has observed, the principle of "continuity as embodied in the fiction of the ether, [. . .] although displaced for scientists by Einstein's special theory of relativity after 1905, continued to play a key role in popular conceptions of reality for several decades."[22] Henderson believes that Boccioni's sculpture *Forme uniche nella continuità dello spazio* was a testimony to this conception.

In their writings, the futurists consistently opposed the positive notion of continuity against the negative one of fragmentation. Boccioni, in *Lacerba*, wrote that "the distances between one object and another are not empty spaces but continuities of matter with different intensity."[23] The understanding of continuity is an exposition of the theosophical doctrine of vibrations.

Advocating for a representation of reality as a continuous blur or wave, instead of the still images he deplored in cubist painting, or the overlapping frames he criticized in Bragaglia and Balla, Boccioni considered the principle of continuity to be part of the spiritual mission of futurist art: "We do not subdivide visual images, we search for a shape, or, better, a single form *[forma unica]* that would substitute the new concept of continuity for the old concept of (sub)division. Just as every subdivision of matter is completely arbitrary, so is every subdivision of motion." In support of these claims, he concluded with a quote from Bergson: "Every division of matter in independent bodies that have absolutely determined surroundings is an artificial division."[24]

Similarly, Soffici in "Raggio" claimed that "the entire universe therefore is a single whole without interruption of continuity," and that "the world is not a molecular aggregate but a flux of energy with varied rhythms, from granite to thought."[25] Soffici did not necessarily take this concept from Bergson; in fact, the title adopted for the reprint of this article is a direct reference to theosophy.[26] After all, the early history of the concept is illustrious and was established long before Bergson's elaborations.

A view of the universe filled continuously with matter is presented in book 4 of Aristotle's *Physics*, where the philosopher denied the Democritean existence of a void that contains no substance. In *Metaphysics* (6, 1, 2), Aristotle differentiated between continuous and discontinuous quantities; later, in *Logic* (5a), he expanded the distinction, explaining that time, space, and geometric line belong to the class of continuous quantities—the class of quantities that have "a common boundary at which their parts join." Aristotle contrasted time, space, and the geometrical line with Poetry, which he considered a discipline dealing with discontinuous quantities, "for its parts have no common boundary" (*Logic* 4b32).[27]

Leonardo da Vinci derived a hierarchy from Aristotle's principle of continuous quantities. In *Il paragone*, a section of his *Trattato della pittura* with which both Boccioni and Russolo were familiar, Leonardo elaborated on what Aristotle had only implied, stating that continuous quantities are superior to discontinuous ones because they are infinitely divisible.[28] The concept of continuous quantities (among these Leonardo included, as Aristotle had done before him, space, time, and the geometric line) refers to the infiniteness—and therefore perfection—of the divine; because of this reference to divine perfection, continuous quantities confer a high metaphysical status to their correlated *scientie mentali* (i.e., Painting for space and Music for time).

In this passage from *Il paragone*, Leonardo explained: "If you [the Musician] say that only the nonmechanical [physical, bodily, material] sciences [liberal arts] are concerned with the mind and that, just as Music and Geometry deal with the proportions of the continuous quantities, and Arithmetic with the proportions of the discontinuous quantities, [so] Painting deals with all the continuous quantities and also with the qualities of the proportions [degrees] of shades and lights and, thanks to perspective, distances as well."[29]

The Leonardo scholar Emanuel Winternitz believed that the continuity of musical flow refers exclusively to the horizontal motion of a melody unfolding in time, moving from one note to the next through the continuum.[30] This continuum is infinitely divisible, exactly as the portion of time in between two instants is infinitely divisible. But for Leonardo, Music could not be continuous only in time, because that would not suffice to explain music's higher status than a discipline such as Poetry, which also unfolds in time. Leonardo believed that thanks to the continuity of Music's spectrum of pitches, that is, pitch-space, Music was continuous not only in time but also—like Painting—in space; Winternitz did not realize this.[31] Whereas Leonardo considered Poetry, although unfolding in time, to be inferior because it lacked a harmonic (polyphonic) dimension (i.e., continuity in pitch space), Painting was for Leonardo continuous in space through perspective, and Music was continuous in the acoustic pitch-space continuum; Leonardo likely derived this comparative ranking from Aristotle. The full exploitation of continuity granted to Painting and Music the power to bombard the viewer or listener with polyphonic, simultaneous harmony, "*in uno medesimo tempo*" (at the same time).[32]

Music is also associated with continuous quantities because it can inhabit pitch space, which, like the space of perspective, is continuous. In the above-cited passage from *Trattato 31 C*, Leonardo implied the notion of the (infinite) divisibility of a musical interval into infinite pitches. Leonardo was interested in this phenomenon for a long time, and he designed a series of instruments (including many variable-pitch percussion instruments) that could produce infinite pitch divisions. Leonardo's instruments had features that Russolo would have described as enharmonic, and this may be the reason why Russolo drew on them for his own constructive principles.[33]

Winternitz does not know how to place Leonardo's variable-pitch instruments and thus wonders, for example, about the reason for what he calls the "glissando flute," one of the projects outlined in Leonardo's Atlantic Codex. Because Winternitz did not think that this instrument could have had a place in any instrumental group known during Leonardo's time, he considers it a *bizarrerie* invented to "amuse the ladies and gentlemen at the court of Lodovico Sforza" and thus an unfortunate example of the "useless researches" Leonardo was occasionally obliged to perform.[34] What Winternitz did not consider is that by fully displaying the principle of continuity not only in pitch space but also in time, these instruments (and with them their creator) projected philosophical, metaphysical, spiritual, and occult ambitions.[35]

The continuous pitch space or, as it can be called, the pitch-space continuum, is equivalent to the futurists' enharmonic space. By reconnecting Aristotle, Leonardo, and Bergson with occult and theosophical thought, the enharmonic system—especially if contrasted with the discontinuity of the tempered system—enacts the spiritual idea of continuity.[36] Enharmony is a spiritual property: being continuous and therefore infinitely divisible, enharmonic space recalls the infiniteness of divine perfection.

The principle of continuity with which the intonarumori spiritualized noise was musically realized on two levels (exactly as Leonardo envisioned it four hundred years earlier, which points to the fact that Russolo drew his inspiration from Leonardo's writings).[37] The intonarumori manifest continuity in time because the noise was held, sustained, and therefore continuous; more important, it is continuous in the infinite pitch-space continuum because the "liberated" noise, intoned enharmonically, could inhabit the continuous and infinite space of all microtonal pitches, and in this space occupy any position within the range of the instrument. It is no surprise that Russolo gave the essence of enharmony the Leonardine name *dynamic continuity*.[38]

The metaphysical superiority of continuous quantities depends on their being infinitely divisible, and thus, as we have seen, perfectly divine. Russolo felt that continuous quantities evoke the perfection of every work of the spirit, be it a divine work *(natura)* or the work of man *(vita)*. Russolo believed that to create a spiritual reality it was necessary not only to reproduce or imitate the noise from nature and life but also, by means of the intonarumori, to infuse the noise with that spiritual property— continuity—that is present in nature and in life. Continuity in time and enharmonic pitch space is a spiritual property because in both it re-creates the perfection of the natural world—broadly understood, the work of man included—and with it, re-creates its spirituality.

Music created according to a "discontinuous" system such as the tempered system can, in Russolo's opinion, only offer a superficial portrait of nature. The art of noises, on the other hand, lives in a continuous pitch space and is thus able to avoid superficial, impressionist imitations. When the noise is intoned enharmonically and changes pitch continuously, it is spiritualized and subjugated as the raw material for a compositional process controlled by the spirits conjured by the artist, a process that dominates, transforms, models, and re-creates.

Like Leonardo's instruments, the intonarumori was not so much a musical instrument as a philosophical-metaphysical one—an instrument endowed with the entirely cosmological ambition of re-creating the continuous structure of the world.[39] Considering that Russolo always took great interest in the science of astronomy, it is not surprising that this cosmological ambition, philosophically promised by the single intonarumori, would correspond with the cosmogonic idea that drove Russolo's spirali di rumori.

The intonarumori moved between the literal and the allegorical. Though it may seem hazardous to associate instruments made of humble materials such as twine, chemically treated skins, wood, and even cardboard with lofty philosophical language, this would not have been the first time. The typically Marinettian "simultaneous portrait" of Russolo's constructing the intonarumori in *La grande Milano*, for example, synthesizes with lucid juxtapositions the spiritual import of Russolo's experiment:

> Luigi Russolo inventor of philosophical systems motors artificial skins musical instruments and first intonarumori
>
> In his dormer window he amazes me by boiling paste to replace the latex on the wheels[40]

Marinetti described the intonarumori as a necessary part of a biomechanical or mechano-philosophical experiment. As a philosophical machine and alchemical experiment in which science and spirituality coexisted in a complex equilibrium, the intonarumori was legitimately positioned within theosophical thought, and it was part of the process of the spiritualization of noise also in its mechanical aspects.

The intonarumori prototype was patented on January 11, 1914.[41] One part of this instrument produced the noise; at this level the excitement of vibrating parts was continuous in time, since it resulted from a wheel put into motion by a crank, which, as in a hurdy-gurdy, could sustain the noise as long as desired.[42] Even more important, though, was the part responsible for intoning the noise. Intonation occurred through a string attached to the membrane that produced and amplified the noise; this string was tightened (thereby stretching the membrane) and shortened at will by means of a movable bridge, by a lever that regulated its intonation. Next to the lever was a graduated scale, which, through a pointer linked to the lever, gave the operator the power to control the pitch of the sound at every moment and therefore to intone fourths or even eighths of a tone; the operator himself did not need to be able to recognize the pitch differences. Normally this mechanism could not produce intervals between pitches by leap but by only gliding. Instead of internal subdivision of the intervals between arrival points or stages inherent in the tempered system, Russolo favored enharmony's essential feature—the glissando between various points of the pitch-space continuum that he called "dynamic continuity." Using language and examples drawn from Leonardo, Russolo wrote:

> It is necessary to keep in mind that Enharmonicism, as a general system and as manifest in the intonarumori, has as its characteristic the possibility not only of fractionalizing into a given number of pitches the interval of a tone, but also of rendering precisely the *becoming* of a tone by another, the shading (so to speak) that one tone makes, to arrive at the tone immediately above or immediately below.
>
> This dynamic passage is not logically divisible, just as the *shading* of color from light to dark is indivisible.[43] Stages or steps can be stabilized, that is, by quarters, eighths, etc. of a tone, but in doing so the pitch's *dynamic continuity* will be broken.
>
> *Dynamic continuity*: here is the essence of Enharmonicism; here is that which differentiates it from music of the diatonic-chromatic system which one could instead call *Intermittent dynamism* or perhaps more exactly *Fragmentary dynamism*.
>
> Now, if a series of *points* has served very well to mark the stages and the steps of the sound in the diatonic system, what could represent the continuity of this sound if not the *line*?[44]

Although Russolo, in describing the features of his enharmonic notation, mentioned a division of the tone into fourths or at the most eighths, it was through the glissando from one pitch to the next that the enharmonic properties could be fully showcased.⁴⁵ This gliding motion, a blur of sound he opposed to pitch stillness and arbitrary pitch divisions, was Russolo's musical equivalent for the dynamic, continuous blur we can see in his painting, or in Boccioni's *forma unica*; fittingly, he notated it in the score with a continuous line. This line represents the glissando, that is, the dynamic continuity of sound in the pitch-space, whereas enharmony is the musical system that allow the continuity, the space in which this continuity can exist and operate. By way of their constructive morphology, the intonarumori celebrate enharmony, sliding from one pitch to the next, in a glissando that reveals the continuity of pitch space beyond all manufactured, structural restrictions, and surely with no regard for equal temperament.⁴⁶

Glissando is so prevalent a feature of twentieth-century music that Douglas Kahn has referred to it, endearingly, as "the modernist glissando."⁴⁷ The similarity between the sliding enharmonic properties of the intonarumori and the glissando in some orchestral works by Ravel is especially striking. In his orchestration of *Gnomus* from Mussorgsky's *Pictures from an Exhibition* (1922), Ravel added glissandi in the strings (gestures not present in the original piano version) to imitate the sinister noise of doors creaking.

A reference to Russolo's intonarumori is even more evident in the score of Ravel's *L'enfant et les sortilèges*. Ravel had the opportunity to hear the intonarumori on June 17, 1921, on the occasion of the first of three concerts of the intonarumori with orchestra at the Théâtre des Champs Elysées in Paris; according to a Parisian music critic, Ravel examined the instruments attentively at the end of the concert and declared that he thought of including them in one of his scores.⁴⁸

In a letter from Russolo to Pratella of August 19, 1921, Russolo says about his *gracidatori* (croakers): "Above all, they are the instruments that enraptured Ravel, who as you know will put the intonarumori in his new compositions."⁴⁹ Russolo mentions no title, but it seems highly probable that one of the scores in question was that of *L'enfant*, which Ravel had just begun to sketch and that absorbed him from 1920 until 1924. In the final version of this score, Ravel used two unorthodox instruments: the *lutheal*, a sort of tack piano, and the flute *à coulisse*, which according to Hugh Davies made its debut in the world of orchestral textures in this work.⁵⁰

In an article dedicated to the *lutheal*, Davies maintains that Ravel originally considered including one of Russolo's intonarumori, the *gracidatore*, as the third nonorthodox orchestral instrument in *L'enfant*.[51] The *gracidatore* would have suited that score, which not only uses noises of mechanical objects and the cries of animals and insects but also includes a procession of *rainettes* (tree frogs). However, Ravel changed his mind. Davies thought that this was a loss. If Ravel had included the *gracidatore* in the score of *L'enfant*, this intonarumori at least would have escaped the fate of the others and there would still be hope of finding a surviving example in some opera house basement. As it was, all were destroyed, probably during World War II.

Ravel may have decided not to include intonarumori in the score of *L'enfant*, but he reproduced not just their timbre but also their enharmonic articulation using the traditional orchestra. This may be the reason why the score of *L'enfant* features frequent glissandi. Thus though physically absent, the intonarumori animate Ravel's score like ghosts, and they may well be partially or indirectly responsible for its unusual timbre and character.

Given Ravel's supreme ability as an orchestrator, his sound reconstructions may be considered a more faithful picture of the intonarumori than any gramophonic recording of the time. The only extant gramophone recording of the intonarumori is not a reliable document because of its primitive recording technique. Fortunately, some sections of Ravel's score can be considered to be "recordings sui generis" of the intonarumori: in their own way, they now offer the best chance to hear what these instruments would have sounded like.[52]

CHAPTER 8

The *Spirali di Rumori*

SPIRALS

On November 1, 1913, *Lacerba* published Russolo's article "Conquista totale dell'enarmonismo mediante gli intonarumori futuristi" (Total conquest of enharmonism through the futurist intonarumori). In it Russolo defines his first two works, *Risveglio di Capitale* and *Convegno d'automobili e d'aeroplani*, as *reti* (networks) of noises. A few months later, on March 1, 1914, *Lacerba* published his "Grafia enarmonica per gl'intonarumori futuristi" (Enharmonic notation for the futurist intonarumori), which includes the two famous pages taken from *Risveglio di una città* (notice the change in title); here, too, Russolo still called his composition a *rete di rumori* (network of noises) (fig. 20).

The term *réseaux*, the French equivalent of *reti*, had made its first appearance in a September 1913 promotional article by Russolo that Marinetti had distributed to the French press. In this article, Russolo referred to the four compositions premiered in the preview concert for the press in Milan on August 11, 1913, as *quatre premiers réseaux des bruits* (four first networks of noises).[1]

This use of the term derives from Marinetti. In his technical manifesto of futurist literature of May 11, 1912, Marinetti defined as "narrow networks" a series of images and analogies in which each is "condensed, collected into an essential word" and placed one after the other "to envelop and grasp all that is most fleeting and elusive in matter." Marinetti here describes objects and the sum of sensations—the confused simultaneous whole of associations—that their motion produces in us.[2]

FIGURE 20. Luigi Russolo, musical example from *Risveglio di una città* (1913), from the article "Grafia enarmonica per gl'intonarumori futuristi" *Lacerba* (March 1, 1914).

RISVEGLIO DI UNA CITTÀ.

Networks was an early designation. In his 1916 *The Art of Noises*, Russolo refers to his pieces as *spirali di rumori* (spirals of noises), without explaining why he had changed his terminology from *reti* to *spirali*.[3] In truth, the designation *spirali di rumori* for Russolo's compositions had appeared in 1913: on a poster designed for the Galleria Sprovieri in Rome, advertising that on December 27, 1913, "Russolo will perform the spiral *Zum Zum Taratrà*."[4]

Both terms—*reti* and *spirali*— refer to the chaotic and dynamic simultaneity of sonic events in Russolo's compositions and thus imply a form of concentration of chaos into unity. But though they were used synonymously, the term *spiral* is more charged with occult and synesthetic allusions than *network*, and it immediately transports the hearer into the sinuous, enharmonic line of *La musica*. The term *spiral* was also rich with alchemical suggestions, as confirmed by its appearance in the novel *L'ellisse e la spirale* (1915) by Paolo Buzzi.[5] Gino Severini even evoked it to portray Russolo's manners, describing them as "subtle, almost spiralic."[6]

From a topological point of view, the spiral has two trajectories: in one direction the line extends toward the infinite, in the other the infinite concentrates to a point.[7] This first motion is centrifugal and seems to refer to the "exploded" shape of the world in its complex variety (think of a Big Bang); the second, centripetal, symbolizes a process of creation carried out with a concentration of energy from external forces into a single point.

Nomen Omen: the spiralic sonic concentration achieved by an orchestra of intonarumori can be considered another level in the experiment of creating life through the intonarumori, a spiritual re-creation of the world first as simultaneous and multiform chaos, and then as substantial cosmological unity.[8] During the execution of the *spirali di rumori*, an entire orchestra of intonarumori aimed at realizing the aesthetic/ontological ideals of simultaneity and dynamism to which futurism aspired.

The concept of "simultaneity"—first introduced as *simultaneity of states of mind* by the futurist painters in the preface to the catalogue for the exhibitions of 1912—designated the overcoming of classical perspective through a multiplicity of perspectives overlapped in an optical-mnemonic synthesis "of what one remembers and what one sees."[9] The catalog states:

> Perspective as it is understood by the majority of painters has for us the same value that they attribute to a project of engineering.
>
> The simultaneity of states of mind in the work of art: here is the intoxicating aim of our art.

Let us explain ourselves further through examples. When we paint a person on a balcony seen from within, we do not limit the scene to what the square of the window permits to be seen, but we force ourselves to give the complex of plastic sensations felt by the painter-standing-on-the-balcony: sunny swarm of the street, double line of houses which stretch to right and left, flowering balconies, etc., which signifies simultaneity of environment, and therefore dislocation and dismemberment of objects, scattering and fusion of details, freed from ordinary logic and independent one from the other.

To make the spectator live at the center of the painting (to go with the expression of our manifesto) it is necessary that the painting be the synthesis of that which one remembers and that which one sees.

Instead of the small excerpt of life, artificially confined as if within the flat scenery of a theater, it is for us necessary to render the unseen which agitates and lives beyond the thicknesses: that unseen which we have at our right, at left and behind us.[10]

The futurists derived the concept of simultaneity from a web of closely linked influences. Scientific influences came from the theories of the fourth dimension and quantum physics, which speculated that parallel realities could exist simultaneously. A second collection of influences was Bergsonian and derived from the theories of psychic time and inner duration, according to which distant events and instants of time can overlap in human brain processes.[11]

A third group of influences, linked to the other two, was occultist. Among the earliest examples of "occult simultaneity" is Russolo's painting *Ricordi di una notte*, exhibited in the shows of 1912 together with Boccioni's well-known example of simultaneity, his 1911 *Visioni simultanee*. Russolo's *Ricordi di una notte* is a pictorial transcription of a metapsychic séance, in which life is re-created on the canvas as a hallucinatory simultaneity of images surfacing in the mind of a "clairvoyant painter." The simultaneity shown reveals the essence of the universe first as monstrous, disordered chaos, then as synthesis carried out by the subject, who comprehends and reconciles the chaos in a process the futurists, as we know, also called congenital complementarism.[12]

In an effort to reproduce reality, cubist painting had already realized a simultaneous superimposition of planes and perspectives from different angles. But cubist simultaneity, with its cold, analytical, objective, static dissection and dismemberment of reality, had nothing in common with futurist simultaneity, which they defined as simultaneity *of states of mind* and understood as an optical-mnemonic synthesis. Futurist painting responded to the analytic coldness of cubism by incorporating into the spatial equation of the superimposition of planes the dimension of Bergson's psychological time, the time of memory and sensation: "It is about uniting with the concept of space, to which cubism limits itself, the concept of time. It is about giving a plastic construction in which the two concepts of space and time balance in turn to resolve into emotion."[13]

Boccioni considered this the way to "approach the concept of a fourth dimension," which was "not a measured and finite [i.e., cubist] fourth dimension [...], but a continuous projection of forces and forms that are intuited in their infinite unfolding. In fact, the single dynamic form [...] is but the suggestion of a form of motion that appears only for an instant before then losing itself in the infinite succession of its variety."[14] By adding to the category of experience the dimension of remembrance, memory, futurist painting acquired a dynamic element that cubist painting—in Boccioni's words a "frozen fabrication of images," simultaneous in space but not in time and therefore essentially static—did not have.[15] Complementing simultaneity with the point of view of the perceiving subject imbued futurist simultaneity with that *dynamism*, which for them constituted the overcoming of cubism.

Time brings simultaneity back to its cause: plastic dynamism. As Boccioni wrote, simultaneity was only "the effect of that great cause that is universal dynamism."[16] Dynamism puts in motion the static representation of simultaneous perspectives, adding the emotive and therefore dynamic element of the subject who grasps them. To illustrate this concept, apropos Carrà's painting *Il ciclista*, Boccioni wrote: "It is the sensation of the race and not the racer that we want to render."[17] The world is therefore re-created by reproducing the synthesis of states of mind that it provokes. The subject is placed at the center of the painting, it is at the center of these movements, bombarded by complementary events, arbiter of a chaos that *is* the world, but that also very possibly he himself generated in the act of perception.[18]

The system appears to be symmetrical; the subject generates the complementary multiplicity, and the subject reconciles it. Reality acquires meaning only when there is a subject to gather its dynamic manifestations (expressed in both the relative and the absolute motion of objects), to gather its unity, to sort the chaos into a cosmos.[19] Time allows the subject—the possessed-artist—to reorder and comprehend reality in its dynamic and continuous unfolding.

Though the term *dynamism* is already found in the technical manifesto *La pittura futurista* (1910), which Boccioni coauthored, it became so central to

Boccioni's personal evolution that he dedicated an entire chapter of his book to the concept and even featured the word in the subtitle (*Dinamismo plastico*). Lucidly, as always, Boccioni opened the chapter by defining the term:

> Dynamism is the simultaneous occurrence of the characteristic motion particular to the object (absolute motion) and the transformations that the object suffers in its changes of position in relation to the mobile or immobile environment (relative motion).
> Therefore, it is not true that to have dynamism, all we need is a breakdown of the forms of an object. Certainly, breakdown and deformation have in themselves the value of motion inasmuch as they break the continuity of the line, they break the silhouette-like rhythm, and augment the collisions and the indications, the possibilities, the directions of the forms. Still, this is not an example of futurist Plastic Dynamism, and the trajectory, the swinging of a pendulum, the change of position from point A to point B are not examples of it, either.
> Dynamism is the lyric conception of forms interpreted in the infinite manifesting of their relativity between absolute motion and relative motion, between environment and object, until they shape the apparition of a whole: *environment + object*. It is the creation of a new form, which renders the relativity between weight and expansion. Between motion of rotation and motion of revolution. In short, it is life itself grasped in the form that life creates in its *infinite succession*.[20]

Balla would not have been in complete agreement with this definition of plastic dynamism. In fact, the concept of plastic dynamism split the group of futurist painters into two divergent poetic camps, which Calvesi has summarized as being represented by the emblematic counterpoint of two opposite (but, I would add, absolutely complementary) figures—Boccioni and Balla.[21] Calvesi described Boccioni's poetics as a "subjective synthesis" in contrast to the "objective analysis of Balla."[22] Both positions were inspired by occult study and practices, but whereas synthesis turned to action, analysis turned toward contemplation.

Boccioni believed that optical-mnemonic synthesis, which is carried out by the subject through plastic dynamism and simultaneity of states of mind (subjective synthesis), had the task of re-creating the world by achieving the essential unity of the whole in the *forma unica* (single form).[23] The principle of unity, a constant in Boccioni's *Pittura e scultura futuriste*, was already present in his Roman lecture of May 1911.[24]

The re-creation of unity was first achieved by a chaotic and irrational mobilization of heterogeneous elements, as if under the influence of a philosophy of Marinettian-Nietzschean action. Boccioni's painting style is in fact a chaotic, whirling, dynamic re-creation of reality, exhibited in such works of monumental, frescolike ambition as *Città che sale* (1910–11), *Stati d'animo I: Gli addii* (1911), and *La risata* (1911). Together with a central theme, which was typically made clear in the title of the work and consisted of a portrayal of visual stimuli, Boccioni's paintings also portrayed his remembrances of earlier visual and emotive suggestions. These remembrances were sometimes clearly connected to the central theme by association, but sometimes the connection was freeform, stream-of-consciousness, chaotic in appearance but actually organized by the subjectivity of the possessed artist. Boccioni believed that the chaos of the world, dynamic both in time and space, can be reordered by an artist-initiate into a single form, a unity that substitutes itself for universal unity, obtained with audacious fusion.[25]

Balla, who considered the universe to be a perfectly ordered harmony, was at the opposite pole. Through analyzing the structure of the cosmos and extracting, adopting, and applying abstract forms, Balla sought to imitate the harmony of the macrocosmic order in the microcosm of objects of art, patiently reconstructing a second, artificial universe by means of artworks that would be samples and models of this same perfect harmony, and populating that harmony one model at a time.[26]

Balla's painting is unquestionably closer to the pictorial meditations of Kandinsky or Delaunay than to the titanic force of Boccioni's fusion. Balla paints not action but contemplation, and patient, objective analysis. Nor does Balla aspire to create cosmic unity but rather to reconstruct models, details, and examples, all pointing to the same universal harmony.

The series *Compenetrazioni iridescenti* (1912–14) is perhaps the purest example of this aesthetic position. In this and other works—from *Fallimento* (1902) to *Un mio istante del 4 aprile 1928 ore 10 più due minuti* (1928)—Balla is just as concerned with time and motion as Boccioni is. Yet space and time are not, as in Boccioni, continuities; rather, they are segmented sections of places and instants. A single instant of time can be sliced and used as an example representing all. Such an instant of time is no longer psychological time, but rather objective time, in which, as in Kant, all the instants are homogeneous points and objectively identical. In these works, time stops, while action, the subjective—and Boccionian—synthesis, gives way to meditation and objective analysis.

The positions are complementary, but the pictorial results are opposites. Balla's paintings resound as deeply rational and objective, glorifying a universe ordered within itself. Boccioni paints a world of irrational multiplicity that requires a subject to reorder it and comprehend its essential unity.

Proof of this contrast can be seen in Boccioni's and Balla's divergent ways of representing dynamism. In Balla's canvases from 1912, movement is an optical superimposition of discontinuous instants in time and space, evidently derived from frame-based image scanning of action. Boccioni's canvases from the same period depict movement as a continuous (i.e., indivisible/infinitely divisible) optical-mnemonic synthesis, which takes into consideration not the phenomenon of motion as divided into various phases but the remembrance of it, and the memory and the associations of the subject perceiving it as space-time continuity.

Russolo, like Boccioni, promoted an idea of art as subjective synthesis, creation of the world in all its dynamic and simultaneous chaos, and able to reach a point of fusion in which the space-time complex becomes synthesized into unity.[27] He continued to consider this aesthetic principle valid even years after the first manifestos and theoretical writings of the futurist painters from the years 1910–12.

On December 15, 1919, Russolo was the first of three to sign a memo (the other two signatorees were Achille Funi and Marinetti) inviting all futurist painters to submit written positions about a division of the "avant-garde and futurist painting" into "four aesthetic currents or trends of pictorial sensitivity."[28] These positions were to be gathered into a manifesto (which, according to Soffici, was never published). In the memo, plastic dynamism is described as the "dynamic synthesis of the universe as forces + simultaneity of time-space + synthesis of form color. Lyricism and modernolatry of the subject."[29] In 1919 Russolo still held the positions he had sided with years earlier. Yet by 1919 he had internalized them to the point of maintaining, orthodoxically, Boccioni's very terminology; given that these guidelines were so central for him, they undoubtedly informed his musical research as well.[30]

SECOND LEVEL: SYNTHESIS

Once the pictorial synthesis of simultaneity and dynamism was defined as an optical-mnemonic "subjective synthesis," the dynamic and simultaneous synthesis offered by the art of noises could be defined as an "acoustic-mnemonic subjective synthesis," a synthesis of what one remembers and what one hears. Decontextualized slivers of reality meet in Boccioni's "fresco" in a nebula that adds them to memories and perceptions in a complex, congenital, spiritual unity elaborated by the inspired artist; similarly, the art of noises decontextualized noise (untied it, that is, from the "causes that produce it").[31]

If the first level of the occult-spiritual operation of the art of noises was the transformation carried out by the intonarumori, whose function was to create a spiritual reality by transfiguring noise, synthesis can be viewed as the second level: as in congenital complementarism, the system is symmetrical. The two levels of this spiritual operation save the art of noises from the charge of being a mere imitation of the noises of the world and a senseless cacophony.

At the first level, through enharmonic intonation, noise became dissociated from the causes that produced it and thus spiritualized. In the second level, which corresponds to the first, the noises produced by the orchestra of intonarumori were superimposed simultaneously and dynamically in seeking to create an autonomous, abstract, spiritual synthesis of multiplicity into unity, chaos into cosmos.[32] Despite Varèse's criticism, the noises in this process were only primal matter—a means, not an end.[33] In Russolo's works, the composer does not abdicate his role; on the contrary, the composer's role is demiurgically expanded.

The following—much misunderstood—passage from *The Art of Noises* acquires new meaning once one understands the spiritual and cosmogonic categories of simultaneity of states of mind (or congenital complementarism) and dynamism:

> Let us cross a large modern capital with our ears more sensitive than our eyes and we will take pleasure in distinguishing the eddying of water, air, or gas in metal pipes, the muttering of motors that breathe and pulse with an indisputable animality, the throbbing of valves, bustle of pistons, shrieks of mechanical saws, starting of trams on the tracks, cracking of whips, flapping of awnings and flags. We will enjoy ourselves by orchestrating together in our imagination the din of rolling shop shutters, slamming of doors, buzzing and foot-stepping of crowds, and the varied hubbub of train stations, iron works, thread mills, printing shops, electrical plants, and subways.
> Nor should the newest noises of modern war be forgotten.[34]

The sublime here is achieved through the bombardment of stimuli (acoustic, obviously, and no longer optical), which Russolo seeks to re-create even in his writing style.

To actuate this effect of bombardment, a simultaneous and synchronic superimposition, Russolo envisioned an ideal orchestra composed almost entirely of intonarumori (the sole exceptions were a few percussion instruments: "two timpani, a sistrum, and a xylophone" as Russolo writes in *The Art of Noises*), because the intonarumori were the only instruments capable of re-creating a spiritual multiplicity that would have had nothing to do with the stylization of reality through imitation offered by means of a traditional orchestra.[35]

A mixed orchestra of traditional instruments and intonarumori, like the one Pratella used for his *Aviatore Dro*, or those used in the 1921 Paris concerts, did not interest Russolo. In *The Art of Noises* he wrote: "I aim and I will always aim to complete and enlarge an orchestra composed *entirely and uniquely* of intonarumori. The more than satisfactory results obtained so far are the best incentives to proceed in this direction, so I am even more convinced that the orchestra of intonarumori is and must remain a separate project from the project of a mixed orchestra, but complete in itself."[36]

The term *orchestrating* indicates that Russolo dreamed of a dynamic fusion of noises. This can be presumed from the fragment of the score of *Risveglio di una città*, in which what matters are not the single events—single pitches and articulations—but rather the synchronic crux of events in unquiet movement. For this reason it makes no sense to try to analyze the piece by transcribing the lines and reducing them to melodies, or transcribing the vertical events and reducing them to chord progressions; this has been done, but Russolo did not conceive his scores in these terms.[37]

The dynamic element, already present in enharmonic intonation—which Russolo called dynamic continuity—here returns as simultaneity, the effect of the mutual clash of sound events, regardless of horizontality and verticality.[38] Simultaneity is an acoustic re-creation of experiencing the world as multiplicity and unity, exactly as in the topological dialectic of the spiral, which projects reality outward and at the same time converges reality in its central point of fusion.

With his *spirali di rumori*, Russolo actuated the simultaneity of space and time that leads to an acoustic-mnemonic synthesis with which he could re-create the world acoustically—first as chaos, then as unity. *The Art of Noises* closes with a promise of ascetic unity, the "lyrical and artistic coordination of the noisy chaos of life" to which Russolo gave the hedonistic name "new acoustic voluptuousness."[39] This ascetic unity would be achieved by letting "vibrate the senses and [...] the brain [...] with the unexpected, the mysterious, the unknown."[40]

A mesmerizing impression of this synthesis and fusion was reported in a review of the first concerts of intonarumori. The conclusion of the performance of *Risveglio di una città* on the August 11, 1913, press concert was described by the anonymous correspondent of the *Pall Mall Gazette* on November 18, 1913, as follows: "Finally, all the noises of the street and factory merged into a gigantic roar, and the music ceased. I awoke as though from a dream."[41]

UNITY

Subjective acoustic-mnemonic synthesis—reaching from multiplicity to unity—can be traced to two sources. Immediately detectable is the one found in Ferruccio Busoni's "Il regno della musica" (The kingdom of music) of March 3, 1910, the epilogue to his "Abbozzo di una nuova estetica della musica" (Outline of a new aesthetics of music).[42] In the final section of this epilogue, perhaps the most extraordinarily messianic and visionary moment in his writings, Busoni trumpeted:

> *Everything resounds* [...] and all the beats are a single thing, a whole. [...]
> And now the *sound* is heard! Innumerable are its voices; compared to them the whisper of harps is a din, the blare of a thousand trombones a chirping.
> All, all the melodies heard before and unheard, all of them none excluded resound together at the same time, they transport you, linger upon you, brush against you [...] they themselves are the souls of millions of beings of millions of epochs. Bring one of these melodies close to your eye, and you will see how it is connected with others, combined with all the rhythms, colored by all the colors, accompanied by all the harmonies, down to the bottom of every depth, up to the arch of every vault of the heavens.
> Now you all understand how planets and hearts together unites into one, and never and nowhere could there be an end, nowhere could there be a boundary. Now you all understand that, in the spirit of the being, the infinite lives complete and undivided; that every thing is at the same time infinitely large and infinitely small; and that light, sound, motion, energy are identical, and that each of them in itself, and all joined together, are life.[43]

Many of the occultist themes in Russolo's thought are present in Busoni's text: synesthesia, correspondence, the principle of energy, space-time continuity, dynamism, subjective synthesis, unity. It is not known whether Busoni and Russolo had a personal relationship: even if they did, it would not have equaled that between Busoni and Boccioni. But Russolo must have known of Busoni's text.

Apart from his affinity for the occult and spiritual, Busoni also had an interest in the division of the tone into microintervals—something that Russolo carried to its extreme logical conclusion—and the two shared a great curiosity for new instruments capable of exploiting this division. Busoni greatly admired Thaddeus Cahill's new instrument, the Telharmonium, with its microintervallic intonation, which Busoni thought supernatural because of its ability to generate "miraculously [. . .] a scientifically perfect sound that never decays, invisible, produced without effort and tireless."[44] On the other hand, Russolo's focus is not on the instruments as such but on the "modes of existence" that the instruments can generate. Russolo's interest in microtonality is expressed through the spiritual, metaphysical, constructive surge that led him to build the orchestra of intonarumori.

The simultaneous-dynamic fusion of sound that Russolo sought to achieve with the orchestra of intonarumori had in all probability yet another source: Leadbeater's *The Hidden Side of Things* (1913), in which Leadbeater collected, as he said in the introductory note, writings that had appeared article form from 1901 on. The book opens with the explanation of the term *occultism*, of which Leadbeater records its Latin etymology (*occultus* = hidden), intended here as the science that proposes to unveil the hidden side of reality. In line with theosophical teachings, Leadbeater emphasized that the deepest knowledge of reality is never intentionally hidden, and that "nothing is or can be hidden from us except by our own limitations."[45]

The fundamental idea of the book is that in the course of existence human beings are constantly influenced by unknown forces. We receive waves from various sources, and they modify the aura surrounding our bodies. We ourselves can be sources of this energy, and we can therefore influence ourselves, and those near to us. The external sources that influence us are many (Leadbeater includes the planets, the sun, nature, spirits of nature, beings we do not see, etc.). Because the understanding of the modalities through which these sources can influence us is of great importance, Leadbeater dedicated a chapter to each.

The chapter dedicated to sound, where Leadbeater expanded the section on sound-forms from the final pages of *Thought-forms*, shows how through sound-forms sound can condition the aura of every individual to be found within their radius. Russolo had this chapter in mind during the time he developed the art of noises, as is clear from chapter 4 of *The Art of Noises*, where he follows Leadbeater's taxonomy of sounds.

In the first paragraph of Leadbeater's chapter "Sound, Color and Form," he presents the theories that underlie *La musica*: sound irradiates both colors and forms. After a few paragraphs that deal with sound-forms produced by more traditional musical compositions ("Religious music," "Song," "Military music"), Leadbeater reviews the forms produced by sounds of natural phenomena such as thunder, rain, the rustling of the wind in the leaves, the cries of wild animals ("Sounds of nature"), cries of domestic animals, and of various tones of the human voice, from laughter to whistles ("Domestic life").[46]

A similar taxonomy can be found in the paragraphs "Noises of Nature" and "Noises of Language" in Russolo's *The Art of Noises*.[47] Similarities between the two texts exist even in the choice of examples. Both Leadbeater and Russolo cite thunder as their first example of noise in sound, and nature, and various other examples are presented with impressive correspondence between the texts (the rustling of leaves and rain, and even the noise of the backwash of waves). A Pan-ic sense of harmony in nature, which Russolo likely derived from Gabriele D'Annunzio, animates both works.[48]

The Pan-ic element recurred in compositions for intonarumori, often in the form of rain, as in Nuccio Fiorda's *Processione sotto la pioggia* (Procession in the rain) for mixed orchestra, played in the Paris concerts of 1921, and *Rain* (*La pioggia*) by Antonio Russolo.[49] Aside from a direct acoustic reference to certain intonarumori and certain registers that the noise-harmonium produced, the recurrence of rain in the titles is also connected to the animist-pantheistic soul that animated futurism, and was probably another symbolist remnant, already observable in other movements in Italian culture in the early years of the twentieth century.[50]

In the emblematically titled *Rain in the Anti-D'Annunzian Pine Forest* (*Pioggia nel pineto antidannunziana*), a work by Buzzi published in *L'Italia futurista* on July 25, 1916, these themes intertwine (fig. 21). Although masked by D'Annunzian parody, this *tavola parolibera* evokes (by different means, of course) a Pan-ic atmosphere similar to that found in D'Annunzio's original—something that brings spontaneously to mind the sapid phrase by Alberto Savino, "scratch a futurist and you'll find a D'Annunzian."[51]

Despite the scarcity of scores for the intonarumori, until now the hint at staff notation that appears in the right margin of *Pioggia nel pineto antidannunziana* has gone unnoticed. It is the accompaniment of Buzzi's icastic poem with an "intonarumori ensemble (*batteria* intonarumori)" composed of "crepitatori + gorgogliatori + ululatori."[52] This brief score, halfway between graphic notation and a typographic *caprice*, has every right to be included among the very rare cases of writing for intonarumori that has survived.

FIGURE 21. Paolo Buzzi, *Pioggia nel pineto antidannunziana*, a *tavola parolibera* reproduced in *L'Italia futurista* (July 25, 1916).

But let us return to Leadbeater. The final paragraph of the chapter on sound is entirely dedicated to what for him are noises, that is, principally the sound of machines. Noises, like sounds, can produce sound-forms that influence us. Many noises have a negative effect on man, because of their negative influx onto the aura. But not all noises are malevolent; some produce sound-forms with the power to positively influence our aura.

Among the noises that project benevolent sound-forms, Leadbeater mentions that of a train in motion. Russolo likewise lists the noise of the train among the mechanical noises, but this is hardly surprising—train references were commonplace in Russolo's historical-cultural context. More significant is that Leadbeater's laconically detached survey of noises of weapons of war (cannons, rifles, and pistols) and the sound-forms they produce, re-echoes distinctly in the chilling and much more developed—but no less detached—paragraph on *i rumori della guerra* (the noises of war) in *The Art of Noises*.[53]

FIGURE 22. Luigi Russolo, *Impressione di bombardamento shrapnels e granate* (1926). Portogruaro, Collezione del Comune di Portogruaro.

In his stunning 1926 canvas *Impressioni di bombardamento shrapnels e granate* Russolo actually painted these noises of the war with shapes that are rather close to Leadbeater's description of the sound-forms generated by warfare noises (fig. 22). Russolo's portrayal of such explosions as violent, red-pointed shapes and his portrayal of their echoes in the crisp air as white-pointed shapes resemble dart-like shapes found in some of the plates in *Thought-forms*.[54]

But above all Russolo draws extensively on Leadbeater's final section, particularly in regard to the concept of a subjective synthesis/fusion of sounds into unity.[55] In this section, Leadbeater concluded:

> There is a yet higher point of view from which all the sounds of nature blend themselves into one mighty tone—that which the Chinese authors have called the KUNG; and this also has its form—an inexpressible compound or synthesis of all forms, vast and changeful as the sea, and yet through it all upholding an average level, just as the sea does, all-penetrating yet all-embracing, the note which represents our earth in the music of the spheres—the form which is our petal when the solar system is regarded from the plane where it is seen all spread out like a lotus.[56]

The vast sound-form created in the fusion of the sounds of the world into a unity, which is a sort of total tuning of the universe, had for Leadbeater a positive influence. The reaching of this form, of this stage, and the consequent influence on the auras of the attending audience, could have been one of the most ambitious goals of Russolo's *spirali di rumori*.

A DIFFERENT MUSIC OF THE SPHERES

If it is true—as I believe it is—that Russolo knew the final passage of Leadbeater's paragraph on noises, then it is easy to understand why he was not interested, as one might expect from a scholar of the occult arts and acoustic science, in constructing a finite musical system traditionally founded on the harmonic series. And in fact the occult musical tradition to which Leadbeater (and therefore Russolo) harked back was not based on the static order of the overtone series of the classical-Pythagorean system but rather on the "dynamic" dialectic of chaos versus cosmos.[57]

In Leadbeater's concluding passage cited above, he did not reach the so-called music of the spheres through a recursive application, at a cosmological level, of the highly rational structure of the overtones series, which would have led him to an eminently static conception (discontinuous, finite) of the universe. Rather, he believes that the "mighty tone" that represents the earth in the harmony of the spheres is the final product of a *process* (hence its dynamic nature) of a synthesis/reordering of a chaotic (infinite, continuous) simultaneity. This process is carried out by the subject who, transported by the divine to a privileged point of observation, can from there grasp the sense of the world (much like in Plato's *Phaedrus*, or Cicero's *Somnium Scipionis*). The subject—the inspired artist—can give a sense to the otherwise undecipherable codex of the world, thanks to metaphysical keys furnished by divine inspiration.

The relationship between these two musical and cosmological conceptions is one of radical opposition: a musical system based on the harmonic series relies passively on an intrinsically ordered, discontinuous, finite cosmos, which is therefore possible to analyze objectively. A musical system based instead on the principles of simultaneity and dynamism relies actively on an infinite and chaotic universe awaiting reordering, re-creation and subjective synthesizing.

Russolo's musical conception was not linked to an "objective analysis," a progressive addition of the first intervals (discontinuous, diatonic even) taken from the overtone series and representing the world by imitation through allegories or models, but to a "subjective synthesis" intended as spiritual/occult creation, fusion of multiplicity (continuous, enharmonic) and chaotic superimposition of all the noises of the world in the cosmological unity of a single "mighty tone."[58]

Enharmonic continuity, though conceptually the opposite of the harmonic series, is no less spiritual. This may have been the spiritual destination that Russolo sought to reach with the *spirali di rumori*. In line with the positions of the Milanese futurist group, this was obviously spirituality of action, not of meditation; and in fact, Russolo preferred the action of synthesis to the contemplation of analysis. After all, the young Russolo had never had much patience or sympathy for contemplative attitudes; in fact, he gives what he called a "Buddhistically drunk" attitude a resounding drubbing in his manifesto of the art of noises.[59]

CHAPTER 9

The *Arte dei "Romori"*

Ed Egli è spento,
l'amico leonardesco
di tutte le arti

—Paolo Buzzi, *Ricordi e presagi*

SUPERNATURAL BUILDING SPEED

Russolo scholars share a particular admiration for the speed with which the artist completed his instrument-building projects.[1] Maffina, for instance, in his biography of Russolo, writes: "It is nothing less than surprising that in such a brief period—not just the crafting time needed for their construction (which was perhaps entrusted to various artisans) but also the study time for understanding the various mechanical principles that would lead to the desired results—Russolo was able to perfect fifteen instruments."[2]

The idea of building new musical instruments occurred to Russolo during the performance of Balilla Pratella's *Musica futurista* at the Teatro Costanzi on March 9, 1913, and he announced his intention a few days later, on March 11, in the *Art of Noises* manifesto. It is well documented that Russolo fashioned the first series of intonarumori at breakneck speed during the next few months. As indicated in Russolo's article "Gl'intonarumori futuristi," he had by the end of May 1913 completed four instruments: the scoppiatore, crepitatore, ronzatore, and stropicciatore.[3] On August 11, 1913, at the Casa Rossa in Milan, the general headquarters of the futurist movement, he presented a special press concert featuring the sixteen instruments that constituted the first complete intonarumori orchestra.[4] Maffina observed: "Despite having grown up in a musical family, Russolo was at that time a painter with only basic music training, so one wonders how he could have acquired the knowledge of acoustics and mechanics necessary for the construction of the intonarumori."[5]

Maffina attributed Russolo's engineering speed in large part to Ugo Piatti, Russolo's acknowledged assistant at the time. Maffina's thesis is contradicted, however, by the categorized lists of the futurist members in periodicals and books printed by Marinetti's Edizioni futuriste di poesia, which serve as a useful barometer for the activities of the evolving movement. There Piatti's name is not included under the rubric "Arte dei rumori" but only that of "intonarumori." This is the rubric an assistant, or mechanic, would belong to; in fact, "docile mechanic" is how Cangiullo referred to him in connection with Russolo.[6] In these lists Russolo incontrovertibly occupies the dominant position. His is the brain behind the project—a fact confirmed by the absence of Piatti's name on all the patents.

Maffina's thesis appears all the more curious given that up to this point Piatti, like Russolo, was "only" a painter—and unlike Russolo, he does not seem to have had any interest or training in acoustics and mechanics (let alone a family musical heritage). Indeed, while overvaluing Piatti's role, Maffina also undervalued the influence of Domenico Russolo. Russolo's father had made and maintained watches and clocks and tuned organs and pianos for a living, and surely this instilled in his son some notion of mechanics and its application to acoustics.

But the father's influence alone could not have been sufficient inducement for Russolo's undertaking so difficult a task and accomplishing it in so short a time. A spiritual guide came to Russolo's help: the legacy and aura of Leonardo da Vinci.

LEONARDO'S TOUCH

Russolo's fascination with occult traditions is demonstrated by his unwavering admiration for the work of Leonardo and for the metaphysical aims that guided his work. Russolo was aware of both Leonardo's experiments with acoustics and his projects for building mechanical musical instruments. They formed the main inspiration for Russolo's intonarumori; the rapidity with which he constructed them was the result of his capitalizing on Leonardo's research.

Russolo did not apply Leonardo's principles blindly; rather, he extended them, integrating them into his own aesthetics of sound. His expansion of Leonardo's ideas remained idiosyncratic, and the result was very much his own. But Leonardo's theory of acoustics was unquestionably an important source for Russolo's revolutionary aesthetics. Leonardo's support for the infinite division of the semitone influenced Russolo's (and perhaps Busoni's) enthusiasm for *enarmonia*, and Leonardo's understanding of "noise" (seen in his differentiation between *strepido* and *romore*) was the germ for Russolo's aesthetics of noises. They further shared an interest in the noises of war; the chapter on that topic in Russolo's *The Art of Noises* likely depended at least as heavily on Leonardo's writings on acoustics and ballistics as on Leadbeater's.

To what extent was Russolo aware of Leonardo's work? Given the conflict between futurism and positivistic science, the figure of Leonardo (who to the layman commonly epitomized the triumph of the "thinking subject") might, at first glance, seem out of place in Russolo's pantheon. Further, the very notion that a futurist would take inspiration from *the past* might seem incongruent.

In fact, Leonardo's place in Russolo's pantheon was entirely appropriate. Leonardo's work was for the most part held in high esteem even in the most radical avant-garde circles of the early twentieth century, including those of the futurists.[7] Leonardo's spiritual side came to futurism through such late nineteenth-century progressive movements as the Decadents and symbolists; the young Russolo, traveling in these circles, was one of the conduits.[8] Within Russolo's set of cultural references, Leonardo was something of an initiate, a man who could sublimate technical knowledge by directing it toward a spiritual goal that was the essence of futurism.

The hypothesis introduced here is primarily supported by circumstantial evidence, for Russolo never directly acknowledged his conscious and intentional borrowings. Proof of Leonardo's influence on Russolo is unlikely to be found, given the nature of the futurist movement's core aesthetics. Nevertheless, my hypothesis explains the coincidences and seemingly unrelated incidents, of which there are too many to ignore.

LEONARDINE PRESENCES

During the summer of 1913, Russolo, with Piatti's help, worked furiously on his intonarumori, but he did not start from scratch. He harnessed Leonardo's acoustical research and some of his specific designs as a starting point for constructing his instruments. It cannot be coincidental that Russolo lived most of his life in Milan, the city where Leonardo worked actively for many years and developed most of his designs for the construction of musical instruments.

Young Italian artists of the beginning of the twentieth century grew up knowing about Leonardo's association with Milan. Boccioni, inviting Gino Severini to Milan in October 1907, used Leonardo's work as bait: "Prepare yourself to see a city that does honor to Italy or, better still, represents [Italy] all by herself. You will also see masterpieces including Leonardo's *The Last Supper* and several of his other works."[9] In his posthumously published diary, *La grande Milano tradizionale e futurista*, Marinetti sees Leonardo's presence everywhere in town, from the locks projected and constructed by Leonardo to "dynamize navigation" on the Naviglio Canal, to the titanic monument to Leonardo da Vinci in Piazza della Scala, where he seems to gaze paternally over the ceaseless intellectual—and sometimes physical—disputes around him.[10]

Russolo's relationship with Milan began in 1901, when he was sixteen. His parents had moved to the city earlier, so that his brothers, Giovanni and Antonio, could attend the conservatory, while Russolo was left with an aunt to finish the seminary in Portogruaro. After joining his family in Milan, he took advantage of the respected Accademia di Brera; though he was never regularly enrolled, he was able, with the aid of friends studying there, to keep up with the syllabi and sneak into some of the classes.[11] It was probably through his contacts with Brera that Russolo's passion for the work of Leonardo began.

Russolo's fervent interest is confirmed in a statement made by his sister, Anna Maria Russolo, in 1947, when she claimed that starting in 1905 Russolo "devoted his time to the study of Leonardo's drawing and sketches."[12] The fact that Anna Maria Russolo mentions "drawing and sketches" instead of paintings or frescos tells us two things: that at this point Russolo was interested in studying Leonardo's process more than its realization, and that he studied Leonardo's process not in the paintings but in Leonardo's codices, where most of the sketches are found.

The interest in Leonardo's process was perhaps first inspired by the young Russolo's restoration work on *The Last Supper*. Typically mentioned in his biographies as a mere curiosity, this experience of restoring art became central to his artistic development. Russolo's wife, Maria Zanovello, writes that he worked under a supervisor named Crivelli in a group that restored both *The Last Supper* and Leonardo's decorations of the *Stanze* in the Sforza Castle. All later biographical essays echo Zanovello but without adding anything more.[13] The name Crivelli seems to be a slip of the pen, for it does not appear in sources about the restoration of *The Last Supper*, and Russolo never mentioned it.[14]

The work of restoration 1904–08 was led, infamously, by Luigi Cavenaghi, the first director of the Scuola Superiore di Arte Applicata all'Industria Annessa al Castello Sforzesco (Advanced School for Arts and Crafts at the Sforza Castle), where Russolo's close friend Carrà had been a student in 1904–05, just before he enrolled at the Accademia di Brera.

Although he never mentioned Crivelli in his writings, Russolo does refer to someone named Cavenaghi in a caustic *bollettino medico* (medical bulletin) written jointly with Carrà for *Lacerba*, where Cavenaghi is called a *stercologo* (stoolologist)—a scathingly scatological assessment of the profession of restorer.[15] Marinetti, in *La grande Milano*, remembers having heard a lecture given by Russolo, probably before the *bollettino medico*, in which Russolo ironically praised Cavenaghi's "creative" restoration project: "Leonardo's *The Last Supper* is a gesticulating agony of colors drowned in the fog of the past. Luigi Russolo talks about that in a crowded lecture on the restorer Cavenaghi and on how a painter's genius affords him the right, the duty, to scrape away and destroy the frescoes of others artists of genius and substitute his own if they demand the same wall. Meanwhile humidity has lifted flakes of color out of the fading, aging plaster."[16]

Russolo would have met Cavenaghi through Carrà in 1904, the year in which Carrà attended the Scuola Superiore and the year restoration work began. We can suppose that the experience of restoration, the only formal study of art Russolo ever had, marked him profoundly. Here Russolo developed a profound, privileged relationship with this famous Leonardo fresco: a relationship that was bound to continue through the years. As documented in his *Al di là della materia*, he returned to the crime scene when he was given a personal tour of the 1924 restoration of *The Last Supper* by the restoration supervisor, Oreste Silvestri.[17]

During his early years in Milan, while engaged in fruitful conversation with art students at the Brera Academy and Sforza Castle School of applied arts, attending classes, and helping with the restoration of *The Last Supper*, Russolo gained familiarity with Leonardo's artworks and became acquainted with his writings, in particular with the *Trattato della pittura*.[18] But it was probably through Giorgio Vasari's *Le vite de più eccellenti pittori scultori e architettori* (translated as *Lives of the Painters, Sculptors and Architects*), which Russolo cites frequently in his writings, that he first learned about Leonardo's musical research.[19] Vasari praised Leonardo's performance abilities and specifically mentions the lyre in the form of a horse's skull, fashioned as a gift for Ludovico il Moro.[20] Vasari's *Le vite* may have piqued Russolo's curiosity and led him to examine Leonardo's codices.

Leonardo's music-related speculations are primarily found in two famous manuscripts: the Codex Atlanticus and Arundel 263. The famous Codex Atlanticus is preserved in Milan's Biblioteca Ambrosiana, to which Russolo had convenient access. A third, lesser-known, codex, the Codex Trivulzianus, which contains many of Leonardo's writings on acoustics, is preserved in the library of the Sforza Castle, where Leonardo worked, Carrà studied, Cavenaghi taught, and Russolo lent his services as assistant restorer.

Both the Codex Atlanticus and the Codex Trivulzianus were available in facsimile, the former promoted by the Accademia dei Lincei and published in the Hoepli edition of 1894–1904, and the latter available in Hoepli's edition since 1891. Three additional manuscripts containing Leonardo's musical projects are preserved in Paris, London, and Madrid—curiously, the only places outside Italy where we know Russolo to have traveled.[21]

The source that was most important for Russolo's development was Arundel 263; folio 175r contains a number of projects for the construction of musical instruments—especially percussion and noise-producing instruments—and reveals mechanical principles that foreshadow the intonarumori (fig. 23). But Arundel 263, which reposed in the British Library, was not available in facsimile until 1923–30.[22] Since Russolo did not visit London until June 1914, when he conducted twelve intonarumori concerts at the Coliseum Theater, how could he have known this codex?

The prominent Leonardo scholar Carlo Pedretti has pointed out that folio 175r was one of several pages from Arundel 263 that Jean Paul Richter, the great pioneer of Leonardo studies, chose to reproduce in facsimile in his *Literary Works of Leonardo da Vinci* (London, 1883). Richter's book was immensely popular, and not simply among Leonardo scholars or restorers: it was nothing short of a blockbuster. Russolo, given his interest in Leonardo's work, would have known it.

The accessibility of folio 175r does not prove that Russolo borrowed from it. But the intonarumori employ a number of mechanical principles akin to those in this folio, including adjustable, telescoping sound boxes, resonating bodies tuned in different ratios, and coiled springs that vibrate against a membrane.

Indeed, as a revealing passage in *Al di là della materia* makes clear, not only was Russolo familiar with Leonardo's manuscripts, but he even admitted that "posterity has finally realized how many treasures of intuition and

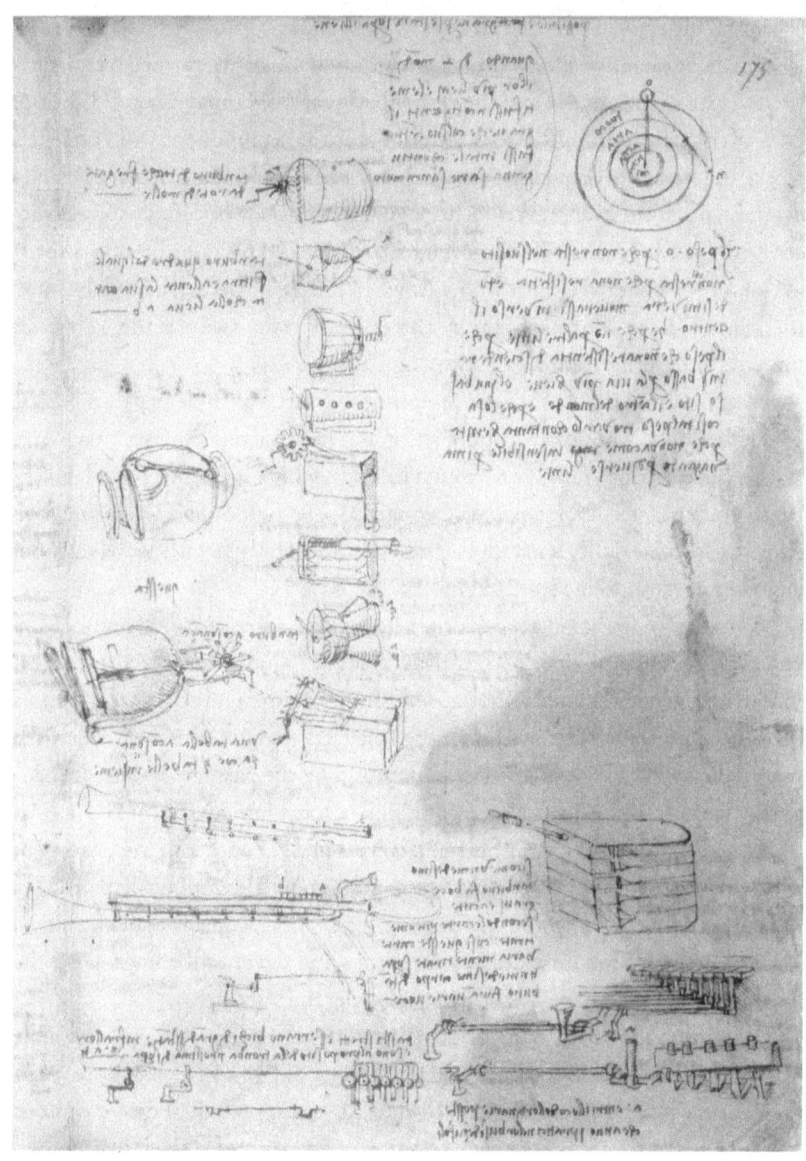

FIGURE 23. Leonardo da Vinci, Codex Arundel 263, fol. 175r. Photo © The British Library Board.

profound observation fill [Leonardo's] manuscripts."[23] Russolo also mentions Leonardo in various other writings, including his last, "L'eterno e il transitorio dell'arte" (The eternal and the transitory in art) of January 1947.[24] Like the Decadents before him, Russolo found a spiritual component in Leonardo's work, and he wrote about the *Mona Lisa* as an example of art that transcends matter, space, time, and every other contingency—a work that aspires, successfully, to the eternal: "Is the *Mona Lisa* beautiful or ugly? Blonde or brunette? Fat or thin? We don't know it, we don't see it. Before her we become the smile, we are the smile, and by the essence of the sweet smile we are all invested and permeated, we are transfigured by it."[25]

Writing similarly of *The Last Supper* as a symbol of the eternal in art, he concludes: "The work of art is pure spirit and lives outside even its own material body, eternally young even though its body, which is matter, is aged, blackened, cracked, as is happening to Leonardo's *The Last Supper*. It becomes in its pictorial materiality a nebulous and evanescent breath without having lost anything of its supreme spiritual life."[26]

What really counts in a work of art is the idea, its spirituality, and not the painting, its materiality (wood, canvas, colors). Painting as object is a fetish that merely generates empty adoration.[27] But if a supreme artist-creator infuses his spirit into the canvas or fresco, the spirit can remain in it even when the materiality of the work of art is compromised by the passage of time. In Leonardo, Russolo saw a creator who could inject spirit into matter.

A meditation on the fight between spirit's permanence and the passing of time rings nicely when it is penned to comment on the work of Leonardo, as he too wrote of time as the supreme enemy: "O Time, consumer of all things! O envious age! Thou dost destroy all things and devour all things, with the hard teeth of years, little by little in a slow death."[28]

Leonardo's idea of time as a continuous and therefore infinitely divisible quantity is closer to Bergson's (and thus Boccioni's and Russolo's) psychological time than to Kant's notion of time as a series of equal discontinuous quantities, a pulse of homogeneous points on a time-line vector.[29] Psychological time, Art time, is the time that creates miracles; it fashions youth from decrepitude, life from death.

That is what wizards such as Leonardo are capable of, as Winternitz has observed about the impressive sketches for the *Study of Madonna with Child and St. John*, in which Leonardo succeeded in "turning the wheel of time in the opposite direction."[30] With a few simple strokes of vivid expressive force,

Leonardo shows us the same figures at different ages: art can thus possess eternal youth, or at least an eternal *spiritual* youth.

For the *inattuale* Russolo, as for Leonardo, the ambitious artifice of creation subverted the conventional notion of *uni-versality* (i.e., directionality) of time.[31] Creation promises that spirit can triumph over directional time, and over matter, surviving even after the death of matter. Clearly, Russolo never ceased being a futurist. Indeed, this is the most moving aspect of futurism: that it is such a vibrant metaphor for eternal spiritual youth, reminding us of that fire.

Further testimony to the connection between Russolo and Leonardo comes from an authoritative contemporaneous source. After Russolo's death, Paolo Buzzi wrote a brief commemorative introduction to Zanovello's biography. In this brief, four-page essay, intended above all to enumerate and celebrate Russolo's achievements, Leonardo's name appears twice; Buzzi reveals the profound similarities of thought process between the two artists, to the point that he involuntarily betrays Russolo's borrowings from Leonardo: "Russolo, the polymath, concerned himself with another avenue of physics: the study of acoustic phenomena. For him the evolution of music, in parallel with the increase of machines developed to help humanity, led to the necessity of increasing the number of sounds and timbres available to composers so as to not avoid but rather seek for a compositional embracing of *noise*. In short, he resembled Leonardo in designing a new lyre for Ludovico il Moro."[32] Buzzi compares the curiosity of Russolo the researcher to that of Leonardo: "In later years he was an apostle of magnetism, and here again I cannot resist the comparison with Leonardo in terms of the multifacetedness of their speculative endeavor when it concerned the enigmas of Nature."[33]

In *Ricordi e presagi*, the tombeau that closes Zanovello's biography, Buzzi invoked Leonardo's spirit one last time, thus framing a book with references to Leonardo. The poems, suggestively, bemoans:

> And He is dead,
> Leonardine friend
> Of all the arts.[34]

INTONARUMORI'S INSIDES[35]

Traces of Leonardo's projects are identifiable throughout Russolo's instrument-building period, which extended from the *scoppiatore* (combuster) of 1913 to the *nuovo istrumento musicale a corde* of 1931. Russolo obtained three patents for the

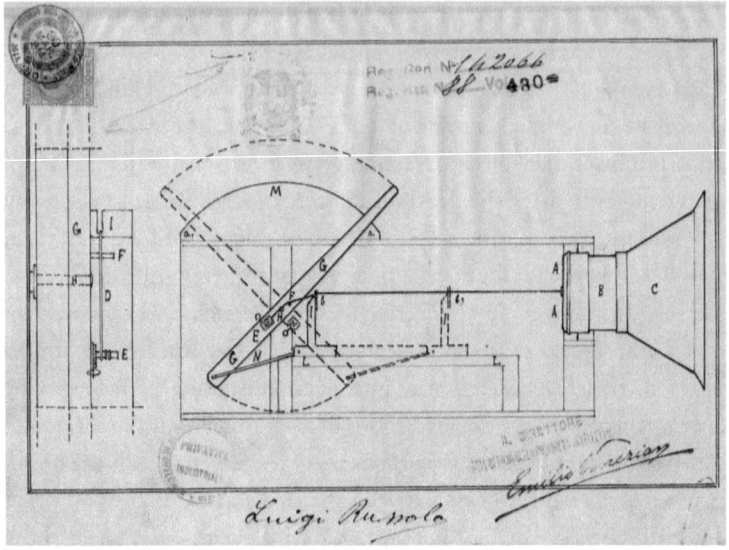

FIGURE 24. Luigi Russolo, drawing for the patent for *Intonatore dei rumori*, Reg. Gen. N. 142066, Reg. Att. 88, Vol. 430, deposited in Milan on March 30, 1914.

intonarumori: in March 1914, October 1921, and November 1921. The projects of 1914 (fig. 24) and November 1921 (fig. 25) concerned essentially the same type of string-based instrument, the only difference being the telescopic sound box added in the November 1921 patent.[36] The patent of October 1921 is for an intonarumori that Barclay Brown, in his English edition of *L'arte dei rumori*, identifies as the *sibilatore* (whistler) (fig. 26).

The *ululatore* (howler), *rombatore* (rumbler), *crepitatore* (crackler), and *stropicciatore* (rubber) all are versions of the January 1914 patent. All the instruments in this group have a string attached to a chemically treated drumskin that Russolo called *diaframma* (diaphragm); the string is set to vibrate by a wheel acting as a continuous bow.

As the name *intonarumori* suggests, noise is "tuned"; this is obtained both by the tension and length of the string and by the tension of the drumskin; in the model with the telescopic resonance box placed behind the membrane (patent of November 1921), the change of pitch is accompanied by a change in length of the resonance box, itself acting on the timbre as a resonance filter. Pitch changes are controlled mechanically by a lever, connected to a needle that, moving along a graduated scale, gave the performer reference points

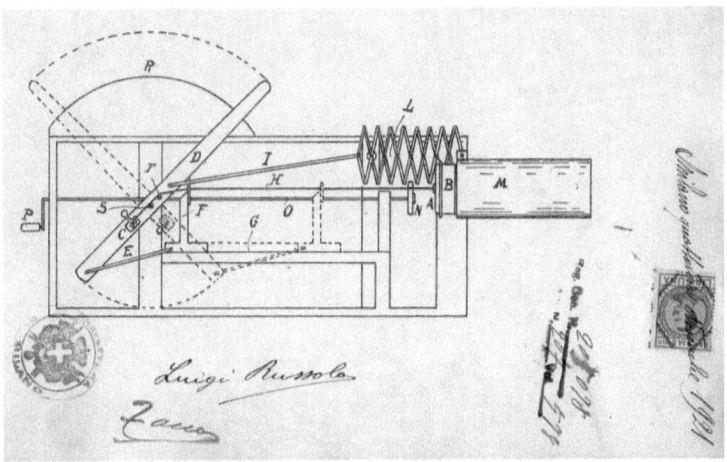

FIGURE 25. Luigi Russolo, drawing for the patent for *Descrizione della prima aggiunta al brevetto depositato l'8/10/1921*, Reg. Gen. N. 205098, Reg. Att. N. 207, Vol. 598, deposited in Milan on November 14, 1921.

for enharmonic intonation. The lever moved continuously, not incrementally, thus affording the kind of uninterrupted microtonality previously referred to as enharmony. Since the lever moved continuously, rather than in spurts, the instrument effectively conquered the enharmonic space.

The intensity, or volume, depended on the pressure of the wheel against the string. This pressure remained unchanged during a performance, though the speed at which the crank was turned, which affected timbre, would have affected the volume as well. The noise produced was dialed on drumskin, shaped or filtered by the sound box connected to it (the sound box was modeled after the Helmholtz resonators, see letter B in figs. 24 and 25), and amplified by a hornlike cone similar to those found in gramophones.

Timbre—the crucial aspect—was determined by the type of wheel (smooth and resin-coated or notched), its material (metal or wood), the position of the wheel in relation to the movable bridge, the type of string, the degree of pressure and speed of the wheel on the string, and, in the November 1921 model, the telescopic sound box acting as a moving harmonics filter (letter M in fig. 25).

The patent does not describe the *ronzatore* (buzzer) or the *gorgogliatore* (gurgler). Though they retain structural similarities with the patented instrument—both have levers and strings attached to drumskins—they differ in

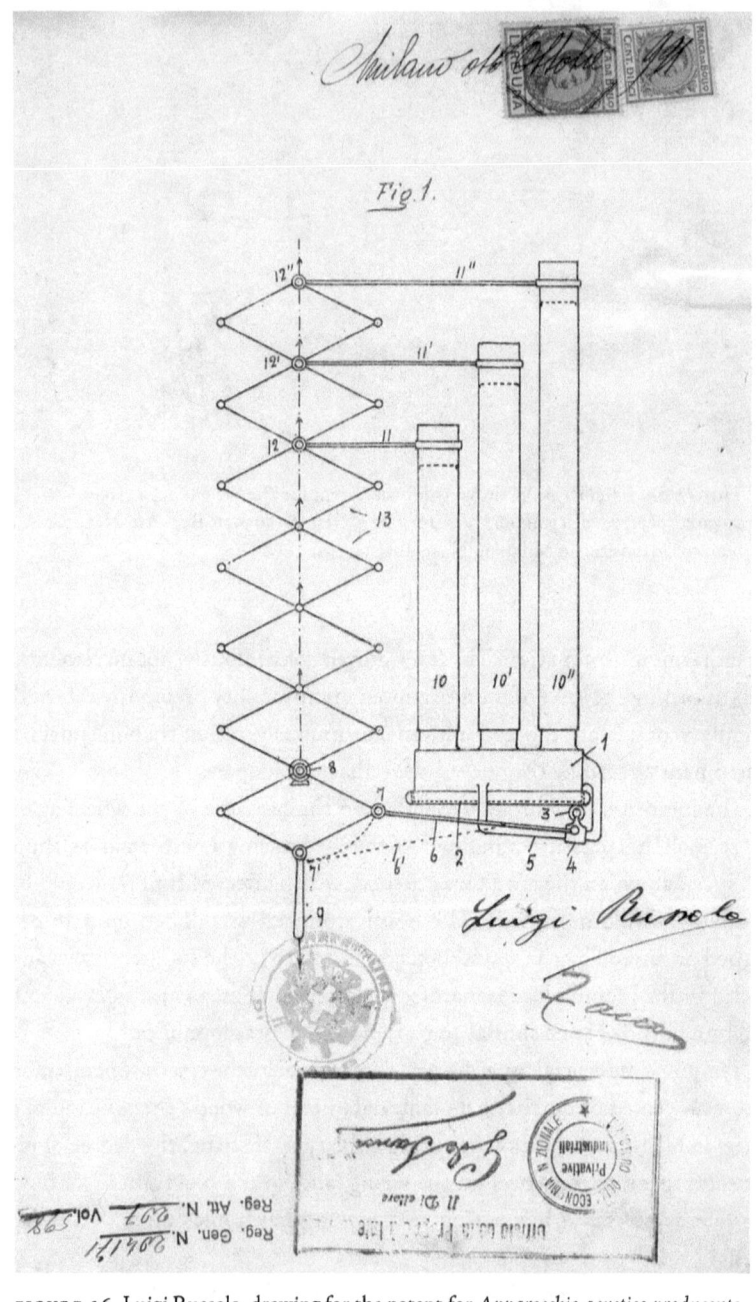

FIGURE 26. Luigi Russolo, drawing for the patent for *Apparecchio acustico producente sotto l'azione di un rumore qualsiasi dei suoni la cui tonalità e il timbro sono definiti*, Reg. Gen. N. 204171, Reg. Att. N. 207, Vol. 598, deposited in Milan on October 8, 1921.

that the agent of vibration is an electric device rather than a wheel; for this reason they use not a crank but a button interface.

Based on photographic evidence—the single extant photograph of the internal mechanism of any of the intonarumori—it is clear that in the ronzatore the sound was produced by an electric bell mechanism whose ball-shaped metal beater, powered by an electric current, was driven to beat against a drumskin whose tension was adjustable by means of the string-and-lever device.[37]

Once the ronzatore was understood, it was possible to reconstruct the gorgogliatore, whose sound was produced by an electric bell mechanism mounted this time so as to beat directly against a string connected to a drumskin with adjustable tension. A coiled spring mounted on the other side of the drumskin, acting as a spring reverb, gave the instrument its characteristic gurgling sound.

For the intonarumori patented in October 1921—this may have been for a later version of the sibilatore—noise was tuned differently. The patent does not specify how the noise is generated, but based on how the sibilatore's principal timbre is described in the *Art of Noises*, it can be assumed that the sound envelope was close to white noise.[38] The performance of an envelope produced by a mechanical white-noise generator would have maximized a complex sound filtering system such as the one found in the patent.

The patent shows how the noise, once generated, was tuned and processed. As in the other intonarumori, the vibrations are tuned by changing the tension of a skin membrane that Russolo here called *diaframma vibratile* (vibrating diaphragm), mounted on the resonance box. The tension of this diaphragm is controlled by a metal roll placed on a guide rail running through the radium, but slightly inclined in respect to the diaphragm: the roll slides across the back, increasing and decreasing its pressure on the diaphragm. An alternative solution, suggested in the patent but not shown in the drawings, controls the tension of the skin with a timpani pedal system.

To filter the tuned noise's timbre, Russolo hypothesized a system of *risonatori sintonici* (syntonic resonators) mounted directly on the resonance box and themselves moving along with the change in tension of the diaphragm and thus entering into a *risonanza composita* (composite resonance) with the vibrations of the diaphragm. These resonators, acting as filters, could be telescoping organ pipes or even strings tuned in various ratios. For the resonators to remain in resonance with the tuned noise as it glides "enharmonically" during performance, a scissorlike device follows the process by continuously varying their tuning according to the tension of the diaphragm.

In the figure included in the patent, Russolo used as an example pipes tuned in harmonic ratios. The presence of pipes in this figure has generated some confusion. Brown believes that the pipes of the sibilatore were fed by bellows, even though the patent shows no need for bellows; bellows are mentioned in the *Pall Mall Gazette* of November 18, 1913, which covered the Casa Rossa press concert. This was the only occasion on which the press was allowed to examine the workings of one of the intonarumori.[39]

Even assuming that this account is reliable, the presence of bellows in a 1913 instrument would not prove that bellows fed pipes in the 1921 patent. Calling the pipes *risonatori sintonici*, Russolo explained that their function was only to modify the timbre, or color, of the sound. The tuning of these pipes is relevant only insofar as it filters the timbre of the tuned, vibrating diaphragm. If strings were to be substituted for pipes, they were likely vibrating sympathetically with the primary medium, the diaphragm.

The resonators were thus not responsible for the production of the sound; if they had been, the sibilatore, based on Russolo's figure, would simply have produced glissandos of major triads—which doesn't sound likely. On the contrary, the alleged bellows observed in one of the intonarumori of 1913 would not have had anything to do with the system of syntonic resonators: it would not explain, in fact, why Russolo would have had to wait almost eight years to patent an instrument using that principle.

The *scrosciatore* (hisser) was not an independent intonarumori but rather an additional register that could be added to both the ronzatore and the sibilatore. When the register of the scrosciatore was added to either of these instruments, a series of strings or even springs were set by a lever to touch the membrane and vibrate against it, as a snare would, thus altering the timbre.

Russolo continued these developments until the early 1930s, designing a number of additional original musical instruments for which he kept improving most of the mechanical principles he had first employed in the intonarumori. In 1921 Russolo began working on a harmoniumlike noise instrument, the rumorarmonio, of which he produced several versions. The third version of the rumorarmonio succeeded not only in combining most of the noises produced by the various intonarumori but also, like the intonarumori, in controlling these noises enharmonically through leverlike interfaces.

In the 1930s Russolo shifted his research from noise-tuning devices to an instrument that exploited the longitudinal mode of vibration of strings. Patented in Paris in 1931 as a *nuovo istrumento musicale a corde* (new string instrument), this device—it was in all probability his last musical project—was an

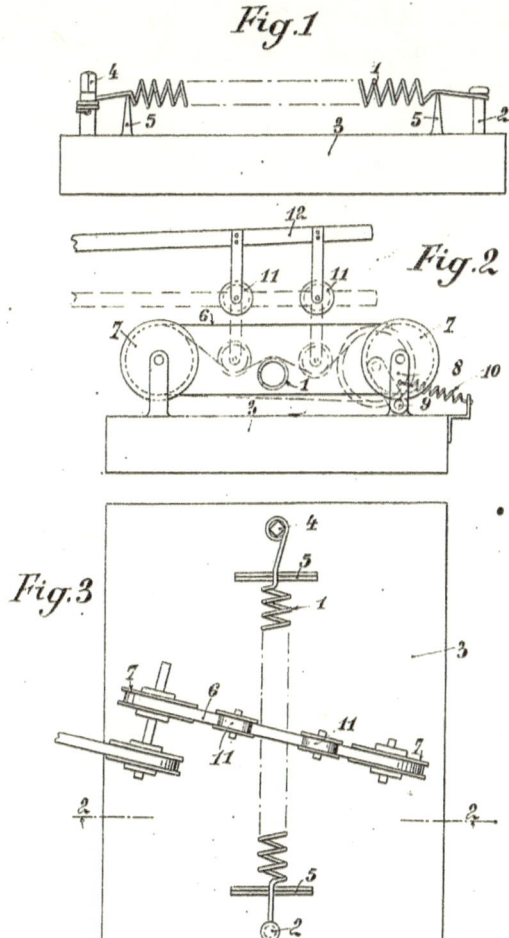

FIGURE 27. Luigi Russolo, drawing for the patent for *Instrument de musique*, N.715.733, requested in Paris on April 20, 1931, deposited on September 29, 1931, and published on December 8, 1931. Archives of Institut National de la Propriété Industrielle.

ingenious "string organ" in which a series of rotating friction belts, controlled by a keyboard, continually excited in longitudinal mode an equal number of steel coiled springs (fig. 27).

Zanovello, inexplicably, called this instrument a *piano enarmonico* (enharmonic piano). Although this name is found in neither the patent nor any of the other writings in which Russolo refers to it—not surprisingly, since the instrument had no enharmonic properties—the "new string instrument" is erroneously called "piano enarmonico" in practically all subsequent secondary sources.[40]

Zanovello suggested that Russolo had built a model with a range of one octave that was later almost completely destroyed.[41] This is inaccurate; in fact, a model with eight keys that Russolo probably rebuilt in 1945, is now preserved at the Russolo Foundation in Varese.[42] This instrument is not, however, the prototype with five keys that Russolo mentioned in the Italian draft for the 1931 patent, and which presumably he had left behind in Paris.[43]

COMPARING THE DESIGN

Leonardo da Vinci's projects involving newly invented musical instruments, like his activity as performer-improviser on the lira da braccio and his studies on acoustics, have been extensively documented by Emanuel Winternitz in *Leonardo da Vinci as a Musician*. Leonardo's projects can be summarized as follows:

1. a mechanical kettledrum activated by a crank to control the beaters;
2. mechanisms for tuning of percussion instruments such that they acquire melodic, harmonic, and enharmonic properties. This was realized in various ways:

    - by mounting differently tuned drums on one support, such that they could be played by one musician;
    - by mechanically modifying the tension of a drumskin with ropes and a screw controlled by a crank, resembling modern timpani;
    - by placing along the drum box lateral apertures that could be opened or closed by the palms of the hands so as to obtain different frequencies and timbre filtering—a sort of drum flute;
    - by controlling three tuned ratchets of different length with the same crank, thus producing a chord of three frequencies;
    - by attaching cones as tuned resonators to the base of a side snare drum;
    - by using devices that could continuously modify the size or the morphology of a sound box, thus affording the instrument enharmonic possibilities by changing actual pitch or filtering the timbre (e.g., an enharmonic ratchet, an enharmonic drum, an enharmonic friction drum, an enharmonic pot drum);

3. instruments where a skin membrane amplifies the noise of horsehair drawn through it (a friction drum) or the noise of coiled springs moved by a crank to scratch against an indented board attached to a drumskin;
4. an "enharmonic" flute;

5. a double-bellows device for organs, allowing continuous feeding of the pipes and thus sustained sound at will;
6. a keyboard instrument, called by Leonardo the *viola organista*, that produced a continuous sound on strings. In the first version, the sound was produced by a bow moving forward and back. Leonardo soon replaced the bow with a wheel that excited the strings, similar to that of the hurdy-gurdy. In the final version he called for a double friction belt, probably made from horsehair or silk thread. The sound was controlled dynamically by pressure on the keys that precisely regulated the pressure of the belt on the strings (like the bow of a violin), making crescendos and decrescendos possible.

Leonardo also developed functional characteristics such as amplifying cones, cranks, and supports designed to free the hands to use drumsticks.

The similarities between Leonardo's mechanical principles and those at the heart of Russolo's projects are striking. Principles common to both include:

- the skin membrane, or drumhead, as a means of amplifying a noise;
- mechanisms to change the tension of the membrane during performance, so as to change the pitch;
- a way to control dynamics through the pressure of a wheel or belt against a string;
- indented or notched friction surfaces;
- rotating sound generators;
- resonating sound boxes with modifiable dimensions, allowing timbre filtering;
- springs vibrating against a membrane;
- tuned resonators applied to a membrane;
- the continuous mechanical beating of a drum;[44]
- continuous sound.

DYNAMIC BOWING

Russolo may have based his rotatory-friction instruments not so much on the hurdy-gurdy as on the more sophisticated principles of Leonardo's *viola organista*. This instrument was most certainly the principal source for Russolo's nuovo istrumento musicale a corde, and constitutes the most obvious point of contact between Russolo and Leonardo. Indeed, the nuovo istrumento is essentially a perfected version of Leonardo's viola organista: a keyboard instrument that produced a continuous sound of strings with a series of friction belts that could also control the dynamic level of every string in real time, according to the degree of pressure applied on the keys. With this characteristic, the instrument, according to Russolo, surpassed the organ:

> [With the nuovo istrumento] one regulates the intensity of sound with a greater or lesser pressure of the belt [against the vibrating body], that is to say pressing with the finger more or less so as to lower the key more or less, as the violin regulates the intensity of the sound with the pressure of the bow against the strings.
>
> Therefore, one can obtain with this instrument all the effects of continuous, sustained chords as in the organ. At the same time one is able to give them all the expression of a violin because every smallest and quickest variation of pressure on the key is immediately reproduced by the belt that thus modifies with great sensitivity the intensity of the resulting sound.[45]

It is useful to compare Russolo's description of the nuovo istrumento with Winternitz's speculation about the dynamic possibilities of Leonardo's viola organista:

> Such an instrument would not have been merely a counterpart of the organ, where ten fingers control numerous pipes, but would have surpassed the organ in one significant aspect: that is, in the flexible dynamics permitting the fine graduation of volume [...]. In Leonardo's viola organista the finger pressure on the keys would have [...] modified the loudness of the tones produced.[46]

It is unclear whether Winternitz understood that the instrument, unlike the piano, could modify dynamics after the keys had been pressed, even though a contact lever for this purpose is shown in another sketch of Leonardo's, also reproduced by Winternitz.[47] Both Russolo, in his patent of 1931, and Winternitz, in describing Leonardo's work, emphasize that the resources of the new instruments surpass those of the organ.[48]

Russolo appears to have studied Leonardo's viola organista projects with great attention: in the second of his detail drawings for the patent for his nuovo istrumento, for example, Russolo used the same perspective as Leonardo had in one of the sketches for the viola in Madrid MS II, folio 76r (fig. 28). Winternitz recognizes three phases in Leonardo's search for an "infinite bow": a true bow moving forward and back, a friction wheel, and a friction

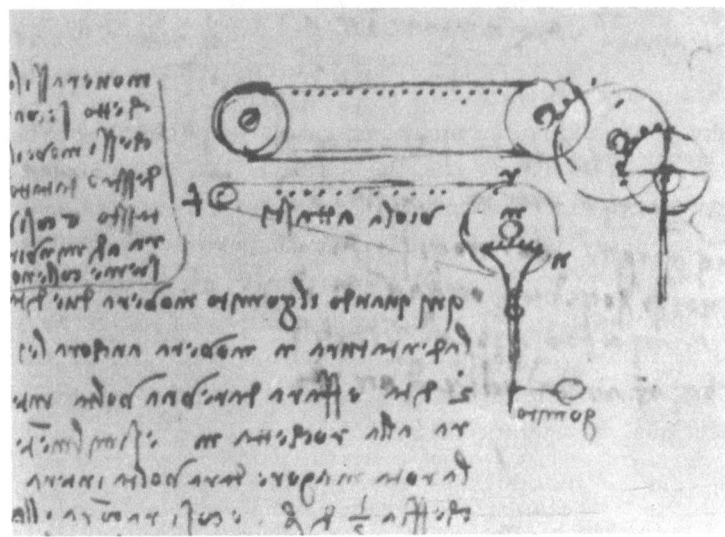

FIGURE 28. Leonardo da Vinci, sketch for the viola organista, from Madrid MS II, fol. 76r.

belt.[49] Russolo, too, who may not have been familiar with the exact progression of the viola organista sketches, curiously progressed from the friction wheel of the intonarumori to the friction belt of the nuovo istrumento.

The viola organista and nuovo istrumento differ significantly in only one respect: in the nuovo istrumento the strings are excited lengthwise. Longitudinal vibration of the string is rare, because this requires very long strings, as an ordinary length would produce pitches that could easily pass beyond the upper audible range.[50] Russolo overcame the problem of string length in a practical way, by using coiled springs of steel thread. Acting like an infinite bow, the friction belt sets the strings to vibrate along the plane of the coil. According to the patent, increased pressure would make the volume louder, an effect that Russolo claimed could be reenforced when traditional lateral vibration is added to longitudinal vibration.

It has been suggested that the intonarumori derived from the hurdy-gurdy, and Winternitz says the same of Leonardo's viola organist.[51] Yet this is true only in the sense that what makes the strings of the hurdy-gurdy vibrate is the cranked wheel functioning as a perpetual-motion bow. But unlike Russolo's and Leonardo's projects, the hurdy-gurdy causes all the strings to vibrate simultaneously; most are drones, with only the so-called melodic strings (usually two strings at the unison) changing pitch. Moreover, the ambitus of the hurdy-gurdy is typically limited to an octave.

Winternitz characterized the hurdy-gurdy as having three distinguishing features: its machinery, its continuous sound, and its reliance on a one-octave melody accompanied by a drone. The first two of these are certainly shared by some of Leonardo's instruments, including the viola organista, and most of Russolo's (the intonarumori, rumorarmonio, and the nuovo istrumento). But Leonardo's projects deliberately avoid drones or fixed pitches, favoring rather mechanisms that allow melodic flexibilities (as in his tuned drums) and independent voice leading (as in the case of the viola organista). Russolo, too, preoccupied with enharmony, never called for the hurdy-gurdy's most obvious aural characteristic: the fixity of the drone.

SOUND SENSIBILITIES

Russolo's borrowings from Leonardo were not limited to principles of construction but extended to matters of acoustics and aesthetics. Chief among these was the notion of enharmony, which, along with the designing and building of enharmonic intonarumori, Russolo considered to be, as he wrote in his 1923 article "L'enarmonismo," his paramount accomplishment. Here, too, he owed a substantial debt to Leonardo, not only as regards the design of instruments that could safely be called enharmonic but also in regard to intention, for Leonardo's attempt to place music in the category of continuous quantity is strikingly close to Russolo's theorization of enharmony.

For both Leonardo and Russolo, building the instruments went hand in hand with the related theorizing. Among the enharmonic instruments Leonardo depicted in Codex Arundel 263 folio 175r are: the timpanilike drum with a crank-turned screw to adjust the tension of the skin; the instrument that Winternitz identifies as a *pot drum*; a type of ratchet; and a drum with a slide window opening into the resonance chamber. All of them were capable of modifying pitch (and/or filtering their timbre) along a continuous spectrum, and thus they were, in Russolo's terminology, enharmonic.[52]

Two instruments designed by Leonardo, sketchily described by Winternitz, seem to have had enharmonic possibilities: a friction drum and a second type of ratchet.[53] In both these instruments, what was probably waxed fabric allowed the performer to modify the dimensions of the body of the instrument during performance, thus gradually filtering the timbre. The performer would have moved a hand inside and outside the instrument, while using the other hand to perform friction on the hairs, or to turn the crank. To stabilize the instruments, the loop of rope designed by Leonardo that Winternitz thought was a handle must instead have been a shoulder or neck strap.

One of the most interesting among Leonardo's enharmonic instruments is what Winternitz called the glissando flute, a sketch of which is found in the Codex Atlanticus (CA folio 397rb). In his explanatory text, Leonardo says that this flute does not change pitch by leap but "in the manner of the human voice" (*nel modo proprio della voce umana*). The instrument can produce microtonal pitches—"You can obtain one eighth and one sixteenth of the tone and just as much as you want" (*possi fare 1/8 and 1/16 di voce, e tanto quanto te piace*)—and, by extensively moving the fingers along the slits, glissandi as well.[54]

Puzzled by Leonardo's flute, Winternitz notes how little it would have had in common with the musical practice of the time: "Such a glissando instrument would have not fitted into the orchestra [sic] of Leonardo's day," Winternitz wrote, naïvely adding: "Could he [Leonardo] have foreseen in a dreamy corner of his incredible brain glissando instruments such as that invented in 1924 by the Russian scientist Lev Theremin?"[55]

Since the slide trumpet and trombone were already in use, the theremin seems hardly relevant.[56] By maintaining that "obtaining an eighth and one sixteenth obviously means [...] to reach the upper octave," Winternitz fails to understand the microtonal implications of this instrument.[57] More important, he does not connect any of these enharmonic instruments with the theoretical base found in Leonardo's writings on acoustics, even though he analyzes these very writings in the last section of his book.[58]

LEONARDO'S ENHARMONY

The notion of a musical system comparable to the one Russolo called enharmonic is implied in Leonardo's *Il paragone*.[59] This treatise in a treatise constitutes that section of his *Trattato della pittura* written to prove that painting has a greater metaphysical status than the other arts. According to Winternitz, however, Leonardo contradicts himself when later in this passage (Trattato 31C) he then recognizes the same status for music: "If you [the musician] say that only the nonmechanical [physical, bodily, material] sciences [liberal arts] are concerned with the mind and that, just as Music and Geometry deal with the proportions of the continuous quantities, and Arithmetic with the proportions of the discontinuous quantities, [so] Painting deals with all the continuous quantities and also with the qualities of the proportions [degrees] of shades and lights and, thanks to perspective, distances as well."[60]

Leonardo believed that music could only achieve the status of painting when it deals with continuous quantities, that is, when it has "continuous flow." As Winternitz has it: "The flow—that is to say the smooth gliding from one tone to the next—elevates music to a *scientia mentale* dealing with continuous quantities, like Geometry and Painting. Thus, to a scientific scrutiny, an equality of rank is established between Painting and Music."[61]

Winternitz defined "smooth gliding" as the unfolding of a melody in time, one note after the other—the kind of a continuity in time that he thinks Leonardo discusses in a passage in Codex Arundel 263:

> Although time is included among the continuous quantities, it does fall—since it is invisible and incorporeal—into the realm of geometry, whose divisions consist of figures and bodies of infinite variety, as a continuum of visible and corporeal things. But only in their principles do they [geometry and time] agree, that is, with regard to the point and the line; the point is comparable to an instant in time; and just as the line is similar to the length of a section in time, so the instants are ends and beginning of each given section of time. And if the line is infinitely divisible, so is the section of time resulting from such division; and if the sections of a line are proportionable to one another, so are the [successive] sections of time proportionable to one another.[62]

Unlike Winternitz, I am convinced that Leonardo in Trattato 31C was referring to the possibility of an infinite (and therefore continuous) microtonal division of a given interval (continuity in pitch space). Since continuous quantities are infinitely divisible—Leonardo discussed this in the passage from Codex Arundel—painting is quantifiable as continuous because of shading (light, shadow) and perspective, a conventional system that allows simultaneous two-dimensional representation of objects that actually exist in a three-dimensional space. Because the lines of a field of perspective are infinitely divisible, the portrayed objects can occupy every position within the simulated field, exactly as they occupy three-dimensional reality.

In Trattato 31C, Leonardo suggested that, just as painting allows and displays all degrees of shadow and light and all degree of distance in perspective, filling the space uniformly and continuously, music can aspire to an equivalent status only when it produces all the intermediate shadings of frequency between two distant pitches. Leonardo believed that music must be continuous not simply in time (as Winternitz maintained) but in that continuous dimension I refer to as pitch space.[63]

Here Leonardo posits a difference of metaphysical status between music and poetry and claims that as music unfolds in continuous pitch space, it occupies a dimension unknown to poetry.[64] Music can live in a continuous dimension when its sounds can inhabit any position of the infinite pitch space, a dimension that is, like perspective in painting, continuous. Just as the perspective line is infinitely divisible, so is the interval in acoustics. Pitch is a continuous quantity because every interval between two pitches is infinitely divisible: possibly it was on this basis that Leonardo explained the difference in status between poetry and music: music's proportions (by which Leonardo must have meant the intervallic proportions) are unknown to poetry.[65]

In the process of demonstrating the difference in status between poetry and music, Leonardo in Trattato 21 introduced the notion of *armonico concento*, which Winternitz describes as the harmony created by proportions between different pitches: a harmony that, according to Leonardo, poetry is not able to create. Leonardo described armonico concento as a phenomenon that hits the senses simultaneously (the eye in painting, the ear in music—but not in poetry). But when read into the context of its time, *armonico concento* can only refer to a broad acceptance of the term *harmony* as a relationship between different pitches in the pitch-space continuum—a harmony of intervals, whether simultaneous or not.

Winternitz sometimes failed to realize that Leonardo's theoretical approach does not place harmony and melody in opposition.[66] However, it is important to remember that in these texts we are not dealing with a question of horizontal and vertical in the modern sense.[67] Armonico concento is a science of intervallic proportions, not necessarily of verticalities. Difference in time is not pertinent, therefore, because intervallic proportions occupy space, not time, and if considered from the point of view of their existence in pitch space, what we currently distinguish as melodic interval and harmonic interval was in Leonardo's time considered one and the same. In the pitch-space continuum, time and space collide.

This intervallic space can be envisaged much as Schoenberg thought of dodecaphonic space, or as Swedenborg thought of skies—a conception that in fact inspired Schoenberg's.[68] Special topological properties apply here: it does not matter if the intervals are horizontal and melodic or vertical and harmonic, nor does their direction matter but only the continuous pitch space that these intervals imply or evoke.[69]

Hence, if any melodic winding usually implies a *harmonic* pitch space (for an arpeggiated chord is still a chord), the melodic winding of a monodic instrument like the glissando flute or the intonarumori showcases the continuousness—what we would call enharmonic—of pitch space. (By the same token, a discussion of form, whether in music or poetry, is not pertinent here, since form, which Leonardo understood to be a different kind of harmony—formal harmony between proximate sections of a poem or a musical work—unfolds continuously only in time and is, in the last analysis, about memory.)[70]

Leonardo believed that poetry, though continuous in time, cannot be continuous in space because it lacks the possibilities provided by pitches and intervals; its lower status is due to the inability to produce armonico concento, that is, it does not function with intervallic proportions. Though music, likewise, unfolds in time, it is active—either harmonically or melodically—in pitch space.[71] By doing no more than operate in the time continuum, poetry cannot inhabit the continuity of infinite pitch space that is the realm in which music operates.

This is why Russolo's and Leonardo's instruments, which can slide or make true glissandi and therefore display enharmonic properties, are so significant. They achieve a functional perfection of musical time and space. In fact, the only way to understand the function of Leonardo's instruments is to consider the music that he dreamed of as continuous not only in time but also in pitch space.[72]

Leonardo's music deals with continuity in two ways. First, by the prolongation of sounds and sustained notes, which he explored with wheels or friction belts and his "perpetual" bellows (a manifestation of the continuity in time).[73] Second, with enharmony, a manifestation of the continuity in pitch space.[74] The relationship with continuous quantities confers spiritual properties on the music because continuity, addressing infinite divisibility, is linked to divine perfection.[75] Russolo may have become attracted to Leonardo's projects precisely because he saw spiritual worth in them.

Russolo's instruments have properties that are similar to those of Leonardo's instruments, manifesting continuity in both time and pitch space. Continuity in time was not a new concept—all music unfolds in time, and instruments that can sustain sound, such as the organ, showcase the property well—but achieving enharmonic continuity in pitch space was a key accomplishment for Russolo, as he proudly confirmed in writings such as "Conquista totale dell'enarmonismo mediante gl'intonarumori futuristi," "Grafia enarmonica per gl'intonarumori futuristi," and the polemic "L'enarmonismo."[76]

Certainly Busoni's *Abbozzo di una nuova estetica della musica* was, with all of its spiritual and metaphysical implications, an important source for Russolo's enharmonic vision. But Leonardo's *Il paragone* is what, above all, echoes in Russolo's writings.[77]

ROMORI VS. RUMORI

When Leonardo discussed noises in his writings on acoustics, he formulated an early aesthetics of the subject. He used two different words for noise: *strepido*, the sound of a loud explosion, and *romore*, a prolonged, less aggressive yet loud sound.[78] Leonardo uses the term *strepido* in contexts like this one: "The tone [*strepido*, or noise] of the bombard directed against water kills all animals that find themselves in such water."[79] *Strepido* is associated with a military explosion, and in fact Leonardo discusses it in his studies of acoustics as applied to the science of war. Winternitz remarks: "As a sought-after technical adviser on artillery and especially as the military engineer for Cesare Borgia, Leonardo was familiar with the functioning of firearms, including naturally the acoustic aspects of firing cannons, and in particular the effect of the length of the gun on the volume of the sound produced and the impact of the atmosphere, misty or clear, on the loudness."[80]

In confirmation, Winternitz cited two passages from Leonardo's writings. One is from the Codex Atlanticus: "Why the short mortar makes a louder explosion when fired than a long one, as one hears it in drawing the breech[es] of the small cannon."[81] The other passage is from the Codex Trivulzianus:

THE NATURE OF THE EFFECT OF THE ROAR OF THE MORTAR [BOMBARDA]

The rumbling [*romore*] of the mortar is caused by the impetuous fury of the flame beaten back by the resisting air, and that quantity of the powder causes this effect because it finds itself ignited within the body of the mortar; and not perceiving itself in a place that has capacity for it to increase, nature guides it to search with fury a place suitable for its increase, and breaking or driving before it the weaker obstacle it wins its way into spacious air; and this not being capable of escaping with the speed with which it is attacked, because the fire is more volatile than the air, it follows that as the air is not equally volatile with the fire it cannot make way for it with that velocity and swiftness with which the fire assails it, and therefore it happens that there is resistance, and the resistance is the cause of the great roar and rumbling of the mortars [grande strepido delle bombarde].

But if the mortar were to be moved against the oncoming of an impetuous wind it would be the occasion of a greater roar [magiore tronito] made by reason of the greater resistance of the air against the flame, and so would make less rumbling [minore romore] when moved in the line of the wind because there would be less resistance. In marshy places or another wide tracts of air the mortar will make a louder report [magiore romore] close at hand.[82]

This passage, so impersonal and detached, can be compared to any number of passages from the chapter on war noises in *L'arte dei rumori*. Showcasing the pedantic analysis of the sound of exploding bombs on the battlefield, Russolo wrote:

The characteristics of the shell's whistling in the air are easily explained by the fact that the velocity of the shell, greatest at the beginning, gradually diminished. Hence, the vibrations of the air—produced by successive impulses of condensation of the air in front of the projectile and consequent rarefaction behind it—follow each other with decreasing frequency and, communicating this way vibrations to the air that are slower and slower, we obtain a gradual lowering of the pitch.[83]

If Leonardo's use of the term *strepido* is charged with militaristic overtones his humorous *romore* described a sustained, albeit bizarre, sound:

DEL ROMORE

If you take a little vessel or another resonant receptacle and cover it with soaked calfskin, and if it is later equipped with a small waxed cord, and if you pull it with a glove coated with a little tar, it will produce a strange *romore*.[84]

Leonardo's *romori* would not, on the face of it, seem to have had much musical promise, and this may very well be the point at which Russolo's and Leonardo's sound sensibilities diverge. However, the term *romore* in Leonardo's definition is connected with music making, and weird *romori* even had a place in some of Leonardo's stage productions.

Leonardo designed and used many instruments (among them friction drums like the one described in the extract above) that produced *romori* for the masked balls and theatrical performances he directed while in the service of the Sforzas. The best documented of these is an entertainment called *Para-

diso, featuring audacious theatrical machines designed by Leonardo, and produced in honor of the Duchess of Milan, on June 13, 1490, at Sforza Castle.[85]

Even after the Sforzas were dethroned, Leonardo found a way to put his skills at the service of his new, foreign patron. This is confirmed by the sketches for a staging of Poliziano's *Orfeo*, produced for the benefit of the French governor of Milan, Charles d'Amboise. In these sketches, contained in Arundel 263 and dated 1506–08 by Carlo Pedretti, Leonardo requested the use of friction drums to evoke the terrifying noises of twelve devils guarding the gates of hell.[86]

This suggestive use of noise and its association with the demonic are topoi that were to recur in later times. Winternitz describes a 1511 rant by Sebastian Virdung against the effect of kettledrums at church, where, he complains, the "horrible noise of these drums [. . .] disturb[s] the pious old people, the sick and the devout in the cloisters who are trying to read, to study and to pray"; in short, they are "an invention of the devil in their suppression of every sweet melody."[87] But a friction drum, with its bizarre, low sound, must have resonated with greater humor than the diabolical seriousness of the timpani.

Winternitz claimed that the Neapolitan *caccavella* may have been Leonardo's source for this bizarre friction drum. The noisemakers from Neapolitan folklore may seem light years removed from Russolo's intonarumori, but the principle of the friction drum—a drumskin that amplifies the noise produced by a string attached on one end—was one of the main features in Russolo's intonarumori, starting with his first patent of January 11, 1914.

The caccavella, heard each September in the procession of the Madonna di Piedigrotta, is one of the many Neapolitan noisemakers glorified by the futurist poet Francesco Cangiullo in his epic poem *Piedigrotta* (1913), possibly the most brilliant example of futurist sound-and-visual poetry. Marinetti and other futurists participated in the first live performance of this poem on March 29, 1914, at the *Salone dell'Esposizione Futurista Permanente* on the Via del Tritone, executing the noisy accompaniment with instruments used during the Neapolitan procession; Cangiullo and Marinetti declaimed the text, with Sprovieri on the *tofa*, Balla on the *putipù*, Radiante on the *triccaballacche*, Depero on the *scetavaiasse*, and Sironi on the *fischiatore*.[88] Russolo must have known of this performance, not only because it featured a number of his close associates but also because it took place in the same venue where three months earlier the intonarumori had made their Roman debut.[89]

If Russolo likely did not superimpose the memory of the enharmonic instruments he found in Leonardo's projects to their more primitive versions from Neapolitan folklore, it is at least safe to assert that the noisy world created by the "dynamic and synoptic declamation" of *Piedigrotta* was an expression of the same aesthetic needs shared by many of the futurists of the time: these needs found their full spiritual realization in Russolo's art of noises.

LEONARDO THE GURU

Russolo's debt to Leonardo thus appears to be more profound and encompassing than would at first have been supposed. In Leonardo's work, Russolo saw the potent spiritual energy that inspired devotion, and he soon came to regard Leonardo as his spiritual guide. This might strike some as a curious proposition, given that Russolo is so closely associated with the iconoclastic futurist fury of the early twentieth century, whereas Leonardo embodies the iconic, fully canonized concept of the Renaissance man. Moreover since neither Leonardo's rigorous scientific research nor Russolo's aggressive futurist aesthetic is traditionally associated with spirituality, it is curious that the connection between the two could have occurred on the plane of common spiritual interest.

Buzzi saw in the eclecticism of these two figures a connection of the spirit that bound their minds together: their encyclopedic, comparativist approach and their flirting with the occult theory of correspondences. Russolo's landscape of interests, like that of Leonardo's, included painting, music, acoustics, metaphysics, astronomy, and the builder's crafts; the two artists also shared a concern for the instruments of war, clockworks, and biomechanic creation.[90]

Leonardine spiritual influence runs like a road map through Russolo's entire career, from the infatuation of his early Milanese years to the veneration for the Renaissance master that is evident in his last writings, prevailing even during the raging futurist attacks against achievements of the past. The evidence of Russolo's occult interests strengthens the connection between Russolo and Leonardo. Yet to fully contextualize Russolo's Leonardine devotion we need to consider Leonardo's spiritual reputation in the years before futurism was founded—a reputation in high bloom in the symbolist milieu that Russolo joined upon his arrival in Milan.

CHAPTER 10

Controversial Leonardo

The futurists took a rather contradictory attitude toward Leonardo, which can only be explained if one separates his work from its canonization. Futurist public attacks on Leonardo centered not on his work but on what he represented of the past. Typically, futurist rage toward the past has been explained through a hermeneutical script by Marinetti, according to which the obsessive shadow of the cultural saints of the past and the adoration of their works—especially in a country with a rich history, such as Italy—were an unbearable weight slowing futurism's dynamic aims.

Marinetti's carefully orchestrated act of turning one's back on the past to deliver oneself from its encumbrances soon became understood (and misunderstood) by the critics as the essence of the futurist movement. Whether consciously or not, he was at least in part responsible for the critical misconstructions; and in regard to futurism's spirituality, this eventually backfired. For many years, his writing, by its very force, dictated in many circumstances the words to his critics, and they believed in his manipulation. Sometimes it is best if authors are not allowed to have the last word on the meaning of their work, for they are often their own worst advocates. Critics of futurism fell under the spell of the propagandistic and rhetorical force of Marinetti's voice, to the point that they believed him blindly and all too frequently read the entire movement through the guidelines that he had established.

Marinetti's smokescreen prevented the critics from applying their hermeneutics to the work itself and caused them instead to divert this hermeneutics onto the rhetoric surrounding the work. This kept them from seeing the contradictions of the movement, instead encouraging the image of a unified front. As a matter of fact, not all futurists hated the past; the more Marinetti proclaimed hatred of the past, the more this proclamation concealed a complex web of psychological conundrums—Marinetti's own insecurity, for one thing, and that of his followers. He feared that his "frail courage" would fail and be defeated at the hands of the past. "Do you want then to waste all your best strengths, in this eternal and useless admiration of the past," he asked in the last section of the founding manifesto of futurism, "from which you come out fatally exhausted, diminished and trampled?"[1] Four years later, in *Lacerba*, Boccioni reasoned likewise, suggesting a process of self-imposed amnesia: "We deny the past because we want to forget, and to forget in art means to renew oneself."[2]

Marinetti acknowledged that if the past is not ignored, forgotten, or destroyed, it can ultimately be kept at bay by paying homage to it, as if it were an insatiable Minotaur: "Museums: cemeteries! . . . Identical, surely, in the sinister promiscuity of so many bodies unknown to one another. [. . .] That one should make an annual pilgrimage, just as one goes to the graveyard on All Souls' Day—that I will grant you. That once a year one should leave a floral tribute beneath the *Gioconda*, I grant you that." Marinetti's fear of the past surfaces here: in his representation of the *Mona Lisa*—one of the few artworks he cited in his 1909 manifesto—as the most authoritative symbol of the art of the past, a terrible deity that needs appeasing, once a year, with flowers.

Modernists attacked the *Mona Lisa* because of the place it holds in the canon: consider Duchamp's suggestive moustaches (every parody, they say, hides admiration).[3] Certainly that painting was an easy target. Ardengo Soffici, in his *Lacerba* column "Giornale di bordo," wrote in the July 15, 1913, issue: "In the tram. —I see written on a wall in big white letters on a blue background: 'GIOCONDA' ITALIAN PURGATIVE WATER. And further down the stupid face of Mona Lisa. Finally! Finally we too are beginning to do good art criticism."[4]

A few months later, on December 15, 1913, in the same column, Soffici returned to the subject with a little acerbic poem on the infamous theft and subsequent retrieval of the painting:

DECEMBER 13.

30,000 people passed before the *Mona Lisa* with hat in hand.

—The press.

They have found it again, the old daub.
The mirror of all the artistic Philistinism.
The touchstone of aesthetic fetishism.
The treasure of literatures.
The magnet of snobbishnesses.
The icon of past-worshipers.
The paradigm of the commonplace.
The sewer of international imbecility.
They have found again the mediocre image of the saccharine-sweet fat lady.
They have found again the *Mona Lisa*.

Also on this page was the following unsigned declaration:

WE FUTURISTS

reunited in extraordinary assembly deplore profoundly the retrieval of the "Mona Lisa" thanks to the double imbecilic act of the *passatista* [passéist] housepainter and we demand for the infamous little painting the prompt reburial in the cemetery-like Louvre Museum.

Soffici's good friend Carrà echoed his anti-academicism in his 1913 manifesto "Pittura dei suoni, rumori e odori," where he calls the use of perspectival illusion a "little game worthy at most of an academician like Leonardo."[5] The *Mona Lisa* was the preferred target but not the only one. Attacks on Leonardo reached the mainstream audience with the publication of *The Study and Criticism of Italian Art* by Bernard Berenson. In a tour de force of negative criticism, Berenson vehemently attacked *The Last Supper*, declaring it nothing less than repulsive. The *Times* of London, scandalized, launched a *Futuristengefahr* (Futurist danger) alarm, suggesting that Berenson was coming dangerously close to the positions of the artistic avant-garde.[6]

LEONARDO THE PROTOFUTURIST

Despite these anti-academic attacks, Leonardo's works were held in high regard by the futurists. When the mask of Marinettian propaganda was dropped, in the intimacy of letters and diaries, and, above all, in the creative and spiritual genesis of the futurists' works, the centrality of Leonardo's influence is undeniable. Calvesi pointed to Leonardo's inspirational role among all futurists:

[Leonardo] remains the one who, before the modern age, occupied himself with vibrations and motions; his "universal dynamism" animates the molecules but sometimes becomes a giant vortex. Not by chance is Leonardo the observer of the flight of birds and prophet of aviation [...].

Bergson himself, whose writings are considered one of the main sources for futurist theories, will be the modern thinker most in keeping with Leonardo. [Like Bergson,] Leonardo considered "motion the cause of every form of life" and called "spiritual virtues" the physical and dynamic forces of which life was for him the most glorious, immense manifestation.[7]

Giacomo Balla was frequently inspired by Leonardo. He told his mother in a letter that while sketching the first of his alchemically influenced *Composizioni iridescenti*, he "held before him a book on Leonardo, like a talisman."[8] Balla even claimed in his diary to be Leonardo reincarnated: "In 1500, they called me Leonardo. [...] after 4 centuries of artistic decadence, I reappeared in 1900 to shout to my plagiarizers that it is time to end it because times have changed. They called me crazy: poor blockheads!!!!!!!!! I have already created a new sensitivity in art that is expression of future ages that will be colorradioiridesplendorideal luminosisssssssssimiiiiii."[9] This quote is even more significant when one considers that Leonardo was credited with being the first scientist to formulate a wave theory of light.[10] Balla also echoes Leonardo in his studies on the flight of swallows and in his *Vortice* of 1911, which can be considered a futurist transcription of Leonardo's projects for flying machines.[11] Lista maintains that Étienne-Jules Marey drew inspiration from Leonardo: similarly, Balla's interest in chronophotography could be understood as indirectly Leonardine.[12]

Furthermore, Leonardo's name is often encountered in Marinetti's personal diaries. In the posthumously published *La grande Milano tradizionale e futurista*, Marinetti characterized the statue of Leonardo in the Piazza della Scala as an authoritative witness smiling over futurist brawls like a benevolent father: "[The statue of] Leonardo da Vinci, boiling in concentric circles around his disciples made of stone, admires it [the revolutionary cyclone] from his privileged place as a genius of simultaneities."[13]

Just as futurists believe that Leonardo's statue magnanimously approved their fight from on high, so too did they consider him a sort of protecting idol for their intellectual movement. Marinetti, again in *La grande Milano*, describes the Milanese cultural environment as being "diplomatic par excellence, because it combines at the table of the attorney Mazza the opposed talents of Don Galbiati, director of the Ambrosiana and Latinist authority,

Marinetti, and the futurists Buzzi [and] Masnata; and all that *under the [protective] light of Leonardo da Vinci.*"[14] Marinetti's Leonardine reverence culminated in the pages of yet another of his posthumous memoires, *Una sensibilità italiana nata in Egitto,* where he considers Leonardo a futurist *ad honorem,* a protofuturist: "They are all deliciously convinced that through a reckless Italian courage which reaches the poetic apex in the midst of dangers, the typically futurist innovative genius of Leonardo da Vinci, Umberto Boccioni, Antonio Sant'Elia, and Marinetti creates a marvelous poetry capable of *synthesizing simultaneously the universe.*"[15]

Marinetti, in placing alongside the names of exponents of the futurist movement the name of Leonardo—a figure that connects spirituality with science and technology—implicitly provided both scientific and a spiritual endorsement to the ambitious futurist goal of (artistic) creation as also being simultaneous synthesis of the universe. In his ability to connect the scientific and the spiritual by means of the technological, Leonardo could not have been a better source of inspiration for the futurists. An indirect acknowledgement of Leonardine devotion in these terms can be found in the article "Futurism, Magic and Life," which Wyndham Lewis wrote in 1914 for the first issue of BLAST. Though technically speaking a vorticist text, "Futurism, Magic and Life" is imbued with the spirit of Italian futurism—though without Marinetti's rhetoric. This may be the one instance where the futurist worship of Leonardo leaks into a text published before World War I:

> I. The Futurist theoretician should be a Professor of Hoffman [sic] Romance, and attempts the manufacture of a perfect being.
>
> Art merges in Life again everywhere.
>
> Leonardo was the first Futurist, and, incidentally, an airman among Quattro Cento angels.
>
> His Mona Lisa eloped from the Louvre like any woman.
>
> She is back again now, smiling, with complacent reticence, as before her escapade; no one can say when she will be off once more, she possesses so much vitality.
>
> Her olive pigment is electric, so much more so than the carnivorous Belgian bumpkins by Rubens in a neighbouring room, who, besides, are so big they could not slip about in the same subtle fashion.
>
> Rubens IMITATED Life—borrowed the colour of it's [sic] crude blood, traced the sprawling and surging of it's [sic] animal hulks.
>
> Leonardo MADE NEW BEINGS, delicate and severe, with as ambitious an intention as any ingenious mediaeval Empiric.[16]

IL LEONARDO

Veneration of Leonardo among the futurists had deep roots in the prehistory of the movement, that is, in the Movimento Fiorentino, a group of intellectuals active in Florence at the beginning of the twentieth century, whose goal was to reawaken Italian cultural life from its gilded sleep. Marinetti eventually made this mission his own.[17]

The Movimento Fiorentino disseminated its ideas most distinctively by means of periodicals. Among them, *Il Leonardo* (1903–07), which distilled the experience of the earlier periodical *Il Marzocco*, became the Florentine movement's most popular publication. Of the first series of *Il Leonardo*, Martin has written that it was "infused with mysticism and D'Annunzian aesthetics."[18] The periodical passed through a more pragmatic second phase but then returned to a mystical-spiritual third phase.

The general editorial tone, determined by the two founders Giovanni Papini and Giuseppe Prezzolini, was "mercurial and polemical," in the tradition of mordant Tuscan invective.[19] The content alternated between philosophy and politics, occasionally dipping into art and literature. Philosophically, *Il Leonardo* affirmed a kind of mystical idealism over the positivism and materialism prevailing in the cultural debate of those years; politically it was nationalist. Its idealism was sui generis; the writers for *Il Leonardo* went to great lengths to exclude, at least in the early phases, the name of Benedetto Croce from their debate, and they frequently critiqued Hegel in their columns.

Papini's imprint determined *Il Leonardo*'s character. His essays emphasized symbolist literature and critical-philosophical literary studies; in many of them, the key voices were those of Bergson, Nietzsche, and Steiner. Though Bergson's philosophical approach in those years had not yet developed into a philosophy of action—his *élan vital* would not take shape until 1907—the periodical rallied behind the critique of positivism and materialism laid out in Bergson's 1896 *Matière et mémoire*.

Il Leonardo's important conjunction of symbolist thinking and condemnation of positivism, along with the influence of Nietzsche, Bergson, and Steiner, anticipated the antimaterialism that futurists, including Russolo, soon espoused. In what was almost a natural progression (and perhaps owing something to the stormy circumstances of the famous brawl of 1911 between Papini and Soffici, on one hand, and Marinetti and Milanese futurists, on the other, and the reconciliation that followed), the positions of the futurists

FIGURE 29. Adolfo De Carolis, header for *Il Leonardo* (1903). Courtesy of the Images Archive of Vallecchi.

and that of the most representative members of *Il Leonardo* converged in 1913 in of Giovanni Papini's and Ardengo Soffici's biweekly publication *Lacerba*.[20]

From the periodical's name *Il Leonardo* to the motto by Leonardo da Vinci reproduced in the header in every issue—*Non si volge chi a stella è fisso* (He does not turn who is fixed on a star)—the homage to Leonardo could not have been more explicit (fig. 29).[21] The motto, adopting the metaphor of sailing that is guided by stars, emphasized the importance of the inner spiritual quest, an undertaking that requires perseverance ruled by firm inspirational principles, especially when it concerns travel toward the Ideal.

At the turn of the twentieth century, Leonardo da Vinci was thought to be the guide who was supposed to rescue the new generation from the stagnation of the Italian cultural swamp. This is clearly expressed in the *Leonardo* group's mission statement—and founding manifesto—which was published in their first issue of January 4, 1903.

SYNTHETIC PROGRAM

A group of youths desirous of liberation, wishing for universality, yearning for a higher intellectual life, gathered in Florence under the symbolic augural name of Leonardo to intensify their own existence, elevate their own thought, exalt their own art.

In LIFE they are pagans and individualists—lovers of beauty and intelligence, adorers of profound nature and the fulfilling life, enemies of every form of Nazarene sheepishness and plebeian servitude.

In THOUGHT they are individualists and idealists, that is to say beyond every system and every limitation, convinced that every philosophy is only a personal way of life—Therefore they reject every other existence outside of thought.

In ART they love the ideal transfiguration of life and fight its inferior forms, they aspire to beauty as evocative portrayal of a profound and serene life.

Among the expressions of their strengths, of their enthusiasms, and of their disdains will be a periodical entitled "LEONARDO."

The signers gathered in Florence in the name of Leonardo considered him not a simple role model but their *nume protettore, spirito-guida*, a god who blessed their pagan *ecclesia*. This evangelic tone recurred in futurist rhetoric not only in the writings of the orphans of *Il Leonardo*—Soffici (in *Pittori e scultori sacri*), Papini, and Prezzolini (whose *La Voce* was conceived as a mission toward moral purification)—but even, and just as forcefully—in those of Marinetti and Boccioni. Veneration of Leonardo as a mystic, or initiate (but also the reliance on him as a banner, protective shield, and talisman symbolizing the power of the Ideal over Matter), had its roots in symbolism and was fully espoused by the European movement of decadentism toward the end of the nineteenth century.[22]

In 1855 the French art historian Alexis-François Rio had described *The Last Supper*, despite its degradation and faded color, as "a great mystical composition." Rio's judgment spread rapidly among adherents of the decadent movement such as Moreau, Walter Pater, and Mallarmé, who read spiritual and occultist meanings into the celebrated fresco; the judgment was later reinforced by Valéry and Freud.

From within turn-of-the-twentieth-century Italian culture, which was clearly infused with symbolist and idealist thought—the most authoritative judgment of the *Last Supper* was offered by the father of Italian decadentism, Gabriele D'Annunzio, who in 1901 emphatically called it a "mirror of the Ideal [. . .] the summit of Art, the vertex of Thought and of Mystery, the visible sign of the Immortal."[23] This opinion must have influenced Papini and Prezzolini, and through them, Russolo.

Il Leonardo was highly esteemed in symbolist, progressive circles such as that around Marinetti's *Poesia*, which Russolo frequented, and he certainly knew about the periodical. Though he was never as intimate with Papini and Soffici as Carrà was, and though he parted ways with them after the quarrels in 1915 between them and Marinetti, Russolo published several articles in their *Lacerba*, and one of these articles included his only surviving musical fragment—the famous seven bars from *Risveglio di una città* of 1913.

Russolo's notion of Leonardo as "spirit guide" cannot but have derived from *Il Leonardo*. This is confirmed in his late period, which was, as is often the case, a time of confessions. In *Al di là della materia*, Russolo places Leonardo among the *fari* (beacons) of the human spirit, in the company of Dante, Shakespeare, and Palestrina.[24] Here Leonardo is still regarded as a "spirit guide," uncorrupted by positivism and materialism, while Russolo's language is that of thirty-five years earlier:

> If his contemporaries did not see anything but the artist in Leonardo, posterity, amazed by his experimental science, ended up wanting to make him into a positivist and even almost a materialist. But this is a clumsy error. His stupendous definition: "painting is poetry that one sees" is an all-inclusive motto and certainly does not mean that poetry and painting must be merely descriptive.
>
> He said "poetry" and not history, description, or speech, because in poetry one presupposes an evasion of the laws of necessity to reach a higher harmony that is spiritual, through the harmony of verses.
>
> (On this definition of Leonardo all painters who make only description or speeches—and they are legion—should meditate!) Leonardo wrote *"He does not turn who is fixed on a star!"* And almost to explain the one and the other he has established the hierarchy that *"our body is ruled by the sky and the sky is ruled by the spirit."*
>
> This hardly amounts to materialism!"[25]

In addition to quoting from Leonardo's *Il Paragone*, Russolo repeats—symptomatically—the motto used by *Il Leonardo* (fig. 29); Papini and Prezzolini's reverence toward Leonardo, which may very well have guided Russolo's lifelong Leonardine investigations, was still imprinted on his mind.

THE REASONS FOR SILENCE

Russolo mentioned Leonardo often, but he never openly acknowledged his debt to him. Could it be that, like his fellow theosophist Giacomo Balla, he believed himself to be Leonardo's reincarnation? Could it be that he self-identified with Leonardo to such a point that he thought it unnecessary even to acknowledge his borrowings?

Russolo believed in reincarnation and wrote at length on this subject in *Al di là della materia*. Nor would this have been the only time that Russolo speculated on his past lives: his friend Nino Frank maintained that Russolo considered himself a reincarnation of Cardinal Richelieu.[26] Russolo believed—another principle derived from theosophy—that a person's thoughts subsist "for a certain time after their emission in and around the places where they emerged [...]. Having the property of being received, [those thoughts] help [...] and go to enrich other men."[27]

A few paragraphs before this passage, Russolo even wrote about a "spiritual conversation" among artists of different epochs as a sort of migration of the spirit, a passing of the baton between one artist of genius and another. Russolo believed that such migration could manifest independently from the means of artistic expression and beyond the sensory field in which these means operate (as in the synesthetic theory of Marinetti's tactilism): "A close kinship, an exchange of spiritual energies, a passage of divine fire occurs therefore between the great artists through the spiritual world where the arts no longer have the diversity of the matter from which they are shaped but rather conserve only their intimate final spirituality."[28]

Russolo must have considered a passage of "divine fire" between Leonardo and himself perfectly plausible, not only because Russolo lived in Milan (where Leonardo worked) but also because of the time he spent in contact with the spirit of Leonardo's oeuvre. He may have thought the *Stanze* of the Sforza Castle to be still imbued with Leonardo's spirit—an idea also explored by the experimental playwright Giovanni Testori, who in one of his theater works staged the sighting of Leonardo's ghost floating over the castle ramparts.[29]

Although this is a fascinating hypothesis, more concrete interpretive pathways ought to be explored. The reader will decide which of these hypotheses is the most compelling, keeping in mind that they may not be entirely incompatible.

Maffina emphasized that "Russolo, in the abundant masses of annotations, writings, and notes on his instrument, is silent on every technical description of the construction."[30] This silence may have been due to Russolo's unconscious embarrassment about the origin of his ideas: heavily marketed as futurist and yet at least in part derived from such a celebrated historical source as Leonardo.

To rely openly on received tradition, especially a canonized one, was contrary to all the principles of novelty and originality that futurists incessantly proclaimed. Official futurist doctrine, though often contradicted in diaries and letters, dictated complete rejection of the past. One could not admit loving Leonardine thought, let alone applying it: the futurists could admire Leonardo privately but had to censure him publicly.

This double standard is one of the many contradictions of the futurist movement, and it points to subconscious denial. There is much to learn from analyzing the reasons for this phenomenon; behind subconscious denial are often ill-concealed traces of personal feelings incompletely suppressed. But analysis can show that subconscious denial often reveals more than it conceals: it always attracts attention and thus often ends up exposing what had been intended to be concealed.

Leonardo = Tradition was the futurists' official equation. They could not openly admit to loving a tradition, for tradition burdened them unbearably. And because it frightened them, they hoped not to have to confront it. This is why the futurists attacked Leonardo publicly, and it may explain why Russolo could not admit a special connection with Leonardo, let alone admit to borrowing from him. Russolo may have been afraid that it would become public that Leonardo's manuscripts were for him a source not only of research objectives but also of construction principles. And though the intonarumori and the nuovo istrumento musicale a corde were not merely replicas of Leonardo's instruments, Russolo may have failed to recognize the extent of his own contribution and therefore feared being deemed unoriginal. It was necessary to keep silent.

Maria Zanovello naïvely recounted an anecdote that reveals Russolo's nervous embarrassment about Leonardo.[31] While reading the galleys of *Al di là della Materia*—notably a section of part 2, "Alla ricerca del bello," which Russolo dedicated to beacons of the human spirit—Zanovello realized that Leonardo da Vinci had not been included in the list. Familiar with her husband's admiration for Leonardo, she was surprised at the omission and resolved to ask him why.

Russolo was unprepared for his wife's question but responded as best he could: "Leonardo is not an artist; he is a scientist." When she reminded him of all that he had taught her of Leonardo's spiritual importance, Russolo grew irritated. All he said, however, was: "To speak of Leonardo is not an easy thing." But knowing that his wife considered him practically infallible, Russolo must have thought that to fail to include a section on Leonardo would make her even more suspicious. As Zanovello recounts, the next day, having thought the matter over, Russolo composed the passage on Leonardo cited above.

Reading those lines, so infused with candid admiration for Leonardo the man and artist, with an understanding of the context in which they were written, leaves a bitter aftertaste of extorted confession. Had Russolo's wife not persisted, there would not be a section on Leonardo in *Al di là della materia*. In all of his writings, this is the only instance in which Russolo explicitly cited Leonardo's manuscripts and revealed his familiarity with them.

Subconscious denial serves well to explain Russolo's silence on the subject of his Leonardine borrowings, but his silence can be read in yet another way. Knowing that he felt protective about the insides of his intonarumori, we can just as reasonably assume that Russolo chose to avoid discussing specific mechanical principles so as not to trivialize the ultimate creative aims of his art of noises.[32] And since Russolo gave a specific meaning to the word *creativity*, these aims may have been for him, at their core, ineffable. Let us unveil them.

CHAPTER II

Third Level

Beyond the process of spiritualizing / sanctifying the noise (first level) and that of synthesizing different noises into unity (second level), Russolo contemplated a third level. During the creative process described so far, the inspired artist is transported to a higher plane of consciousness, which allows him to comprehend the world from a privileged point of view. At this stage the artist enters a new level, one in which he can communicate with the spirits of the dead he has conjured up, who fluctuate in the same plane, awaiting reincarnation.[1] The intonarumori were thus intended as a portal to the beyond; the disturbing brute materiality of their noise was the call that conjured the spirits—a futurist, simultaneous, and dynamic call that was to guide the artist-creator in his process of transformation.

Testimony of mediumistic music—that is, music produced at séances where a medium-musician plays under spirit dictation—became increasingly popular from mid-1800 on, and in Russolo's day the practice would not have been unusual.[2] The most convincing testimony of Russolo's mediumistic music practices once again comes from Paolo Buzzi, Russolo's intimate friend from the time of their first futurist struggles until Russolo's last years in Cerro di Laveno.

RUSSOLO WOUNDED

On December 17, 1917, while defending the summit of Monte Grappa at Malga Camperona from the Alpenkorps' offensive—a key moment of the *battaglia d'arresto* that finally succeeded in halting the Austro-German offense after the bloody Caporetto—Lieutenant Luigi Russolo of the Sixth Alpine Battalion "Val Brenta" was wounded in the head by the explosion of a grenade. In a futurist announcement of January 1918 celebrating his heroism in combat, for which he was decorated with a silver medal, Buzzi wrote of his friend in a brief text titled "Russolo ferito" (Russolo wounded): "Wherever he passed, with his hobnailed boots, there was a burst of sparks which resembled a halo [...]. But also his brain added to it the aureole of ingenious scintillations." Buzzi also remembered Russolo as "the thin, electric Russolo living in our plane, who painted blue concentric atmospheres of music using elusive flashes of the paintbrush and conducted orchestras of intonarumori in theaters worldwide with gestures that recalled those of the Spirits conjured up by the tongue of Swedenborg."[3]

This concise portrait effectively summarizes many of the characteristics discussed in the course of this book—and in much the same order. As in the self-portraits, this image of Russolo is surrounded by an aura (halo, aureole), which spiritualizes and transfigures it. Russolo, a true "skeletal sorcerer," is gifted with special powers, a form of energy that builds a protective halo around him.[4] Buzzi portrays Russolo almost as an antenna, or lightning rod, electrified and galvanized by sparks of the energy he both attracts and returns. His most ambitious painting, *La musica*, is evoked in Buzzi's passage through its most indelible traits: the concentric aura around the central figure of the canvas and the enharmonic, ineffable continuity of the blue band, a sinuous sound-form.

In its literal sense, the last phrase of Buzzi's description quoted above depicts Russolo in the act of developing spiritualistic features while conducting the orchestra of intonarumori. But if one reads the text in its simultaneity, without paying too much attention to its syntactic links and focusing instead on the chain of analogies typical of Words-in-Freedom, one can enter the experience of the intonarumori as a conjuring essence. The gestures Russolo makes in conducting the *spirali di rumori* are here even compared to those Swedenborg made in invoking his "Spirits."

Although Buzzi's description does not address the way the art of noises operates, it unquestionably shows how the art of noises was perceived by Russolo, his closest futurist comrades, and the audience of "initiates" (to quote *commendator* Amann in Cameroni's trial) who followed Russolo's gestures on the podium; as they saw it, Russolo, through the orchestra of intonarumori, invoked and communicated with spirits.

Given the comparisons with Swedenborg, I should explain that he believed that angels communicate with human beings using a language that differs from human language in only one aspect: that angels can express in one minute what men cannot express in half an hour, and with few words they express what would take many pages to describe. It seems as if Swedenborg's angelic language possessed characteristics uncannily similar to futurist simultaneity and synthesis.

THE CITY AWAKES

The energy from the spirits that the artist-creator gathers through the intonarumori produces both thought-forms and sound-forms, radiating vibrations that influence the aura of all persons within their field of action.[5] Besant's and Leadbeater's *Thought-forms* defines "externalized" thought-forms as abstract and reproducing states of mind that can also assume the contours of material objects and bodies.[6] According to Leadbeater's *The Hidden Side of Things*, these objects or bodies can materialize by drawing around themselves a veil of physical matter, whereupon they can incarnate.[7]

Boccioni, in referencing such processes, used the expression *materializzazione medianica* (mediumistic materialization), whereas Marinetti employed the equivalent term *esteriorizzazione della volontà* (exteriorization of will).[8] In *Al di là della materia*, Russolo adopted the expression *esteriorizzazione della sensibilità* to describe the process whereby the etheric double materialized. He had been interested in the subject since at least 1910, the year of the *Autoritratto (con doppio eterico)*.[9] It follows that, for Russolo, when sufficient spirit energy was developed during the occult process of the intonarumori, the spirits could materialize and become incarnate.

A last and decisive example shows that the art of noises can legitimately be interpreted as an occult operation. Buzzi's poem "Russolo" reinforces the hypotheses of this book and at the same offers an interpretation of the title of Russolo's most famous *spirale di rumori*, *Risveglio di una città*, which is in line with these hypotheses. The poem reveals the occult meaning of *awakening* as materialization and incarnation.

RUSSOLO

Hero sharpened by the whirled anguish
Of every moment, you, seek
The newest acoustic buzz
In the clash of the noises. You, watch
With the eyes of the mental basilisk
The magnificent scenery of hurricanes
And listen, listen
To the mystical orchestral pits of thunders and rains:
And you descend, with quick pupils of yellow amber,
To the orchestras of the factories and the shipyards:
And listen, listen
To the convulsions of tormented iron:
May the wheel that rumbles always be
The tenor that dominates the concert!
Luigi, the *ululatore* is the oracle
Of the God who inspires you and who will render you justice.
The abyss, our illustrious Relative, is grateful to you.
I hear the only true musics: those
That the dead hear,
Over their heads, under our feet.
The future City awakens
In an explosion that invites
The cemeteries to masked balls of power and desire![10]

SETTING THE RECORD

This poem, in French, appeared for the first time in 1950 in an issue of *Cahiers d'art* dedicated to Italian art of the first half of the twentieth century, primarily futurism. In this issue, the poem is presented as part of Buzzi's *Les médaillons*, a mysterious collection that the author dated 1909 and for which no other information exists.[11] The poem was subsequently reprinted in Zanovello's biography, following Buzzi's preface, but without a date or information about its provenance. Maffina, who also reprinted the poem, considered 1909 to be improbable, but he did not suggest an alternative.[12]

Although it may not be possible to date the poem definitively, it is important at least to restrict the range of possible dates. The poem mentions one of Russolo's intonarumori, the ululatore, a term that made its first appearance in the article "Grafia enarmonica per gl'intonarumori futuristi," published in the *Lacerba* issue of March 1, 1914. Presumably, therefore, Buzzi wrote his poem after this date; thus 1909 could not be the date of creation.

But the poem cannot have been written later than 1921, for in that year Russolo renounced the attempt to perfect individual intonarumori, and he occupied himself thereafter almost exclusively with merging the various timbres (and constructive principles) of the intonarumori into a single instrument, the rumorarmonio.

In an uncanny poetic leap, Buzzi compared an intonarumori (the wheel that rumbles) to a tenor soloist, and he wished the instrument triumph in concert performances to come. Assuming that Buzzi's phrase the "wheel that rumbles" refers to the ululatore mentioned in the following verses, the comparison is appropriate, for Russolo considered the ululatore to be the most "musical" of the intonarumori because it produced a ululation that he thought "almost human."[13]

It is unlikely that the pieces for mixed orchestra that were performed in the 1921 Paris concerts featured the ululatore in the preponderant role it must have had in the spirali di rumori of 1913–14 (it also had a principal role in the *Risveglio di una città* fragment). Therefore it can safely be concluded that Buzzi's poem was written in the years immediately following the Great War, a period when Russolo (and Buzzi) still hoped that the intonarumori would be successful.

The same issue of *Cahiers d'art* that published the Russolo poem also published a second poem by Buzzi, also identified as belonging to the collection *Les médaillons* and dedicated to Boccioni, who died during World War I after falling from a horse. The poem includes vivid references to horses, and images of death and rebirth, which would indicate that it was written after Boccioni's death.

This suggests that *Les médaillons* was a commemorative diptych written after 1916, and perhaps in 1918 at the conclusion of World War I, to honor the heroism of two futurist soldiers who had been particularly close to Buzzi: one fallen and the other severely wounded. Considering the similarities of theme and style (let alone title) with Buzzi's text "Russolo ferito," I propose that the date of composition of "Russolo" was either 1918 or 1919.

Stylistic Reverberations

The style of Buzzi's poem is indebted to symbolist poetry, from which Buzzi never entirely freed himself. In the frequently repeated "Écoute, écoute," followed by the liquid reference to rain, we hear D'Annunzio's *repetitio* of the word *ascolta* in his "La pioggia nel pineto" (1902) but also a distinct echo of the opening lines of Aloysius Bertrand's poem "Ondine," from his posthumous prose ballad collection *Gaspard de la nuit* (1842).

Born in Piedmont as Louis-Jacques-Napoléon Bertrand, Aloysius Bertrand died of tuberculosis in Paris in 1841 in relative obscurity. His prose poems, filled with fantastic themes and open rebellion against the tyranny of classic French alexandrine verses, were rediscovered by and deeply influenced symbolist poets, above all Baudelaire and Mallarmé.

Buzzi would have been familiar with Aloysius Bertrand via Baudelaire, but also via Ravel. The poem "Ondine" was reprinted in its entirety as an epigraph to the movement of the same title that opens the original Durand edition of Ravel's piano triptych *Gaspard de la nuit* (1909). Ravel's triptych derived its title and soul from Bertrand's seminal ballad collection. Each of the three movements of the piano composition closely follow the corresponding ballads from Bertrand's book. Even an apparently exterior means such as the much celebrated (and imitated) piano virtuosity of Ravel's work, ranging between velocity and fear and reaching melting-point temperatures to sublimate into the supernatural, bring the prophetic, presymbolist quality of Bertrand's literary vision into full focus.

Buzzi's indirect reference to Ravel the *sorcier* and his *sortilèges*—Russolo finally ended up meeting Ravel in person in 1921—through one of Bertrand's most symbolist, uncanny works resounds all the more appropriately for being part of a poem dedicated to Russolo, who would not have missed the reference.

Along with references to Baudelaire's sources, Buzzi also makes prominent references to Baudelaire's poetry. In 1921 Buzzi published his Italian translation of Baudelaire's *Fleurs du mal* for the Istituto Editoriale Italiano, and it is plausible that he might have been working on the translation at the time he wrote his poem to Russolo. Buzzi's immersion in the world of Baudelaire (a world that was already well known to him) had to have left visible traces in his writing, particularly in a poem written in the French language. The poem "Russolo" is fully under the visionary influence of *Fleurs du mal* and also echoes *Le crépuscule du soir* and *Le crépuscule du matin*, of the *Tableaux Parisiens*, as well as *Danse macabre*. This influence is concentrated in Buzzi's use of charged words, of indisputably Baudelairian provenance, such as *abîme*.[14]

Hermeneutic Oracle

With "Russolo," Buzzi summarized and interpreted Russolo's musical activity in an occult key. I should like to return to the poem and emphasize with italics the passages that overlap with the various aspects I have discussed in this book.

> RUSSOLO
> Hero sharpened by the whirled anguish
> Of every moment, you, seek
> The newest acoustic buzz
> In the clash of the noises. You, watch
> With the eyes of the mental *basilisk*
> The magnificent scenery of hurricanes
> And listen, listen
> To the *mystical orchestral pits* of thunders and rains:
> And you descend, with quick pupils of yellow amber,
> To the orchestras of the factories and the shipyards:
> And listen, listen
> To the convulsions of tormented iron:
> May the wheel that rumbles always be
> The tenor that dominates the concert!
> *Luigi, the ululatore is the oracle*
> *Of the God who inspires you and who will render you justice.*
> The abyss, our great Relative, is grateful to you.
> I hear *the only true musics:* those
> That the dead hear,
> Over their heads, under our feet.
> *The future City awakens*
> In an *explosion* that invites
> The cemeteries to masked balls of power and desire!

The poem opens by presenting the dedicatee, Russolo, the restless hero with the fatal basilisk gaze, involved in exploring the profundity of sound. Next, the poem evokes nature as spectacle (*décor, Golfes mystiques*). The Wagnerian expression "Golfes mystiques" (a chain of metonymies: mystic gulf = orchestral pit = orchestra = sound and noise) associated with peals of thunder and rain confirms the central proposition of *The Art of Noises*: a revaluation of noise as sound and therefore as material suited for music.

Considered more carefully, this section of the poem is imbued with occult themes. First, it brings the reader back to the pantheistic atmosphere of *Linee-forza della folgore*. Second, the sinuosity of line that the image of the gulf suggests, united to the adjective *mystic*, goes back to the theory of sound waves as vibrations that potently manifest in the grandiose spectacle of natural forces, of which thunder is the primary expression.[15]

Even more charged are the lines *Luigi, l'ululeur est l'oracle / Du Dieu qui t'inspire*, which describe the intonarumori as a true portal to the beyond, through which communication between the artist and the spirits can be instituted, be these, as theosophy claimed, spirits of nature, or spirits of the dead awaiting reincarnation. The term *oracle* comes from the Latin *oraculum*, which derives from the verb *orare* and therefore etymologically refers to a mysterious voice of supernatural origin providing responses about unknown events. This passage is even more appropriate to Russolo, because the intonarumori in question is the ululatore, which Russolo described as a "mysterious, suggestive instrument" that, just like the spirits conjured up by Swedenborg, emits "an ululation" that is "*almost* human."[16]

Russolo believed firmly in the possibilities of communicating with the dead and expressed himself on the subject *apertis verbis* many times, beginning with the letter to Margherita Sarfatti of August 22, 1916, in which he claimed to be in mediumistic contact with the spirit of the recently deceased Boccioni. His interest in spiritism continued throughout the 1920s, and in his late Parisian years he participated in the séances of the medium Madame Lazare on rue des Mathurins, near the Madeleine church. Finally, from the 1930s until his death, spiritism was a focus of his studies.[17]

If the intonarumori could become the oracle that spoke through the mouths of the spirits, then the art of noises was the privileged base on which to construct communication between the world of the living and the beyond. According to Buzzi, Russolo's *musiche uniche e vere* were expressions coming from the beyond that only the enlightened among the living, the artists-clairvoyants, could understand: noises transfigured by transferring vital energy and re-creating spiritual life that for the living anticipated the beyond, and for the dead recalled and promised life.

The re-creation of spiritual life carried out by the intonarumori was the path that, as the final consequence of the materialization of thought-forms, conducted the dead toward reincarnation. The life created by the intonarumori can, then, be considered the life of spirits incarnating from the beyond. In the end, Buzzi's poem reveals exactly that: the energy created by an orchestra of intonarumori could produce an explosion so powerful as to bring cemeteries back to life.

This was the occult side of *Risveglio di una città*, a Romeroesque *Dawn of the Dead*, in which a city of the dead is reanimated by energy that is channeled by machines producing an explosion of noise. This explosion of energy, coming from the force and desire of the spirits for incarnation, generates that overflowing and disturbing "artificial" (biomechanic?) multiplicity—represented by the procession of masks to restage the notorious trope of the Danse Macabre—that finds its synthesis in the cosmogonic unity of the City of the Future.

FUTURIST VERTIGOES

In 1924 Buzzi consolidated the position expressed in his poem "Russolo" by stretching the poem into a novel, *Cavalcata delle vertigini* (Ride of the vertigoes), in which the war hero, aptly named Marzio, is a literary transposition of Russolo. In the preface, Buzzi wrote: "Having found a marvelous specimen, given to me by the war among my great friends in art (must I say it? Luigi Russolo), I made him the chrysalis of an imaginary cocoon that would have needed to be as luminous as a halo."[18]

In the book, essentially a fantastic and philosophical novel with occasional incursions into the erotic, Marzio represents a total artist who has constructed and conducts, under the effect of a mediumistic trance, an orchestra of intonarumori. A bullet implanted in his brain blesses him with exceptionally powerful spiritual gifts and at the same time kills him periodically; as a result he cyclically reincarnates in almost every chapter.

Cavalcata delle vertigini lingers on descriptions of mediumistic phenomena, galvanization, spirit materialization, and reincarnation. Chapter 5, for instance, bears the emblematic title "Musica e metempsicosi" (Music and metempsychosis). Chapter 16, "La novissima orchestra" (The all-new orchestra), is worth recounting for the connections to the present discussion.[19]

On the snowy peak of the Monte Bianco—described as the ultimate symbol of spiritual elevation and supreme summit of "an orography of spirits," where "one lives a life at the same time divinely carnal and humanly astral"—Marzio/Russolo conducts his own creation, the orchestra of intonarumori, in "full consciousness of his hyperdynamic force."

The inspired orchestra conductor is described as "a bundle of nerves galvanized by an electrical current of one hundred thousand *ampères*." He is an antenna elevated on "a majestic podium," picking up energy "from the direct light of the stars" and instilling it into the orchestra, which appears to be "operated by electrical forces." In this process of possession, Marzio/Russolo is transfigured. He is no longer "the man of bone, nerves, and flesh." He becomes "the man-battery. A bundle of electric wires passed through by all the most mysterious and complex intersections of thousands and thousands of *volts*."

And once again, this process, both spiritual and technological—one might call it biomechanization—is what leads to spiritual elevation: "The man, thus galvanized, seems to hurl himself, with his conducting gestures, into the sky." (Even if cemeterial themes are not as pronounced in this chapter as elsewhere in the novel, their echo is always present and surfaces with the topos of galvanic awakening.)

Once spiritual elevation is reached, creation can be achieved in all its synesthetic luxuriance: "When sounds, ably regulated by the technical ability of the performers, are abandoned to their aerial destiny, one hears that all life finds again its breaths, its tremors, its harmonies; certainly also scents and colors. 'Awakening of a modern capital.'"

The composition *Risveglio d'una capitale moderna* (Awakening of a modern capital), whose title is an intentional reference to Russolo's *Awakening of a City*, aims to concentrate "on the snow-white summit of Europe [. . .] all the sound waves of the human labyrinth" so that, while conducting, Marzio/Russolo can swim over a boundless "polyphonic and polyethereal ocean."

Buzzi describes Marzio/Russolo's visionary composition as "the symphony of the morning of Life offered with the original elements: the ecstatic music reproducing sounds and noises of the cosmos, renewed and revealed in its very miracle of genesis, simultaneously simple and complex." Enraptured by this description, Buzzi sings visionarily—and martially, in line with Marzio's etymology—about this sound fusion: "One of the supreme pleasures denied to Hector Berlioz, who in the *Treatise of Instrumentation* complained that he could not find the musical means to render, accurately, the sound of a thousand rifles operated by a regiment on the Esplanade des Invalides, turned a smile—full, vehement, cosmic, and astral—on Marzio standing on his fantastic podium, which the stars illuminated like miraculous lightbulbs."

ART OF NOISES AND REINCARNATION

Buzzi thus understood the art of noises as an experiment in alchemical creation: the noise first comes to be spiritualized through the intonarumori; on a second level, the chaotic multiplicity of noises produced by the orchestra of intonarumori comes to be transfigured through simultaneity and dynamism into a synthesis that fuses the opposites into unity. Then in the third level, the spirits of the dead, which supplied the energy for the first two levels, reach their objective through the medium of the possessed artist, achieving incarnation. The explosion of noises, according to Buzzi, is what furnishes the surge for this last operation of transformation.

Leadbeater believed that the spirits could not incarnate themselves out of nothing but needed to find physical, corporeal matter.[20] And it is here that this process of transformation crosses the line into black magic. The reanimation of the dead through a concentration of energy (in this case magnetic) is an example of the phenomenon of magnetism. Russolo dedicated numerous pages of *Al di là della materia* to the Austrian doctor Franz Anton Mesmer and to the analysis of Mesmer's method of magnetization, but he would also have known of the practices of magnetization through their popularization by way of the Hoepli manual by Giulio Belfiore, *Ipnotismo e magnetismo* (Hypnotism and magnetism).[21]

Mesmer and his studies were cited by the counts Ginanni Corradini in their *Metodo* of 1910. In *Arte dell'avvenire* of the same year, Ginna and Corra translated mesmerism into a practical occult tool that in the hands of the inspired artist could activate the reanimation of "the dead things of nature."[22] The ambition of creating life as a biomechanical experiment of reanimating cadavers returns frequently in Marinetti, who in *Guerra sola igiene del mondo* of 1915 claims that the futurists have the power to awaken mummies through the electricity of their gestures: "Everywhere, we saw growing in a few hours the courage and the number of men who are truly young, and [we saw] the galvanized mummies that our gesture had extracted from the ancient sarcophagi becoming bizarrely agitated."[23]

In *La Radia*, the manifesto drawn up together with the occultist Pino Masnata, Marinetti expanded on this idea and wrote of the "overcoming of death 'with a metallicization of the human body and the capturing of the vital spirit as machine force.'"[24] The words he quoted come from another futurist manifesto that appeared in the same year as *La radia*: *Il macchinesimo* (Machineism, 1933), signed by the sculptor Renato di Bosso and the poet Ignazio Scurto. In *Il macchinesimo*, di Bosso and Scurto proposed an originally futurist—and metallic—alternative to cremation, that unquestionably reads as an alchemic transformation. This is one of the most extreme, quasi-cartoonish representations of the futurist occult experience. It also shows how much larger a circulation (and grotesque a deformation) some of Russolo's ideas, including the musical ones, had achieved by the 1930s.

Machineism

BEGINNING OF A NEW ETHIC AND END OF THE WORLD

I have pondered over the actualization of this new ideology thanks to the enthusiasm of a faith and with projects and architectonical displays that are not meant by the artist to be mere empty decorative exercises but are instead created as a MACHINEANTROPOS for the MACHINEISM! They are the result of a perfect sympathy between my modern, futurist spirit and the mechanical state of mind.

This new futurist ethics will be the beginning of a new civilization and will also be the last funeral service mankind will ever perform, because my thought, sped up by a profound conviction of spirit, is projected in the mechanical future and infuses in me such clairvoyance that it suggests to me the striking prophecy of a NOT-SO-DISTANT END OF THE WORLD!

This prophecy should not be confused with the cruel, martyrizing predictions of religions founded over the terror that divinity instills in the believer! The catastrophic epilogue that will instantaneously stall the path of human civilization, erasing, in a huge pyrotechnic scenery, human history, I foresee to take place in the time in which the MACHINANTROPI, having reached the highest point of their development, will be able to obtain such knowledge as to permit them to take full control of natural forces now still unknown, forces whose measureless powers, getting in contact with one another, will magnify to the point of determining the total combustion and the FINAL EXPLOSION!

RITUALS AND MANIFESTATIONS OF MACHINEISM

The MACHINANTROPOS, once he has concluded his life cycle, will be conducted to the METALLIZATORY or Mechanical Temple where a speaker cone will amplify, for the audience's benefit, the last will and last greetings of the dead; the will would have been transferred to a phonograph record that the MACHINANTROPOS will have pressed and deposited, while still alive, with a reliable attorney. (The record will substitute for the hard copy of the testament.)

While this thrilling recording is broadcast to the audience attending the ceremony, the open casket will be laid over the RADIOPHORE or altar of mechanical civilization. When the MACHINANTROPOS, with his voice, has sealed this first manifestation of his demonstrating the existence of a mechanical hereafter, from the MOTORARMONIUM will rise, softly, a caressing, motoristic buzz that, vibrating, will gradually increase in volume while the casket is carried by the transmigration officers inside a long hallway, at the entrance to which those present at the ceremony will be asked to stop, and in which, by moving through predetermined, subsequent areas of increasing darkness, the corpse will disappear.

Finally, the body of the MACHINANTROPOS, running on an inclined plane, will end up immersing itself in a crucible filled with burning metal, where the useless matter will dissolve almost instantly, while the metallic essence of the departed will be catalyzed [sic] in the brand new metal. At this point, the METALHARMONIUM WILL SONORIZE, with the highest scream, the culmination of the fusion ceremony, and will soon after slowly fade into silence.

A few hours after the transmigration ceremony, the tiny metallic soul of the MACHINANTROPOS will be incorporated in the new matter. A small tag recording the name and the vital statistics of the deceased will be incised by pressing a small part of the liquid metal, and it will be filed in the METAL TAGS LIBRARY.

From this point the MACHINANTROPOS will start his own SPIRITUAL MECHANICAL HEREAFTER IN A PRACTICAL MECHANICAL HERE AND NOW, because the portion of the metal not used in the tag will recuperate its useful, productive function as a machine or part thereof. And so, the few microparticles of metal contained in the transmigrated human body will continue, when transplanted into the body of other men, to run toward the future. This process will definitively eliminate the cumbersome occupation of vast surfaces of land for the repellent and absurd conservation of human bodies in fatal decomposition."[25]

This manifesto included a (supposedly) intimidating photograph representing an imposing "motoristic musical instrument that will sonorize the death."[26] To top it off, it had a foreword by Marinetti, boasting that "The IDEA of mechanization of the dead obtained by metallizing their essence may seem insane, but when seriously studied and pondered, it can offer UNFORESEEABLE ideological and practical solutions!"[27]

Marinetti's position would not have surprised anyone. In fact, a first, embryonic manifestation of the concepts found in *Il macchinesimo*, and part of the origins of the futurist movement (the foundation manifesto of February 20, 1909), was Marinetti's description of his car accident, a true archetype—before Warhol, before Ballard—of the many car crashes in twentieth-century art history and culture.

After the accident, the car, which had fallen into a ditch, was fished out, in the presence of a crowd of curious onlookers, with the aid of enormous iron nets:[28] "The car slowly came up from the ditch, leaving in the bottom, as if they were scales, its heavy bodywork of common sense and its soft upholstery of comfort. They thought it was dead, my beautiful shark, but a caress from me was enough to *revive it; and there it was, resuscitated*, running again on its mighty fins!"[29]

By the 1930s, this enthusiastic lightheartedness was gone, and the political atmosphere had changed sharply. When in 1933—the year Russolo moved permanently back to Italy—Ginna in *L'uomo futuro* spoke again of reincarnation, it was clear that the alchemical and occult plan of futurism had become subordinate to the aims of the Fascist regime.[30] Embodying as it does Mussolini's desire of forging anew the Italian race of the future, the *uomo futuro* constituted the embryonic stage of Fascism's racial campaign, something that is also evident in the frightening warnings to the Italian Jewish community of forced racial assimilation that were proclaimed in *La radia* in that same year 1933.[31]

Notwithstanding Ginna's aspiration to perfect the human by creating a biomechanical man of the future, no one looking back can feel empathy for his homunculus, for it is an idiot under the orders of the Duce, a frightening automaton whose direct precedent was not the intonarumori but the infernal metallic war animal produced in "millions of unities" promised by the *Ricostruzione futurista dell'universo* in the wake of World War I.

In 1913, though, with that war still around the corner, and future political directions (let alone involuntary parodies à là Ginna) still impossible to predict, futurists could still optimistically believe in a renewed art, a renewed sovereign Italian nation, a renewed humanity, and a renewed future, and they hoped for the spiritual energies and occult means to make these hopes real. Yet no oracle came to warn Russolo of the imminent deaths of Boccioni, Sant'Elia, and Carlo Erba, nor did the aura around his body protect him in battle from a forehead wound that left him convalescent for over a year.

INTONARUMORI AND THE UNCANNY

Although unable to protect Russolo, some kind of supernatural aura enveloped the intonarumori, as even the contemporary press could not avoid acknowledging. In a *Daily Graphic* article published on the occasion of Russolo's concerts of June 1914 at the Theatre Coliseum, the arrival of the crates of intonarumori in London was described as "the materialization of a nocturnal nightmare."[32] In a later review of the first of the three concerts at the Théâtre des Champs Elysées in 1921 which appeared in *L'Avenir* on June 19 of that year, the commentator perceived them as something ominous: "These terribly mechanical intonarumori appeared somewhat frightening."[33]

The intonarumori do indeed sound disturbing in the only surviving gramophone recording of 1921, which reproduces two of the pieces for mixed orchestra played in the Paris concerts: *Corale* and *Serenata*, by Antonio Russolo. The recorded sound of the intonarumori can be described as a disturbing spiritual intrusion in a context otherwise so annoyingly conventional and mundane that it is almost anodyne. The intrusion creates an effect that at first sounds humorous but is actually uncanny.

The term *uncanny* points to the noted Freudian dialectic of *heimlich/unheimlich*, or revealed/occult, two terms in opposition that resolve into the same disturbing outcome.[34] Think of an automaton: it is uncanny because of the strident presence of familiar, humanlike features that hide the unfamiliar, mechanical element that animates it. The cohabitation of the *heimlich* of external human features and the *unheimlich* of the internal mechanism frightens the viewer the moment he becomes aware of such coexistence and the fact that something is not as it seems, that something is wrong.

The Freudian *uncanny* is the horror of the unfamiliar busting into the familiar, the feeling of danger in a place considered safe, the private (as in familiar *and* occult) becoming the place of the obscene. The uncanny can derive from the unpleasant surprise of discovering the prosaicness of a mechanical interior, the discovery that what we thought spiritual—the soul moving the body of the automaton—is nothing but a grotesque camouflage or mechanical travesty. It can be the unsettling feeling of having been tricked.

An exhumation, understood as unveiling of the internal mechanism, is always an obscene, trivial, and fundamentally melancholic operation. In his own private *Genesis*, the 1909 manifesto, Marinetti lingered ingenuously over this horror when he described the car departing without its outer body or any padding to hide the internal mechanism. But, unlike Marinetti, Russolo was troubled by the dialectic of *heimlich/unheimlich*, revealed/occult, and especially by how this external/internal dilemma played out in the intonarumori.[35]

Obscene was the pressing request of the audience in the Storchi Theater, who interrupted Russolo and Piatti during the ritual solemnity of their presentation of the intonarumori prototype, trivially demanding to see the insides of the instruments: "It's a trick, it's a trick! Open the box!!"[36] And both obscene and melancholic was Michel Seuphor's description of the insides of the later rumorarmonio, which speaks of frightening mechanical "intestines."[37]

To his credit, Russolo was sufficiently aware of the *heimlich/unheimlich* dialectic and its place within futurist aesthetic discourse to refer to it in writing. He opened his French article "Les bruiteurs futuristes italiens," published in the *Revue de l'Epoque* in July of 1921, with Marcello Fabri's definition "FUTURISM MAKES THE EFFORT TO RENDER SIMULTANEOUSLY THE INTERNAL

AND THE EXTERNAL, THE PSYCHIC AND THE PLASTIC [. . .]. THROUGH THE INTERPENETRATION OF PLANES AND VOLUMES, IT ATTEMPTS TO REALIZE AT THE SAME TIME THE FAMILIAR AND THE UNFAMILIAR."[38] Russolo must have thought Fabri's catechism of plastic dynamism a fitting introduction to the theory of the art of noises. Yet the reference in this quote to the simultaneity of intimacy and strangeness cannot but evoke Freudian ghosts.

Because of the mechanical nature of their internal devices, their strong supernatural charge, and the secrecy with which Russolo treated the occult aspects of the project, the intonarumori transport the listener into the arena of modernist alienation, that mechanical anguish of modernism—a true *angoscia delle macchine,* to borrow the title of a futurist play by Ruggero Vasari—that in futurism seems to materialize everywhere we look.

The intonarumori were and are disturbing for yet another, subconsciously perceived, reason. Critical reflections of modernism have successfully linked the anguished obsession of modernist aesthetics for machines and automatic movements—Ravel's and Stravinsky's works provide convincing examples of this obsession—with the repression of romantic aesthetics and sentimentality, which for the modernists represented a past that should best be forgotten.[39]

Far from being the crucible for an artist-creator's subjective synthesis of reincarnation, the intonarumori became a vehicle for modernist dehumanization, symbol of the obliteration of the (human) self caused by technological alienation. An attempt to recover this lost humanity by opening the box and unveiling its mechanism is a futile operation, one that haunts us with its horror. Today, the City of the Future that populates itself with the dead brought back to life is no longer a paradoxical image. The reanimated dead represent the past—the nineteenth-century sentimentality repressed by modernist mechanisms, by automata—that has returned to torment us.

Conclusion

Materialist Futurism?

Se i contemporanei non hanno capito in Leonardo che l'artista, i posteri sbalorditi della sua scienza sperimentale hanno finito col voler fare di lui un positivista e anche quasi un materialista.

—Luigi Russolo, *Al di là della materia*

The question whether there are such things as black or red magic, mediumistic séances or ideoplastic materializations, is not germane to my discussion. But what about the intonarumori? Were they or were they not a "portal to the beyond"? Or were they only a metaphor for it? That, too, does not matter. Artworks are screens over which artists project their (he)art's desires, their poetics: considered from this point of view, artworks are always revelatory. What really matters—and what I have proposed—is that Russolo and other futurists believed in these occult concepts from the very beginning.

Russolo's theosophy is the key that allows us to identify, decode, and contextualize the occultist interests that were ever present in his work: from his printmaking and paintings (*Maschere, autoritratto [con doppio eterico], La musica,* etc.) to his theoretical writings on music.

Although examples cited in *Thought-forms* percolated into *The Art of Noises,* which borrows concepts and structures from *The Hidden Side of Things,* Russolo chose not to highlight his occult poetics nor to mention theosophy explicitly in his theoretical writings about music. Yet, as we know, the futurists had no qualms about acknowledging occult influence. Theosophy, among other forces, had helped them reclaim both spirituality and the occult, allowing the futurists to view these thought systems not as musty old traditions but rather as expressions of the latest frontiers of science.

Since spiritual and scientific goals were fully accepted within the futurist movement and are found, explicitly or implicitly, in most of the initiatives promoted by futurism, Russolo did not need to justify or explicitly state the occultist poetics underlying the art of noises. I was, however, principally concerned with discovering the various floating fragments of Russolo's poetics, and from them reconstructing a mosaic: for this side of my work, explanations about the lack of an explicit exposition of Russolo's modalities and operations are therefore not so essential.

If many of the pieces of this mosaic were eventually covered up in the second half of the twentieth century, this was not Russolo's fault. In fact neither Russolo, nor the other futurists, considered the connections between futurism and the occult to be per se shameful: futurism as a materialistic movement was a creation of modernist critics.

After World War II, and once the general interest in theosophy had waned, modernist criticism of futurism entirely missed the futurists' equation "Occult = Science." By confusing futurist science with positivistic science, these critics dismissed or even censored the references to the occult and the irrational, which can be found everywhere in futurist works, and relegated all such references to the margins of critical discourse, instead forefronting a materialist reduction of machine and technology in their interpretive frame of the futurist movement. Those phases of the futurist movement in which the influence of the occult was unarguable they attacked as evidence of reactionism, postromantic or late nineteenth-century regurgitation, or, incongruently, regressive "abdication of the spirit of the avant-garde."[1]

Modernist criticism likely promoted this particular critical reading with the good intention of redeeming futurism as a progressive, modernist force in the eyes of the postwar international artistic community. Consciously or not, this was done to enable a discussion on futurism—which obviously has some merit—in a post-Resistance climate when openly to address or discuss or study anything relating to fascism was considered taboo in Italy.[2]

Wishing to save the futurist movement from its uncomfortable connections with any form of fascism, modernism tended in the process to erase any reference to spiritual or irrational philosophy, and this was done in the name of a rational materialism that the futurists themselves, Russolo above all, would have abhorred.[3] During this critical process some aspects of futurism (such as the worship of the machine) were inflated to excess, while, with the same casualness, others were put to death. Such was the price of rehabilitation.

Some may object that modernist critics were not the only ones responsible for portraying futurism as materialistic, and it might even be argued that Marinetti's rhetoric played a major role in this portrayal. Could it be that Marinetti and his scholars were swimming, so to speak, in the same modernist "waters" and so contributed to the affirmation of the materialistic interpretation of futurism? Or maybe this interpretation was the result of Marinetti's self-construction, his self-serving, myth-producing rhetoric? Marinetti is an easy scapegoat, but I would like to argue otherwise.

He may have been responsible for lobbying to erase the past, but if so, he could not also be charged with erasing the spiritual. In fact, Marinetti talked openly and consistently about the occult, in connection not simply with the symbolic foundational act of the movement but also with the 1912 breakthrough of the Words-in-Freedom theories, *La radia* of 1933, and beyond.[4] True, Marinettian rhetoric placed machines front and center in the movement's image, but the futurists' machine—represented by Marinetti as that of Prampolini and Russolo—was not materialistic, bourgeois, fordist-rational comfort but rather the means to a spiritual, occult end.

Is this, then, one of futurism's many contradictions?[5] Could it be that Marinetti allowed modernist critics to consider futurism materialistic, and that he accepted the misunderstanding purely for purposes of publicity? Regardless of whether this was the case, it is a fact that modernist critics exploited the ambiguity, lifting the weapon with which they were to make futurism "occult-free" from Marinetti's own rhetorical arsenal.

For the futurists, originality was of such fundamental importance (in a number of cases futurists backdated their works) that any relation with the past was vehemently deemed to be conservative and dishonorable. Since the occult can be understood as a source of wisdom received from the past, modernist criticism, using the reductive equation "Occult = Past," rejected any reference to the occult within futurism, considering it to be *passatista* (passéist).

Given modernism's built-in materialism, modernist critics must have felt vicariously embarrassed by the spiritual and occult components of futurism. In unceremoniously lumping the occult together with the past, they made, to use a fitting Italian expression, "di tutta un'erba, un fascio."

Marinetti and the futurists considered principally those aspects of the occult that had been confirmed by the latest and most surprising discoveries of modern science; they never understood the occult as something from the past, and thus they never espoused the "Occult = Past" equation.[6] Yet modernist critics deliberately misread the occult influence, considering it an embarrassing, if occasional, debt to the past and abdication of that innovative (and thus rational and materialistic) spirit that was expected always to propel the avant-garde. Modernist critics hijacked and turned back toward the occult the same rhetorical weapon futurists had directed toward the past: in short, Marinetti's rhetoric and strategy backfired.

The elements for a reading of the art of noises in spiritual terms, which are present in the sources, were quickly dismissed, if mentioned at all. For example, Lista first hints at Russolo's interest, starting circa 1910–11, in "the studies of metapsychics and Eastern doctrines." But he leaves this thought unexplored, setting it aside as a reflection of a broader interest that was common to all members of the futurist group.[7] Some pages later, however, Lista declares that Russolo's late interest in spirituality should be discounted because it was regressive.

This example helps to explain the critical vacuum around the art of noises and the occult in the modernist Russolo scholarship established by Lista, Maffina, and Brown—authors whose work remains among the most substantial musicological contributions to Russolo studies to date and continues to be the starting point for subsequent investigations.

This book should not be perceived as an attack on modernist critical ideologies. I have not wished to exploit Russolo's misfortunes at the hands of his critics for an epistemological assault but have been primarily focused on studying Russolo's poetics to uncover new materials and initiate a new basis for discussion.

Modernist criticism used futurism's self-professed ideology to construct an image of Russolo as an innovator of genius and acclaim the inventor as "the first major exponent of musical synthesis itself."[8] But it was modernist ideology that led to the suppression of the other, and no less important, sides of Russolo's operation. By placing the analytic focus on materialistic—and technological—innovation and ignoring the proximity between technology and occult's rhetorical approach, modernist criticism transformed the art of noises into a materialistic feast. This misunderstanding obliterated the fact that the futurist future was by and large a spiritual one, and that futurist machines were only the medium through which to explore spirituality.

If in considering the spiritual link between Russolo and Leonardo one were to substitute Leonardo's name for Russolo's, the following passage from

Russolo's *Al di là della materia* suddenly sounds tragically autobiographical, both foreseeing and attacking his future critical fate: "If his contemporaries understood in Leonardo only the artist, posterity, amazed by his experimental science, ended up wanting to make him into a positivist, even almost a materialist."[9]

Thus in the end Russolo became subject to the same critical reductivism that he had diagnosed in Leonardo's critics. In the narrow reading of a futurist universe, constricted between the binaries of a materialist techno-idolatry and the blind cult of science—a *scientismo* that is far removed from what most of the futurists believed, and a cult to which Russolo never subscribed—there was no space for the ouija board of the séances, the divinatory responses of a medium, the dialogue with the dead or, more generally, parascience—all things that the futurists pursued.

The portrait of Russolo as a materialist scientist was thoroughly convenient to modernist criticism. Modernist critics preferred to see him as a scientist who worked intensely with the sole objective of replacing the old instruments of the orchestra with new, noise-producing ones, and creating an orchestra to execute his futurist music with the objective of achieving sound innovations.

This portrait, which has survived until now, is partially true but incomplete and much too reductive.[10] Yet if we can free ourselves from the heavy modernist baggage that is still so much a part of the critical discourse surrounding futurism, then a new impression of Russolo's image, enhanced by new interpretive angles such as those I have indicated here, can begin to materialize.

NOTES

INTRODUCTION

1. Maria Zanovello, *Luigi Russolo: L'uomo, l'artista* (Milan: Cyril Corticelli, 1958), 78–79; henceforth Zanovello, *Luigi Russolo*.

2. Luigi Russolo, *Al di là della materia* (Milan: Bocca, 1938); quoted from the second edition (Milan: Luciano Ferriani editore, 1961), 102–3.

3. Giovanni Lista, "Russolo, peinture et bruitisme," in Luigi Russolo, *L'art des bruits* (Lausanne: l'Age d'Homme, 1975), 28; henceforth Lista, "Russolo, peinture et bruitisme." This judgment was later echoed by other scholars. See Piera Anna Franini, "Il futurismo in musica fra rivoluzione e tradizione: Terza parte," *Musicaaa!* 3, no. 8 (1997): 26.

4. Barclay Brown was the first to point out "Russolo's role in creating the first musical synthesizer"; see Brown, introduction to Luigi Russolo, *The Art of Noises*, trans. Barclay Brown (New York: Pendragon Press, 1986), 1.

5. These interests will include such alternatives spiritual practices as remote healing, spirit conjuring, etheric doubling, ectoplasmic materialization, sun gazing, palm reading, yoga meditation, etc. Because of the syncretic nature of the occult field of inquiry, more an all-encompassing ocean than a univocal stream of study, I prefer to let the term *occult* (as well as the discipline that studies it, *occultism*) define itself, with all its manifold and even contradictory allure, in the following pages than reveal it in a narrow definition. In this way I pay homage to the term's etymology.

6. A case in point is Anna Gasparotto's thorough examination of Russolo's late philosophy in the MART 2006 catalog (cited in n. 10), research that shows how Russolo's spiritual and occult research is now taken more seriously. But if Gasparotto's scholarship is presented in parallel with Russolo's visual art explorations of the 1940s, no contribution in MART employs spirituality as an access key to a deeper understanding of Russolo's futurist activities. Daniele Lombardi's brief contribution to studies of Russolo's futurist investigations in the realm of sound, which is also included

in the catalogue, only makes passing reference to Russolo's spirituality and does not provide any kind of interpretation of his sound theory. Instead, it mostly list facts and notions previously available in print, including some which meanwhile had already been corrected by my *Luigi Russolo and the Occult* (e.g., Russolo's 1931's *nuovo istrumento musicale a corde* is here still referred to as *piano enarmonico*).

7. The word *intonarumori* first appears as *apparecchi intonarumori* (noise intoner instruments) in Russolo's article "Gl'intonarumori futuristi," dated May 22, 1913, and published in *Lacerba* on July 1, 1913. Since the word *apparecchi* was implied, it soon would be omitted. In the course of this book I will use the word *intonarumori* for both the singular and plural forms, as it is in Italian (e.g., "il singolo [apparecchio] intonarumori," or "un'orchestra di [apparecchi] intonarumori"). *Lacerba* is available in facsimile (Milan: Mazzotta, 1970).

8. Zanovello, *Luigi Russolo*, 21. Throughout this book, italics are mine unless otherwise noted.

9. Gianfranco Maffina, *Luigi Russolo e l'arte dei rumori: Con tutti gli scritti musicali* (Turin: Martano, 1978), 115, 117; henceforth Maffina, *Luigi Russolo e l'arte dei rumori*. All quoted passages from *The Art of Noises* are based on the Barclay Brown translations (see note 4), which I edited when needed. Italics are mine unless otherwise indicated.

10. Daniele Lombardi, "Tanto rumore per nulla?" in Luigi Russolo, *Vita e opere di un futurista* (Milan: Skira, 2006), 118; henceforth MART. Franco Tagliapietra, "Riflessioni sulla pittura: Teoria e produzione dal dopoguerra al 1930," in *MART*, 56. In her essays for this catalog, Anna Gasparotto recognizes that Russolo's late spiritual interests were rooted in his early Milanese years, but by claiming that they were the result of his early Milanese milieu and "resurfaced" later, that is, that Russolo had "pushed them aside" until he "revisited" them in Paris as part of his "curious and detailed investigations," she implies that his occult interests skipped the futurist years altogether; Gasparotto, "Da Parigi a Tarragona al rientro in Italia," in *MART*, 69, 85, and "Cerro di Laveno e il lago Maggiore: L'incontro e la conversazione con un gruppo di amici, la pittura 'classico-moderna,'" in *MART*, 98.

11. For the titles and dates of Russolo's artworks, I rely on the chronology Franco Tagliapietra prepared for *MART*.

12. Maffina, *Luigi Russolo e l'arte dei rumori*,16.

13. I first proposed the notion of a continuity in Russolo's interests in my 2004 PhD dissertation. Russolo himself was aware of the continuity; see Luigi Russolo, "Catalogo della Galleria Borromini di Como," partially reproduced in Maffina, *Luigi Russolo e l'arte dei rumori*, 122. In his diaries, Russolo wrote: "Despite the apparent differences of my occupations, there is a unity in my life"; diary entry of July 31, 1934, quoted in Gasparotto, "Da Parigi a Tarragona al rientro in Italia," in *MART*, 87n54. For a more in-depth discussion of Russolo's concept of *unity*, also a Boccionian keyword, see my chapter 8. The realization of continuity (and coherence) in Russolo's early and late investigations led Gasparotto to a conclusion about the substantial unity of Russolo's undertakings that agrees with mine, and she gets there by a similar path, though she does not consider apply her findings to Russolo's futurism; see Luciano Chessa, "Luigi Russolo

and the Occult" (PhD dissertation, University of California, Davis, 2004), 2, 7; Gasparotto, "Riprese, approfondimenti, nuovi orientamenti: Alcune considerazioni su riflessioni ricorrenti e modalità espressive negli scritti," in *MART,* 67; and Gasparotto, "Da Parigi a Tarragona al rientro in Italia," in *MART,* 85.

14. Futurists, likely influenced by French symbolists, adopted synesthesia—which clearly has an occultist provenance—in their art and made it one of the cardinal point of their poetics. A first trace of synesthesia in Russolo's output is his 1910 oil painting *Profumo,* which is imbued with symbolist and occult resonances alike.

15. The synthesizer-like qualities of the intonarumori, alleged by Barclay Brown and others, were achieved mechanically. They arose from Russolo's systematic and taxonomical (but also ecumenical!) approach to sound. Naturally, a single intonarumori would mechanically "synthesize" only one kind of sound; but these instruments displayed synth-like properties as a whole. This was the case until Russolo in the 1920s built the rumorarmonio, an instrument that combined all the timbres of the individual intonarumori and controlled them through a keyboard interface (a change that curiously resembles Moog's conceptual departure from Buchla). See Brown, "The Noise Instruments of Luigi Russolo," *Perspectives of New Music* 20 (1981–82), 48; and Brown, introduction to Russolo, *The Art of Noises,* 1, 2.

16. In the passage quoted above from the introduction to his French translation of Russolo's book *L'art des bruits* (1975), Lista provided the classic example of this modernist ideology in defining Luigi Russolo's later interest in the occult as a regressive phase, or, more precisely, as an "abdication de l'esprit d'avant-garde" (Lista, "Russolo, peinture et bruitisme," 28). Very likely, Lista's unexpressed fear of a connection between Russolo's later occult theories and fascism played a role in the formulation of this judgment. The phrase "abdication of the spirit of the avant-garde" is edited out in the updated version of the essay, in Giovanni Lista, *Luigi Russolo e la musica futurista* (Milan: Mudima, 2009), which awkwardly omits any discussion of Russolo's post-1930 work.

17. In fact the opposite is true: for instance, on the title page of the publication *Arte fascista,* published by the Sindacati Artistici Torino in December 1927, Russolo's name is prominently displayed (see figure 2).

18. For this reason I wrote of that connection in depth in a separate essay, which follows the development of Russolo's aesthetics after 1921 in the context of his developing political philosophy.

19. Futurists considered the occult a progressive force, a spiritual expression of the newest, yet unexplored, frontiers of science.

20. Luigi Russolo, "L'arco enarmonico," *Fiamma* 2, no. 1 (January 1926).

CHAPTER 1

1. Maurizio Calvesi, *Il futurismo: La fusione della vita nell'arte* (Milan: Fratelli Fabbri Editori, 1967; 1975), 228; henceforth Calvesi, *Fusione.* Calvesi's critical work on futurism decisively showed the movement's aesthetic positions in all their density and

contradictions. His research led to a far more complex image of futurism than that of the modernism-inspired critics.

2. Many of the futurists' sources—including Henri Bergson and Charles Webster Leadbeater—were at opposite poles in respect to materialism. To Marinetti, the machine was a metaphor for spiritual energy, akin to Nietzsche's *action*. For Boccioni, a similarly spiritual dynamic ideal was represented by a horse (see Calvesi, *Fusione*, 64).

3. In Edgar Varèse, "VERBE," *391* [vol.] 5 (1917): 42.

4. Gino Severini was one of the few to object to Marinetti's censorship of and interpolations to his writings; according to Calvesi, this explains why Severini's 1913 manifesto "Le analogie plastiche del Dinamismo" remained unpublished (see Calvesi, *Fusione*, 78).

5. The volume *Pittura e scultura futuriste (Dinamismo plastico)* (Milan: Edizioni futuriste di "Poesia," 1914) is reprinted in Umberto Boccioni, *Gli scritti editi e inediti*, ed. Zeno Birolli (Milan: Feltrinelli, 1971), 75–204; henceforth Boccioni, *Scritti*.

6. Calvesi, *Fusione*, 48.

7. Calvesi, *Fusione*, 39.

8. Among them should be mentioned the influence on both Marinetti and Boccioni of 1905 Einstein's special theory of relativity.

9. In fact, a variety of scientists of the time such as Wilhelm Röntgen, Camille Flammarion, Thomas Alva Edison, and Cesare Lombroso conducted research on the margins of what was considered "science," in effect blurring the lines between occultism and official science.

10. A partial list would at least include Hertz's electromagnetism, Röntgen's X-rays, Becquerel's radioactivity, Curie's radium, Marconi's radio waves, but also the non-Euclidean geometries promoted by Gauss, Lobachevsky, Bolyai, Riemann; Einstein's relativity, Planck and Bohr's quantum theory, Heisenberg's indetermination principle, etc. See Flavia Matitti, "Balla e la Teosofia," in *Giacomo Balla 1895–1911: Verso il futurismo*, ed. Maurizio Fagiolo dell'Arco (Venice: Marsilio, 1998), 41; henceforth Matitti, "Balla e la Teosofia." See also Giuseppe La Monica, "Il tempo e lo spazio morirono ieri," in *Il futurismo* (Milan: Fratelli Fabbri Editori, 1976), 49; henceforth La Monica, "Il tempo e lo spazio morirono ieri."

11. Cited in Linda D. Henderson, *Duchamp in Context* (Princeton, NJ: Princeton University Press, 1998), 6; henceforth Henderson, *Duchamp in Context*.

12. In 1892, Gaetano Previati was the only Italian painter invited to participate in the exhibition of painters affiliated with Joséphin Péladan's Rose+Croix. See Matitti, "Balla e la teosofia," 41. Boccioni was aware of this, and it is certainly because of Previati that he mentioned the "pittura dei Rosa Croce" at his 1911 lecture at the Circolo Artistico in Rome. The full text of that lecture can be found in Boccioni, *Altri inediti e apparati critici*, ed. Zeno Birolli (Milan: Feltrinelli, 1972), 11–29; henceforth Boccioni, *Altri inediti*.

13. Germano Celant, "Futurismo esoterico," *Il Verri* 15, nos. 33–34 (October 1970): 109; henceforth Celant, "Futurismo esoterico."

14. See especially the first chapter in Henderson, *Duchamp in Context*, "Duchamp's

First Quest for the Invisible: X-Rays, Transparency, and Internal Views of the Figure, 1911–1912."

15. Celant, "Futurismo esoterico," 113.

16. Umberto Boccioni, Carlo Carrà, Luigi Russolo, Giacomo Balla, and Gino Severini, "La pittura futurista: Manifesto tecnico," in *I manifesti del futurismo: Prima serie* (Milan: Edizioni futuriste di "Poesia," 1913), 28; henceforth *I manifesti del futurismo*. If not Russolo, Boccioni may have been the author of this sentence. He will refer again to X-rays and Röntgen in his critical text for *La risata* in the catalog for the 1912 Sackville Gallery futurist exhibit. Moreover, the reference to "opacità dei corpi" recurs verbatim in the text of Boccioni's lecture in Rome in May 1911. For a transcription of a newspaper article that was found in Boccioni's documents, entitled "I misteri della radioattività" (The mysteries of radioactivity), see Boccioni, *Scritti*, 442.

17. See "La pittura futurista: Manifesto tecnico," in *I manifesti del futurismo*, 27, 28, 30.

18. Marianne W. Martin, *Futurist Art and Theory* (Oxford: Clarendon Press, 1968), 53; henceforth Martin, *Futurist Art and Theory*.

19. My book will privilege these three critical sources (Calvesi, Fagiolo dell'Arco, and Celant) rather than Cigliana's book, because they focus on the group of futurist painters. The type of information that can be obtained from these sources is more useful for a research that aims to redraw a map of Russolo's influences. Ginna, Corra, Balla, Soffici, and Russolo were all, directly or not, influenced by theosophical writings. We cannot therefore exclude the possibility that other futurists may not have been equally interested in theosophy. Others who are known to have been interested in the occult arts include Marinetti, Boccioni, Carrà, Severini, Bragaglia, Romani, Buzzi, Valeria, and Settimelli.

20. Marinetti had after all modeled futurism on symbolism from the beginning, deriving not just fundamental philosophical and aesthetic elements but also promotional strategies. The writer Jean Moréas founded *Symbolism* on 18 September 1886 with a manifesto published in the Parisian newspaper *Le Figaro*; Marinetti chose the same literary genre and international forum to launch futurism.

21. Calvesi proposed that Marinetti's knowledge of Einstein came by way of Minkowsky; see Calvesi, *Fusione*, 37.

22. La Monica, "Il tempo e lo spazio morirono ieri," 49. La Monica adds that Boccioni makes this assumption a central point of both his poetics and his art. I find that this is evident from an analysis of "Stati d'animo: quelli che vanno" and "Stati d'animo: quelli che restano" of 1911, in which the central subject is always in movement, either because the observer, standing still, is watching a subject in motion, or because the observer, in motion, is watching a still subject. See also Martin, *Futurist Art and Theory*, 93–95, 112–14.

23. Calvesi, *Fusione*, 39.

24. Calvesi, *Fusione*, 39. This denial of the independent existence of matter, as well as of the dualistic opposition of matter and movement, is also found in a series of lectures that Rudolf Steiner presented around 1908 at the Architektenhaus in Berlin. As Sixten Ringbom notes, for Steiner "there is no such thing as matter; Spirit and Spirit

only, exists, but it exists in varying degrees of condensation." Ringbom, "The Sounding Cosmos: A Study in the Spiritualism of Kandinsky and the Genesis of Abstract Painting," in *Acta Academiae Abonensis*, series A, 38, no. 2 (1970), 68; henceforth Ringbom, "The Sounding Cosmos." Marinetti's denials about the nature of matter and movement, and especially the belief in the existence of various degrees of condensation (and of the principle of continuity), would become important points in Boccioni's theoretical writings. See Umberto Boccioni, "Fondamento plastico della scultura e pittura futuriste," *Lacerba* (March 15, 1913); henceforth Boccioni, "Fondamento." Similar ideas are found in the article "Raggio" by Ardengo Soffici, which was later reprinted under the title "La teosofia nel futurismo" in the periodical of Roman theosophical writings, *Ultra*. Steiner was well known among futurists, and I believe that Boccioni and Russolo may have even attended his lectures in Milan in 1912. Furthermore, Mario Verdone claims that Ginna, Corra, and Sprovieri were familiar with his work; see Mario Verdone, introduction to Arnaldo Ginna and Bruno Corra, *Manifesti futuristi e scritti teorici*, ed. Mario Verdone (Ravenna: Longo, 1984), 27; henceforth Ginna and Corra, *Scritti*.

25. The very existence of primal matter, another name for ether, would be seriously questioned by Einstein's theories.

26. In Filippo T. Marinetti, *Teoria e invenzione futurista* (Milan: Mondadori, 1968; 6th ed., 2005), 125; henceforth Marinetti, *Teoria e invenzione futurista*. A further point of contact between Marinetti's Words in Freedom and the occult is suggested by Calvesi in a 1975 article in which he claimed that behind the automatic writing that Marinetti described in 1912 was the influence of mediumistic writing, which Calvesi thought was "directed" by spirits to a medium in a trance state, filtered by way of Bergson's concept of "intuition" and the Romantic theory of "inspiration." See Calvesi, "L'écriture médiumnique comme source de l'automatisme futuriste et surréaliste," *Europe* 53 (1975): 47; henceforth Calvesi, "L'écriture médiumnique."

27. Marinetti, *La grande Milano tradizionale e futurista: Una sensibilità italiana nata in Egitto* (Milan: Mondadori, 1969), 104; henceforth Marinetti, *La grande Milano*.

28. Marinetti, *Teoria e invenzione futurista*, 209. These words likely inspired a number of John Cage's projects, including his amplification of a wood in Ivrea, Italy, in 1984. He employed Marinetti's and Masnata's language and rhetoric to describe this project to the Italian press; see "Arriva John Cage: 'Sonorizzerà' un bosco?" *Il Secolo* (Genoa), April 28, 1984.

29. Marinetti, *Teoria e invenzione futurista*, 209.

30. According to Calvesi (*Fusione*, 39), Boccioni was interested in X-rays since 1910.

31. The futurists' interest in synesthesia, and in the theory of vibrations implied by synesthesia, is crucial in explaining Russolo's intellectual evolution (think of his paintings *Profumo* and *La musica*, for instance). Russolo probably began to study acoustics and the synesthetic theory of vibrations through Röntgen's theories of the vibration of ether and how these would be historically interpreted to explain the phenomenon of ectoplasms. The connection between Röntgen's theories and the ectoplasm is mentioned in Celant, "Futurismo esoterico," 113.

32. The scapigliatura was a northern Italian literary movement of the second part of the nineteenth century. The scapigliati took as a model the French maudit poets and their bohemian lifestyle.

33. Found, among others, in Busoni's "Il regno della musica (epilogo della nuova estetica)" [The kingdom of music (epilogue of the new aesthetics)].

34. Marinetti, "Tattilismo," in *Teoria e invenzione futurista*, 178. (The excerpts from "Tattilismo" are from pages 177–79.) This catastrophic hypothesis shows a debt to the early twentieth-century trope of thermodynamic death, the end of the world through entropy, as found in Flammarion's writings. See the chapter on Flammarion in Bruce Clarcke and Linda D. Henderson, *From Energy to Information: Representation in Science and Technology, Art and Literature* (Stanford, CA: Stanford University Press, 2002); henceforth *From Energy to Information*.

35. In this case also, as in the case of ether, a reduction takes place: just as all matter can be reconducted to ether, so all senses can be reconducted to the sense of touch.

36. In fact, Marinetti encouraged the "avoidance of [...] variety of colors in the tactile tables."

37. See Marinetti, *La grande Milano*, 58.

38. To invoke Balla was by no means a casual choice.

39. Marinetti, *Teoria e invenzione futurista*, 196–97.

40. This will also occur in his *Mafarka il futurista*, in which a wooden puppet—reminiscent of Pinocchio?—comes to life thanks to the transfer of psychic energy from the father, Mafarka, to the son, Gazurmah. Once born, Gazurmah will aspire to fly.

41. In *Guerra, sola igiene del mondo*, in Marinetti, *Teoria e invenzione futurista*, 299–300.

42. In Marinetti, *Teoria e invenzione futurista*, 206. The project of metallizing the human body is expanded *ad absurdum* in "Il macchinesimo," a futurist manifesto by Renato Di Bosso and Ignazio Scurto of the same 1933.

43. "Prime battaglie futuriste" in *Guerra sola igiene del mondo*, Marinetti, *Teoria e invenzione futurista*, 239.

44. In Marinetti, *Teoria e invenzione futurista*, 231.

45. This opening sentence of Boccioni's posthumous *Note per il libro* includes his most strenuous attacks against philosophical systems that dominated in the second half of the nineteenth century: idealism, materialism, and positivism, against whose rationality Boccioni (and the whole futurist movement) were fiercely opposed. See also Boccioni, *Altri inediti*, 72–74.

46. On Steiner's Architektenhaus lectures, see note 24. To futurists' ears, the term *spirito* must have sounded too reminiscent of Hegel's idealism. At the "serata futurista" that took place at the Teatro Costanzi in Rome, Papini said: "What matters is to have an Absolute Principle—whether this is God or the Spirit, this is essentially the same—and it is also important for men to be happy in the worship of this good and high principle." See Calvesi, *Il futurismo* (Milan: Fratelli Fabbri Editori, 1970), 16; henceforth Calvesi, *Futurismo*.

47. Boccioni, "Fondamento."

48. Boccioni, "Fondamento."

49. Ardengo Soffici, "Raggio," *Lacerba* (July 1, 1914).

50. Soffici, "Raggio." This is not the first time that Soffici addressed occult themes in his writings; on synesthesia, see Soffici's article "La pittura futurista" in *Lacerba* (December 15, 1913). Several years later, Russolo echoed Soffici's words in his late philosophical work *Al di là della materia*: "You should feel your Self becoming a power, a solar center around which gravitate the body, the mind, feelings and thoughts!" Russolo, *Al di là della materia*, 2nd ed. (Milan: Luciano Ferriani editore, 1961), 144; henceforth Russolo, *Al di là della materia*.

51. Boccioni, "Fondamento." As Boccioni wrote in his "Manifesto tecnico della scultura futurista," the lecture in Rome took place in May 1911 at Rome's Circolo Artistico (Boccioni, *Altri inediti*, 11–29). The term "trascendentalismo fisico" might be derived from Lombroso's "Ricerche sui fenomeni ipnotici e spiritici," published in 1909; see Henderson, *Duchamp in Context*, 117–18. Celant provides a short quotation from this passage by Boccioni, erroneously claiming that the lecture was held in 1915. Marinetti (*La grande Milano*, 83) mentions a photographic plate, in a passage describing Russolo in the process of building the intonarumori.

52. Boccioni, *Scritti*, 203.

53. In "Note per il libro," from *Pittura e scultura futuriste*, reprinted in Boccioni, *Altri inediti*, 76.

54. In Maurizio Fagiolo dell'Arco, "Boccioni, Beyond Painting," *Art International* 11, no. 1 (1967): 19; henceforth Fagiolo dell'Arco, "Boccioni, Beyond Painting."

55. Matitti, "Balla e la teosofia," 43, and Fagiolo dell'Arco, "Boccioni, Beyond Painting," 19.

56. Calvesi, "L'écriture médiumnique," 45.

57. Kandinsky wrote about this in his journal; see Ringbom, "The Sounding Cosmos," 51–52. Ringbom also mentions that Kandinsky studied criminology in Lombroso's manuals.

58. Celant, "Futurismo esoterico," 111.

59. For Bragaglias's articles, see Simona Cigliana, *La seduta spiritica* (Roma: Fazi, 2007), 295.

60. Calvesi, *Fusione*, 107.

61. Cited in Calvesi, *Fusione*, 109.

62. See Annie Besant and Charles W. Leadbeater, *Thought-forms* (Wheaton: Theosophical Publishing House, 1999), 21 (henceforth Besant and Leadbeater, *Thought-forms*); and Robert Galbreath, "A Glossary of Spiritual and Related Terms," in *The Spiritual in Art: Abstract Painting 1890–1985* (New York: Abbeville Press, 1986), 390 (henceforth Galbreath, "A Glossary of Spiritual and Related Terms"). According to this theory, though everybody can produce thought-forms, only the clairvoyant has the power to see them with the naked eye, and certainly only a medium can gather the power to materialize them.

63. See Giovanni Macchia, *Pirandello o la stanza della tortura* (Milan: Mondadori, 1981), 54.

64. Boccioni, "La pittura futurista (conferenza tenuta a Roma nel 1911)," in Boc-

cioni, *Altri inediti*, 11; the lecture is from pages 11 to 29. Unless otherwise indicated, all subsequent Boccioni quotes in the text are from this lecture.

65. The claim that the painting took many years to complete is found in Paolo Buzzi, "Souvenirs sur le futurisme," *Cahiers d'art* 25 (1950): 26; henceforth Buzzi, "Souvenirs sur le futurisme."

66. See Martin, *Futurist Art and Theory*, 93, 106.

67. This concept will percolate in Marinetti's "Tattilismo." See also Russolo's theory of "colloquio spirituale," a spiritual dialogue among artists across history, in Russolo, *Al di là della materia*, 210.

68. *Intuition* is a Bergsonian keyword.

69. Boccioni, *Altri inediti*, 86. "Gives the eye the power to perceive the invisible," reports a variant.

70. The concept of *unità* is further explained in a phrase that Boccioni wrote in the preparatory notes for his Roman lecture but did not include in the final version, "aspiring to unity as universal vibration"; see Boccioni, *Altri inediti*, 35.

71. Boccioni, Carrà, Russolo, and Severini. "Presentazione alle opere esposte alla Sackville Gallery," in *Archivi del futurismo* 1, ed. Maria Druidi Gambillo and Teresa Fiori (Rome: De Luca, 1958), 110; henceforth *Archivi del futurismo* 1.

72. Boccioni, *Altri inediti*, 34.

73. The notion of a utopian overcoming of the five senses returns in Marinetti's "Tattilismo." The notion of hypersensitivity was already in the technical manifesto of futurist painters published the year before; see *I manifesti del futurismo*, 28.

74. Boccioni, *Altri inediti*, 35.

75. This analysis is found in Calvesi, *Fusione*, 112.

76. Henderson, "Vibratory Modernism," in *From Energy to Information*, 131.

77. Celant, "Futurismo esoterico," 111n11.

78. Celant, "Futurismo esoterico," 111n9.

79. Cf. Fagiolo dell'Arco, *Compenetrazioni iridescenti* (Rome: Bulzoni, 1968), 12; henceforth Fagiolo dell'Arco, *Compenetrazioni*. Balla's portrait of Ghilarducci is mentioned in Celant, "Futurismo esoterico," 111n11.

80. Celant, "Futurismo esoterico," 111.

81. See also the amplification of this effect in the series of photographs made by the ambassador Cosmelli, a friend of Balla. In these photographs, Balla is shown first with *Ritratto della madre* and then with *Fallimento*. See Fagiolo dell'Arco, *Balla pre-futurista* (Rome: Bulzoni, 1968), 4, 5; henceforth Fagiolo dell'Arco, *Balla pre-futurista*.

82. Fagiolo dell'Arco, *Balla pre-futurista*, 28; Fagiolo dell'Arco, "Giacomo Balla verso il futurismo," in *Giacomo Balla 1895–1911: Verso il futurismo*, ed. Maurizio Fagiolo dell'Arco (Venice: Marsilio, 1998), 20; henceforth Fagiolo dell'Arco, "Giacomo Balla verso il futurismo."

83. This is according to Elica Balla; see Fagiolo dell'Arco, *Balla pre-futurista*, 28.

84. In Balla, Elica. *Con Balla* (1984), cited in Matitti, "Balla e la teosofia," 43. *Trasformazione forme spiriti* is the title of a cycle of paintings that Balla produced between 1916 and 1918.

85. Soffici and Balla were not the only futurists to participate in the group's activities. Around 1910–14, before moving to Florence, Maria Crisi (later Ginanni) attended lectures by Besant and Steiner at Gruppo Roma's center. Julius Evola collaborated intensively with the group from 1922 to 1927, and it is probable that futurists from the Roman area such as Depero, Bragaglia, and Prampolini, who gravitated into Balla's orbit and were evidently interested in the occult, also had relationships with Gruppo Roma.

86. Matitti, "Balla e la teosofia," 44. Steiner frequently visited Italy. In 1912, he gave lectures on life after death and reincarnation in Milan.

87. The swastika was associated with the cult of light among the Zoroastrians, so the origins of the symbol could be Indo-Iranian. The Indo-Iranians were a Sumerian-Akkadian people, originally from Iran, who in the Bronze Age (ca. 1700 to 1300 B.C.) migrated to India, where they mingled with the native population of Dravidian stock. In India the Sumerian-Akkadian language of the Indo-Iranians gave rise to Sanskrit; the origin of the term swastika, translatable as "lucky charm," is in fact Sanskrit.

88. Helena P. Blavatsky, *The Theosophical Glossary* (London: Theosophical Publishing Society, 1892), 315.

89. Illustration 35 in Matitti, "Balla e la teosofia," 40. The disc with horizontally spread-out wings was one of the symbols of the sun. The Belgian religious archeologist and freemason Eugène Félicien Albert, Count Goblet d'Alviella, in his 1891 book *La Migration des Symboles* claims that both the gammadion-swastika and the circle with wings spreading out horizontally represent the sun as the supreme and almighty life force, the highest deity. For this, see Count [Eugène] Goblet d'Alviella, *The Migration of Symbols* (London, 1894), facsimile ed. (Wellingborough, UK: Aquarian Press, 1979); see esp. chapters 2 (*On the Gammadion, or Swastika*) and 6 (*On the Winged Glove, the Caduceus, and the Trisula*).

90. I am not the first to have noted the importance of light in Balla's works. Dell'Arco cites three works by Balla as examples of this interest: *Il pertichino* (1898), *Fiera di Parigi* (1900), and *Lavoro* (1902). See Fagiolo dell'Arco, *Compenetrazioni*, 13. See also Sergio Poggianella's brief article "Okkulte Elemente und das Licht im Werk Ballas," in *Okkultismus und Avantgarde: Von Munch bis Mondrian 1900–1915* (Frankfurt: Schirn Kunsthalle, 1995), 459–65; henceforth *Okkultismus*. It should also be mentioned that the rising sun appearing in Previati and Pellizza had socialist associations, something that Balla and Boccioni surely absorbed.

91. See Fagiolo dell'Arco, *Balla pre-futurista*, 24. Marinetti named one of his daughters Luce.

92. On the chronology of these paintings, see Calvesi, *Fusione*, 98ff.

93. On the victory of electric over natural light, see Calvesi, *Fusione*, 337n28.

94. Calvesi, *Fusione*, 52.

95. See Fagiolo dell'Arco, "Giacomo Balla verso il futurismo," 23.

96. Matitti, "Balla e la teosofia," 42; Robert C. Williams, *Artists in Revolution: Portraits of the Russian Avant-garde, 1905–1925* (Bloomington: Indiana University Press, 1977), 104.

97. Bragaglia's *Forme e pensiero—visione spiritica* is mentioned in Matitti, "Balla e la teosofia," 41.

98. A similar procedure can be found in one of Russolo's self-portraits from 1912–13, *Io dinamico*.

99. In *Demolizione della casa di Balla* of 1926, cited in Fagiolo dell'Arco, *Compenetrazioni*, 25.

100. Maurizio Fagiolo dell'Arco, *Omaggio a Balla* (Rome: Bulzoni, 1967), 62.

101. Matitti, "Balla e la teosofia," 43.

102. Fagiolo dell'Arco, *Compenetrazioni*, 25.

103. Balla's pantheism and panpsychism is noted in Fagiolo dell'Arco, *Compenetrazioni*, 26. On Anton Giulio Bragaglia's pantheism-inspired periodical *La ruota*, of which he was the editor, see Calvesi, *Fusione*, III, 213–14. On Pratella and pantheism, see the next chapter.

104. Calvesi, *Fusione*, 119.

105. Calvesi, *Fusione*, 128.

106. Alchemy was considered the preeminent hermetic science because it was believed during the Renaissance that Hermes Trismegistus was the founder of alchemy. I believe that Balla may have first become interested in alchemic creation because it was a metaphor for artistic creation—which, after all, is Romanticism's perception of alchemy, all the way to Goethe's *Faust*.

107. Galbreath, "A Glossary of Spiritual and Related Terms," 368.

108. Leonardo, a sort of futurist *ante litteram* who occupied himself with science, alchemy, and art, became an important reference figure for several futurists. We know from a letter that Balla wrote to his mother, quoted in Fagiolo dell'Arco, *Compenetrazioni*, 13, that Balla had a book by Leonardo before him as a talisman while working on the first *Compenetrazioni iridescenti*. In the biographical note quoted above, Balla proclaimed himself a reincarnation of Leonardo.

109. Cited in Fagiolo dell'Arco, "Giacomo Balla verso il futurismo," 17.

110. Fagiolo dell'Arco, *Compenetrazioni*, 13.

111. Fagiolo dell'Arco, "Giacomo Balla verso il futurismo," 23.

112. Fagiolo dell'Arco, *Compenetrazioni*, 25.

113. Matitti, "Balla e la teosofia," 42. Flammarion was a member of the Theosophical Society. On Balla and astronomy, see Fagiolo dell'Arco, *Compenetrazioni*, 26.

114. See the facsimile of the manifesto reproduced in Maurizio Fagiolo dell'Arco, *Balla: Ricostruzione futurista dell'universo; Scultura teatro cinema arredamento abbigliamento poesia visiva* (Rome: Bulzoni, 1968); henceforth Fagiolo dell'Arco, *Balla: Ricostruzione futurista dell'universo*.

115. See the facsimile of the manifesto in Fagiolo dell'Arco, *Balla: Ricostruzione futurista dell'universo*.

116. Cangiullo was the first to call Balla a "magician"; see Fagiolo dell'Arco, *Compenetrazioni*, fig. 8.

117. Fagiolo dell'Arco, *Compenetrazioni*, 34.

CHAPTER 2

1. Arnaldo and Bruno Ginanni Corradini used various pseudonyms, most often Arnaldo Ginna and Bruno Corra, which were coined by Giacomo Balla and inspired by gymnastics (*ginnastic*) and running (*corsa*), respectively. On Ginna's and Corra's precocious interest in the occult, see Mario Verdone, "Abstraktion, Futurismus und *Okkultismus*—Ginna, Corra und Rosà," in *Okkultismus*, 477–97.
2. Celant, "Futurismo esoterico," 112. It is possible that the futurists of the Milanese group were familiar with occultism at first hand, through symbolism or scapigliatura. They may have known the same sources that the Corradini brothers knew.
3. In Ginna and Corra, *Scritti*, 74, magnetism is distinguished from hypnosis. Russolo in *Al di là della materia* would later make the same distinction very clearly.
4. Ginna and Corra, *Scritti*, 68. These concepts are also found in two *Lacerba* articles, Soffici's "Raggio" and Boccioni's "Fondamento."
5. Ginna and Corra, *Scritti*, 25.
6. *Opera d'arte dell'avvenire* is the Italian title of Wagner's *Das Kunstwerk der Zukunft*.
7. Ginna and Corra, *Scritti*, 112.
8. Ginna and Corra, *Scritti*, 106.
9. Ginna and Corra, *Scritti*, 106.
10. Ginna and Corra, *Scritti*, 108; epigraph on p. 105. The spiritually charged quote from Mazzini, which will disappear in the second edition of the pamphlet, suggests a further point of contact between the counts Ginanni Corradini and freemasonry. Mazzini was a freemason but also a theosophist and friend of Helena Blavatsky. On Mazzini and the occult see the chapter "Giuseppe Mazzini e la reincarnazione," in Simona Cigliana, *La seduta spiritica* (Rome: Fazi, 2007), 223–32.
11. Ginna and Corra, *Scritti*, 152. From here the next step would be Marinetti's *tattilismo*.
12. Daniele Lombardi, *Il suono veloce: Futurismo e futurismi in musica* (Lucca: LIM Ricordi, 1996), 162; henceforth Lombardi, *Il suono veloce*.
13. In the same year as *Musica cromatica* (1912), Leonid Sabanejew's famous article "Prometheus von Skrjabin" was published in Kandinsky's and Marc's almanac *Der Blaue Reiter* (Munich: Piper, 1912), 107–24.
14. Ginna and Corra, *Scritti*, 161.
15. It would go beyond the scope of this book to discuss in detail the many attempts throughout history to establish connections between colors and music, which include the coeval and theosophically inspired experiments of Kandinsky, Schoenberg, and Scriabin, as well as the earlier ones of Louis-Bertrand Castel, Isaac Newton, and Marin Cureau de la Chambre. For more information, see Cretien van Campen, *The Hidden Sense: Synesthesia in Art and Science* (Cambridge, MA: MIT Press, 2007) and Thomas Hankins and Robert Silverman, *Instruments and the Imagination* (Princeton, NJ: Princeton University Press, 1999).
16. Ginna and Corra, *Scritti*, 187.
17. Ginna and Corra, *Scritti*, 195.

18. Ginna and Corra, *Scritti*, 202. In the original Italian, this last sentence—"Dipingo quindi non gli atteggiamenti di un umano, contorto dal dolore, ma la vibrazione della sua anima dolorante o il DOLORE STESSO"—reads like an echo of a passage in the technical manifesto of futurist painting of five years earlier: "The pain of a man is for us just as interesting as the one of an electric lamp, which suffers, and agonizes, and screams in excruciating expressions of pain" (Il dolore di un uomo è interessante, per noi, quanto quello di una lampada elettrica, che soffre, e spasima, e grida con le più strazianti espressioni di dolore); see "La pittura futurista: Manifesto tecnico," in *I manifesti del futurismo*, 29.

19. Ginna and Corra, *Scritti*, 197.

20. Ginna and Corra, *Scritti*, 197. Compare this description with the passage in Boccioni's 1911 Roman lecture where he evokes the image of the artist as gifted with "clairvoyant eyes" (*occhi veggenti*); Boccioni, *Altri inediti*, 29.

21. Ginna and Corra, *Scritti*, 197.

22. Ginna and Corra, *Scritti*, 202.

23. Ginna and Corra, *Scritti*, 201. In the version of *Pittura dell'avvenire* published in installments in *L'Italia Futurista* in 1917, Ginna's relationship with theosophy is more tense, perhaps because of Steiner's split from the Theosophical Society. The issue of July 1, 1917, includes the strong statement: "I hope that the very old and superstitious theosophists, so old that they are falling apart, will stop preaching fear and digging into the rotten mummy that Indian philosophy is." This attack on Indian philosophy is aligned with Steiner's position at the time.

24. This affinity was to remain problematic for Ginna for years to come. Many years later, in 1967, he signed an open letter titled "A proposito di 'Arte dell'avvenire,'" in which he claims to have painted his first abstract painting in 1908, before being aware of Kandinsky's work; see Ginna and Corra, *Scritti*, 268. For a relevant statement of 1959 by Giuseppe Sprovieri, the official gallery representative of the futurist painters in Rome, see Ginna and Corra, *Scritti*, 251–52. Sprovieri claims that Ginna was the first abstract painter in Italy to have been publicly shown at an exhibit in 1914. Interestingly, this exhibit also presented some of Kandinsky's paintings.

25. If Boccioni was indeed the target, Ginna's attack was not entirely accurate. Although "states of mind" was a key concept in Boccioni's aesthetics, he, like Russolo, was never interested in purely abstract painting.

26. Ginna and Corra, *Scritti*, 203.

27. Ginna and Corra, *Scritti*, 202.

28. Ginna and Corra, *Scritti*, 217.

29. Ginna and Corra, *Scritti*, 234.

30. Ginna and Corra, *Scritti*, 234.

31. Ginna and Corra, *Scritti*, 237. This quote is taken from the epigraph of Marinetti's *Futurismo e fascismo*, where it appears directly below the dedication of the book to Mussolini; see *Teoria e invenzione futurista*, 489. Marinetti reused the quote in his 1929 *Marinetti e il futurismo*; there he introduced it by claiming that "among the many definitions of futurism, the one given by the theosophists is the one I prefer"; *Teoria*

e invenzione futurista, 583. In none of these writings, however, is a source provided for the epigraph.

32. Verdone, introduction to Ginna and Corra, *Scritti*, 8.
33. Verdone, introduction to Ginna and Corra, *Scritti*, 9.
34. Verdone, introduction to Ginna and Corra, *Scritti*, 12.
35. Ginna and Corra, *Scritti*, 168.
36. Ginna and Corra, *Scritti*, 265–67.
37. Lista, *Le futurisme: Création et avant-garde* (Paris: Les Éditions de l'Amateur, 2001), 73; henceforth Lista, *Futurisme*. Boccioni must have known Kandinsky in 1913, because he attacks him in his book (see Calvesi, *Fusione*, 70).
38. Maffina, *Caro Pratella* (Ravenna: Edizioni del Girasole, 1980), 27–29.
39. Francesco Balilla Pratella, "Manifesto dei musicisti futuristi," in *I manifesti del futurismo*, 43.
40. See Luigi Rognoni's essay in the 1980 CRAMPS double LP recording *Antologia sonora: Musica Futurista*. This recording has been rereleased on CD by the record label EDEL (CHSCD 046/047) with original artwork and the full reprint of Rognoni's essay.
41. Maffina, *Luigi Russolo e l'arte dei rumori*, 12.
42. Rodney Johns Payton, "The Futurist Musicians: Francesco Balilla Pratella and Luigi Russolo" (PhD dissertation, University of Chicago, 1974), 51–52; henceforth Payton, "The Futurist Musicians."
43. Lombardi, *Il suono veloce*, 57.
44. Pratella, *Scritti Vari*, 116–31. For an English translation of this essay, see Payton, "The Futurist Musicians," 133–49, appendix 6.
45. Compare this to the passages from Ginna's *Pittura dell'avvenire* cited earlier in this chapter.
46. *I manifesti del futurismo*, 48.
47. *Lacerba* (February 28, 1915).
48. Lombardi, *Il suono veloce*, 37.
49. Pratella, *Autobiografia* (Milan: Pan editrice, 1971), 163.
50. Pratella, *Autobiografia*, 164. The various stages of the ascension of the soul ought to be a clear reference to Plato's Phaedrus.
51. Payton, "The Futurist Musicians," 86.
52. These stage directions can be read both in the libretto (pages 8–11) and in the score (pages 1–53). I cite here from Pratella, *Edizioni, scritti, manoscritti musicali e futuristi*, ed. Domenico Tampieri (Ravenna: Longo, 1995), 458–59; henceforth Pratella, *Edizioni*.
53. Corra and Ginna, who had already worked for a couple of years within these synesthetic coordinates, may have first encountered *Prometheus* through the abovementioned article by Leonid Sabanejew (see note 13). It is very likely that *Poem of Fire* was a central topic of conversations between Pratella and the Corradinis.
54. See Payton, "The Futurist Musicians," appendix 6, 144–45.
55. Payton, "The Futurist Musicians," appendix 6, 139. The quoted letter from

Marinetti to Pratella, of February 14, 1912, is found in Domenico Tampieri, "Catalogo cronologico degli scritti e delle trascrizioni musicali di F.B. Pratella editi dal 1900 al 1995," in Pratella, *Edizioni*, 412–13.

56. On Ricciardi's relationship with the Pratella of *Giallo pallido*, see Lia Lapini, "Un musicista sulle scene futuriste," in Pratella, *Edizioni*, 69.

57. On futurism in Florence and its relationship with the occult, see Mario Verdone, "Abstraktion, Futurismus und *Okkultismus*—Ginna, Corra und Rosà," in *Okkultismus*, 478–97.

58. Bruno Corra, *Sam Dunn è morto* (Milan: Einaudi, 1970), 69.

59. Ginna and Corra, *Scritti*, 208.

60. This can be easily compared with the concept of unity expressed by Boccioni in his 1911 Rome lecture.

61. Arnoldo Ginna, "Il coraggio nelle ricerche di occultismo," in *L'Italia Futurista*, May 6, 1917.

62. On panpsychism, see the expanded English version of Celant's article "Futurismo esoterico" in Germano Celant, "Futurism and the Occult," *Artforum* 19 (1981): 37. The article lists several scientists who were interested in occultism, including the psychiatrists and neurologists Lombroso, Morselli, Marzorati, Pappalardo, and Vassallo, the scientists Richet, Crookes, La Fontaine, Maxwell, and Zollner, and the astronomers Schiapparelli and Flammarion.

63. Her actual name was Maria Crisi. She adopted the second name Ginanni in the years that she was Arnaldo Ginna's companion, and later she kept it as a pseudonym.

64. Maria Ginanni, "Il gambo del mondo," in *Montagne trasparenti* (Florence: Edizioni de L'Italia Futurista, 1917).

65. Silvia Evangelisti, "Geometrien der Psyche im Werk Romolo Romanis," in *Okkultismus*, 81–92.

66. Martin, *Futurist Art and Theory*, 71.

67. See Calvesi, *Fusione*, 214. See also a discussion of Leonardo's experiment on radial propagation of vibrations (irradiation of waves) in sand on a flat surface when the surface is hit by a hammer, in Emanuel Winternitz, *Leonardo da Vinci as a Musician* (New Haven and London: Yale University Press, 1982), 111; henceforth Winternitz, *Leonardo da Vinci as a Musician*. According to Winternitz, this experiment by Leonardo anticipated Chladni's experiment.

68. Martin, *Futurist Art and Theory*, 71.

69. *I manifesti del futurismo*, 154. The use of the verb *intuire* seems to point to Bergson's notion of intuition.

70. By defining all man-made mechanical products as *il regno meccanico*, Carrà considered the machine to be part of Nature.

71. *I manifesti del futurismo*, 156.

72. Compare this to Glauco Viazzi, ed., *I poeti del futurismo* (Milan: Longanesi, 1983), 307–13; henceforth Viazzi, *I poeti del futurismo*. *Guerrapittura* is available in facsimile, in an edition published by S.P.E.S. in Florence.

73. *Archivi del futurismo*, 1:76ff.

74. *Archivi del futurismo*, 1:210.

75. Calvesi, *Fusione*, 95.

76. Marinetti and Fillìa [Luigi Colombo, pseud.], "Manifesto dell'arte sacra futurista," in *I futuristi*, ed. Francesco Grisi (Rome: Newton, 1990), 87.

77. Celant, "Futurismo esoterico," 112. On D'Annunzio's séances, see Matitti, "Balla e la teosofia," 44. (For more on Russolo's séances, see chapters 3 and 11).

78. Enrico Crispolti, "Giulio Evola" *La Medusa* 40 (1963).

79. Balla and Depero signed themselves "Futurist Abstract Painters" in the 1915 manifesto "Ricostruzione futurista dell'universo"; see the facsimile in Fagiolo dell'Arco, *Balla: Ricostruzione futurista dell'universo: Scultura teatro cinema arredamento abbigliamento poesia visiva* (Rome: Bulzoni, 1968).

80. Zanovello mentions that Russolo's library included books by Evola; see Zanovello, *Luigi Russolo*, 77. The first philosophical works by Evola, which were also known to Ginna, were published beginning in 1927 by the same Milanese publisher, Bocca, with whom Russolo in 1938 published the first edition of his *Al di là della materia*. In 1919 works by Russolo and Evola were presented side by side at the *Grande Esposizione nazionale futurista*, which opened in Milan at the ex–Caffè Cova before going on tour to Genoa and Florence. It is not known whether Russolo and Evola met on that occasion.

81. Calvesi, *Fusione*, 156, 339n126.

82. Severini coined the term "absolute realism," according to Calvesi, *Fusione*, 144.

83. Calvesi recalls that, just as Bergson did, Boccioni believed that matter becomes life through action. Through the animation of matter and the identification of matter with energy, the futurists "point to the image of the 'absolute reality,' 'superreality,' the integrated reality of time and space, object and subject, external and internal data." Calvesi, *Fusione*, 145.

84. Soffici, "Al di là della pittura," *Mediterraneo Futurista* 4 (1938); cited in Calvesi, *Fusione*, 145.

85. *Archivi del futurismo*, 1:588.

86. This article is reprinted in Umbro Apollonio, *Futurismo* (Milan: Mazzotta, 1970), 168–71.

87. The original article is found in *Noi* (Numero speciale, I, II serie, n. 6/9, 1924), 12. *Noi* is available in facsimile (Florence: S.P.E.S., 1981).

88. *Noi* (May 1923): 2.

89. *Noi* (June–July 1923): 3.

90. Enrico Prampolini, "The Aesthetic of the Machine and Mechanical Introspection in Art," *Little Review* 11 (1926): 10.

91. Viazzi, ed., *I poeti del futurismo*, 113.

92. Numerous examples could be cited; I will discuss the two poems dedicated to Russolo in chapters 9 and 11.

93. Viazzi, ed., *I poeti del futurismo*, 121–22. The reference to the lyre as a machine was already in Buzzi's *Inno alla Poesia nuova*; cf. Viazzi, ed., *I poeti del futurismo*, 122, with the anthology Marinetti, ed., *I poeti futuristi* (Milan: Edizioni Futuriste di "Poe-

sia," 1912), 107; henceforth Marinetti, ed., *I poeti futuristi*. Buzzi often read *Inno alla poesia nuova* during the many *serate futuriste* (futurist evenings). If the connection between these lines and Russolo's musical research could be confirmed, one could conclude that Russolo was in 1912 longing for an occult music of machines. Indeed, my analysis of Russolo's painting *La musica* confirms this hypothesis (see chapter 4).

94. In Russolo's compositions, the spirali di rumori, he refurbished the notion of harmony of the spheres by synthesizing many chaotic noises in cosmological unity. For a fascinating treatment on the harmony of the spheres, see the classic book by Leo Spitzer, *Stimmung: Storia semantica di un'idea* (Bologna: Mulino, 1967)

95. Viazzi, ed., *I poeti del futurismo*, 128.

96. Buzzi was one of the few friends from Russolo's youth who remained close to him in his late years. For many years, Buzzi rented a summer house near Russolo's cottage in Cerro di Laveno. On the later stages of the friendship between Russolo and Buzzi, see Gasparotto in MART, 107–9. Buzzi's novel *Cavalcata delle vertigini* (Foligno: Campitelli, 1924; henceforth Buzzi, *Cavalcata delle vertigini*) also suggests his close friendship with and admiration for Russolo; Marzio, the protagonist of the novel, was directly inspired by Russolo.

97. "Manifesto della aereopittura," in Francesco Grisi, ed., *I futuristi* (Rome: Newton, 1990), 101. A detailed chronology of Marinetti's published poetry is provided in Viazzi, ed., *I poeti del futurismo*, 21.

98. On Scriabin's alcohol abuse, see Boris de Schloezer's classic biography, first published in French in 1976, and in English translation as *Scriabin: Artist and Mystic*, trans. Nicholas Slonimsky (Berkeley: University of California Press, 1987).

99. In *MART*, 19n22. *Testa e fiore* is reproduced on page 131; for a reproduction of the sleeping female that Tagliapietra has identified as *Morfina*, see 132.

100. Giovanni Lista records on the subject that "Maria Ginanni, Irma Valeria, Bruno Corra, Oscar Mara, Arnaldo Ginna, Mario Carli and Remo Chiti, the poets and the writers of the Florentine group who for the most part were from Ravenna, [...] held séances, practiced mediumistic [i.e. automatic] writing and indulged in experiences of hallucinations caused by the use of drugs." Lista, *Futurisme*, 265.

101. Ginna and Corra, *Scritti*, 265–67.

102. Bruno Corra, *Sam Dunn è morto* (Milan: Einaudi, 1970), 38.

103. Lista (in *Futurisme*, 266) adds to those I have discussed the names Pino Masnata, Benedetta [Cappa], Giuseppe Steiner, Emilio Notte, Luigi Rognoni, and Oswaldo Bot.

104. This concept is very much present in Russolo's metaphysical system, as evident from his works.

105. Boccioni's chilly line on cubism is quoted in Boccioni, "Fondamento," *Lacerba* (March 15, 1913).

106. Reference to the opposition between Boccioni and Balla is first found in Calvesi, *Fusione*, 127. See also Fagiolo Dell'Arco, *Compenetrazioni*, 12. The very concept of subjective synthesis (*sintesi soggettiva*) can be found in Boccioni's "La pittura

futurista," in *Altri inediti*, 16, and his "Note per la conferenza tenuta a Roma 1911," in Boccioni, *Altri inediti*, 35.

107. Balla's obsession with detail can be noted in *Fallimento* (1902), but it is structurally fully exposed in *Un mio istante del 4 aprile 1928 ore 10 più due minuti* (1928), where Balla's self-portrait appears isolated and almost trapped between two opposed forces, visually represented as symmetrical and convergent. With a deductive operation, this instant in time that Balla painted brings us back to universal dynamism by implying and exemplifying it. Boccioni's titanism is displayed fully in his *Città che sale* of 1910–11 and *Stati d'animo I: Gli Addii* of 1911.

CHAPTER 3

1. Russolo described his friendship with Boccioni in an article emblematically titled "La voce lontana," which he wrote in 1933 for *Dinamo futurista*, a periodical edited by Depero; the article was reprinted in Maffina, *Luigi Russolo e l'arte dei rumori*, 263).

2. This may have been an unconscious politico-philosophical position. Already in his 1962 *Opera aperta*, Umberto Eco, addressing the orphism of Mallarmé's *Livre*, declared that "every aspiration of the artist to clairvoyance, even though poetically productive, always sounds somewhat equivocal." Eco, *Opera aperta* (Milan: Bompiani, 2006), 50.

3. See Gary Lachmann, "Ready to Rumble," *Wire* (December 2003): 30–35, and Carlo Piccardi, "Futurismo," in *Dizionario enciclopedico universale della musica e dei musicisti*, ed. A. Basso, *Il lessico* (Turin: UTET, 1985), 2:307–17.

4. The first issue of *Ultra* (January 1907) carries the mission statement of the editorial board: "This periodical aims to bring to all its readers the *message of the soul*. This message tells us that man is more than a mere clothed animal, because in his intimate nature he is divine even though his divinity is hidden by a veil of flesh." In Matitti, "Balla e la teosofia," 44. This statement resembles what Russolo wrote in the last section of *Al di là della materia*. Writing about the men of the future, Russolo argued that "man, who will certainly still be made of his exterior clothing of flesh and bones, will have understood by then that this exterior vest is only a simulacrum, a bark, a transitory phase that hides what man truly is." Russolo, *Al di là della materia*, 395.

5. Celant, "Futurismo esoterico," 112–13, 115. Celant omitted the first quote in the English version of the article as it appeared in *Artforum*, but he does not add anything on Russolo; Germano Celant, "Futurism and the Occult," Artforum 19 (1981).

6. In Zanovello, *Luigi Russolo*, 86. In this review, Carrà writes a contradictory statement, claiming that in *Al di là della materia* Russolo had found a "*new orientation, after futurism*"; Zanovello, *Luigi Russolo*, 85.

7. See Lista and Franini, whom I quote in the introduction. In later research, Lista more openly acknowledged a connection between the avant-garde and occult arts, though in his 2009 essay on Russolo he refrains from addressing the topic. This modernist critical stance was shared by other Russolo scholars (Maffina, Franini) and has dominated Russolo scholarship up to the present.

8. This may have been for fundamentally political reasons. An equation can easily be drawn from occultism and irrational thought to fascism. Furthermore, the neopositivism and neorationalism that has characterized post–World War II Western culture, and may be seen as a philosophical reaction to the horrors and excesses of Fascist and Nazi totalitarianism, has also produced a "modernist" critical climate that tended only to reward what is scientific, rational, or "progressive." Despite the best intentions, this modernist approach has rescued from the futurist movement only, or mostly, pragmatic aspects such as exaltation of technology and has consequently sacrificed the irrational or spiritual side, building an image of futurism that, though not corresponding to reality, is still the dominant one today.

9. Zanovello, *Luigi Russolo*, 17.

10. Zanovello, *Luigi Russolo*, 12. The title for this piece, like the titles of most of Russolo's other pieces, was likely suggested by Marinetti. The reference to Rimini's Hotel Kursaal cannot but have come from Marinetti. In a photograph from his prefuturist years, reproduced in Marinetti, *La grande Milano*, 131 (photograph 11), the fiery poet is portrayed in an impeccable summer outfit while sitting at the table of the Hotel Kursaal's terrace, a location that will enter collective memory thanks to the opening scene of Fellini's *I Vitelloni*.

11. Information about the organ of Portogruaro was provided to me by Professor Luigi Russolo (no relation to the subject of this book), organ professor at the Trieste Conservatory. Thanks also to Professor Andrea Macinanti, organ professor at the Bologna Conservatory.

12. This is true at least of the first two models. In the 1927 version, levers were substituted for the keyboard to allow those shadings of microtonal pitch that the futurists would call "enarmoniche." See Brown, introduction to Russolo, *The Art of Noises*, 16.

13. Quoted in Maffina, *Luigi Russolo e l'arte dei rumori*, 190 (Maffina published the text but not the patent drawing, which was at first thought lost). This project, whose patent Russolo never registered, offers an insight into his understanding of the construction principles of the pipe organ. His modification was designed to allow an organ pipe to obtain multiphonics. The additional pitch could be tuned over the fundamental according to the ratios $1/2$, $2/3$, $3/4$, $4/5$, etc., to produce a relationship of octave, fifth, fourth, third, etc. This project constituted for Russolo a remarkable construction saving. At the end of the text, he added a variation, based on a simpler principle: since two pipes can be contained one inside the other, they can both exploit the same breath emission. From the combination of the two versions presented in the project, Russolo claimed that with two pipes—one inside the other—up to four distinct sounds can be produced with the same breath.

14. Zanovello, *Luigi Russolo*, 41.

15. Ester Coen, "Les futuristes et le moderne," *Les Cahiers du Musée National d'art moderne* 19–20 (June 1987): 62.

16. In Calvesi, *Futurismo*, 21.

17. Lista, "Russolo, peinture et bruitisme," 12–13.

18. Jean-Marc Vivenza, "L'art des bruits: Historique et theórie du bruitisme futuriste," *Inter* 76 (Summer 2000): 47.

19. Celant, "Futurismo esoterico," 115.

20. Martin, *Futurist Art and Theory*, 90.

21. Martin, *Futurist Art and Theory*, 70–71.

22. Martin, *Futurist Art and Theory*, 92–93. Boccioni's quote is found in Boccioni, *Altri inediti*, 11.

23. Verdone, "Abstraktion, Futurismus und *Okkultismus*—Ginna, Corra und Rosà," in *Okkultismus*, 488.

24. Lista, "Futurismus und *Okkultismus*," in *Okkultismus*, 435.

25. Quoted in *MART*, 85–86.

26. The only other work on this topic is Diego Collovini's book *Luigi Russolo: Un'appendice al futurismo* (Venice: Supernova, 1997). Scholarly reluctance to address Russolo's connections with fascism may also explain the reluctance to investigate Russolo's late works.

27. Zanovello, *Luigi Russolo*, 31.

28. Russolo expressed this idea in his "Catalogo della Galleria Borromini di Como," cited in Maffina, *Luigi Russolo e l'arte dei rumori*, 122.

29. On Russolo's harsh critique of the Novecento group, see Maffina, *Luigi Russolo e l'arte dei rumori*, 304. Funi was the only exponent of Novecento with whom Russolo stayed on good terms. On November 7, 1920, Russolo wrote a laudatory review for the periodical *La Testa di Ferro* of the October 1920 Achille Funi exhibit curated by Margherita Sarfatti. The review is reproduced in *MART*, 65.

30. We know from a letter by Russolo, written in Paris on July 1, 1927, that he was not proficient in German (see Maffina, *Luigi Russolo e l'arte dei rumori*, 279). It is therefore likely that he read Nietzsche in D'Annunzio's translations. As for Poe, Russolo certainly read his writings in the Italian translation by Decio Cinti. Cinti's translation of a collection of Poe's tales was in fact one of the few works of fiction that Russolo owned. According to Gasparotto, Poe might have been the source for Russolo's early etching and aquatint *Donna pipistrello* (Bat woman), of 1907; see *MART*, 86. Marinetti mentioned Poe in his "Manifesto tecnico della letteratura futurista" of May 11, 1912 (see *I manifesti del futurismo*, 97), and he mentioned him again a couple of years later in his article "Contro il decadentismo" (Against decadentism) in *L'Italia Futurista*, but on that occasion he attacked Poe.

31. See Geurt Imanse, "Occult Literature in France," in *The Spiritual in Art: Abstract Painting 1890–1985* (New York: Abbeville Press, 1986), 355f.

32. Buzzi, in the poem "Russolo," compared a concert of intonarumori with a dance macabre; see chapter 11.

33. Martin, *Futurist Art and Theory*, 34.

34. Diane Lesko, *James Ensor, the Creative Years* (Princeton, N.J.: Princeton University Press, 1985), 43. It is interesting to compare this position with two different statements by Russolo on the aging of *The Last Supper*. In the first, recorded by Marinetti in his *La grande Milano*, 118–19, the young Russolo argued in favor of replacing

aging (and aged) frescoes with the work of young artists. In the second, contradictory, opinion, the older Russolo wrote about the contrast between the aging of the material body of *The Last Supper* and the eternal spiritual power of that work; see Russolo's last writing, of 1947, "L'eterno e il transitorio nell'arte," in Maffina, *Luigi Russolo e l'arte dei rumori*, 315.

35. Calvesi, in *Fusione*, 52, noted the influence of scapigliatura—in particular Emilio Praga's Satanism—within the futurist movement.

36. In Carrà, *La mia vita* (Milan: Rizzoli, 1945), 88. Carrà mentioned Romani in the chapter that discusses his years in Brera's Art Academy from 1906 on.

37. Lista, "Russolo, peinture et bruitisme," 15. 1910 was the year when, according to Lista, Russolo began to take an active interest in spirituality. However, Lista set this date slightly earlier in *Okkultismus*, where he links Russolo's early *Autoritratto con teschi* (which he incorrectly believed was painted in 1909–10) with Russolo's interest in the occult (Lista, "Futurismus und *Okkultismus*," in *Okkultismus*, 435).

38. Russolo could have known the French edition of this text, which had appeared by 1905.

39. See Martin, *Futurist Art and Theory*, 92–93.

40. The influence of Romani is not particularly surprising, especially given the deep friendship that bound him to Russolo. See Silvia Evangelista, "Dal simbolismo alla non figurazione e ritorno: Il percorso artistico di Romolo Romani," in *Romolo Romani*, ed. Silvia Evangelisti, Renato Barilli, and Bruno Passarani (Milan: Mazzotta, 1982), 23. Evangelisti emphasizes Russolo's and Romani's common interest in the vibration of light and sound waves, and in ways of portraying them in painting.

41. Piselli's hypothesis is described in Ethel Piselli, *Luigi Russolo: Incisore e pittore 1907–1913* (Bornato in Franciacorta: Sardini Editrice, 1990), 20–23.

42. See reproductions of Romani's works in Giorgio Nicodemi, *Romolo Romani* (Como: Cairoli, 1967) and *Romolo Romani*, ed. Evangelisti, Barilli, and Passarani.

43. Silvia Evangelisti, "Geometrien der Psyche im Werk Romolo Romanis," in *Okkultismus*, 83. The term *ideoplastica*, together with its synonym *eteroplastica*, and intended in this occultist sense, is from Boccioni: "Our futurist audacity has already forced opened the gates of an unknown world. We are creating something that is similar to what the physiologist Richet [Nobel Prize in 1912] has called *heteroplastic* or *ideoplastic*. For us, the mystery of the medianic materialization is certainty, a clarity." Boccioni, *Scritti*, 203, 457n11. On Romani and Palladino, compare Romani's *Ritratto di Giosuè Carducci*—one of the "masks" that Romani made for *Poesia* (October 1906–January 1907 issue)—with one of the "ideoplastic" medallions produced by Palladino; see Evangelisti, "Geometrien der Psyche im Werk Romolo Romanis," in *Okkultismus*, 84. Romani painted many other mysterious manifestations, including the demoniac mask in the upper right corner of his phantasmal *Ritratto di Dina Galli* of 1906. These works by Romani may well have been the main influence on Russolo's mystical mezzotint *Il Redentore* of 1907, a mask-like print of the barely identifiable features of Jesus's face, and probably an allusion to the Shroud of Turin.

44. See Boccioni, *Scritti*, 203.

45. Masks are also found in Russolo's painting *Giovane romantica* of 1941. Tagliapietra has mentioned that Ilaria Schiaffini linked *La musica* to theosophy (*MART*, 41n58).

46. Maffina, *Luigi Russolo e l'arte dei rumori*, 289.

47. Buzzi, in a 1921 article cited in Zanovello, *Luigi Russolo*, 30–31. The reference to the "intellectual goatee" but also the reference of the skulls as masks, together with the reference to music (Verdi chorus), leaves us uncertain on whether Buzzi may here be overlapping the memory of the 1908 *Autoritratto* with that of the later *La musica*.

48. Giovanni Lista, "Futurismus und Okkultismus," in *Okkultismus*, 435.

49. Zanovello, *Luigi Russolo* , 39.

50. A discussion of the skull is pertinent in analyzing Russolo not only for anatomical and structural but also for metaphysical and symbolic reasons. Emanuel Winternitz has written that "Leonardo is well known as a master in drawing skulls, apparently being attracted by their structure and complex curvature of surface with its interplay of light and shadow." According to Winternitz, people used animal and human skulls throughout the Renaissance, both as decoration and as an object for meditation. See "The Mystery of the Skull Lyre," in Winternitz, *Leonardo da Vinci as a Musician*, 39. I have dedicated chapters 9 and 10 to the relationship between Leonardo and Russolo.

51. Igor Stravinsky, *Conversations with Igor Stravinsky*, ed. Robert Craft (London: Faber and Faber, 1958), 93.

52. Russolo did not have much respect for the term "studio" or for the very existence of a market for sketches as finished artistic products. See Russolo, *Al di là della materia*, 247–48. It is possible that this work and others are forgeries.

53. This is especially surprising given that 1911 marks the turning point of De Chirico's career.

54. See the reproduction in *MART*, 173. The red-chalk drawing (*sanguigna*) technique, especially when used for self-portraiture, may be another of the many influences of Leonardo da Vinci, whose self-portrait in red chalk was immensely popular.

55. In Calvesi, *Fusione*, 111.

56. Buzzi, "Russolo ferito (January 1918)," in *Archivi del futurismo*, 1:378.

57. See Lista, "Russolo, peinture et bruitisme," 28, 139.

58. We know that the painting was shown at Milan's *Prima Esposizione d'Arte Libera* of April 1911, as it is mentioned in a series of reviews of the exhibit: one by Filippo Quaglia in the newspaper *Avanti!* of June 11 and one by Enrico Cavicchioli from June 15, 1911, both reproduced in the catalog (p. 53) of the exhibit *Luigi Russolo: L'arte dei rumori 1913/1931*, curated by Maffina in 1977 for the Venice Biennale. A third review, from Ardengo Soffici in *La Voce* of April 20, 1911, is cited in Maffina, *Luigi Russolo e l'arte dei rumori*, 35.

59. Muldoon and Carrington, *The Projection of the Astral Body* (London, 1929), pl. 9. Cited in Katharine V. Tighe, "Primitives of a Transformed Sensitivity: Italian Futurism and Occultism" (MA thesis, University of Texas, Austin, 1994), 80.

60. According to Gasparotto, another painting that present a series of projections on the aura is the above-mentioned *Giovane Romantica* of 1941; see *MART*, 70.

61. The chronology of this work is particularly uncertain. Zanovello claims 1909 as the year it was painted, Lista 1910, Maffina 1912, and Tagliapietra 1910–11.

62. Zanovello, *Luigi Russolo*, 23. Flavia Matitti considers the canvas an example of the futurists' interest in mediumistic phenomena, and for that reason is cited by Lista. See Matitti, "Balla e la teosofia," 43, and Lista, "Futurismus und *Okkultismus*," in *Okkultismus*, 439.

63. Apollinio, illustration 55. See also *MART*, 171.

64. Maffina, *Luigi Russolo e l'arte dei rumori*, 289.

65. In my dissertation I argued that it could perhaps be dated to the period that preceded his stay at Thiene (1922). In the letter of December 5, 1929 (cited in Maffina, *Luigi Russolo e l'arte dei rumori*, 289), Russolo wrote that the "portrait with the shadow (ritratto con l'ombra)" was part of a stock of paintings that he left as a temporary deposit for the unpaid last three months' rent with the landlord of his Milanese studio in via Stoppani, where he and Piatti had built the intonarumori.

66. See the author's foreword in Charles W. Leadbeater, *The Hidden Side of Things* (Adyar: Theosophical Publishing House, 1913), 3; henceforth Leadbeater, *The Hidden Side of Things*.

67. The Milanese publisher Bocca, also Evola's publisher, had a large number of books on occultism in his catalog.

68. Russolo, *Al di là della materia*, 102–5. According to Besant and Leadbeater in *Thought-forms*, the mental body and the astral body are the main components of the aura (Galbreath, "A Glossary of Spiritual and Related Terms," 390).

69. Russolo, *Al di là della materia*, 103.

70. Russolo, *Al di là della materia*, 116.

71. Zanovello, *Luigi Russolo*, 78–79.

72. Zanovello, *Luigi Russolo*, 24.

73. Martin, *Futurist Art and Theory*, 71.

74. *MART*, 88n92.

75. Lista, *Futurisme*, 58. The term *metapsychic* was first introduced by the Nobel laureate Charles-Robert Richet, a physiologist who studied anaphylaxis but was also a scholar of medianic and paranormal phenomena. Boccioni cited Richet in his *Scritti*, 203. See also Boccioni, *Scritti*, 457n11.

76. *Ricordi di una notte* share common traits with Boccioni's *Notturno*, which was also painted in 1911. Among these traits are the subject and composition, with the female figure in the foreground. Boccioni's *Notturno* is less chaotic than Russolo's.

77. Although Russolo voiced his dislike of the term *cacophony*, it is useful in this context.

78. Bergson, quoted in Martin, *Futurist Art and Theory*, 91.

79. This simultaneous chaos is related to the following passage from *The Art of Noises*: "We will enjoy ourselves by orchestrating together in our imagination the din of rolling shop shutters, slamming of doors, buzzing and foot-stepping of the crowd, the varied hubbub of train stations, iron works, thread mills, printing shops, electrical plants, and subways. Nor should the newest noises of modern war be forgotten."

Russolo, quoted in Maffina, *Luigi Russolo e l'arte dei rumori*, 131. The futurist painters adopted the phrase "synthesis of what one remembers and what one sees" in February 1912; see Boccioni, Carrà, Russolo, Balla, and Severini, "Prefazione al catalogo delle esposizioni di Parigi, Londra, Berlino," in *I manifesti del futurismo*, 61. Optical-mnemonic synthesis was another expression to indicate the simultaneity of states of mind; see Boccioni, *Altri inediti*, 12. Yet another equivalent was the expression *complementarismo congenito* (congenital complementarism), a concept introduced in the technical manifesto of futurist painting of 1910.

80. Cited in *Archivi del futurismo*, 1:112.

81. Boccioni attacked Anton Giulio Bragaglia and photodynamics, which he had created, because the discipline was based on the principle of optical frame–based *scomposizione del movimento* (breakdown of movement). Boccioni felt that this technique portrayed reality in a far too cold, mechanical, impersonal, analytical way. In his works, Boccioni wanted to portray the subject together with the subject's experiences and reaction to movement: he intended to paint, in other words, a personal selection of positions—from among the infinite positions of a body in motion—that the subject's memory decided to retain. He preferred optical-mnemonic synthesis, the combination of what the subject sees and remembers. Calvesi claimed that Boccioni's attack on Bragaglia's photodynamics hid an indirect attack against Balla, who had produced a painting that imitated photographic perception, that is, showed him using his eye as a camera. See Calvesi, *Fusione*, 114–16, 127–28.

82. *Una-tre teste* closely resembles Boccioni's *Visioni simultanee* and *La strada entra nella casa*, both painted the year before.

83. Martin, *Futurist Art and Theory*, 150. According to Maffina (*Luigi Russolo e l'arte dei rumori*, 333), only two fragments survived. However, Russolo, as he had done before, re-utilized the back of the central panel of the painting one year later to paint *I tre pini* (1944). This central panel, which was discovered under a thick, uniform coating of paint during the 2005 restoration of *I tre pini*, was shown at the 2006 Russolo retrospectives; see Tagliapietra, MART, 34, 42. Other fragments of the painting from the two side panels mentioned in Maffina have appeared in internet auctions. Leadbeater's essay on sonic forms is found as a chapter of his *The Hidden Side of Things* of 1913, but based on what Leadbeater claims in the introduction to the book, the essay had appeared earlier in *The Theosophist*.

84. Henry Adams hailed electricity as a "god" of the new century, and he adored the dynamo, which he first saw at the Paris World Exposition of 1900; cited in Fred K. Prieberg, *Musica ex machina* (Turin: Einaudi, 1963), 89.

85. Luckily, the center of the canvas survived. I will discuss the principle of synthesizing multiplicity into unity later in this book.

86. Besant and Leadbeater, *Thought-forms*, 43. In the preface of the volume, Annie Besant explains that "the drawing and the painting of the thought forms observed by Mr. Leadbeater or by myself, or by both of us together, has been done by three friends—Mr. John Varley, Mr. Prince and Miss Macfarlane." Though it is impossible to validate the authorship of these works, we can surely attribute to Besant and Lead-

beater, if not the actual execution of drawings and paintings, then surely the shapes, colors, formal organizations, and ideas portrayed in them.

87. Leadbeater, *The Hidden Side of Things*, 204.
88. Leadbeater, *The Hidden Side of Things*, 208.
89. See Evangelisti, "Geometrien der Psyche im Werk Romolo Romanis," in *Okkultismus*, 23.
90. In Lista, *Futurisme*, 58.
91. This is one of the most often cited statements from the 1910 technical manifesto of futurist painting.
92. Martin, *Futurist Art and Theory*, 149.
93. Martin, *Futurist Art and Theory*, 150.
94. The mezzotint version is close to Boccioni in the choice of subject, direction of the profile (turned toward the right), and characteristic, arched shape of the frame. In pictorial specifics, however, the oil-on-canvas version is closer to Boccioni's study: both paintings are executed with the same technique, their dimensions are similar, as is the subject, and they both exploit the same diffraction of light waves, which is clearly derived from Italian divisionism.
95. In Zanovello, *Luigi Russolo*, 24.

CHAPTER 4

1. Buzzi, "Souvenirs sur le futurisme," 26.
2. The authenticity of this version has been disputed.
3. Martin, *Futurist Art and Theory*, 89.
4. The concept of materialization is frequently found in theosophical literature. Russolo borrowed it when he wrote in *Al di là della materia* of the materializations of the etheric double carried out on the physical plane. Boccioni (*Scritti*, 203) mentioned materialization in his *Pittura e scultura futuriste*). Another term for materialization was *esteriorizzazione*, which Marinetti used in his "Guerra, sola igiene del mondo" (in *Teoria e invenzione futurista*, 299) and Russolo in his *Al di là della materia*, 102. On the materialization in theosophy, see Leadbeater, *The Hidden Side of Things*, 88.
5. Maffina, *Luigi Russolo e l'arte dei rumori*, 20.
6. Russolo also studied violin at an early age under the guidance of his father, and he continued to play; on Russolo's violin, see Carlo Carrà, *La mia vita* (Milan: Rizzoli, 1945), 153.
7. According to Buzzi, the masks converge "from every directions toward the head of the player, a head functioning as a black pivot"; Buzzi, "Souvenirs sur le futurisme," 26.
8. Calvesi, *Fusione*, 104.
9. Zanovello, *Luigi Russolo*, 26. Zanovello dated the review in June 1910, but this is obviously a mistake.
10. Ibid., 26–27.
11. Ibid., 27–28. This unsigned critical note accompanied the reproduction of Rus-

solo's painting in the December 9, 1920, issue of *Poesia*. In 1933 Russolo sent this critical note to Depero with his signature. See Lista, "Russolo, peinture et bruitisme," 152n10.

12. Ibid., 28. Zanovello dates the comment in 1916, which is impossible, as the ex–Caffè Cova exhibit took place in 1919.

13. Calvesi, *Fusione*, 152.

14. Ibid., 214.

15. Martin, *Futurist Art and Theory*, 90.

16. Lista, *Futurisme*, 60. Carrà's interpretation is mentioned in Simona Cigliana, *Futurismo esoterico: Contributi per una storia dell'irrazionalismo italiano tra Otto- e Novecento* (Naples: Liguori, 2002), 302. I could not find this citation in any of Carrà's writings

17. The first edition of *Arte dell'avvenire* adopted Mazzini's epigraph: "The Arts need someone who can re-tie them. This person will come."

18. Ginna's reading list is cited in Celant, "Futurismo esoterico," 112.

19. Ginna and Corra, *Scritti*, 265–67.

20. Besant and Leadbeater, *Thought-forms*, 66–76.

21. Besant and Leadbeater, *Thought-forms*, 66.

22. As late as 1946, Russolo painted two musician-inspired, symbolical portraits, of Mt. Rushmore–kitsch proportions, titled *Beethoven* and *Bach*; for reproductions of these two late paintings, see *MART*, 186–87.

23. Besant and Leadbeater, *Thought-forms*, 67.

24. Leadbeater, *The Hidden Side of Things*, 195.

25. Leadbeater, *The Hidden Side of Things*, 196.

26. Calvesi mentions the existence, documented from at least 1853 on, of a mediumistic musical practice within spiritualist movements. This practice he divides into three categories: "music that manifests itself without instruments; music that manifests itself with instruments but without the material aid of the medium; and music that manifests itself through the automatism of the medium-pianist." Russolo's *La musica* belonged firmly in the third category. Surprisingly, in this brief article concentrating on automatic writing, Calvesi ("L'écriture médiumnique," 47) mentioned neither the painting nor Russolo's musical activities.

27. The word *enharmonic* is used synonymously with *microtonal*. Russolo adopted the term *enarmonia* to refer to a musical system that employs the division of the whole step into infinite microintervals, which can be produced by instruments that have the capability to glide (*glissando*) between pitches.

28. Though music creates sound-forms, spiritual music is what actually provides the fuel for the spirits to materialize. Spirits materialize via thought-forms, not via sound-forms. The specificity of the reading just offered is both consistent with and demanded by the "scientific" specificity that is always found in theosophical prose, with which Russolo was well familiar. This detailed reading was thus within Russolo's horizon of cultural references.

29. Lista, *Futurisme*, 60.

30. Besant and Leadbeater, *Thought-forms*, 27.

31. Cited in Gasparotto, *MART*, 81. Curiously, Gasparotto misses this almost lit-

eral reference to *La musica* and instead links this text to Russolo's 1941 *Giovane romantica*, a painting that she considers the "pictorial translation" of these words.

32. Besant and Leadbeater, *Thought-forms*, 11–12; Galbreath, "A Glossary of Spiritual and Related Terms," 390.

33. The "flexible blue ribbon" description comes from a review of the painting by Attilio Teglio, cited in Zanovello, *Russolo*, 26.

34. Cited in Zanovello, *Luigi Russolo*, 13.

35. Maffina, *Luigi Russolo e l'arte dei rumori*, 141; Helmholtz is mentioned on page 140.

36. Lista, "Russolo, peinture et bruitisme," 153. Although Helmholtz's research was undoubtedly important for Russolo—this is also attested by an important mechanical feature of the intonarumori, whose sound box is essentially a Helmholtz resonator—equally influential on Russolo was Leonardo's research in acoustics.

37. Leadbeater, *The Hidden Side of Things*, 195–96. The book was printed in 1913, but it includes articles published from 1901 on.

38. See Winternitz, *Leonardo da Vinci as a Musician*, 109–11.

39. I discuss the *spirale di rumore* in depth in chapter 8.

40. Buzzi, "Russolo ferito (January 1918)," in *Archivi del futurismo*, 1:378.

41. Cited in Maffina, *Luigi Russolo e l'arte dei rumori*, 164. Continuity, a concept that carries philosophical and occult implications, is also found in Leonardo da Vinci's writings, which is probably where Russolo encountered the concept. In his Roman lecture of May 1911, Boccioni prophesied a period when "pictorial works will be whirling musical compositions of enormous colored gases"; Boccioni, *Altri inediti*, 11. Given Buzzi's statement that Russolo worked on *La musica* for years, and knowing that Russolo showed the first version of the painting in May 1911, it may well be that Boccioni in this passage in his lecture had the synesthetic features of *La musica* fresh in his mind. It could therefore be concluded that this Russolo work influenced both Boccioni's lecture and his theory.

CHAPTER 5

1. Maffina, *Luigi Russolo e l'arte dei rumori*, 18. On Russolo's technical limitations, see Martin, *Futurist Art and Theory*, 70. Though Russolo may well have been technically weak, technique is not everything. Given that history of the arts in the twentieth century is not so much a history of technically executed virtuosic artifacts as it is a history of ideas, Russolo more than deserves his place.

2. Martin, *Futurist Art and Theory*, 91.

3. Maffina, *Luigi Russolo e l'arte dei rumori*, 16.

4. Cited in Maffina, *Luigi Russolo e l'arte dei rumori*, 134.

5. Quoted in Zanovello, *Luigi Russolo*, 13.

6. His leaning toward science, and his adoption of a trial-and-error-based procedure, does not, of course, make him a positivist scientist. Russolo was anxious to keep the internal mechanism of the intonarumori hidden from the players and listeners ,

designing his instrument cabinets to that end, because he wanted the intonarumori to provide a magical experience. Russolo operated within what Umberto Eco defined as the construct of miraculous technology—technology as magic; see Eco, "Scienza, tecnologia e magia," in *A passo di gambero* (Milan: Bompiani, 2007), 103–10, esp. 106. This attitude is confirmed by the orphic character of Russolo's language and aims. On the orphic, see the passage from Umberto Eco's *Opera aperta* quoted in chapter 3.

7. Marinetti, "Quinte e scene della campagna del battaglione lombardo volontari ciclisti sul lago di Garda e sull'Altissimo: La presa di Dosso Casina II," *Gazzetta dello sport* (February 7, 1916); reprinted in Enrico Crispolti, "Zang Tumb Tuum I futuristi vanno alla guerra. Giochi, burle e travestimenti dei futuristi del battaglione ciclisti," *Bolaffiarte* 79 (May 1978): 15.

8. Francesco Cangiullo, *Le serate futuriste* (Naples: Editrice Tirrena, 1930), 183.

9. Russolo, *Al di là della materia*, 184.

10. Zanovello, *Luigi Russolo*, 19.

11. Zanovello, *Luigi Russolo*, 62. The appellation "magician" occurs among other futurists as well; on one occasion Cangiullo called Balla "mago" (see Fagiolo dell'Arco, *Compenetrazioni*, fig. 8).

12. Marinetti, *La grande Milano*, 106.

13. Russolo's letter to his wife of July 1, 1927, is quoted in Maffina, *Luigi Russolo e l'arte dei rumori*, 278. The practice of improvisation was common among futurists; this is confirmed by Mario Bartoccini's and Aldo Mantia's 1921 manifesto "L'improvvisazione musicale," which some consider to be the first avant-garde statement about improvisation.

14. Maffina, *Luigi Russolo e l'arte dei rumori*, 34.

15. Marinetti, *La grande Milano*, 83.

16. See Nietzsche's *Unzeitgemäße Betrachtungen*. The common Italian translation for Nietzsche's title is *Considerazioni inattuali*. The paragraphs on Nietzsche are my personal reaction to Nietzsche's ideas after having reread them in an effort to understand how the futurists might have interpreted them. I may have been influenced by Nicola Abbagnano's interpretation of Nietzsche. The reader will be well aware that there is ongoing debate among philosophers about the interpretation of Nietzsche's thought. Obviously, there is no opportunity to review that debate here.

17. In futurism's founding manifesto of 1909, for instance, Marinetti attacked the "heavy bodywork of common sense" as useless.

18. Marinetti's mention of the noise harmonium (rumorarmonium) in this passage is not chronologically accurate, as Russolo did not start to work on the instrument until 1921. Marinetti's lapse here may be the result of writing a diary entry in retrospect. Like many of Marinetti's texts, *La grande Milano* was mostly dictated, and work on this text—which involved his wife, Benedetta, his two daughters, Vittoria and Ala, and the Venetian nurse who took care of Marinetti at that time—occurred primarily in Venice between October 1943 and August 1944; see Marinetti, *La grande Milano*, xix, xx.

19. Zanovello, *Luigi Russolo*, 91.

20. Quoted in Maffina, *Luigi Russolo e l'arte dei rumori*, 292.

21. Zanovello, *Luigi Russolo* , 19.

22. Celant, "Futurismo esoterico," 111n9.

23. Among the pre-Hoepli writings, see Giovanni Guglielmo, "Sui raggi catodici, sui raggi Roentgen e sulle dimensioni e la densità degli atomi," *Rendiconti della R[eale] Accademia dei Lincei: Classe di scienze fisiche, matematiche e naturali* 8, no. 1, series 5, fasc. 8 (1899): 379–85.

24. Henderson, *Duchamp in Context*, 5.

25. Quoted in Maffina, 139–43. Although Russolo is actually advocating for a separation between sound and noise, Russolo's argument is de facto contemplated by Helmholtz when he claimed that "noises and musical tones may certainly *intermingle in very various degrees, and pass insensibly into one another,* but their extremes are wildly separated." See Hermann L. F. Helmholtz, *On the Sensation of Tone as a Physiological Basis for the Theory of Music* (New York: Dover, 1954), 7. It is likely that Russolo read Helmholtz indirectly, by way of popularizations such as those published by Hoepli.

26. On Duchamp's influence on X-rays, see the chapter "Duchamp and Invisible Reality 1911–1912," in Henderson, *Duchamp in Context*, 3–28.

27. This concern for deep reality is comparable to the interest, also shared by artists of the period, in theories on the fourth dimension and non-Euclidean geometries.

28. In "La pittura futurista: Manifesto tecnico," in *I manifesti del futurismo*, 28.

29. Quoted in Maffina, *Luigi Russolo e l'arte dei rumori*, 134.

30. See Henderson, *Duchamp in Context*, 7.

31. Celant, "Futurismo esoterico," 113n18.

32. Celant, "Futurismo esoterico," 113n18. Among the four scholars cited by Celant, Lombroso was well known to Italian readers interested in parapsychology and spiritualism; the young Balla was among his students at the Turin Academy (Celant, "Futurismo esoterico," 111).

CHAPTER 6

1. Russolo, "Conferenza sull'architettura tenuta da Russolo alla Galleria Borromini di Como nel 1944," in Maffina, *Luigi Russolo e l'arte dei rumori*, 307.

2. This position is frequently found in futurist writings from various periods.

3. Quoted in Maffina, *Luigi Russolo e l'arte dei rumori*, 133. Despite Russolo's emphasis here and in the following excerpt, he has been misunderstood. Among the most famous example of this misunderstanding is the attack by Edgar Varèse, in his article in "VERBE," *391* [vol.] 5 (1917): 42.

4. In Maffina, *Luigi Russolo e l'arte dei rumori*, 134.

5. In Maffina, *Luigi Russolo e l'arte dei rumori*, 177.

6. In Maffina, *Luigi Russolo e l'arte dei rumori*, 135. A similar concept is also repeated at the closing of *L'arte dei rumori* (176).

7. Russolo, "L'architecture musicale et le rumorharmonium," *Circle et carré* 1 (March 15, 1930); reprinted in Maffina, *Luigi Russolo e l'arte dei rumori*, 220.

8. *Lacerba* (May 15, 1914); reprinted in Maffina, *Luigi Russolo e l'arte dei rumori*, 46.

9. Carrà, "Piani plastici come espansione sferica dello spazio," *Lacerba* (March 15, 1913).

10. Carrà, "Piani plastici come espansione sferica dello spazio," *Lacerba* (March 15, 1913).

11. Besant and Leadbeater, *Thought-forms*, 66–76; Leadbeater, *The Hidden Side of Things*, 195–210.

12. A subject gifted with particular psychic powers in a state of trance can create fluctuating thought-forms endowed with the power to overcome the barrier of the aura; he can instill them with his spirit through etheric waves—vibrations—and make them materialize. This theory can be found in various theosophical writings, including Leadbeater's *The Hidden Side of Things*.

13. See the facsimile of this manifesto in Fagiolo dell'Arco, *Balla: Ricostruzione futurista dell'universo*.

14. In Maffina, *Luigi Russolo e l'arte dei rumori*, 163.

15. In Maffina, *Luigi Russolo e l'arte dei rumori*, 175–76.

16. In Marinetti, *Teoria e invenzione futurista*, 106; reprinted in Maffina, *Luigi Russolo e l'arte dei rumori*, 156.

17. Russolo, *Al di là della materia*, 201.

18. Quoted in Maffina, *Luigi Russolo e l'arte dei rumori*, 266. The addition of word to sound, color, clay, or marble, as another material element to be subjugated in the artistic process, is related to Marinetti's classification of onomatopoeiae in "Lo splendore geometrico e meccanico e la sensibilità numerica."

19. Quoted in Maffina, *Luigi Russolo e l'arte dei rumori*, 306–7.

20. Maffina, *Luigi Russolo e l'arte dei rumori*, 122.

21. Maffina, *Luigi Russolo e l'arte dei rumori*, 314–15. These pages rephrase a position on Leonardo's *Last Supper* that is already present in Russolo, *Al di là della materia*, 272.

22. Steiner, "Investigations into Life between Death and Rebirth," in *Life between Death and Rebirth: Sixteen Lectures by Rudolf Steiner* (New York: Anthroposophic Press, Inc., 1968), 3–30; henceforth Steiner, *Life between Death and Rebirth*.

23. I use the term *theosophical* here because Rudolf Steiner in 1912 was still operating within the Theosophical Society. The tensions between Steiner and Besant can be traced back to 1907, but Steiner did not officially leave the society until 1913. Only then did he found the Anthroposophical Society. See Floyd McKnight, *Rudolf Steiner and Anthroposophy* (New York: Anthroposophical Society in America, 1967), 22.

24. "Investigations into Life between Death and Rebirth," part 2, in Steiner, *Life between Death and Rebirth*, 25.

25. "Investigations into Life between Death and Rebirth" part 1, in Steiner, *Life Between Death and Rebirth*, 6.

26. Steiner's later condemnation of mediums, states of trance, and spiritualism is mentioned in Galbreath, "A Glossary of Spiritual and Related Terms," 370.

27. Russolo's letter to Margherita Sarfatti, dated August 22, 1916, is reprinted in Maffina, *Luigi Russolo e l'arte dei rumori*, 269. "Him" is capitalized in the original.

28. Russolo's eulogy is presented in Maffina, *Luigi Russolo e l'arte dei rumori*, 266. Russolo was familiar with the language used in séances, having participated in several in Paris in the mid-1920s.

29. Marinetti, *La grande Milano*, 104.

30. Russolo in Maffina, *Luigi Russolo e l'arte dei rumori*, 135.

31. "L'allegra serata futurista al teatro Storchi," *La gazzetta dell'Emilia* (June 3, 1913); reprinted (without the author's name) in Maffina, *Luigi Russolo e l'arte dei rumori*, 29–31.

32. Although the tone of the article may have been ironic, the journalist never questioned the honesty and earnestness of Russolo and his assistant, Piatti. In fact, the article only sounds ironic because of the contrast between Russolo and Piatti's almost pedantic seriousness and the audience's ferocious sarcasm. Because I shall focus on the portrayal of Russolo's behavior throughout the evening, I have edited out all the sections in which the journalist describes the audience. Audience reactions did not differ significantly from those at subsequent intonarumori performances, and they are well documented in articles and books that deal with futurist performances.

33. For a sample of this review, see Maffina, *Luigi Russolo e l'arte dei rumori*, 44.

34. In *L'Italia* (October 11, 1914); see Maffina, *Luigi Russolo e l'arte dei rumori*, 55–57.

CHAPTER 7

1. *Risveglio di una città* is the only spirale by Russolo of which at least a fragment remains. This fragment, consisting of seven bars (see *Lacerba* [March 1, 1914]), is not definitively known to be the opening of the piece, though this is frequently claimed.

2. Françoise Escal, "Le futurisme et la musique," *Europe* 53 (1975): 92f; henceforth Escal, "Le futurisme et la musique." Escal quotes Russolo's point 6 of the manifesto *The Art of Noises* from the French edition translated by Maurice Lemâitre. As the original Italian text differs somewhat from the Lemâitre translation, I have retranslated this excerpt. For the original text, see Maffina, *Luigi Russolo e l'arte dei rumori*, 134.

3. Escal, "Le futurisme et la musique," 93.

4. The study of alchemy was revived in the occultist circles of Milan in the early years of the twentieth century by Angelo Marzorati, standard-bearer of panpsychism and other occult activities with which the futurists were familiar. See Lamberto Pignotti and Emanuela Andreani, "Paolo Buzzi, 'L'ellisse e la spirale film: Parole in libertà,'" in Buzzi, *L'ellisse e la spirale* (Florence: S.P.E.S., 1990), liv; henceforth Pignotti and Andreani, "Paolo Buzzi, 'L'ellisse e la spirale.'" See also Celant, "Futurismo esoterico," 109f.

5. On the alchemical *vas* in the context of futurism, see Pignotti and Andreani, "Paolo Buzzi, 'L'ellisse e la spirale,'" liv–lv.

6. According to Besant's and Leadbetter's *Thought-forms*, the aura is composed of different bodies that could become a background against which several states of mind project thought-forms. See also Galbreath, "A Glossary of Spiritual and Related Terms," 390.

7. This is what Giovanni Macchia declared in his theosophical elaborations in *Piran-*

dello o la stanza della tortura (Milan: Mondadori, 1981), 60. Pirandello's interest in the occult is well documented. For a brief time in the late 1920s—but before 1929, according to the diary of the actress (and Pirandello's muse) Marta Abba, as well as the testimony of the writer Paola Masino—Pirandello's Parisian agent was the same Guido Torre who, according to Maffina, introduced Russolo to magnetization in the early 1930s.

8. Soffici, "Raggio," *Lacerba* (July 1, 1914).

9. Boccioni, "Il cerchio non si chiude," *Lacerba* (March 1, 1914).

10. From chapter 7 of *The Art of Noises*, quoted in Maffina, *Luigi Russolo e l'arte dei rumori*, 176. Russolo's aggressive operation forces noise to be "enharmonically" intoned. Russolo's chapter title, "La *conquista* dell'enarmonismo," is similarly militaristic, and chapter 5 is entirely dedicated to the noises of modern warfare.

11. Marinetti, *La grande Milano*, 104.

12. See Steiner's two-part Milan lecture of October 26 and 27, 1912, "Investigations into Life between Death and Rebirth," in Steiner, *Life between Death and Rebirth*, 3–30. Particularly pertinent to my discussion is part 2 (18–30).

13. See Leadbeater, "How We Are Influenced: By Sound," in Leadbeater, *The Hidden Side of Things*, 198.

14. Quoted in Maffina, *Luigi Russolo e l'arte dei rumori*, 176.

15. Quoted in Maffina, *Luigi Russolo e l'arte dei rumori*, 142. In this passage, nature (which here stands for divine creation) and life (i.e., human creation) are presented as models that ought to be imitated and secure the "naturalness" of enharmony. Russolo's claim that enharmony is "natural" (in several subsequent paragraphs, he even poses enharmony against the "artificiality" of the temperate system) should not confuse us. Russolo was not seeking a blind imitation of nature but only the re-creation of some of its properties, with the aim of controlling them. The paradox, in fact, is that to create life artificially he must begin by employing natural properties (i.e., subjugate natural elements).

16. Pratella, "La musica futurista: Manifesto tecnico," in *I manifesti del futurismo*, 46–47.

17. By the turn of the century, several composers had theorized and proposed microtonal systems to expand pitch resources. (Ferruccio Busoni, whose work was well known to the futurists, was among those who explored the possibility of composing music with microtonal pitches.) Russolo, in a 1923 revindication of his work titled "L'enarmonismo" (reprinted in Maffina, *Luigi Russolo e l'arte dei rumori*, 211), claimed to have been the first not only to have designed and built "musical instruments that are capable of producing a concrete realization of this [...] enharmonic theory" but also to have lectured and published a theory of enharmony "understood not only as a fragmented and occasional subdivision of a tone in steps that are smaller than the semitone but as a whole system."

18. Maffina, *Luigi Russolo e l'arte dei rumori*, 161–62. This chapter had appeared as an article in the November 1, 1913, issue of *Lacerba*, where it carried the title "Conquista totale dell'enarmonismo mediante gli intonarumori futuristi."

19. In Maffina, *Luigi Russolo e l'arte dei rumori*, 158–59. Inexplicably, Barclay Brown omitted the last few words of this excerpt in his translation. Russolo's insistence on

the "artificiality" of the division of an octave into semitones operated by the temperate system (he refers to this twice in the same section) suggests that the term *artificial* had a negative meaning for him. This implies another critical take against materialism; the term *artificiale*, could have been taken directly from Bergson's argument against the "artificial" division of matter and in favor of continuity, which Boccioni cited in *Lacerba* (March 15, 1913).

20. Quoted in Maffina, *Luigi Russolo e l'arte dei rumori*, 160.

21. On sirens, studied by Helmholtz and used by Varèse in his compositions, and on glissandi in modern music and *The Art of Noises*, see Douglas Kahn, *Noise, Water, Meat: A History of Sound in the Arts* (Cambridge, MA: Massachusetts Institute of Technology, 1999), 72–100; henceforth Kahn, *Noise, Water, Meat*.

22. Henderson, "Ether and Electromagnetism: Capturing the Invisible," in *From Energy to Information*, 97. The theremin, an instrument that produces only glissandi, was also called *aetherophone* (Winternitz, *Leonardo da Vinci as a Musician*, 193).

23. Boccioni, "Fondamento," *Lacerba* (March 15, 1913). A few months later, Carrà invoked "the continuity and simultaneity of the plastic transcendences of the mineral world, vegetal world, animal world, and mechanical world"; Carrà, "La pittura dei suoni, rumori e odori," in *I manifesti del futurismo*, 156.

24. On the term *artificial*, which Bergson employed negatively to describe the division of matter, and on how Russolo used the term in his *L'arte dei rumori* to designate negatively the arbitrariness of division (in this case of the semitone), see note 19. Opposing enharmonic continuity (natural and spiritual) against chromatic fragmentation and subdivision (materialistic and artificial), Russolo applied Boccioni's theory of the continuity of the individual form (likewise spiritual and natural) rather than Balla's and Bragaglia's fragmented, frame-based representation (which he, like Boccioni, considered materialistic and artificial). In this instance, too, Russolo embraced Boccioni's subjective synthesis leading to unity rather than Balla's objective analysis tending to multiplicity.

25. Soffici, "Raggio," *Lacerba* (July 1, 1914).

26. For the reprint, see the Roman periodical *Ultra*.

27. On these quotations from Aristotle, see Winternitz, *Leonardo da Vinci as a Musician*, 216. Presumably, Russolo was familiar with Aristotle's *Metaphysics* and *Logic*. Buzzi mentioned Aristotle among Russolo's late influences; see Buzzi's introductory note in Zanovello, *Luigi Russolo*, 13.

28. Winternitz, in *Leonardo da Vinci as a Musician*, 221–22, quotes another section taken from Leonardo's notes included in Arundel 263, a codex now owned by the British Library. In this passage, Leonardo claims that time, as the line in geometry, is a continuous quantity precisely because the interval between two instants in time is infinitely divisible.

29. From *Trattato della pittura* 31 C, as quoted in Winternitz, *Leonardo da Vinci as a Musician*, 215.

30. Winternitz, *Leonardo da Vinci as a Musician*, 216.

31. Winternitz, who does employ the categories of "art in space versus art in time"

when he paraphrases a passage of *Trattato* 23 (Winternitz, *Leonardo da Vinci as a Musician*, 208), surprisingly fails to consider music as continuous in pitch space.

32. From *Trattato* 21, as quoted in Winternitz, *Leonardo da Vinci as a Musician*, 205. Winternitz (205, 208, 211) is confused by Leonardo's notion of *armonico concento*. Yet this notion is far less ambiguous if applied to intervals regardless of their direction (i.e., ignoring the distinction between harmonic and melodic intervals). Admittedly, Leonardo's *Trattato della pittura* was published after the artist's death, and Leonardo never produced a systematic revision of the work for publication. The text he left behind is full of contradictions, and it is often difficult, if not downright impossible, to follow Leonardo's thinking. For the purposes of the present discussion, it is important to point out that, just as Leonardo considered painting to be continuous because of the shades of colors (Leonardo called this *ombre e lumi*), so Russolo considered music to be continuous in timbre, and he believed that this manifestation of continuity erases the traditional distinction between sound and noise (something that will become a key concept in Russolo's art of noises). Interestingly, Russolo utilizes the example of shades of colors, but he does not compare color shades with sound colors (timbre) but only with enharmony (see Russolo as quoted in Maffina, *Luigi Russolo e l'arte dei rumori*, 164). (Harry Partch used the color-sound metaphor in the opening pages of his *Genesis of a Music* to advocate for microtonality,). The discussion of musical continuity also relates to a discussion of "sliding" in modern compositions, including discussions about sliding in pitch, tempo, and dynamics as addressed in Nancy Yunhwa Rao, "Cowell's Sliding Tone and the American Ultramodernist Tradition," *American Music* (Fall 2005): 281–323.

33. See chapter 9 for my comparison of Russolo's and Leonardo's instruments.

34. Winternitz, *Leonardo da Vinci as a Musician*, 192–93.

35. This would not have been the first time that musical instruments served as metaphors of the universe; consider, for example, the monochord, between Marin Mersenne and Robert Fludd. The concept is linked with the Pythagorean association of music and astronomy, famously stated at the closing of Plato's *Republic* and echoed in Cicero's *Somnium Scipionis* of *De Republica*. Music as a discipline of the quadrivium implied proportion of musical intervals corresponding to cosmological proportions and distances between planets. The assumption is that continuity (and infinity) of enharmonic space is related, allegorically or magically, with the continuity (and infinity) of cosmic space. Given that Leonardo was interested in the issue of continuity at various levels, surely he was also interested in continuity in time. Several instruments designed by Leonardo could sustain notes. Among these projects is that of the *viola organista*, a project that occupied Leonardo for many years, and an air chest bellow that can produce a continuous flux of air. "With this one, the flux of air will be continuous," Leonardo wrote (quoted in Winternitz, *Leonardo da Vinci as a Musician*, 197).

36. Counterbalancing enharmonic *and* temperate systems bears some relationship with counterbalancing analog and digital systems.

37. Russolo had read Leonardo's *Il paragone*.

38. Quoted in Maffina, *Luigi Russolo e l'arte dei rumori*, 164.

39. As in Mersenne's monochord. In fact, the intonarumori were, from one point of view, a new type of monochord. On Mersenne, see note 35, above. See also Kahn, *Noise, Water, Meat*, 73–79.

40. Marinetti, *La grande Milano*, 99. Marinetti described Russolo's studio/laboratory in via Stoppani as follows: "I enter Russolo's workshop with Boccioni and Armando Mazza. Yellow green red pink piling of futurist intonarumori. Buzzing, bursting, howling, whistling. The inventor oversees the cooking of a noise drumskin. — Stop! Leave the acid and motors alone! Tonight we will stage a very violent demonstration against Austria!" *Marinetti e il futurismo* and *8 anime in una bomba*, in Marinetti, *Teoria e invenzione futurista*, 596, 878. This passage indicates the color scheme Russolo adopted for the intonarumori, but there is more. Russolo, without going into detail, also frequently wrote about his experimenting on custom-made chemical baths for his drumskins (he started calling them diaphragms as of the *Lacerba* article of July 1, 1913) to make them more resistant to stretching. Marinetti confirms that Russolo's chemical baths involved dipping and cooking the drumskins in a latex-like paste. The use of latex (india rubber) was suggested to Russolo by Hermann L. F. Helmholtz, who, in his classic *On the Sensation of Tone*, mentions an experiment in which a "vulcanised india-rubber membrane" is used as a vibrating surface to test sympathetic vibrations; see Helmholtz, *On the Sensation of Tone as a Physiological Basis for the Theory of Music* (New York: Dover, 1954), 41–42. Helmoltz's experiment with the vulcanized latex membrane constituted another way of illustrating the phenomena Chladni had discovered with his figures, which Helmholtz quotes in these very pages. Russolo mentions Chladni's figures in the same chapter of *The Art of Noises* in which he quotes *On the Sensation of Tone* (see Maffina, *Luigi Russolo e l'arte dei rumori*, 169), which indicates that he could well have learned of Chladni's plates from Helmholtz, and also that he may have begun experimenting with latex membranes after having read about them there.

41. Quoted in Maffina, *Luigi Russolo e l'arte dei rumori*, 178–79. The majority of the intonarumori are variations on this model. All of the intonarumori exhibited, each in its own way, continuity in time and space.

42. Russolo was also interested in continuity in time; in praising the ululatore (howler), he wrote with excitement about this instrument's ability to hold "a long note, even a very long one, at will"; quoted in Maffina, *Luigi Russolo e l'arte dei rumori*, 169.

43. These words can be compared with the passage in which Leonardo described the continuity of painting in shades of "shadows and lights" *(ombre e lumi)* and in distances between points within the rules of perspective; Leonardo also discussed continuity of line. See Winternitz, *Leonardo da Vinci as a Musician*, 215–16, 221.

44. Quoted in Maffina, *Luigi Russolo e l'arte dei rumori*, 164–65. The argument against the "dinamismo frammentario" has Leonardine echoes and similarities with Boccioni's attack on Balla's frame-based breakdown of movement.

45. Franco Casavola stressed this point in an article on Russolo written for Mario Carli's and Emilio Settimelli's futurfascist newspaper *L'Impero* of June 2, 1925. In comparing the "whole enharmony" allowed by Russolo's instruments—which Russolo called *concezione totale*—to the limitation of the division of tone into quarter tones that

is called for in "Hába's piano and Baglioni's harmonium," Casavola adds that in Russolo's instruments, "the rigid, uneven, tough, and angular profile of the scale disappears to leave space for a smooth and harmonious [read: enharmonic] line"; quoted in Maffina, *Luigi Russolo e l'arte dei rumori*, 103. Russolo mentions the division into quarters and eighths of a tone in *The Art of Noises*; see Maffina, *Luigi Russolo e l'arte dei rumori*, 166.

46. Douglas Kahn explained the glissando in these terms in his *Noise, Water, Meat*, 83–84. Though Russolo is cited in this chapter, Kahn, primarily interested in issues related to timbre, does not mention Russolo in discussing the continuity of enharmonic space; rather, he quotes Russolo in relation to another principle of continuity that Russolo was concerned with: the principle that erases the distinction between sound and noise (Kahn, *Noise, Water, Meat*, 80). Russolo often reminded his readers that the distinction between sound and noise is merely conventional, and that from an acoustics standpoint there is no difference between the two. The distinction is a cultural one. Likely guided by his research with the CRT oscilloscope, Russolo claims that an absolute distinction cannot be made because even though a noise usually generates a sound wave with a more complex shape than that of a musical tone, a dividing line (edge) between the two cannot be established. Both in fact occupy the same timbral space, which is a continuous dimension. Because the distinction was subjectively and culturally determined, Russolo advocates the inclusion of noises into the palette of sounds used by the modern composer.

47. Kahn attributes the popularity of glissando among modernist composers, including Russolo, to Helmholtz's sirens; see Kahn, *Noise Water Meat*, especially "Resident Noises," 79, and "The Gloss of the Gliss," 84.

48. In *Comoedia* (June 19, 1921), a Parisian music critic wrote that Ravel "has requested to observe all the instruments after the performance, one by one, and he has expressed the desire to employ some of them in one of his next scores." Russolo repeated this quote in his article for *L'Impero* of January 11, 1927 (quoted in Maffina, *Luigi Russolo e l'arte dei rumori*, 214). Zanovello cites an article from the journal *La Renaissance* of July 2, 1921, in which a Parisian journalist reported Ravel's interest in the enharmonic features (*l'échelle de leur tonalité*) of Russolo's intonarumori; see Zanovello, *Luigi Russolo*, 59–60.

49. In Maffina, *Luigi Russolo e l'arte dei rumori*, 86; see also 79.

50. In Hugh Davies, "Maurice Ravel and the *lutheal*," *Experimental Musical Instruments* 4, no. 2 (August 1988): 12. The flute à coulisse was designed specifically to produce glissandi; conceptually it is similar to Leonardo's "glissando flute."

51. Hugh Davies, "Maurice Ravel and the *lutheal*," *Experimental Musical Instruments* 4, no. 2 (August 1988): 12. Davies likely deduced this from what Russolo claimed in his letter to Pratella, though Davies does not quote the letter, and though the letter does not directly mention *L'enfant*.

52. Many are the points in *L'enfant* in which Ravel re-creates the sound (mostly glissandi) of the intonarumori: the impressive duet of the cats (Durand edition, 126–31); the imitation of birdsong produced by the flute à coulisse (132); the equally impressive procession of *rainettes* (134–36 and 150–54); the trees and the beasts (138–41 and

192). Although a detailed discussion of these passages is impossible here, it is worth noting that Ravel's score evokes a supernatural atmosphere. Carolyn Abbate has discussed the disturbing side of this score, where inanimate objects and beings frightfully reanimate like the dead rising from their tombs, or like voices rising from a gramophone; see Abbate, "Outside Ravel's Tomb," *Journal of the American Musicological Society* 52, no. 3 (1999); henceforth Abbate, "Outside Ravel's Tomb." Abbate views both a tomb and a gramophone as means to preserve, shape, (re-)create something that is gone. The intonarumori certainly possess a quality of the uncanny, perhaps because Russolo intended them to be used as crucibles for (re-)creation.

CHAPTER 8

1. Quoted in Maffina, *Luigi Russolo e l'arte dei rumori*, 177.
2. Marinetti, "Manifesto tecnico della letteratura futurista," in *I manifesti del futurismo*, 90–91.
3. Maffina, *Luigi Russolo e l'arte dei rumori*, 136.
4. Claudia Salaris, *Il futurismo e la pubblicità: Dalla pubblicità dell'arte all'arte della pubblicità* (Milan: Lupetti, 1986). On the basis of this poster, I can add the spirale *Zum Zum Taratrà*, whose curiously onomatopoeic title was most likely invented by Marinetti, to the list of lost Russolo scores, which had previously been limited to the four compositions premiered at the August 11, 1913, Milanese press concert: *Réveil de capitale*, *Rendez-vous d'autos et d'aéroplanes*, *On dîne à la terrasse du casino*, and *Escarmouche dans l'oasis*.
5. On the relationship between Buzzi's novel *L'ellisse e la spirale* and alchemy, see Pignotti and Andreani, "Paolo Buzzi, 'L'ellisse e la spirale,'" liv–lv. This novel (like other works by Buzzi, especially *Cavalcata delle vertigini*) includes references to Russolo's musical research. See, for example, the chapter titled "La diana enarmonica," in Buzzi, *L'ellisse e la spirale* (Florence: S.P.E.S., 1990), 213–49.
6. Quoted in *MART*, 42n104.
7. On the centripetal and centrifugal direction of movement, see Boccioni, *Scritti*, 119. Marinetti, in the manifesto "La distruzione della sintassi" of May 11, 1913, declared that he was tired of the shape of the spiral and preferred the shape of the straight line; see *I manifesti del futurismo*, 136. On the other hand, Carrà, in "Pittura dei suoni, rumori e odori" (August 11, 1913), included the spiral among the dynamic (and therefore higher-ranked) shapes; see *I manifesti del futurismo*, 155.
8. I have used the term *re-creation* intentionally, to pose Russolo's operation of "re-creating" the world against Balla's and Depero's "reconstruction" of the universe. The term *reconstruction* suggests a process in which, once the abstract equivalents of the shapes found in the universe have been isolated, the universe can be reproduced in detail, via the sample, through a patient multiplication of the sample. This is different from the ambitious aim of re-creating the simultaneity of the entire universe through synthesis and again illustrates the opposition between Balla's objective analysis and Boccioni's subjective synthesis.

9. Boccioni, Carrà, Russolo, Balla, and Severini, "Prefazione al catalogo delle esposizioni di Parigi, Londra, Berlino," in *I manifesti del futurismo*, 63. The writing technique "stream of consciousness" could be considered a literary parallel to this concept

10. "Boccioni, Carrà, Russolo, Balla, Severini, "Prefazione al catalogo delle esposizioni di Parigi, Londra, Berlino, [...]," in *I manifesti del futurismo*, 63.

11. For more on this subject, see Martin, *Futurist Art and Theory*, 91.

12. The reference to the painter as clairvoyant is mentioned in Boccioni. *Altri scritti*, 34.

13. Boccioni, *Scritti*, 180.

14. Boccioni, *Scritti*, 150. The *intuited* in the quote is a Bergsonian term for *captured*.

15. Boccioni, "Fondamento," *Lacerba* (March 15, 1913).

16. Boccioni, *Scritti*, 176.

17. Boccioni, *Altri inediti*, 26. Though Carrà was no longer aligned with the aesthetic positions of futurism after 1915, he was, as late as 1958, still defending the spirituality of plastic dynamism; in his introduction to the Russolo retrospective at the Galleria Barbaroux in Milan, he declared: "Plastic dynamism was not the cinematographic reproduction of the physical phenomenon. [...] In other words, it was implicit in Luigi Russolo a mystical philosophy of nature charged of a psychic power." Quoted by Gasparotto in *MART*, 90.

18. This self-generative process may very well be the ultimate sense of the futurists' congenital complementarism.

19. On the relative and absolute motion of the object, see Boccioni, *Scritti*, 134.

20. Boccioni, *Scritti*, 149.

21. The counterposition is critically useful, but it should not be forgotten that Boccioni was Balla's most important pupil, and both aesthetics were to a degree intertwined.

22. Calvesi, *Fusione*, 127, and Fagiolo dell'Arco, *Compenetrazioni*, 12. Admittedly, Calvesi's polar opposition is a simplification of Boccioni's and Balla's thought; and though it is (like all deliberately weak theories) critically useful, it cannot take into account the diachronic development of their respective poetics (especially those of Balla, who was active for decades). Both of these artists occasionally departed from the positions described by the polar opposition.

23. In Boccioni's writings, the notion of *single form* is also connected with the concept of *congenital complementarism*, which can be best understood as a sort of fusion of (apparent) opposites. *Unity* was a central concept for Busoni, whose interest in futurism started early; of the futurists, he connected most with Boccioni. His admiration for Boccioni (he bought some of his paintings, including the famous *Città che sale*) turned in the last year of Boccioni's life into actual friendship, of which perhaps the most significant testimony is Boccioni's vibrant 1916 portrait of Busoni, one of his last masterpieces.

24. Boccioni, *Altri inediti*, 14.

25. The idea of *substitution* is derived from Calvesi. He explained that whereas Pascoli's onomatopoeiae were "imitative," Marinetti's were "substitutive" *(sostitutive)*; see Calvesi, *Fusione*, 149, 151. It is also worth noting that Boccioni's polymaterism and Mari-

netti's onomatopoeiae (especially the abstract onomatopoeia) stand in close relation to Russolo's art of noises.

26. There are occasional exceptions to the polar opposition of Boccioni and Balla. For example, Boccioni, in "Fondamento," aspires to the "creation of autonomous organisms built with abstract elements of reality." Subjective synthesis and objective analysis may on occasion start their process from the same point, with abstract elements of reality, though the former then re-creates reality by producing and reconciling the conflict among these elements and achieving the *forma unica*, whereas the latter patiently reconstructs reality through a series of samples.

27. For this reason Russolo could not accept the idea of "cacophony" (in fact, he did not have much respect for the word *cacophonic*); see Maffina, *Luigi Russolo e l'arte dei rumori*, 135. Because Boccioni was so close to Russolo (they were both living in Milan and in daily communication), it is sometimes impossible to determine with certainty which ideas were Boccioni's and which Russolo's. Beyond a certain point, it is in fact rather difficult to distinguish among Russolo's, Marinetti's, Carrà's, Romani's, and Boccioni's ideas. With time, the majority of futurism's ideas have unfortunately been attributed to the two most charismatic figures, Marinetti and Boccioni. (As Kahn recalls in *Noise Water Meat*, 138 and 393, the theories in *The Art of Noises* have often been attributed to Marinetti.) It is both necessary and useful, when at all possible, to try to attribute authorship of these ideas properly.

28. "Circolare di L. Russolo, A. Funi e F.T. Marinetti," *Archivi del futurismo*, I, 383.

29. In "Circolare di L. Russolo, A. Funi e F.T. Marinetti," *Archivi del futurismo* I, 383. The term *synthesis* was to become a keyword in Russolo's aesthetics in the early 1920s and according to Tagliapietra and Gasparotto, it aligned Russolo with the theoretical positions of the art critic and curator Margherita Sarfatti. Synthesis was certainly central in the futurist manifesto "Contro tutti i ritorni in pittura," which was signed by Dudreville, Funi, Russolo, and Sironi on January 11, 1920, though both Tagliapietra and Gasparotto have argued that it was mostly Russolo's work; see *MART*, 45–48 and 59–67.

30. *Modernolatria* was a typically Boccionian term; see Boccioni, *Scritti*, 203.

31. Quoted in Maffina, *Luigi Russolo e l'arte dei rumori*, 176.

32. Boccioni noted the correspondence between these two levels; he described the enharmonic intonation of a single intonarumori using the categories of simultaneity and dynamism. (Boccioni, *Scritti*, 178.)

33. Edgar Varèse indirectly attacked *The Art of Noises* when he wrote: "Why do you Italian futurists merely reproduce from the flux of our everyday life what is superficial and annoying?"; see Varèse, "VERBE," *391* 5 (1917): 42. Over time, Varèse changed his mind, and toward the end of the 1920s, the two musicians became friends. On December 27, 1929, at the Russolo concert that accompanied the opening of the exhibit of futurist painting in Paris at *Galerie 23*, Varèse briefly introduced two of the instruments that Russolo had engineered, the noise harmonium and the enharmonic bow. (The poster for this event is reproduced in Maffina's 1977 catalog, 66.) Russolo and Varèse remained in touch until at least 1934, as documented by letters, later published in Lista, 143–49.

34. Quoted in Maffina, *Luigi Russolo e l'arte dei rumori*, 131.

35. For a list of the instruments that Russolo would accept to accompany the intonarumori (incidentally, all percussion instruments), see Maffina, *Luigi Russolo e l'arte dei rumori*, 172.

36. Quoted in Maffina, *Luigi Russolo e l'arte dei rumori*, 172.

37. See Edward Venn, "Rethinking Russolo" *Tempo* 64, no. 251 (January 2010): 8–16. After reducing Russolo's seven bars into a conventional score, Venn proceeded to analyze and criticize harmonic and voice-leading choices from the transcription; he treated the intonarumori without any regard to timbre, as if they were merely sirens, and went to the absurd length of finding a "tonic" of E minor in the second bar. Opining that Russolo was "not a particularly inspired composer," he proceeded to prove it by looking for compositional "weakness" and "mistakes" with the pedantry of a *novellus* Théodore Dubois. Venn argued that the piece "deploys all the resources" far too soon ("Clearly the city is awaking quickly!" he states), evidently forgetting that he is not analyzing a whole composition but only a musical example of seven bars, the length of which in terms of absolute time is actually impossible to determine, as Russolo did not indicated in this excerpt any tempo or metronome markings.

38. Russolo introduces the *Dynamic continuity* in Maffina, *Luigi Russolo e l'arte dei rumori*, 164.

39. Quoted in Maffina, *Luigi Russolo e l'arte dei rumori*, 176.

40. Quoted in Maffina, *Luigi Russolo e l'arte dei rumori*, 175.

41. Quoted in Brown, introduction to Russolo, *The Art of Noises*, 5.

42. In answer to this essay, Hans Pfitzner published his famous *Futuristengefahr* (Futurist danger). Busoni answered him in June 1917 with an open letter that is a masterpiece of elegance and irony; see "Lettera aperta a Hans Pfitzner," in Busoni, *Lo sguardo lieto*, 109–11. On the cross-pollination between Busoni and Russolo, see Lombardi, *Il suono veloce*, 76. Lombardi, analyzing the common ground between the two artists, also pointed to the substantial difference between them. He shows that Busoni operated a "nonhistorical" synthesis of past and future, and Russolo is entirely driven by "an iconoclast fury." To my way of thinking, both Busoni and Russolo operated in the fields of a "nonhistorical" synthesis (or asynchronous, *inattuale* synthesis). Both of them, more or less openly, more or less painfully, revealed a comparable attraction for the cultural traditions (musical, philosophical) of the past.

43. In Busoni, "Il regno della musica (epilogo della nuova estetica)"; reprinted in Busoni, *Lo sguardo lieto*, 71–72.

44. Busoni, "Abbozzo di una nuova estetica della musica,"; reprinted in Busoni, *Lo sguardo lieto*, 68n18.

45. Leadbeater, *The Hidden Side of Things*, 4.

46. In these two paragraphs, Leadbeater classified as "sounds" some acoustic phenomena that Russolo, perhaps more terminologically conservative, considered to belong to the category of noise: natural sounds such as that of wind or the sea, and those produced by savage and domesticated animals—even the sound of the human voice.

47. Compare Leadbeater, *The Hidden Side of Things*, 204–10, with the Russolo quote in Maffina, *Luigi Russolo e l'arte dei rumori*, 143–58. Russolo mentioned animal sounds in the sixth *famiglia* of noises, a taxonomy previously published in his 1913 manifesto. See Maffina, *Luigi Russolo e l'arte dei rumori*, 133.

48. The word "Pan-ic" is used here to translate the Italian *pànico*, which is a term that refers to a sense of deliberate downward canceling of the self, a primordial togetherness, that man feels when he is at one with nature. It is therefore distinct from *pantheistic*, a term that implies more of a religious, certainly upward motion of the soul towards the divine in nature. The original Italian word refers the Greek god of nature, Pan.

49. Fiorda's *Procession* is mentioned in Maffina, *Luigi Russolo e l'arte dei rumori*, 77. Russolo cited Antonio Russolo's *La pioggia* in a letter to his wife of July 1, 1927 (Maffina, *Luigi Russolo e l'arte dei rumori*, 278–79). In this letter Russolo describes the concert he gave at the Sorbonne the previous week, and mentions *La pioggia* among the pieces he played with the noise-harmonium. A recording produced in 1997 by the Russolo Foundation in Varese includes a version of *La pioggia* for voice, piano and three intonarumori; the recording dates that work in 1914, which seems highly implausible.

50. A good example is the Florentine group Leonardo and, among the futurists, Pratella, who professes himself to be *pantheistic* in his letter to *Lacerba* of February 28, 1915.

51. This quote was brought to my attention by the Savinio scholar Luca Valentino of the Conservatory of Alessandria, Italy.

52. In *L'Italia futurista* (July 25, 1916).

53. Interestingly, Leadbeater, in *The Hidden Side of Things* (279), includes an entire section on war, in which he even cites the same battle of Tripoli that futurist scholars would have been familiar with through Marinetti's 1911 poetical reportages.

54. Tagliapietra (in *MART*, 53) describes the painting only briefly, missing the link between this canvas and the section on the noises of the war in *The Art of Noises*.

55. Evidence of this subjective approach can be found in the first sentence of this quotation, in which Leadbeater stresses the point that, to capture the sense of unity, it is necessary to have a higher, privileged point of view.

56. In Leadbeater, *The Hidden Side of Things*, 210.

57. If it is true that Russolo "nourished himself with the essential Pythagorean doctrine" (Buzzi, quoted in Zanovello, *Luigi Russolo*, 13), we must also say that Russolo's own version of the monochord, the intonarumori, did not divide the string (the space) into finite discontinuous intervals (the ratios of the harmonic series) but rather divided it infinitely, throughout the enharmonic continuity.

58. Russolo did not refer, as Leadbeater does, to the harmony of the spheres. However, it is fair to read in the concept of Russolo's synthesis an echo of that principle of reordering multiplicity in unity, which for Leadbeater produces the frequency of resonance of each planet.

59. Russolo, cited in Maffina, *Luigi Russolo e l'arte dei rumori*, 131.

CHAPTER 9

1. Barclay Brown, in the introduction to his translation of Russolo's *The Art of Noises* (3), mentions the "astonishing speed" at which Russolo conceptualized and built the intonarumori. Carlo Piccardi has written that the process was "immediato"; Piccardi, "Futurismo," in *Dizionario enciclopedico universale della musica e dei musicisti,* ed. A. Basso (Turin: UTET, 1985) 2:309.

2. Maffina, *Luigi Russolo e l'arte dei rumori,* 26.

3. "Gl'intonarumori futuristi" was published in the *Lacerba* issue of July 1, 1913, but it is dated May 22, 1913.

4. The fact that the construction of the instruments was announced on March 11 and the completed instruments presented on August 11 is not coincidental. On Marinetti's numerological fixation on the number 11, see Calvesi, *Fusione,* 336n28.

5. Maffina, *Luigi Russolo e l'arte dei rumori,* 27.

6. Francesco Cangiullo, *Le serate futuriste* (Naples: Editrice Tirrena, 1930), 248.

7. See, for example, the discussion of the relationship between Leonardo and Duchamp in Henderson, *Duchamp in Context.*

8. Russolo, like other futurists, had an early creative phase with a symbolist thrust. Symbolism remains the father (albeit often unacknowledged, even oedipally repressed) of the creative behavior of several futurists. On the spiritual consideration of Leonardo's work by late nineteenth-century movements, see Pietro C. Marani, "Leonardo, i moti e le passioni: Introduzione alla fortuna e sfortuna del Cenacolo," in *Il genio e le passioni, Leonardo e il Cenacolo: Precedenti, innovazioni, riflessi di un capolavoro,* exhibit catalog, ed. Pietro Marani (Milan: Civico Museo d'Arte Contemporanea 2001), 29–38; henceforth Marani, "Leonardo, i moti e le passioni."

9. *Archivi del futurismo,* 1:228.

10. Marinetti, *La grande Milano,* 69, 173. Marinetti mentioned Leonardo and his machines on page 187.

11. According to Marianne Martin, Carrà was one of these friends. Martin cites Buzzi's article in *Cahiers* as a source; see *Futurist Art and Theory,* 70n2. However, I was unable to locate in Buzzi's article the information quoted by Martin.

12. Quoted by Tagliapietra in *MART,* 16.

13. See Zanovello, *Luigi Russolo.* This account is repeated in Lista, "Russolo, peinture et bruitisme"; Maffina, *Luigi Russolo e l'arte dei rumori*; Martin, *Futurist Art and Theory*; Tagliapietra, *Luigi Russolo: Pittore musicista filosofo* (Treviso: Europrint, 2000); and elsewhere.

14. The extensive report on *The Last Supper* produced by the Lombard public administration, contemporaneously with Cavenaghi's restoration, never refers to Crivelli in the course of a very detailed account of every single restoration up to the date of publication. See Achille Patroclo, ed., *Le Vicende del Cenacolo di Leonardo da Vinci nel secolo XIX* (Milan: Ufficio Regionale per la Conservazione dei Monumenti della Lombardia, 1906). Yet in the very years in which Leonardo is working on *The Last Supper* and the *Stanze* of the Sforza Castle, he is also painting the famous *La Belle Ferronnière,* which is believed

to be the portrait of Lucrezia Crivelli, the mistress of Ludovico il Moro, Duke of Milan, who was also Leonardo's boss at the time. Since Russolo was involved in the restoration of both *The Last Supper* and the *Stanze*, I suspect that this is perhaps where the name Crivelli came from. It is not the only incorrect information in Zanovello's biography.

15. *Lacerba* (September 1, 1913).

16. Marinetti, *La grande Milano*, 118–19. All that now remains about this lecture is a brief text that is known through a copy made by Boccioni. Because of Boccioni's handwriting, and because Marinetti, who sorted Boccioni's papers after his death titled it "Ricerche sull'arte di Russolo," the writing was misattributed to Boccioni by Zeno Birolli, who published it, although expressing some perplexity over its authorship, in his collection of Boccioni's posthumous writings. In this text, Russolo makes a list of several fourteenth-, fifteenth-, and sixteenth-century frescoes that have been destroyed or painted over by subsequent artists, as a sort of Darwinist justification for futurism: "Thus we know that where Michelangelo painted his *Last Judgment*, there was already a fresco by Perugino. Likewise, Raphael scraped away from the Vatican's Raphael Rooms other frescoes by Sodoma and even some by his own mentor, Perugino." In Boccioni, *Altri inediti*, 50; Marinetti eventually recycled the Raphael/Sodoma argument in his manifesto "Dopo il teatro sintetico e il teatro a sorpresa noi inventiamo il teatro antipsicologico astratto di puri elementi e il teatro tattile," reprinted in *Teoria e invenzione futurista*, 173. Yet in describing the "gesticolante agonia di colori," Marinetti (or Russolo, if Marinetti was citing him verbatim) was directly quoting from—and directly aligning himself with—Bernard Berenson's famous attack on *The Last Supper*. In *The Study and Criticism of Italian Art*, Berenson writes of the (now much studied and praised) fresco's position of the characters: "What a pack of vehement, *gesticulating*, noisy foreigners they are, with faces far from pleasant, some positively criminal, some conspirators, and others having no business there"; quoted in Marani, "Leonardo, i moti e le passioni."

17. Russolo, *Al di là della materia*, 272.

18. Besides Carrà and Piatti, Romolo Romani, another friend of Russolo from the prefuturist years, also admired Leonardo's work. See the section on the young Romani in Giorgio Nicodemi, *Romolo Romani* (Como: Cairoli, 1967).

19. For Russolo's references to Vasari, see Maffina, *Luigi Russolo e l'arte dei rumori*, 306; see also Russolo, *Al di là della materia*, 210.

20. Giorgio Vasari, *Le vite de piv eccellenti architetti, pittori, et scvltori italiani*, ed. Corrado Ricci (Milan: Bestelti e Tumminelli, 1927), 8:17; henceforth Vasari, *Le vite*). See also the chapter "The Mystery of the Skull Lyre" in Winternitz, *Leonardo da Vinci as a Musician*, 39–72.

21. Russolo went to Paris, London (in 1914), and Spain (in 1932). In Spain we know from *Al di là della materia* that he visited the Prado museum; see Russolo, *Al di là della materia*, 184. On the same page Russolo claims to have seen all of Titian's paintings that were to be found in European museums. This voracious, almost compulsive collecting of knowledge is characteristic of him (another example is his sudden interest in dairy art that Russolo's wife described in Zanovello, *Luigi Russolo*, 19). Russolo may

well have hunted all over Europe for manuscripts of Leonardo that contained musical instruments.

22. The full title of the 1923–30 facsimile is *Codice Arundel: I manoscritti e i disegni di Leonardo da Vinci pubblicati dalla Reale Commissione Vinciana*, vol. 1, *Il codice Arundel 263 del Museo Britannico*, Riproduzione fototipica con trascrizione diplomatica e critica, part 1 [–4] (Rome: 1923 [–1930]). Arundel 263 famously contains preparatory studies for *The Last Supper*. Given Russolo's special association with this work, we assume that Russolo was aware of the existence of this codex by 1904. See Pedretti in *Leonardo da Vinci: Il Codice Arundel 263 nella British Library, Edizione in facsimile nel riordinamento cronologico dei suoi fascicoli*, ed. Carlo Pedretti, with transcription from the manuscript and critical notes by Carlo Vecce (Florence: Giunti, 1998), 14.

23. Russolo, *Al di là della materia*, 270.

24. Maffina, *Luigi Russolo e l'arte dei rumori*, 347. Though Baudelaire's name is not mentioned in this essay, the subject matter and especially the two keywords in Russolo's title, *eterno* and *transitorio*, were surely lifted from Baudelaire's well-known essay "Le peintre de la vie moderne" ("The Painter of Modern Life"), published in installments in *Le Figaro* on November 26, November 28, and December 3, 1863; see Charles Baudelaire, *Selected Writings*, (London: Penguin, 1972), 402–3. Writings in which Russolo make a passing reference to Leonardo are the reviews "La mostra di Achille Funi," *La Testa di Ferro*, November 7, 1920; "L'arte è creazione, non è plagio," *L'Impero*, April 7, 1926; "Il Novecento italiano," *La Borsa*, March 4, 1926; and "Conferenza sull'architettura tenuta da Russolo alla Galleria Borromini di Como nel 1944," reprinted in Maffina, *Luigi Russolo e l'arte dei rumori*, 306; as well as three letters to Edgar Varèse of January 14, February 8, and March 22, 1934 (see Lista, *Luigi Russolo e la musica futurista*, 145–48).

25. Quoted in Maffina, *Luigi Russolo e l'arte dei rumori*, 314.

26. From Russolo's "L'eterno e il transitorio dell'arte," quoted in Maffina, *Luigi Russolo e l'arte dei rumori*, 315. This position on *The Last Supper* differs significantly from the one Russolo apparently held many years earlier (see Marinetti, *La grande Milano*, 118–19). The version we have of Russolo's lecture (see note 16 above) does not mention Leonardo's *Last Supper*. This may be yet another instance of Marinetti's creative paraphrasing or manipulating facts to advance his modernist agenda. He "edited" most of the writings of his futurist associates in his activities as a publisher. Gino Severini was one of the few to object to Marinetti's interpolations in his writings; Calvesi claims that this explains why Severini's manifesto of 1913, "Le analogie plastiche del dinamismo," was not published; see Calvesi, *Fusione*, 78.

27. It is striking that this thought, written almost thirty years after the 1909 manifesto, more gently rearticulates—and fully illuminates—one of the manifesto's central and most provocative enterprises: destroying the museums. Since the passing of time would destroy art, we cannot cling to its exterior materiality, and neither should we worship it. It is the spiritual power of the artworks that we have to absorb, and embrace, if even to direct it, as the 1909 manifesto states, toward the creation of new art.

28. Leonardo, Codex Atlanticus, folio 71r, translated by Richter and quoted in Winternitz, *Leonardo da Vinci as a Musician*, 224.

29. Leonardo's notion of time as continuous is found in Arundel 263; see Winternitz, *Leonardo da Vinci as a Musician*, 221. See also Leonardo's definition of time and psychological time in Codex Atlanticus, which seems to anticipate Bergson (and therefore Boccioni).

30. Winternitz, *Leonardo da Vinci as a Musician*, 228.

31. On the term *inattuale*, see chapter 5.

32. Buzzi, introduction to Zanovello, *Luigi Russolo*, 11–12. The reference to the lyre betrays Buzzi's familiarity with Vasari. In Buzzi's poem "Inno alla poesia nuova" of 1912, he presents both "the Machine" and the Russolo-inspired sound produced by it, as "our days' Lyre." By associating the noise of an engine to the lyre, that is, the bard's accompanying instrument, Buzzi implies that the noise of machines must inspire today's poetry as the lyre inspired classical poetry. See the anthology *I poeti futuristi*, ed. Filippo T. Marinetti (Milan: Edizioni Futuriste di "Poesia," 1912), 107. Buzzi's poem, in evoking the music of the spheres, is imbued with occult suggestions (Viazzi has appropriately written of its "cosmic-esoteric dimension"; see Viazzi, ed., "I poeti del futurismo," 114). Russolo read Vasari, as he quotes Vasari's *Le vite* in *Al di là della materia*, 210.

33. Quoted in Zanovello, *Luigi Russolo*, 13–14.

34. Zanovello, *Luigi Russolo*, 95. This poem is rich in allusions and influences, from D'Annunzio to Mallarmé. These references, so synesthetically rich, are a perfect homage to Russolo. Furthermore, the poem presents a landscape of great beauty: lush and green, but with a variety of shadows and light, in the visual realm; the mention of the intonarumori offers the aural, and the garden with perfume of laurel provides the olfactory.

35. The overview of the intonarumori I offer here is the result of a research grant from Performa 09, the Biennial of Performance Arts in New York City, which commissioned me to direct a new reconstruction project of the intonarumori. With full support from RoseLee Goldberg and Esa Nickle from Performa, Frank Smigel from SFMOMA, and Johannes Goebel and Micah Silver from EMPAC, I was able to reconstruct for the first time the earliest intonarumori orchestra of sixteen instruments that Russolo unveiled on August 11, 1913, at the Casa Rossa. Much was learned during the reconstruction process, which was executed under my supervision by the luthier Keith Cary and with help from Dna Hoover. In an earlier stage of construction, help came from EMPAC's Bill Bergman and Jenni Wilga, and in a later stage from Nora Cary and Ellen Fullman. I am indebted to the scholarship of Barclay Brown and Hugh Davies, and to Pietro Verardo's intonarumori reconstruction—a partial one, but the first ever attempted—that I was able to visit while being interviewed by the BBC in summer 2009.

36. Giovanni Lista, in his *Luigi Russolo e la musica futurista* (Milan: Mudima, 2009), 183, disagreed with Maffina and claimed that he was the first scholar to have, in 1975, published Russolo's patents. This may be the case; however, Lista misdated the first patent (rather than January 11, 1914, the actual date was March 30, 1914) and gave the wrong classification number for the October 8, 1921, patent (rather than 420171, vol. 895, the actual number is Reg. Gen. N. 204171, Reg. Att. N. 207, vol. 598). As these are similarly

wrong in Maffina, it is likely that both Maffina and Lista relied on the same second-hand source (perhaps Zanovello's files) instead of the primary source.

37. This photo was first published in Maffina's catalog for the Venice Biennale Exhibit of October–November 1977, *Luigi Russolo: L'arte dei rumori, 1913–1931*, 55.

38. The sibilatore, the most complex of Russolo's intonarumori (and the one with the most extensive pitch range), had two registers plus an additional stop, the same scrosciatore (hisser) that was also employed in the gorgogliatore (gurgler).

39. Brown, introduction to Russolo, *The Art of Noises*, 5.

40. Including Lombardi's essay in *MART*, 117.

41. Zanovello, *Luigi Russolo*, 77.

42. Maffina's 1977 catalog reproduced a picture of this model with a caption indicating that Russolo reconstructed this prototype in Cerro di Laveno in 1945 according to the 1931 patent.

43. Russolo's draft for the 1931 patent is quoted in Maffina, *Luigi Russolo e l'arte dei rumori*, 225. The Fondo Russolo of MART [Rus 2.3.16] has preserved an unpublished manuscript with five detailed sets of computations, which may be the calculations to determine the diameter and thickness of coils and other parameters required to build the five-keys prototype. Further research is needed to validate this hypothesis.

44. Compare Russolo's ronzatore with the mechanical kettledrum sketched in Leonardo's Codex Atlanticus or the "enharmonic" pot drum sketched in Arundel 263 (both reproduced in Winternitz, *Leonardo da Vinci as a Musician*, 169, 181–82). The main difference seems to be that Russolo used an electric motor instead of a crank.

45. Quoted in Maffina, *Luigi Russolo e l'arte dei rumori*, 224–25.

46. Winternitz, *Leonardo da Vinci as a Musician*, 155, 164.

47. Winternitz, *Leonardo da Vinci as a Musician*, 153 (fig. 17).

48. However, the desire to improve on the organ was widespread. Cahill was motivated by this wish when he developed his telharmonium; see Busoni, "Abbozzo di una nuova estetica della musica," in *Lo sguardo lieto: Tutti gli scritti sulla musica e le arti*, ed. Fedele d'Amico (Milan: Il Saggiatore, 1977) 68n18.

49. The first two phases happened quite quickly, as documented in Codex Atlanticus, folio 218r.

50. One of the few successful instruments to use longitudinal vibration is Ellen Fullman's long string instrument, created at the beginning of the 1980s, and tuned in just intonation. Fullman designed her instrument with strings more than one hundred feet long. She played by walking a platform placed under the strings forward and back along their length, sublimating with the gracefulness of her motion what might seem the logistical problem of impractical dimensions.

51. On differences between the intonarumori and the hurdy-gurdy, see for instance Lombardi, *Il suono veloce*, 39.

52. Winternitz, *Leonardo da Vinci as a Musician*, 181–83, 179.

53. Winternitz, *Leonardo da Vinci as a Musician*, 185.

54. Winternitz, *Leonardo da Vinci as a Musician*, 192; CA folio 397rb is reproduced on p. 194.

55. Winternitz, *Leonardo da Vinci as a Musician*, 192.

56. In the explanatory text of Codex Atlanticus, folio 397rb, Leonardo explained that the glissando feature is achieved by moving "la mano su e giu, come alla tromba torta, e massime nel zufolo a" (the hand up and down [along the slits] just as with the *tromba torta* and even more so in the *zufolo* a); Winternitz, *Leonardo da Vinci as a Musician*, 192. These *tromba torta* and *zufolo* can be, respectively, an early example of a slide trumpet and of a flute *à coulisse*.

57. Winternitz, *Leonardo da Vinci as a Musician*, 192. He was here likely thinking in terms of natural harmonics.

58. Winternitz, *Leonardo da Vinci as a Musician*, 204–23.

59. Both notions are in fact based on the assumption that pitch space is continuous, and that every selection of pitches (i.e., every scale) extracted from this continuity is therefore arbitrary. Leonardo also discussed continuity in Codex Arundel 263; see Winternitz, *Leonardo da Vinci as a Musician*, 221.

60. Leonardo, *Trattato* 31C; see Winternitz, *Leonardo da Vinci as a Musician*, 215–16 (translation by Winternitz).

61. Winternitz, *Leonardo da Vinci as a Musician*, 216.

62. Winternitz, *Leonardo da Vinci as a Musician*, 221.

63. For a brief mention of this division of art in space and art in time, see Winternitz, *Leonardo da Vinci as a Musician*, 208. Pitch-space is a continuous space: the pitch is a continuous quantity because an interval between two pitches is infinitely divisible.

64. Winternitz was not convinced by Leonardo's argument; see Winternitz, *Leonardo da Vinci as a Musician*, 208–9.

65. Winternitz noted that Leonardo thought of intervals as the relationships between notes of different pitch; Winternitz, *Leonardo da Vinci as a Musician*, 206, 206n4). On the difference in status between Poetry and Music, see Leonardo, *Trattato* 21; Winternitz, *Leonardo da Vinci as a Musician*, 205–6.

66. Winternitz, *Leonardo da Vinci as a Musician*, 211.

67. This opposition was unknown in Leonardo's day; see Winternitz, *Leonardo da Vinci as a Musician*, 205n3.

68. Franco Ballardini, *Swedenborg e il falegname: Poetica, teoria e filosofia della musica in Arnold Schönberg* (Modena: Mucchi Editore, 1988).

69. The current difference between melodic and harmonic intervals is a difference in time and not pertinent in this discussion. However, the relationships among pitches are always considered to be harmonic relationships, even when the sounds occurs one after another, because the comparison between subsequent notes that are different in pitch is measured within the field of harmony, here understood—*repetita juvant*—as the science of intervallic proportions and not as the science of verticalities.

70. Leonardo, in *Trattato* 30 and 32, acknowledged for music the existence of harmony of proportions in time between consecutive sections of a piece, but he did not acknowledge the same for the poetry. This conclusion did not satisfy Winternitz. On these aspects, see Leonardo, *Trattato* 21 and 23, and Winternitz's comments on them in *Leonardo da Vinci as a Musician*, 205–9.

71. Even when only melodic, music is never exclusively about time, for melody always implies harmony; this is true of musical practices even after Leonardo's time.

72. Leonardo, in Codex Arundel 263, writes directly about time as a continuous quantity (see Winternitz, *Leonardo da Vinci as a Musician*, 221); Leonardo's understanding of pitch-space continuity, though not openly stated, can be evinced from his discussion.

73. Leonardo discusses sound that fades away, for example with the plucked strings of a lute, in *Trattato* 29 (see Winternitz, *Leonardo da Vinci as a Musician*, 210–11). Leonardo considered this sound volatility, or fading, to be music's main problem (see Winternitz, *Leonardo da Vinci as a Musician*, 208); this may explain why most of Leonardo's instruments are capable of sustaining sound.

74. Winternitz, *Leonardo da Vinci as a Musician*, 216.

75. In fact, it is in proving that time is a continuous quantity that Leonardo claims that continuous quantities are infinitely divisible. This passage is in Codex Arundel 263 and reprinted in Winternitz, *Leonardo da Vinci as a Musician*, 221.

76. All reprinted by Maffina.

77. Compare Leonardo's definition of music as capable of making invisible things visible (*figuratione [. . .] delle cose invisibili*) in *Trattato* 32 (reprinted in Winternitz, *Leonardo da Vinci as a Musician*, 217) with the quotation from Leonardo that defines painting as poetry made visible (*pittura è una poesia che si vede*), in Russolo, *Al di là della materia*, 270.

78. Winternitz, *Leonardo da Vinci as a Musician*, 104, 105, 183.

79. Translated in Winternitz, *Leonardo da Vinci as a Musician*, 104.

80. Winternitz, *Leonardo da Vinci as a Musician*, 120.

81. Winternitz, *Leonardo da Vinci as a Musician*, 122.

82. Translated in Winternitz, *Leonardo da Vinci as a Musician*, 105.

83. Quoted in Maffina, *Luigi Russolo e l'arte dei rumori*, 151. On Russolo's analysis of the battlefield, see Marinetti, "Quinte e scene della campagna del battaglione lombardo volontari ciclisti sul lago di Garda e sull'altissimo: La presa di Dosso Casina," part 2, *Gazzetta dello sport* (February 7, 1916); reprinted in Enrico Crispolti, "Zang Tumb Tuum I futuristi vanno alla guerra. Giochi, burle e travestimenti dei futuristi del battaglione ciclisti," *Bolaffiarte* 79 (May 1978): 15.

84. Quoted and translated in Winternitz, *Leonardo da Vinci as a Musician*, 105.

85. See Winternitz, *Leonardo da Vinci as a Musician*, 183.

86. See Carlo Pedretti, "'Non mi fuggir, donzella . . . ,' Leonardo regista teatrale del Poliziano," in *Arte lombarda*, n.s. 128 (2000): 7–15. I am indebted to Professor Pedretti for this information.

87. Quoted in Winternitz, *Leonardo da Vinci as a Musician*, 177–78.

88. These instruments are all rather noisy. The name *fischiatore* already seems a potential name for an intonarumori.

89. Piedigrotta's performance left yet another mark: in 1915 Giacomo Balla designed, built, and decorated an instrument called the *ciac-ciac*, which was based on

the triccaballacche; this instrument is now preserved in the Museo degli Strumenti Musicali in Rome.

90. On Leonardo and clockworks, see Winternitz, *Leonardo da Vinci as a Musician*, 137; Zanovello has documented that watch- and clock-making was the Russolos' family business. Leonardo's interest in automata is well known, and is even, famously mentioned by Vasari. As we have seen, the dream of "creation" developed in a different way in Russolo's mind, because of his interest in theosophy. On Leonardo and "creation," see the passage from *BLAST* quoted in chapter 10.

CHAPTER 10

1. Marinetti, "Fondazione e manifesto del futurismo," in *I manifesti del futurismo*, 7–8.
2. Boccioni, "Fondamento."
3. For more information on Leonardo as prefuturist, see Henderson, *Duchamp in Context*.
4. This advertising campaign offered an easy target for ferocious futurist irony. Marinetti reused the phrase "'GIOCONDA' ACQUA PURGATIVA" in his manifesto on "Teatro di varietà."
5. Carrà, "La pittura dei suoni, rumori e odori" in *I manifesti del futurismo*, 153.
6. Quoted in Marani, "Leonardo, i moti e le passioni," 29–38.
7. Calvesi, *Futurismo*, 10. Leonardo's spiritual side can also be observed in his research on hydraulics, for he considered water to be a creature always in motion, gifted with a spiritual virtue and power.
8. Quoted in Fagiolo dell'Arco, *Compenetrazioni*, 13.
9. Quoted in Fagiolo dell'Arco, *Omaggio a Balla* (Rome: Bulzoni, 1967), 62.
10. Winternitz, *Leonardo da Vinci as a Musician*, 104n9.
11. Reproductions of *Vortice* are included in Calvesi, *Fusione*, 267. Leonardo's influence on Balla's flying swallows was also noted in Fagiolo dell'Arco, "Giacomo Balla verso il futurismo," 23.
12. The connection between Leonardo and Marey is debated in Lista, *Futurisme*, 63.
13. Marinetti, *La grande Milano*, 173.
14. Marinetti, *La grande Milano*, 33; italics in original.
15. *Una sensibilità italiana nata in Egitto*, in Marinetti, *La grande Milano*, 256. Particularly insightful is the aim of "synthesizing simultaneously the universe."
16. Wyndham Lewis, "Futurism, Magic and Life," *BLAST* 1 (June 20, 1914): 132 (facsimile repr., Santa Rosa: Black Sparrow Press, 1997); boldface and capitals follow the original. This text was published about a week before the murder of Archduke Franz Ferdinand.
17. For an introduction to the Movimento Fiorentino, see the chapter "New Directions: The Florentine Movement" in Martin, *Futurist Art and Theory*, 19–27.
18. Martin, *Futurist Art and Theory*, 20.
19. Martin, *Futurist Art and Theory*, 20.

20. On the brawl of 1911, see Martin, *Futurist Art and Theory*, 81. With *Lacerba*, Soffici and Papini finally separated from Giuseppe Prezzolini and *La Voce*. Papini and Prezzolini had founded the periodical *La Voce* in 1908 after Prezzolini dreamed of a gramophone through which a mysterious voice suggested, like an oracle, that he do so; see Martin, *Futurist Art and Theory*, 26. *La Voce* was dominated by Prezzolini's personality. The periodical's main concerns were sociology and politics, and little space was dedicated to the arts. This led to the split between Papini and Prezzolini. Even though Papini never considered himself a futurist and, in fact, maintained a slightly ambivalent position (he claimed in *Lacerba* that he could offer a more objective critique of futurism precisely because he had never actually been a futurist), he was sufficiently aligned with futurist aesthetics to transform *Lacerba* into the official organ of the futurist movement for a few years. As he himself claimed, this was a time in which he shared most of the futurists' ideas, values, objectives, and cultural references.

21. The header of *Il Leonardo* was a symbolically elaborate engraving designed by Adolfo De Carolis.

22. See Sandra Migliore, *Tra Hermes e Prometeo: Il mito di Leonardo nel Decadentismo Europeo* (Florence: Olschki, 1994).

23. Cited in Marani, "Leonardo, i moti e le passioni." 29–38. Marani explains that the history of the worship of this work had begun in 1498, with the first enthusiastic comments by Luca Pacioli.

24. The term *fari* is already found in Papini. In 1906 he published his first philosophical book, *Il crepuscolo dei filosofi*, in which he attacked the work of *sei fari* (six beacons) of contemporary culture (Kant, Hegel, Schopenhauer, Comte, Spencer, and Nietzsche), and declared the entire discipline of philosophy dead, favoring instead what he called "vital irrationalism." But in the mid-1930s Russolo's iconoclastic past was far behind him and he gives the expression *fari* a positive spin, likely modeling the section on *i fari dell'umanità* on Édouard Schuré's *The Great Initiates*, a book that we know Russolo had read (see Zanovello, *Luigi Russolo*, 77).

25. Russolo, *Al di là della materia*, 269–70.

26. Lista, "Russolo, peinture et bruitisme," 140.

27. Russolo, *Al di là della materia*, 246–47.

28. Russolo, *Al di là della materia*, 210. It is particularly meaningful that in the following paragraph, on the same page, Russolo again mentions Leonardo and quotes him.

29. Giovanni Testori, "Reliquiae fugientes," cited in Marani, "Leonardo, i moti e le passioni."

30. Maffina, *Luigi Russolo e l'arte dei rumori*, 27.

31. Zanovello, *Luigi Russolo*, 83–84.

32. According to an unsigned article in the *Pall Mall Gazette* of November 18, 1913, Russolo gave the general public the opportunity to examine the insides of the intonarumori on only one occasion, the press concert of August 11, 1913; at all other times he kept the boxes carefully occulted. See Brown, introduction to Russolo, *The Art of Noises*, 5.

CHAPTER II

1. See Steiner's previously mentioned lecture "Investigations into Life between Death and Rebirth," in Steiner, *Life between Death and Rebirth*, part 2I, 18–30.

2. Calvesi mentioned the music produced in séances, and its popularity, in his study on the automatic writing techniques of the futurists and surrealists; Calvesi, "L'écriture médiumnique," 47. Calvesi focused his article on literature, and he does not discuss futurist music, let alone link Russolo's art of noises to the conjuring of spirits.

3. Buzzi, "Russolo ferito [January 1918]," in *Archivi del futurismo*, 1:378.

4. The expression "skeletal sorcerer" is one of Marinetti's "simultaneous portraits" of Russolo; Marinetti, *La grande Milano*, 106.

5. See Leadbeater, *The Hidden Side of Things*, 198.

6. Besant and Leadbeater, *Thought-forms*, 27; these forms were actually meant to offer models for the painter.

7. See Leadbeater, *The Hidden Side of Things*, 88, 121.

8. See *Guerra sola igiene del mondo*, in Marinetti, *Teoria e invenzione futurista*, 299–300. For "mediumistic materialization," see Boccioni, *Scritti*, 203.

9. For "exteriorization of sensitivity," see Russolo, *Al di là della materia*, 102. Russolo's wording is likely derived by the 1895 Albert de Rochas's book *Extériorisation de la sensibilité*, also quoted by Cesare Lombroso.

10. *Cahiers d'art* 1 (1950): 85–86; italics in the original. This translation has been revised with the help of Pierina Demelas and Karen Vanhercke. The original reads:

> Héros aiguisé par l'angoisse
> Tournoyante de chaque heure, toi, cherche
> L'acoustique ivresse la plus nouvelle
> Dans le heurt des bruits: toi, regarde
> Avec les yeux du basilic mental
> Le décor magnifique des ouragans,
> Et écoute, écoute
> Les Golfes mystiques des tonnerres et des pluies:
> Et descends, avec de lestes pupilles d'ambre jaune,
> Aux orchestres des usines et des chantiers:
> Et écoute, écoute
> Les convulsions du fer déchiré:
> Et que le volant qui mugit soit pour toujours
> Le ténor qui domine le concert!
> Luigi, l'ululeur est l'oracle
> Du Dieu qui t'inspire et te rendra justice.
> L'abîme t'est reconnaissant, notre grand Parent.
> J'entends les musiques uniques et vraies: celles
> Qu'entendent les morts
> Sur leurs têtes, sous nos pieds.
> La Capitale future se réveille
> Dans une explosion qui invite
> À des bals masqués de force et de désir les cimetières!

11. A collection of poems with the title *Les Médaillons* does not appear in Viazzi's catalog of Buzzi's works; see Viazzi, ed., "I poeti del futurismo," 23–24.

12. Reprinted in Maffina, *Luigi Russolo e l'arte dei rumori*, 125–26.

13. Russolo, quoted in Maffina, *Luigi Russolo e l'arte dei rumori*, 169.

14. I am indebted to Professor Pierina Demelas for first pointing out to me the influence of Baudelaire's poetry on Buzzi.

15. References to thunder are found in both Russolo's and Leadbeater's work.

16. Russolo in Maffina, *Luigi Russolo e l'arte dei rumori*, 169. Russolo also claimed that the ululatore has "something that might remind you of the siren"; furthermore, Buzzi wrote in his 1912 "Inno alla Poesia Nuova": "Today's Lyre is the Machine. [...] a sound of a thousand sirens" (*La Lira è la Macchina, oggi.* [...] *un anelito di mille sirene*); in Marinetti, ed., *I poeti futuristi*, 107.

17. On Russolo séances at Madame Lazare's, see Lista, "Russolo, peinture et bruitisme," 28.

18. Buzzi, foreword to his *Cavalcata delle vertigini*.

19. Buzzi, *Cavalcata delle vertigini*, 81–86.

20. Leadbeater, *The Hidden Side of Things*, 88.

21. Belfiore's Hoepli manual is cited in Celant, "Futurismo esoterico," 111. Russolo's passages on Mesmer are in Russolo, *Al di là della materia*, 45–51, 156. Russolo's sections on Mesmer, the apostle of magnetism, and Charcot, the founder of hypnotism, seem directly to summarize notions learned from Belfiore's manual, which was a best seller that went through four editions in fifteen years.

22. *Ipnotismo e magnetismo* is mentioned in *Arte dell'avvenire*, 1910; see Ginna and Corra, *Scritti*, 106. Russolo would have known either the first edition of 1898 or one of the popular and frequent reprintings.

23. Marinetti, *Teoria e invenzione futurista*, 239.

24. "La radia," in Marinetti, *Teoria e invenzione futurista*, 206.

25. In *Il futurismo a Verona* (Florence: Electa, 2002) 65–67. The portion quoted here is the first half of the manifesto which is signed by Di Bosso. Scurto's part 2 is on pages 68–70. I am indebted to Professor Marco Mancin for pointing me to this text.

26. In *Il futurismo a Verona* (Florence: Electa, 2002), 67.

27. Quoted in Antonio Latanza, "Al di là della Musica, al di là del Suono: L'accordatura dell'Universo, Magia naturale e umana," in "i suoni, le onde" *Rivista della Fondazione Isabella Scelsi* 11 (semester 2, 2003): 18.

28. For a picture that testifies to this moment, see Marinetti, *The Futurist Cookbook* (San Francisco: Bedford Arts, 1989), 10.

29. "Fondazione e manifesto del futurismo," in *I manifesti del futurismo*, 5.

30. For Ginna's *L'uomo futuro*, see Ginna and Corra, *Scritti*, 234.

31. Marinetti, *Teoria e invenzione futurista*, 206.

32. Susan Wilson, "Futurismo e futuristi a Londra," in Pratella, *Edizioni, scritti, manoscritti musicali e futuristi*, 90.

33. Maffina, *Luigi Russolo e l'arte dei rumori*, 80.

34. Here I use the word *occult* in its literal sense, as in "hidden from sight." This

choice, especially at this point of the book, is not coincidental. The term *occult* in its multifaceted acceptations encapsulates perfectly the connection between Russolo's interest in occult art and futurists' process of subconscious denial by which they hide traces of the past from sight—though not their occult interests!—thereby *occulting* them.

35. Russolo was reluctant to show the insides of the intonarumori. One could be tempted to read this reluctance as a manifestation of what Eco diagnosed and criticized as the mediatic "sale" of the image of technology as magic. In today's society, users should not be distracted by the long chain of causes and effects that science, through its method of *provando e riprovando* (trying and retrying), ought to sort. Everything should happen *magically*, at the click of a mouse, and the inner workings should be disguised. See Umberto Eco, "Scienza, tecnologia e magia" in *A passo di gambero: Guerre calde e populismo mediatico* (Milan: Bompiani, 2007), 103–10. However, I doubt that Russolo was simply moved by a desire to protect his construction tricks for commercial exploitation. I prefer to think that his protective anxiety derived from the desire not to trivialize what he considered to be the metaphysical aims of the operation of his art of noises.

36. Maffina, *Luigi Russolo e l'arte dei rumori*, 30.
37. Lista, "Russolo, peinture et bruitisme," 136.
38. In Maffina, *Luigi Russolo e l'arte dei rumori*, 184.
39. See, for instance Carolyn Abbate, "Outside Ravel's Tomb."

CONCLUSION

1. Lista, "Russolo, peinture et bruitisme," 28. To be fair, Lista was commenting on Russolo's activity after the 1930s—and it is debatable whether that phase was futurist or not. However, late occult themes (e.g., the etheric double, or a spirit abandoning the dead body) are distinct reprises of earlier, and even futurist, themes. This thematic coherence raises doubts about reading Russolo's final activities as an abdication.

2. This history has not been concluded. Even though no longer enforced, the charge of *apologia di fascismo* is in fact still part of the Italian penal code.

3. Modernist critics would have been aware that the occult influence in futurism also spawned such unfortunate monsters as Ginna's *futurfascist* homunculus. But although Russolo, too, eventually aligned his occult leanings with fascism, not all occult spirituality led the believers to reactionary, authoritarian regimes.

4. The 1912 breakthrough and subsequent subdivision of Marinetti's aesthetics into two parts, before and after the Words in Freedom, is the premise of Leonardo Tondelli's superb *Futurista senza futuro: Marinetti ultimo mitografo* (Florence: Le Lettere, 2009).

5. Marinetti acknowledged that contradictions have a role in the art/life process: "Create by living. Sometimes contradict yourself." See Marinetti, *Marinetti e il futurismo*, in *Teoria e invenzione futurista*, 583.

6. The equation "Occult = Past" certainly would not have appealed to Marinetti and his companions. When they gave space to spiritual figures of the past (e.g., Leo-

nardo), they did so in diaries and letters but not in their manifestos, and when they did it was only to claim the past as part of a lineage of progressive, futurist thought *ante litteram*, that is, as protofuturism.

7. Lista, "Russolo, peinture et bruitisme," 12–13.

8. Barclay Brown claimed Russolo as the father of musical synthesis; see Brown, "The Noise Instruments of Luigi Russolo," *Perspectives of New Music* 20 (1981–82): 48.

9. Russolo, *Al di là della materia*, 270.

10. Examples of this modernist partial portrait, focusing narrowly on technical novelty or lack thereof, include Gary Lachmann, "Ready to Rumble," *Wire* (December 2003): 30–35, which celebrates Russolo as a "futurist too far ahead of his time"; and Edward Venn, "Rethinking Russolo," *Tempo* 64, no. 251 (January 2010): 8–16, who just as modernistically complains that Russolo was not modern *enough*.